A PEOPLE
WITHOUT
A COUNTRY

Other titles by Gerard Chaliand

Armed Struggle in Africa
Peasants of North Vietnam
The Palestinian Resistance
Revolution in the Third World: Myths and Prospects
Terrorism: From Popular Struggle to Media Spectacle

A PEOPLE
WITHOUT
A COUNTRY

THE KURDS AND KURDISTAN

EDITED BY
GERARD CHALIAND
Translated by Michael Pallis
Foreword by David McDowall

OLIVE
BRANCH
PRESS

An imprint of Interlink Publishing Group, Inc
NEW YORK

First American edition published 1993 by
OLIVE BRANCH PRESS
An imprint of Interlink Publishing Group, Inc.
99 Seventh Avenue • Brooklyn, New York 11215

The article entitled "The Kurdish Republic of Mahabad" by A. Roosevelt, Jr. first appeared in the July 1947 issue of *The Middle East Journal*. Reprinted by permission. The article entitled "Operation Provide Comfort: False Promises to the Kurds" (Original Title: "The False Promises of Operation Provide Comfort") by Bill Frelick, appeared in the May/June 1992 issue of *Middle East Report*. Copyright © by Bill Frelick. Reprinted by permission.

Originally published in French by François Maspero under the title
Les Kurdes et le Kurdistan
First published in English by Zed Books, 1980

Library of Congress Cataloging-in-Publication Data
Kurdes et le Kurdistan. English
A people without a country : the Kurds and Kurdistan / A.R.
Ghassemlou . . . [et al.] ; edited by Gerard Chaliand ; translated by
Michael Pallis. — 1st American ed.
p. cm.
Translation of: Les Kurdes et le Kurdistan.
Includes bibliographical references and index.
ISBN 1–56656–114–0 — ISBN 0–940793–92–X
1. Kurds. 2. Middle East—Ethnic relations. I. Ghassemlou,
Abdul Rahman. II. Chaliand, Gerard, 1934. III. Title.
DS51.K7K86313 1992
956'.0049159—dc20   92-14618
CIP

Cover design by Linda Dalal Sawaya

Printed and bound in the United States of America

10 9 8 7 6 5 4 3 2 1

Contents

Regions Populated by the Kurds

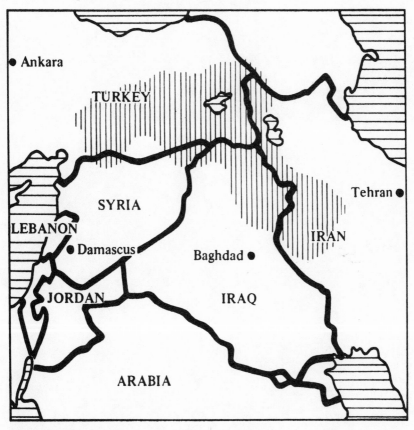

|||||||||| Regions inhabited by the Kurdish Nation

Foreword

David McDowall

Towards the end of March 1991 over one and a half million Kurds fled across the snow-clad mountains of Kurdistan in search of safety from the forces of Saddam Hussein. Had it not been for television, these fugitives would probably now be either dead or refugees bereft of hope outside Iraq. For it was television news bulletins which brought the horrific ordeal of the Kurds into homes across Europe and America. And it was the outrage of ordinary people at Saddam Hussein's onslaught and at the Allies' passivity, which finally compelled Western governments to provide protection to the Kurds inside Iraq.

Television created a powerful image of Kurdistan in the popular imagination of the West, in a way that a succession of uprisings in Iraq, Turkey and Iran had previously failed to do. When Iraq repeatedly used gas against the Kurds in 1987–88, there was insufficient television coverage to mobilize public opinion. Even after Halabja in March 1988, where at least 5,000 perished, and after the final Iraqi offensive the following August, Security Council members and other states avoided offending Iraq and its Arab allies for fear of damaging their economic and political interests in the region. When Kurds reported in 1989 that over 3,000 villages and towns had been razed by Saddam Hussein, they were treated with skepticism, as if Western governments could not easily have verified such assertions by satellite photography. When it was possible for journalists to travel through Kurdistan in spring 1991, the truth of Kurdish claims was belatedly confirmed. Since then, credence has also been given to Kurdish claims that 200,000 or more men, women and children were liquidated in the infamous *anfal* operations, 1987–88.

Although they currently enjoy Allied protection, the Kurds of Iraq lack any guarantees for the future. If Turkey refuses to renew the six monthly agreement whereby the Allied aircraft use Incirlik airbase, the Kurds will lose their protection and Saddam Hussein will be tempted to attack them again.

As time passes and the public begins to forget about them, the Kurds feel more vulnerable. For without public interest, Western governments may feel able quietly to withdraw from what may seem like a political quagmire. It should be remembered that Western governments have only involved themselves in the tragedy of Kurdistan with reluctance. They do not wish to see the integrity of either Turkey or Iraq (not to mention other countries where Kurdish minorities exist) compromised by Kurdish separatism.

There are a number of reasons why it is crucial that public opinion should remain well-informed and vigilant about the Kurdish situation. At the humanitarian level a clear moral responsibility rests upon the electorates of parliamentary democracies to ensure that their governments are responsive to the humanitarian dimension of international affairs. It is public silence which permits reluctant governments to disregard international responsibilities, and informed and articulate public opinion which goads them into action.

Then there is the question of international law and norms of behavior. The West allowed Iraq to violate with impunity the 1925 Geneva Protocol on Chemical Weapons, the Universal Declaration of Human Rights, and (arguably) the 1948 Geneva Convention on Genocide with regard to its Kurds. When agreed international standards and conventions are not upheld they are inevitably weakened. Governments should not be allowed to collude with violators in the erosion of these standards. Once again, when governments fail to act, it is the public which must persuade them to take law observance seriously. The story of Kurdistan, like that of Palestine, demonstrates all too clearly the tragic consequences of inertia.

Finally, there is the political dimension. The Kurds claim the right to self-determination. Whether one supports the idea of an independent Kurdish state or of guaranteed autonomy arrangements for areas where the Kurds form a clear majority, it is vital that the international community helps the parties concerned find a peaceful and productive formula whereby approximately 23 million Kurds can play a full part in the development of the Middle East.

At the time of the 1991 Peace Conference, one senior British official forecast with great prescience that "failure to deal adequately with the Kurdish question will leave a permanent sore threatening forever the peace of the Middle East." His warning was not heeded at the time, and has subsequently been tragically fulfilled. Can this running sore now be healed? In Turkey the growing disaffection of over 10 million Kurds threatens a destructive inter-communal conflict unless a process of reconciliation and political rearrangement can be embarked upon. External encouragement in that process remains crucial. In Iraq, the failure to bring the government and its Kurds into peaceful coexistence may lead to even greater humanitarian tragedies than those already experienced. It is too easy to assume that once Saddam Hussein is removed, the Kurds will be able to resolve their problems with a successor government. This is open to question.

The problems which exist between governments and the Kurds, be it in Turkey, Iraq, Iran or elsewhere, cannot be lightly dismissed in simplistic denunciations. The bases of mutual distrust are longstanding and complex. If these problems are to be resolved, as they must be for any process of peaceful conciliation, it is likely that this will be partly because the Kurdish question is better and more widely understood. It is for this reason that this new edition of *A People without a Country* is vitally important.

Introduction

Gerard Chaliand

Minorities Without Rights

Ever since the question of the colonies was settled more or less throughout the world, a particular problem has increasingly come to the fore, especially in the Afro-Asian countries: the problem of oppressed minorities. Ethnic, linguistic or religious minorities are demanding the right to be themselves and to control their own destiny. They insist on reminding us that they form a majority in their own territories, or when they are scattered over a wider area, demand the right to preserve their own identity.[1]

In international assemblies the "right of people to self-determination" is frequently invoked, but always rather vaguely. In principle this right is guaranteed by international law,[2] but its content is actually non-existent and it is well known to depend more often than not on a balance of forces measured in terms of armed strength. Paradoxically, human beings as groups turn out to have fewer rights than individuals — unless they form a state. It is from this absence of their own states that the minorities of the world are suffering today, in that sovereign states, particularly in the Third World, are denying them even cultural rights.

Nations, in the full sense of the word, first appeared during the 18th and 19th centuries in the West, as historic communities politically and economically cemented by a national state and a national market. This model of the nation-state came to be adopted everywhere once the colonial empires of the 19th and 20th centuries had collapsed in Latin America, in Central Europe, in Asia, in North Africa and even in places where the nation had no real existence, as in Tropical Africa. The majority group's nationalism and impulse to centralize resulted more or less everywhere in the oppression of minority groups, a feature accentuated by the fact that the newly independent countries assimilated the modern state's repressive methods more easily than any stress on citizens' rights.

Throughout the world the oppression of minorities manifests itself to varying extents and in a wide variety of forms, including:

Discrimination: rejection of those who belong to a given group.

Cultural oppression: deprivation of the minority's right to use its own language in schools, in publications and in dealings with the administration.

Economic oppression: a systematic bias against the interests of the minority.

Physical oppression: massive implantation of the majority ethnic group or occupation of the minority's territory by means of population transfer.

Genocide: the attempt to eliminate the minority community as a whole.

The diversity of the problem implies that solutions must also be wide ranging, from independence or autonomy to simple preservation of the minority's identity. Yet even cultural rights, which should constitute an *inalienable minimum*, are denied to minorities in several states, notably the ex-colonial ones. The fact is that during the last three decades it has been far easier for a country to achieve formal independence from an ex-colonial power than for a minority to obtain a measure of (effective) autonomy within a Third World state. The reaction to demands of every kind has been almost universally negative.

Tens of millions of people are still being denied the right to use their own language and to have an identity of their own.[3] Leaving aside the right to self-determination, which remains largely hypothetical in practical terms, it would seem that there is an urgent need to define a body of minimal rights, which would be defensible in international law.[4] These rights should include:

Non-discrimination: the right to equality, to identity, or to assimilation (if that is what is wanted).

Inalienable cultural rights: the right to study in one's own language at school, and to use it on broadcasts, in publications and in dealings with the administration.

The right to an equitable share of the country's national wealth.

The right of extra-territorial minorities to preserve their identity within the confines of sovereign states.

International institutions are still incomplete and ineffective when it comes to dealing with matters which come under the heading of "internal affairs." It is essential that international legislation be reinforced, stipulating the rights of minority peoples and groups, notably in cultural matters, and ensuring that the movements representing such minorities are at last assured of a hearing before the various international assemblies. The current tendency is very much in the opposite direction: at the moment the most elementary human rights are denied to combatants or victims involved in domestic armed conflicts.[5]

Nationalism is an ideology which claims to represent the supreme value for the state, and sometimes for its citizens; it can thus justify any injustice, however extreme. The proposition is inadmissible in general, and becomes intolerably so when the majority group's nationalism invokes "reasons of state" (or even "the revolution" and "socialism") to justify denying a minority people the right to transmit and enrich their culture.

Whatever injustices the bourgeois democracies perpetrate upon their minorities, they do allow for a margin of action and for possible improvements which are left largely up to the minorities concerned to campaign for. The "socialist" countries admitted the principle of cultural rights and, in general, applied it, which was already something, although it did not eliminate the fact that the effective status of many minorities in these countries was inequitable, notably in the USSR, where the scale of the issue became apparent when one considered that one Soviet citizen in two was not Russian. Most Afro-Asian states have now achieved independence; unfortunately there has been an increasing tendency for these states to be despotic ones, in the sense that shifts in power are invariably achieved by violence, and political criticism is usually dealt with by repression. This way of doing things is based on an inherited conception which presents hierarchy as an essential ingredient in human reality. Citizens remain subjects, and conceive of themselves as such.

The minorities, which were tolerated by the authorities in the past as long as they gave their allegiance to the weakly centralized states and empires which prevailed at the time, have now become an obstacle to the more extensive form of control which the new states are seeking to impose. This is heightened by the fact that the very notion of minorities having *rights* is alien to a tradition in which the normal practice has been for the despot to distribute favors amongst the leaders of the minorities he used or tolerated. Indeed it is difficult to see how the rights of minorities could be recognized when the mass of the people in the majority are themselves treated like children and addressed only in the hocus-pocus language of nationalist rhetoric.

Public Opinion and the Minorities

In the West, left and liberal-minded people in general, especially in the Scandinavian and Anglo-Saxon countries, have usually supported or at least expressed some sympathy with struggles against both European colonialism and U.S. policies in such places as Vietnam. But as soon as the problem shifted to Biafra, Southern Sudan, Kurdistan or Eritrea — in short, whenever the national question was raised *within* a Third World country — this section of public opinion has tended to remain silent and confused. The reasons for such hesitation include a lack of knowledge of the historical context, a shortage of information, and the effectiveness of the established state's propaganda, especially when it is a state which claims to be pursuing the revolution. Some westerners are opposed to any form of balkanization, for strategic reasons; others fall back on conformism and are content to judge an issue according to who is supporting whom (which often leads to further confusion); there are also those whose support for a state or a group of states is assured in advance, and who will assess a situation accordingly (for some people Arabism is revolutionary by definition, just as any opposition to the policies of the Israeli government seems inherently anti-semitic to others). Finally, most people are wary of giving their support to an insufficiently radical or even conservative minority movement struggling against a state which claims to be anti-imperialist or revolutionary. Such caution ignores the basic issues, which are that a minority is being *oppressed*, even if it is in the name of socialism; that its right to preserve its cultural identity is absolute; and that its right to self-determination has usually been denied for so long that armed struggle has become the only form of freedom left to it.

It is quite true that some of the minority movements in conflict with established states seem more reactionary in their alliances and more conservative in their social policies and ideology than the states which oppress them — although appearances are sometimes deceptive. Nonetheless, these movements' demands for self-determination and cultural rights are nearly always fully justified. During the 1960s, in Southern Sudan, an armed movement struggling against the ethnic, religious, economic and cultural oppression practiced by a central state which was leftist in orientation at that time, was supported by Haile Selassie's Ethiopia, Israel, a few European mercenaries and the funds of the Catholic Church. But this does not change the fact that Southern Sudan was oppressed and that it was only after a prolonged armed struggle that the Sudanese government very grudgingly granted it a minimum of autonomy. So one should always examine the relationship between a state and its minorities *before* applying ideological criteria, since such relations are oppressive more often than not.

The History of the Kurdish Movement

In this context, the Kurdish people have the unfortunate distinction of being probably the only community of over 15 million persons which has not achieved some form of national statehood, despite a struggle extending back over several decades. The Kurdish national question has constantly been on the agenda ever since the collapse of the Ottoman Empire after the First World War and the ensuing colonial repartition of the Middle East. Since then the Kurdish people have been divided amongst four separate states, namely Turkey, Iran, Iraq and Syria. (There is also a Kurdish minority in the former Soviet Union.) In Turkey, Iran and Syria, they are deprived of the most elementary rights, including the rights to learn their own language at school and to safeguard their cultural identity. In Iraq, population transfers affecting certain oil-rich or frontier areas have considerably reduced the "autonomous region." However, the Kurds are recognized as an entity and do enjoy certain cultural rights.

The Kurds are a mountain people whose economy is mainly based on agriculture and pastoralism. Since antiquity they have occupied a vast area known as Kurdistan, although this geographical term, which designates a mountainous zone reaching from south-eastern Turkey through the northernmost areas of Iraq and well into eastern Iran only covers a part of the regions peopled by Kurds. There are Kurds from the Taurus mountains to the western plateaus of Iran and from Mount Ararat to the foothills adjoining the Mesopotamian plain.

The Kurds speak an Indo-European language which, like Afghan and Persian, is part of the Iranian group of languages. Unlike the Persians, the Kurds are Sunni Muslims. The first recorded text in Kurdish goes back to the

7th century; ensuing literary works were both abundant and of high quality, notably Ehmed Khani's 17th century masterpiece, *Memozin*.[6] From the 11th century onwards, following a decline in the power of the Caliphs, several Kurdish principalities emerged. Although the Kurdish contribution to Muslim culture has not been a major force, it has by no means been negligible. At the beginning of the 16th century, when the Ottoman Empire sought to resist the rising power of the Shiite Persia, it secured the support of the Kurdish principalities. The Persian armies were defeated and the Kurdish princes continued to reign over the territory of Kurdistan in accordance with the pact established with the Sublime Porte, thereby shoring up the eastern frontiers of the Empire. Indeed the Kurdish principalities maintained their prerogatives right up until the beginning of the 19th century.

During the last century, the Sublime Porte became anxious to centralize its threatened and decadent Empire. In an effort to ensure the fullest possible control over its domains, it sought to subjugate the Kurdish principalities. The reaction to the Sultan's encroachments was a series of revolts led by the traditional chieftains (1826, 1834, 1853–55, 1880). These insurrections kept to the traditional pattern: they were struggles against a state authority which was encroaching upon established rights. There was no parallel with the movements inspired by that great European 19th century ideology, nationalism. The traditional chieftains were defending their prerogatives against a central authority, and whilst they certainly did rely on specific local characteristics, they had no wider demands and no modern political vision.

The Kurdish press first emerged in 1898. Following the Young Turk Revolution of 1908, this press began to develop, and in Constantinople it contributed to the debate on national problems. But the Kurdish modernizing elite made up of urbanized elements was still very small. After the defeat and collapse (on October 30, 1918) of the Ottoman Empire, which had sided with the Central Powers, President Woodrow Wilson, in his "Program for World Peace" (Point 12), declared that the non-Turkish minorities of the Ottoman Empire should be granted the right of "autonomous development." Section III, Article 62–63 (Kurdistan) of the Treaty of Sèvres, signed by the Allies and the Turkish government on August 10, 1920, specifically stipulated that the Kurds were to be allowed "local autonomy." The Treaty, which was actually very unfair towards Turkey, was never applied because the subsequent War of Independence (waged with Kurdish support) changed the whole situation and enabled Mustafa Kemal to impose different terms at the Treaty of Lausanne, signed in 1923. Meanwhile, Britain had detached the overwhelmingly Kurdish vilayet (province) of Mosul from Turkey and attached it to Iraq, which was then a British mandate, in order to seize control of the Mosul oilfields. When the frontiers between Turkey and Syria were drawn up, three areas settled by Kurds were integrated into Syria under French mandate. The division of the Kurdish people was complete.

As early as 1924, Kemalist Turkey passed a law forbidding the teaching of Kurdish in school. Later, Article 89 of the Turkish law concerning political parties and associations stipulated that such organizations "must not claim that there are any minorities in the territory of the Turkish Republic, as this would undermine national unity." The regime crushed three major national insurrections, in 1925, 1930 and 1935, deprived the Kurds of all rights, and imposed on them the euphemistic reference "mountain Turks." In the meantime, several hundred thousand Kurds were deported to central and western Anatolia. From 1925 to 1965 Kurdistan was a "military area" to which foreigners were denied access. In the years 1960 to 1980, despite periods of relative political liberalism, the Kurdish national problem, which involves more than 20% of the population, was mentioned publicly only once. This was in 1970, when the Turkish Workers Party passed a resolution recognizing the *existence*(!) of the Kurdish people and the legitimacy of its democratic demands. The Party was banned as a result.

In Iran, the Kurds manifested their opposition to Reza Shah's centralizing policies by a series of revolts during the 20s and 30s. In 1941, the British and the Soviets invaded Iran to prevent Reza Shah's pro-Axis sympathies turning into a military alliance. Free from central control, the Azerbaijanis and the Kurds each began to organize, and in December 1945 the Kurds proclaimed the Mahabad Republic. It lasted for a year, until the Shah's troops overran it and executed its leaders. Mustafa Barzani and a hundred followers managed to escape to the Soviet Union.

The Shah's policy (until his overthrow in 1979) was somewhat more flexible than the Turkish one, but still granted practically no rights to the Kurds — or to any other minority. It is worth remembering that the Persians are far from being the majority in Iran, even though they dominate it.

The Franco-Turkish Treaty of 1921 incorporated three Kurdish areas — Djezira, Kurd-Dagh and Arab-Pinar — into Syrian territory. In 1963 a plan to Arabize parts of Djezira was launched. It was revived in 1967. Officially the project of creating an "Arab belt" all along the frontier was dropped in 1976, but the Kurds still have no rights at all in Syria.

In terms of cultural rights, the position of the Kurds would seem to be better in Soviet Armenia than anywhere else.

Iraq (the old vilayets of Baghdad and Basra) was detached from the Ottoman Empire at the end of the First World War. Britain, the mandate power, eventually annexed the oil-rich Kurdish vilayet of Mosul. In 1922, a joint Iraqi-British declaration recognized the Kurds' right to "form a Kurdish government within the Iraqi frontiers." Despite Kurdish uprisings in 1919 and 1923, the League of Nations allocated the province to the new state for 25 years in 1925, with the recommendation that the Kurds should be granted a degree of autonomy and various cultural rights. These cultural rights were, in fact, granted by the British occupying authorities. The Kingdom of Iraq became nominally independent in 1931 but remained under British influence until the July 1958 Revolution.

Once the mandate had come to an end, the Iraqi government sought to establish its control over the northernmost areas of the province; the Barzanis, led by Mustafa Barzani, revolted in 1922 and were crushed by the British Royal Air Force. They rose up again in 1943 and eventually moved into Iran, at the time of the Mahabad Republic (1945).

The 1958 Revolution defined Iraq as a country made up of "two peoples," the Arabs and the Kurds. Mustafa Barzani returned from the USSR. But relations with the Qasim government deteriorated very quickly and in 1961 the Kurds launched a war of liberation to secure autonomy within the framework of the Republic. Between 1961 and 1968 the armed struggle waged by the Kurds caused the fall of four Iraqi regimes, until the presently dominant wing of the Baath came to power in July 1968. In March 1970, the new regime signed an agreement with the Kurdish leaders promising autonomy for Kurdistan in all areas of Iraq which a projected census would establish as having a mainly Kurdish population. This census, which would have been decisive in the oil-rich Kirkuk area, was never carried out. Conflict broke out once more when, in March 1974, the Baghdad government decided to implement unilaterally a restricted form of autonomy. The war, in which the Kurdish movement enjoyed the tactical support of the Iranian regime — and the covert support of the U.S. — came to an end with the March 1975 Algiers agreements between Iran and Iraq. A prisoner of its own alliances, the Kurdish movement, led by Barzani, opted for surrender.

Right from the mid-1960s, the Kurdish national movement received aid from Iran, as part of an attempt by that country to weaken Iraq, its opponent in various border disputes and litigation over navigation rights. In exchange for this aid, Barzani contributed to freezing the situation in Iranian Kurdistan, and even went so far as to execute or hand over to the Shah some Iranian Kurdish cadres who also favored insurrection against the Iranian state. According to the CIA,[7] the Shah had informed Baghdad as early as December 1972 that he was prepared to cut off all aid to the Kurds if Iraq would consent to negotiate. The Pike Report to the U.S. Congress reveals that the Kurdish leadership received secret Washington funds amounting to $16 million between 1972 and 1975. Indeed, even the State Department was not informed of these high level dealings conducted by Nixon and Kissinger through the intermediary of the CIA. For the Americans, the point of these operations was not to contribute to the setting up of an autonomous Kurdish state, but to weaken Iraq, an ally of the USSR from 1972 until the late 1980s. The report indicates that Barzani had made it known that he had absolutely no faith in the Shah, but that the U.S. had guaranteed that the flow of Iranian aid would not be interrupted abruptly.

The March 6, 1975 Algiers agreement between Iraq and Iran put an end to the struggle led by Mustafa Barzani, a struggle in which the Kurdish forces were organized in classical military units and were thus heavily dependent on the logistics and supplies provided by Iran.

Shortly afterwards, and for more than a year, the Iraqi government proceeded to implement a policy of Arabization in the oil-rich and the frontier Kurdish areas such as Kirkuk, Khanaqin and Sindjar. Hundreds of thousands of Kurds, at a conservative estimate, were deported to the south or to the shrunken "autonomous region" which the Baghdad government had allocated to them. Kurdish officials were transferred to Arab Iraq and replaced by Arab officials faithful to the government. Towns and villages in parts of Kurdistan were renamed. Kirkuk became El-Taamin. The autonomy of the Kurdish area was restricted to the operations of an executive body appointed by Baghdad and a legislative body following government guidelines. But at least cultural rights were maintained. Limited and spontaneous guerrilla activity broke out again in the summer of 1976. However, the Iraqi Army remained in control, and even built several strategic hamlets to enable it to patrol the Kurdish areas more effectively. In parallel, some effort was made towards reconstruction and the implantation of a few small industrial plants.

After this disaster, the Kurdish national movement inevitably underwent a profound crisis, which took the form of a split into three factions, each of which has published more or less radical critiques of the events which led up to the present situation. The three groups are the Democratic Party of Kurdistan, "provisional leadership"; the Kurdistan Patriotic Union; and the Democratic Party of Kurdistan, "preparatory committee."

The Weaknesses of the Kurdish National Movement

The Kurdish movement collapsed in the 1970s and 1980s not because it had established "unnatural" alliances but because it did not take the ambiguity of these alliances sufficiently into account and seek to ensure its own military and political autonomy. Its weakness stemmed from the limitations of the movement itself. Although a genuinely national movement, it has never been able (or attempted) to radicalize itself in order to develop an organic link between the masses and a people's army fired with a revolutionary national ideology. On the contrary, an increasingly orthodox army failed to establish real contact with a largely passive population of refugees. The deadweight of a tribal mentality, of the notables and of the corruption of various military cadres contributed to the perpetuation of the traditional relations. True, other movements suffering from these disadvantages have succeeded in other contexts, but the exceptionally difficult geopolitical conditions under which the Kurdish movement labored called for something very different. A revolutionary ideology and a degree of modernity were lacking in the Kurdish leadership, and this may well have had something to do with the generation to which its main leader belonged.

Through the centuries, the Kurdish national movement has consistently manifested itself somewhat belatedly compared to the movements of the majority peoples of the surrounding areas. This is attributable to the economic, social, political and cultural level attained by Kurdish society. A mountain people, and, like nearly all mountain peoples, relatively backward, with a very small elite, the Kurds have historically been overtaken and crushed by the old, well-established statist tradition of the Persians and, to an even greater extent, by that of the Turks. At the time of the First World War, the Kurds were clearly well behind in development as compared to the other national movements within the Ottoman Empire, notably in the Balkans and eastern Anatolia. Kendal[8] correctly highlights the Kurdish movement's political inability to seize the historic opportunity which presented itself during the brief period of political vacuum from 1918 to 1920, following the collapse of the Empire. Throughout the first half of this century, the Kurdish revolts remained largely traditional uprisings.

Conditions were different in Iraq, a newly formed state in which, until 1968–70, the Kurds faced a state apparatus which was not yet firmly established. But this ceased to be the case under the government of Saddam Hussein, who, with the British, can in some senses be called the architect of the Iraqi state. Furthermore, it is in Iraq that the proportion of Kurds·in the population is most favorable to their cause (1 in 3 as opposed to 1 in 4 or 5 in Turkey and 1 in 6 in Iran).

The second wave of nationalism in the Orient came after the Second World War. Despite its considerable failings, the Mahabad Republic was an expression of this wave, in that it concretized a national project, albeit one without very clearly defined perspectives. Its ideology remained traditionalist, especially in matters of social class. In the end, for a variety of reasons, the Republic collapsed without a fight.

The Kurdish movement in Iraq from 1958 to 1975 continued to reflect the backwardness of Kurdish society. The leadership never managed to set itself the goal of rising above its own society, carrying the masses with it, as other revolutionary leaderships succeeded in doing elsewhere.[9] Combined with the severe geopolitical handicaps, this is the crucial point which underlies the main weaknesses of the Kurdish national movement: *its elites were backward*, and this historical inheritance has perpetuated the crisis of Kurdish society and weighed heavily on the course of its national destiny. A traditionalism in values, mentality and behavior has still not been replaced by an alternative conception of things. Instead there has been merely a degree of adaptation to the codes of modernity; however the knowledge and use of this ritual modernity engenders no real change. The fundamental values are still those of yesterday: tactical cunning instead of political analysis, clientist maneuverings instead of political mobilization, and a few revolutionary slogans instead of a real radical practice.

What the Kurdish movement in the second half of this century has lacked, both quantitatively and qualitatively, is a mainly petty-bourgeois modernist intelligentsia. Even when they were present, such elements remained powerless. But if they can find a way of establishing links with the masses, they should be able to play a decisive role in the next phase of the national movement.

It is up to the Kurdish national movement to define and articulate a double strategy: on the regional and international levels, in the pursuit of cultural rights and recognition of a Kurdish entity; on the level of each of the four states concerned, in association with local democratic forces, to bring about a change in the status quo.

After an introduction covering the history of the Kurdish people under the Ottoman Empire, which provides the overall historical context, the texts in this work deal with every aspect of the Kurdish question from the end of the First World War to the collapse of the armed struggle led by Mustafa Barzani in Iraq (1975). The book's originality lies partly in the fact that it covers the Kurdish communities in Turkey, Iran and Iraq, as well as the Kurds of Syria and the USSR, and partly in that these questions are dealt with by Kurdish intellectuals who provide a critical examination of the national movement's heritage.

Notes

1. Cf. ideas expressed in "Les Kurds et le droit des peuples minoritaires," *Le Monde*, March 17, 1976 and in "Des minorites encombrantes," *Le Nouvel Observateur*, July 12–18, 1976.
2. As in the United Nations Charter, Articles 1 and 55; the right to self-determination is recognized by the UN General Assembly's Resolution 2625/xxv, October 24, 1970.
3. "Certain ethnic groups are well treated by the dominant nations only to the extent that these groups accept abandoning their culture, their mother tongue, their history and their literature, in other words to the extent that they accept assimilation. We have a duty to encourage these ethnic groups to oppose assimilation, to develop and enrich their mother tongue, their literature and their culture. Only in this way can world culture develop, enrich itself and serve humanity" (Article 18 of the Statutes of the Human Rights Commission).
4. Cf. *Declaration universelle des droits des peuples*. July 4, 1976 (Section vi on Minority Rights, Articles 19–21), Maspero (Paris; 1977).
5. Except under a colonial administration, a foreign occupation or a racist regime; minorities are thereby excluded from the scope of the law. Cf. the International Red Cross's diplomatic conference on human rights in war time, Geneva, April–May 1977; details in *Le Monde*, June 9, 1977.
6. Roger Lescot, *Mame Alan*, a collection of oriental writings. Institut Francais de Beyrouth, *Textes Kurdes*, Vol. II, 1942.
7. The Pike Report reproduced in *The Village Voice*, New York, February 23, 1976.
8. Cf. "Kurdistan in Turkey" in this volume.
9. Vietminh or NLF in Vietnam, Amilcar Cabral's PAIGC, the Eritrean PLF, etc.

1

The Kurds under the Ottoman Empire

Kendal

The present situation of the Kurdish people can only be understood in its historical context, notably in the light of the events of the last hundred years.

From Ottoman Cosmopolitanism to Ethnic Nationalisms

The Ottoman Empire, having failed to adapt to the Industrial Revolution, undermined by internal contradictions (the maintenance of a gigantic army, a "statist" landholding system which prevented an evolution towards capitalism, the sclerosis of scientific and philosophical thought due to absolutism, etc.) and harassed by Austria and expansionist Czarist Russia, finally began to fall apart during the 19th century.

Under the pretext of renovating and modernizing the Empire, Britain imposed unequal treaties and "reforms" (Tanzimat, 1839) which, added to previous capitulations, furthered the process of disintegration.

From 1878 the finances of an insolvent, ruinously indebted Ottoman Empire came under the control of a European Council for the Ottoman Debt made up of representatives of the creditor nations (Britain, France, Germany, Austria and Italy). The Ottoman Bank, a private establishment operating on Anglo-French capital, obtained the exclusive right to issue currency. The exploitation of minerals, railways and external trade passed entirely into European hands. Foreign advisers were imposed on the Army and the administration. Lord Stratford Canning, the British Ambassador to Istanbul, was charged with supervision of the "proper implementation of the reforms" and could make and break ministries at will. The dominated peoples of the Balkans, who had always considered the Ottoman Empire as an apparatus for repression and tax collection, made the most of the new balance of forces and launched national liberation struggles. At the other end of the Empire, the Kurds began to agitate as well.

As a reaction to the foreign influx and the creeping colonization of an

11

Empire whose anachronistic structure was being undermined by nationalism, there emerged another nationalism, a defensive and conservative *Ottoman* nationalism. From 1865 onwards, the upholders of "Ottomanism" (Namik Kemal, Zia Pasha) — the New Ottomans, as they came to be known — were beginning to ask themselves how to go about modernizing the Empire, eliminating the prevailing misery, corruption and aimlessness, and ridding themselves of the Sultan's absolutism and arbitrariness. They suggested that the adoption of a "good" constitution, which recognized the equality and freedom of all nationalities in the Empire would put an end to "separatism." Such a constitution would also promote education and "enlighten minds," thereby enabling the "Ottoman nation" to achieve a Western level of civilization.

This constitutionalist movement recruited its partisans from the ranks of the young officers and intellectuals.[1] By the 1890s it was calling itself the "Young Turk" movement. The Ottoman bourgeoisie, the social base of the movement, was heterogeneous in the extreme and seriously divided amongst itself by divergent interests. It was made up of three main groupings: (1) The (Christian) Greek and Armenian merchants, who were the privileged, if not the only, intermediaries of Britain and France, and who were the most prosperous; (2) The Ottoman civil and military comprador bureaucrats who benefited from foreign commissions and bakshish and had strong links with European interests; and (3) The puny Turkish commercial bourgeoisie, whose interests were slighted by a system geared to those of the foreign powers (the Jewish merchants, laboring under the same disadvantage, were also members of this group).

Contradictory and antagonistic interests led to a split in the Young Turk movement in 1902. The aspirations of the first two of the above groups for *political* freedom and stability (i.e. elimination of arbitrary rule) found expression in the tendency formed around Prince Sabhattine, which eventually emerged as the Freedom and Conciliation Party (*Hurriyet ve Hilaf Partisi*). It campaigned for a liberal Turkey under British protection, where power would be held by the most competent without discrimination on grounds of race or creed. Under the prevailing conditions, this would have amounted to acceptance of the dominance exercised by the essentially non-Muslim cosmopolitan bourgeoisie.

As for the Muslim bourgeoisie's demands, these were for a *national* economy and for a constitutional state, and were put forward by the majority wing of the Young Turks who kept the original name of the organization once the Prince's friends had left; they were the Ottoman Society of Union and Progress (*Osmani Ittihet ve Terakki Cemiyeh*), or more popularly the Union and Progress Committee.[2] The fashionable watchword of the day was a call for "Muslim firms, Muslim banks, Muslim factories and Muslim merchants." Replacing the New Ottomans' *Ottoman* nationalism, the Unionists represented a *Muslim* nationalism; the next stage of the process was the emergence of a *Turkish* nationalism. The Unionists sought to preserve the unity of the Muslim peoples of the Empire. They were particularly concerned about national independence and categorically rejected all foreign intervention. Many Arab, Kurdish and Albanian intellectuals joined the Turkish elements as militant members of Union and Progress. Furthermore, this organization had reached an agreement with the Armenian and Bulgarian Social Democrats to overthrow Sultan Abdulhamid II, the symbol and incarnation of "oriental" despotism, and to elect a representative assembly which would adopt a constitution recognizing and guaranteeing freedom and formal equality for all the peoples of the Empire. Having little faith in the unificatory virtues of a formal equality of peoples, the Sultan preferred to believe that pan-Islamism was the only ideology which could preserve the Islamic conglomerate which the Empire had effectively become by the end of the 19th century. In order to face up to the "Christian menace," what was required was a political union of all Muslims under the authority of the Caliph — who just happened to be the Sultan himself. This pan-Islamism was actively supported by Germany, which was seeking to colonize Anatolia and Mesopotamia (exemplified by its building of the Baghdad railway).[3]

In July 1908 the Unionists came to power through a military coup. This marked the beginning of the *Turkish* bourgeois revolution, which only came to an end after fifteen tumultuous years, with the final victory of Mustafa Kemal in 1923. In its early stages it aroused general enthusiasm and was hailed by all the nationalities concerned as the beginning of a new era. The imperial *iradeh* (edict) proclaiming the constitution led to emotive displays of fraternization.[4] Five months later, elections were held and parliament convened. Certain democratic liberties were granted to the non-Turkish nationalities, notably the right to publish and teach in their own languages. This phase of relative freedom, unprecedented in the annals of the Ottoman Empire, was ephemeral. Before long the autonomist Albanian movement, which was calling for the election of an autonomous Albanian assembly, was crushed; the intellectuals of the other nationalities, who had worked with such conviction and devotion for the victory of what they had thought of as an "egalitarian revolution," began to quit the Unionist ranks in droves. From then on, they opted for separation and the independence of their own people. Albania and Bulgaria won their independence during the Balkan Wars of 1912–13. In its turn the Arabian peninsula was swept by insurgency.

The constitution and the "new spirit" had revealed themselves to be inoperative and the myth of Ottoman unity had been shattered. The Union and Progress Committee adopted a much harder line. All non-Turkish associations, publications and schools were banned. Now made up exclusively of Turkish nationalists, the Unionists proclaimed pan-Turanism as their official ideology. In fact, even long before this proclamation, they had been applying it in practice, thereby finally breaking all their links with the other nationalities. Largely inspired by pan-Germanism, this tendency sought to found a great Turanian Empire stretching from European Turkey to the steppes of Central Asia.[5] Sultan Rashid, who came to the throne following the overthrow of the pan-Islamist Abdulhamid, was himself strongly inclined towards the Turkish nationalists' pan-Turanian theories. The pan-Turanian Empire which the Turkish nationalists dreamt of — and still dream of — was in no way ethnically homogeneous: between Turkey and Turania (Azerbaijan,

Uzbekistan, Turkmenistan, Kirghizia, etc.) there lay Armenia and Kurdistan, populated by non-Turks. On the eve of the First World War, the Unionist leaders had found their own solution to this problem; to use the war in order to destroy these national entities, by physical liquidation if possible; and, if not, then by massive deportation geared to thinning them out as much as possible.[6] The Armenians who, as Christians, were considered to be unassimilable would be exterminated. The Kurds, on the other hand, were to be dispersed, deported or liquidated as required.

The Origins of the Kurdish National Movement

Although the idea of being part of a Kurdish national community emerged very early amongst certain literate members of the community, the formation of a social base for nationalism is a relatively recent development in Kurdistan, for a variety of historical reasons, first amongst which is the special status which Kurdistan enjoyed within the Ottoman Empire.

The Status of Kurdistan

The history of Kurdo-Ottoman relations goes back to the early 16th century. At the time Kurdistan, with its countless principalities and fiefdoms, was in a constant state of war with the Shah of Persia, who sought to annex it.

During the Perso-Ottoman battle of Tchaldyran (north of Kurdistan) in 1514, the Kurdish chieftains fought alongside the Ottoman Sultan Selim the Cruel and contributed to his victory. As a result, Selim the Cruel concluded a pact with the main Kurdish lords. The fact that the Kurds, like the Ottoman Sultan, were Sunni Muslims, while the Shah was a Shiite, must also have played some part in bringing the Kurds round to the Ottoman side.

The Kurdo-Ottoman pact formally recognized sixteen independent principalities of various sizes, about fifty Kurdish sanjaks (fiefdoms) and a number of Ottoman sanjaks.[7] The powerful princes of southern Kurdistan were given independent status and enjoyed all the attributes of sovereignty: they could strike coinage, and the Friday public prayer (the *Khutba*) was recited in their name. They were not accountable to the Sultan, nor did they have to pay him tribute. But — and this was important — they were bounden not to rise against the Porte and not to modify the frontiers of their "state," supposedly so as to protect the rights of adjoining principalities but actually to prevent the emergence of a centralized state in Kurdistan.

The most inhospitable areas, where any form of military control seemed quite spurious, were set up as Kurdish sanjaks and left to the Kurdish Beys (often tribal chiefs) who became vassals of the Porte. The Beys had a free hand within their fiefdoms and their power was hereditary. In exchange for their privileges, these irrevocable and irremovable Beys were expected to fight as *sipahi's* or knights in the imperial campaigns, notably those against Persia. These Ottoman sanjaks covering about a third of the territories of Ottoman Kurdistan (the northern regions and part of the valleys of the Tigris and Euphrates, as well as important urban centers such as Kiyurbekir, Siirt,

Mardin, Kharput, etc.) were administered according to the standard pattern of Ottoman rule.

"Feudal" Kurdistan

This status was for the most part respected by both sides until the beginning of the 19th century. Most of Ottoman Kurdistan, broken up as it was into principalities and sanjaks, was effectively independent. As a general result of this independence, a specifically Kurdish literature, culture and civilization grew up and blossomed. In it, one can find Sufi (Bateh), mystical (Jazari, Beyazidi), patriotic (Khoni, Koyi), and revolutionary (Feqiheh, Teyran) orientations.

Certain Kurdish towns such as Bitli, Djazireh and Hakkai, the capitals of the most powerful Kurdish states, were important cultural centers where poets, musicians and scientists were protected and encouraged. The more ambitious amongst the latter would sometimes go to Constantinople in search of a wider reputation (people like Fuzuli, Nabi, Nefi, etc.).

The Kurdish kinglets held court in a style which was just as splendid and luxurious as that of their contemporaries. The clichés spread abroad by certain travelers and missionaries since Marco Polo, depicting the Kurds as savage nomads living lives of banditry and pillage, were quite inaccurate. During this period, which is known as the Kurdish cultural renaissance and the golden age of Kurdish "feudalism," the society was practically cut off from the outside world. Far from the capitals, sheltered from any threat of invasion which might have jeopardized their sovereignty, the Kurdish princes, whose horizons often extended no further than their own frontiers, proved incapable of uniting their people under a single central authority. The quarrels over supremacy and precedence endemic to feudalism set them against one another, and the pact with the Sublime Porte also prevented them from coming together and uniting. In addition, one Sultan fanned divisions and rivalries with a positively Byzantine cunning and, as guarantor of the status quo, opposed any modification of it. To go against the authority of the Sultan-Caliph, "God's shadow on Earth," was quite unthinkable for these would-be pious princes — as long, that is, as he did not attempt to infringe on their prerogatives. Their consciousness of *Umma* (Islamic community) far outstripped any Kurdish national consciousness, if it ever existed for them as such.

Even though subjective factors, such as the ambitions of the princes and the influence of religion, played an important role in inhibiting the development of a Kurdish national consciousness which could have acted as the basis for setting up a Kurdish national state, the main obstacle was the socio-economic structure of Kurdistan itself. At the time, most of the population were farmers and pastoralists. The main form of organization was tribal. The rulers of the Kurdish sanjaks were nearly always the chiefs of the most important tribe in the area. This was also true of the kinglets, who headed confederations of tribes, of which they were the customary chieftains.

Tribalism seems to have been the main barrier to the emergence of a national consciousness: even the powerful grip of religion upon the Kurdish people was merely one of its corollaries. We believe that this same feature was mainly responsible for the failure of nearly all the revolts and insurrections aimed at setting up an independent and united Kurdish state which broke out in the early 19th century and which all eventually collapsed due to betrayals, switching of allegiances, divisions amongst the Kurds themselves, and the tribal ideology.

Pastoralism, the economic basis for tribalism, was for centuries the main activity in the uplands of Kurdistan. The rugged slopes of the mountains and valleys which make up most of the country are not propitious for agriculture, which was practiced mainly in the valleys of the Tigris and Euphrates. The use of grazing land, the long treks through an inhospitable landscape and the need to protect the herds all contributed to making pastoralism a community activity, requiring strong and durable links between the members of that community. The clan based on blood ties, and its more developed organizational form, the tribe, met these needs exactly.

Just like any other form of social organization, the tribe has its own system of values, geared to ensure its self-preservation. Traditional pastoralism requires no formal education. Its techniques, which are particularly unsusceptible to changes, do not call for the acquisition of new knowledge. Furthermore, even if members of the tribe should wish to educate themselves, the need to travel would make it very difficult. Only town dwellers and settled agricultural village communities are in a position to enjoy the privilege of education. The mountain tribes have few contacts with the outside world and they live an isolated existence in symbiosis with their natural environment. Members of a tribe who, day in day out, confront the harsh conditions of life and the pitiless forces of nature have a paramount need for a simple explanation of the world which offers some hope of another easier life.

Once convinced, they will defend their conviction with their lives, just as they will never allow anyone to besmirch the honor of the tribe. Manicheism is another characteristic of this mentality. If members of a tribe are convinced that someone is telling the truth, they will stake everything on that person's word — as honor requires — and will discount any other possibility. The harmful consequences of such a mentality, which is quite obviously incapable of coping with the complex and subtle factors that come into play during a national liberation struggle, were to handicap all Kurdish uprisings during the 19th century and most of the 20th century as well.

The concept of "I" hardly exists in the context of a tribal culture's value system: "we" (the tribe) predominates. Individuals define themselves entirely in terms of their tribe. They are first a member of this or that tribe, then a Muslim, a Yezidi, or a Christian. The sense of being a member of a national group, a Kurd for instance, comes a very poor third. Any other tribe whatsoever, even one which is of the same religion and nationality, is inferior to their own, and its members will be seen as necessarily potential and intrepid adversaries or even enemies.

As a form of social organization the tribe is already a proto-state. It manages production, keeps the peace internally and organizes defense. The chief of the tribe, who often also fills the role of religious leader, embodies executive power; his orders have the force of law. The tribal system of values, internalized and adopted by all its members, its traditions and mores all weld the tribe into a unity committed to following the lead given by the chief. He acts as a screen between the tribe and the outside world. There is no hope of getting the members of the tribe to support any course of action without the assent and participation of the tribal chieftains.

Unfortunately, the chiefs are divided amongst themselves by quarrels over supremacy and grazing land, by vendettas and by sectarian conflicts, and can come to an agreement — and a short-lived one at that — only very rarely, for instance when they feel threatened. It does not take much for a difference of opinion to turn into a matter of honor and pride, for old enmities to re-surface, shattering a fragile unity. In such cases this or that tribe will go over to the forces of some foreign aggressor simply so as not to fight alongside tribes which it has quarreled with and considers as its worst enemies. The history of Kurdistan is full of this kind of treason and disunity. There is no point in expecting some sort of national consciousness to graft itself upon a monolithic and inert tribal consciousness.

The 19th Century Uprisings

It was within this frozen dynamism that a divided, scattered and still largely tribal Kurdish society entered the 19th century. But, right from the first years of that century, new elements began to break into this stagnant universe. To begin with, there was the Ottoman intervention in the affairs of the Kurdish princes.

As the Sublime Porte's grip in Europe began to slip, it sought to recruit new troops to bolster its failing empire. It was then that the Porte turned to Kurdistan as the only unexhausted source of manpower, thereby infringing on the privileges of the Kurdish feudalists.

Western penetration, in the form of missions, consulates and schools, also began to manifest itself as early as 1835. Throughout the century, Kurdish territory was to be used as the theater for the Russo-Turkish (1828–30, 1877–78) and Turko-Persian wars, bringing in their wake a level of destruction and pillage which eventually awakened feelings of exasperation and hostility towards the Ottoman authorities amongst the Kurdish population. New developments such as greater contact with the outside world, Mehmet Ali's successes in Egypt, etc., finally began to have an impact on the Kurdish feudal chieftains, whose privileges were being threatened. The defense of these privileges, the stubborn refusal to pay any tribute whatsoever or to furnish the Porte with soldiers was to be the driving force of over fifty insurrections which broke out during the century.

What were the distinctive features of these uprisings? The first point is that they were geared to the creation of an independent Kurdistan, and led by feudalists whose main concern was to preserve and extend their own privileges. In this regard it is worth nothing that, apart from a few spontaneous *jacqueries*, they all started in independent principalities. The "states" of Baban

Soran, Hakkari, Bahdinan (Amadiya) and Bohtan — all fiefs which were the pride of Kurdish "feudalism" — were the starting points for all the main insurrections.[8] If these insurrections failed, it was because of a dearth of political experience, the absence of any overall program or military strategy, the lack of foreign support and, above all, the tribal ideology which spawned innumerable splits and betrayals. Faced with a danger which threatened all of them, the Kurdish chieftains nonetheless went into battle as a disjointed force. Despite themselves, they played into the hands of the Sultan, who deployed great ingenuity in playing them off one against the other, so as to subordinate them all.

The Baban Revolt

The first important Kurdish revolt of the 19th century broke out in 1806 in the principality of Baban, under the leadership of Abdurrahman Pasha. The principality, which Suleiman the Magnificent had established following the annexation of southern (Iraqi) Kurdistan, had developed considerably during the 17th century and played an important part in the political affairs of the area during the second half of the 18th. The Baban, an ambitious warlike tribe, had extended their territories at the expense of the Ottoman Empire and Persia. They were also builders, as can be seen from their numerous *medresseh*'s, their works of art, and particularly from the town of Suleimanieh (the present principal city of Iraqi Kurdistan), which they built as their capital and a monument to their greatness. When Ibrahim Pasha Bebe, the founder of Suleimanieh, died, the Ottoman authorities, worried by the power of the Babans, attempted to impose Khalid Pasha, a member of a rival Kurdish tribe, as Emir. The slight affronted Abdurrahman Pasha, Ibrahim Pasha's nephew; he stabbed the Turkish governor of Koy Sanjak and defeated Khalid Pasha's forces. For three years he led an offensive against the Ottoman armies allied with those Kurdish tribes who had joined them out of rivalry with the Babans. Eventually, he was defeated and took refuge in Iran towards the end of 1808.

Meanwhile, the Ottoman troops had reinforced their presence in the north of Kurdistan, under the pretext of containing Russia's aggressive ambitions. Extortionate taxation, pillage and the military occupation itself provoked uprisings in several provinces of Erzurum and Van, starting in 1815. Iranian Kurds and Armenians took part in these revolts, which were mainly attempts by the population to defend itself. There was another wave of rebellion during the 1828–29 Russo-Turkish War, which was fought in this part of Kurdistan, bringing desolation and misery again to the people of the region. However, these spontaneous and local movements lacked precise goals and died out fairly quickly.

Mir Mohammed's Attempted Conquest of Kurdistan

The center of gravity of the Kurdish uprisings remained in the mountain fastnesses of southern Kurdistan. After the Baban rising, Mir (Prince)

Mohammed, sovereign of the principality of Soran, lying between the Great Zab and the Iranian frontier, also attempted to take advantage of the Ottoman Empire's difficulties and create an independent Kurdistan. A descendant of the famous Saladin, his dream was to secure for his dynasty the honor of having realized Kurdish unification and independence. The time was ripe. Weakened as they were by the recent war with Russia, the Ottoman forces were also having to contend with the troops of Mehmet Ali, Viceroy of Egypt.

Inspired by the example of Mehmet Ali, Mir Mohammed established armaments factories in his capital, Rawanduz, to turn out his own rifles, ammunition and even cannon. More than two hundred cannons were made in this way, some examples of which can still be seen in Rawanduz and in the Baghdad Museum. At the same time the Mir was working towards the creation of a regular army. Having thus prepared himself, he embarked upon the conquest of Kurdistan. By the end of May 1883, his army, with its 10,000 cavalrymen and 20,000 well-trained infantrymen, had brought the whole of southern Kurdistan under his control and had reached the frontiers of the principality of Bohtan. The Emir of this principality, Bedir Khan Bey, was a powerful chieftain. Mir Mohammed's aim was to unite all the Kurdish chieftains who resented the interference of the Ottomans, but not to extend his own sphere of influence by force. To avoid useless internecine conflict, he invited the Prince of Bohtan to conclude a political alliance against the Porte. But this Prince had his own dreams of one day becoming King of Kurdistan. He rejected the alliance,[9] which would have involved the supremacy of the lord of Rawanduz, although he did send his brother, Seyfeddine, as a form of symbolic support. The Mir also sent ambassadors to the Iranian Kurds, hoping for their assistance in his cause.

Mir Mohammed's activities did not pass unnoticed. The Sultan sent Rashid Pasha with his Siras troops, joined by the armies of the Walis (Governors) of Mosul and Baghdad, to put an end to this threat to the Porte's authority. The Kurdo-Ottoman War raged on throughout the summer of 1834. Von Moltke, at the time a young captain in the Ottoman Army, described the situation: "The battles were very bloody: the Kurds put up a heroic resistance. The Ottoman soldiers had to fight for thirty or forty days to take possession of every insignificant hillock."[10] Throughout the war the regular Kurdish forces were supplemented by guerrilla units. Eventually the exhausted and demoralized Ottoman troops withdrew.

Taking advantage of the respite, the Mir set about the liberation of Iranian Kurdistan, starting from October 1835. He conquered it from end to end and advanced to the borders of Southern Azerbaijan. Everywhere he was greeted as a liberator by the Kurdish populations.[11] After a series of unsuccessful efforts at repelling the Kurdish forces, Persia called upon its "protector," Russia, to provide assistance.

At the beginning of the summer of 1836, there were rumors of a forthcoming Ottoman campaign against Rawanduz. Aware of the danger of having to contend with both Persia and the Ottoman Empire, and fearing especially the latter, the Mir withdrew to his capital with the bulk of his troops. He then attempted to play on the rivalry between Persia and the Empire, seeking to divide his enemies. Messengers were sent to the Shah informing him that the Mir would acknowledge Iranian sovereignty and pay tribute if the Shah would wage war against the Empire and provide the Kurds with material assistance for their own military campaign. But the Persian court was not to be duped so easily. Its differences with the Empire seemed minor compared with the "Kurdish peril" and the Mir's proposition was rejected.

The Kurdo-Ottoman war broke out again, with renewed intensity, towards the end of July 1836. Mir Mohammed had consolidated his capital's defenses. Under the leadership of Ahmed Bey, the Mir's brother, the Kurdish Army, 40,000 strong, sallied forth against the Turkish Army and forced it to retreat. The Ottoman leadership then resorted to a ruse. They invoked religion, calling on the Mir to stop the war and to seek "a reconciliation amongst Muslims." This appeal impressed the mullahs and other religious figures in the Mir's entourage, who exercised considerable spiritual influence over the masses. One mullah, by the name of Khati, who is now considered a traitor by most Kurdish authors, pronounced a *fatwa* (religious decree) which was binding upon all the faithful: "He who fights against the troops of the Caliph is an infidel." The Mir, for all that he was sincerely committed to Islam, was not taken in. Despite Mullah Khati's *fatwa*, he refused to negotiate with the Ottoman Pasha. However, he did not dare attack the religious authorities, for fear of losing the support of the masses.

In the end, deserted by his own people, he had to surrender. He and his family were sent to Istanbul, where Sultan Mahmoud II harangued him about Muslim solidarity and fraternity; meanwhile, the Sultan's armies were pillaging Kurdistan and leaving a trail of fire and blood. After six months of exile in Istanbul, Mir Mohammed was allowed to return to Kurdistan. On the way back (in 1837) he was assassinated by the Sultan's men in Trebizond. The legendary Mir Mohammed was gone, but all over Kurdistan new sparks of revolt and resistance were setting the country ablaze: in the north, in Erzincan, Beyazit and Erzurum; in the center in the province of Bitlis. The Ottoman artillery pounded dozens of villages into the ground and the rebel leaders, Temur Bey and Redjeb Bey, were taken prisoner and hanged. Deprived of its leaders, the revolt collapsed from within. In the east violent conflict broke out in the spring of 1837 between the Ottoman forces and two Kurdish tribes, the Resohkotan and Bekiran of Pasur (today's Kulp, in the province of Diyarbekir). This campaign gradually extended southwards. Before attacking Bohtan, the Ottomans set about the "definitive pacification" of southern Kurdistan, where revolts led by Said Bey of Bahdinan (Amadiya) and Ahmed Bey of Ravanduz, Mir Mohammed's brother, had broken out once again.

Bedir Khan Bey's Revolt

Bedir Khan Bey was born in 1802 in Djazireh, capital of the principality of Bohtan. His family was one of the most powerful in Kurdish "feudalism," hereditary chieftains of the Bokhti tribe and rulers of the principality since the 14th century[12] (with a few interruptions during the occupations by Tamburlane and the "White Sheep"). The court there, held at Djazireh, was prosperous and flourishing. Bedir Khan acceded to power on his father's death in 1821. He organized the most warlike tribes of his territory in a disciplined regular army, established close links with Nurulah Bey, prince of Hakkari and with Mahmoud Khan of Mukus (central Kurdistan), and bided his time.

The Ottoman defeat at Nizib gave him his chance.[13] He moved fast: by the end of 1840 he had extended his influence over all of Ottoman Kurdistan, and struck alliances with the Beys of Kars (northernmost Kurdistan) and with Emir Ardelan (Iranian Kurdistan). According to Safrastian the Armenian, Bedir Khan Bey was an entirely just ruler, not only towards the Kurds but also towards the Armenians, Assyrians, Chaldeans and others. "Christians enjoyed freedom of religion, were allowed their places of worship, in Djazireh as elsewhere, and were in no way discriminated against," according to the report of a Russian traveler of the time who was full of praise for the order, justice and peacefulness which prevailed in the territories controlled by Bedir Khan, in marked contrast to the disorder, injustice and corruption which was the rule in the Ottoman and Persian Empires.[14]

Bedir Khan's fairness and honesty assured him genuine popular support and enabled him to iron out the last wrinkles of conflict between the various communities of Kurdistan. But it was not in itself enough miraculously to eliminate all the divisions and rivalries of a feudal society. These rivalries re-emerged when it came to the trial of strength with the Ottoman forces under Osman Pasha the Lame. The war raged on until the summer of 1847. In the meantime, acting at the request of the Ottoman authorities, English and American missionaries implanted in Kurdistan had set about turning the Christian tribes against the Kurdish leader, and in the end they succeeded. The Christian tribes refused to participate in the battles and stopped paying taxes to Bedir Khan Bey right in the middle of the war.[15]

The war entered its third year, and still no military resolution was in view. Famine, exhaustion and epidemics ravaged both sides but, unlike the Ottomans, the Kurds could not obtain supplies and reinforcements. As the pressure mounted, intrigues and divisions began to emerge. Towards the beginning of summer in 1847, Osman Pasha managed to convince Bedir Khan's nephew, Yezdan Sher, who commanded the eastern flank of the Kurdish forces, to go over to the Ottoman side. The way to Djazireh was wide open.[16] Betrayed by his own nephew, who took with him half of Bedir Khan's forces, the prince left the capital for the more easily defensible fortress of Eruh, where he made his last stand. In the end, he was forced to surrender, and was exiled to Varna and then to Candia (Crete). He was later deported to Damascus, where he died in 1868.

Yezdan Sher was made Governor of Hakkari by the Ottoman government. In 1849 the Porte deported Sherif Bey, Prince of Bitlis, to Istanbul, and replaced him with an Ottoman Wali. One by one, the independent Kurdish principalities were annexed to the Porte. But the Ottoman war of conquest had lasted more than forty years.

The struggle for an independent Kurdistan did not come to an end with the fall of these principalities. It broke out again a few years later, under the leadership of the very same Yezdan Sher whose ambition had led him to betray his uncle, Bedir Khan. Fearing his influence over the Kurdish population, the Porte had stripped him of his functions as Governor of Hakkari in 1850. In 1853, when the Ottoman Empire went to war with Russia, important sections of the Kurdish population refused to take part, even though the Sultan had pronounced it a *jihad* (holy war). The agents of the Czar were no more successful in attracting the Kurds over to the Russian camp, despite all the financial inducements they proffered.

Yezdan Sher (Yezdan the Lion)

Yezdan Sher sought to take advantage of the Russo-Turkish war to channel popular discontent and to set up an independent Kurdistan with himself as King.

In the spring of 1855, he launched into the struggle, at Bitlis. At the head of about 2,000 warriors, he seized the town, expelled the Turkish Governor, installed a Kurd in his place, and marched on to Mosul, which he captured without great difficulty. The arms and munitions seized from this important Ottoman military base enabled him to equip an army of 30,000 partisans, which went on to liberate Siirt, the administrative and military center of the Ottoman occupation in Kurdistan. The struggle was over amazingly quickly, even though Siirt was defended by the conjoined forces of the Walis of Siirt and Baghdad. Within months a vast area from Baghdad to Lake Van and Diyarbekir had come under Yezdan Sher's control, arousing high hopes and many illusions amongst the population. People old enough to bear arms came from all over Ottoman Kurdistan to join his forces; by the end of summer 1855, he had over 100,000 men under his command.[17]

As the winter drew near, the Russians withdrew to their winter quarters, granting the Porte the respite it needed to deal with the insurrection in Kurdistan. Britain and France, allies of the Empire in the Crimean War against Russia, had no reason to welcome the emergence of an independent Kurdistan which might well fall under Russian influence. The British emissary, Nimrud Rassam, set off from Mosul in 1855 with plenty of cash in his coffers and demanded to be received as a mediator at the headquarters of the Kurdish movement. After visiting the tribal chieftains one by one, offering bribes of guns, gifts and money, he set about persuading Yezdan Sher to settle the question of independence through Kurdo-Ottoman negotiations with the British as mediators. Some tribal chiefs accepted the British bribes and refused to carry on with the struggle. As for Yezdan Sher, he may have been an intrepid warrior chief, but he knew little of diplomacy. He believed in Rassam's promises and in the good intentions of "civilized Britain." He had still received no answer to the letter sent to the Russian rulers appealing for their aid.[18] Furthermore, he believed that, as in the case of Greece and Egypt, an independent state could only be set up with the support of a European power.

He set off with Rassam for Istanbul to begin the British sponsored negotiations with the Porte; the moment he arrived at the Ottoman capital, he was imprisoned. His leaderless troops wandered about in the mountains for a while and eventually dispersed.

The Revolt of 1880 (Sheikh Obeidullah)

The last important Kurdish revolt of the 19th century broke out in 1880 under the leadership of Sheikh Obeidullah, involving both the Ottoman Kurds and those of Iran. Obeidullah was the son of Sheikh Taha, whom Khalfin has designated as "the Kurds' greatest spiritual leader." When his father died, Obeidullah inherited his goods as well as his religious influence, which was mediated by the powerful Naqchebendi fraternity. He in turn became "the spiritual leader of Kurdistan."

In December 1872, the Persian government had demanded payment of taxes from the Kurds of Urmieh and Khoy. The Kurds refused outright, and declared that their taxes were paid to the Sheikh, whose father had obtained this privilege in 1836 from Shah Kadjar. Faced with this popular opposition, the Persian authorities sent in the army. The Sheikh, whose authority had been slighted, appealed to the Porte to intervene and obtain reparations from Persia. The Ottoman government sent the Wali of Erzurum to plead the Sheikh's cause in Tehran, but his mission proved abortive: the Shah rejected Obeidullah's demands.

The incident revealed to the Sheikh the fragility of his own power. Hoping to secure Ottoman assistance in his struggle with Persia, the Sheikh sent an admittedly small force to participate in the Russo-Turkish war of 1877–78, which was fought in northern Kurdistan. This war caused much death and destruction in Kurdistan, and led to what was probably the worst famine the Kurdish people had known for centuries. The Ottoman soldiers and officials, whom the Porte could no longer pay, proceeded to terrorize the population, extorting supplies and money. Revolts broke out in Dersim, Mardan, Hakkari, Bahdinan, etc. In these times of trouble, the disciples' hopes turned to the Sheikh, in whom they saw a liberator as well as a spiritual leader. The Sheikh sent an ambassador to Istanbul to demand that the persecution of his people be ended and damages paid for the havoc which had been wreaked. At the same time, he prepared himself for a trial of strength, recruiting from both sides of the border. The Sheikh established contacts with the Sherif of Mecca and the Khedive of Egypt, hoping to obtain their support, and he sent emissaries to the Russian consuls in Erzurum and Van to assess the feelings of the Czarist government on the Kurdistan issue. But Russia had only very recently come to the end of a war with the Ottoman Empire and was fully occupied putting down the Turkoman revolt. On the other hand, the English Vice-Consul came from Van to visit Obeidullah in 1879.[19] After this visit, the Sheikh's forces received weapons and ammunition from the British. These arrived under the cover of famine relief, supposedly without the knowledge of the Ottoman authorities. In fact, the Porte was well aware of what was going on and intended to divert Obeidullah's wrath against Persia.

In early August 1880, 220 tribal chieftains and sheikhs gathered at Chemdinan to work out a battle plan.[20] Obeidullah soon dropped the idea of making war against Persia and the Ottomans simultaneously as too dangerous, and decided to attack Iran first.

The offensive was launched in October 1880. The Kurdish troops, 80,000 strong, quickly liberated Saoudjboulak (Mahabad), Meyandiya and Maragheh, and drew near to Tabriz, the capital of Azerbaijan. But lacking discipline and carried away by their easy victories, the Kurdish soldiers indulged in pillage and did not go on to conquer Tabriz, an important stronghold whose capture might have had a considerable influence on the outcome of the war. Panicstricken, the Shah fulminated at the Porte and insisted that it put an end to the Sheikh's activities. Obeidullah's rapid successes, his great popularity and his intention to set up an independent Kurdistan had begun to worry the Turkish government, who had originally believed that they could use the Sheikh as a weapon against Persia. They therefore began to mass troops in Kurdistan, encircling the Kurdish forces. Caught between the Ottoman army and the Shah's, which had been reinforced by a few hostile Kurdish tribes, the Sheikh ordered his officers to evacuate the territories he controlled and pull out of Iran. The Porte took no punitive measures against Sheikh Obeidullah and his entourage. The Ottoman government felt it might be useful to keep the Sheikh's forces as a weapon against Persia should the need arise. Sultan Abdulhamid II showed himself to be both cunning and paternalistic. He sent presents to the Kurdish chieftains and invited the Sheikh to visit him.

Sheikh Obeidullah's arrival in Istanbul sparked off a veritable diplomatic battle between the Ottoman and Persian Empires. The Sultan's ambassador in Tehran demanded that Iran should compensate the Sheikh for the damages he had suffered in 1870, 1876 and 1881. Influenced by Russia, Iran retorted by demanding compensation for the losses incurred during Obeidullah's campaign in Azerbaijan. In August 1882, right in the middle of this diplomatic fight, the Sheikh slipped away from Istanbul. The Kurdish leader no longer had any illusions about the possibility of liberating his people with the help of the Sultan. He now sought to free himself first from the Ottoman yoke, possibly with the support, or at least the neutrality, of Russia. But Russia was too well pleased with the advantages of its "protection" of Iran and its power play in Turkey to engage in new, and possibly unprofitable, adventures. The Porte caught wind of Obeidullah's negotiations with the Russians and, in October 1882, sent troops to arrest him. He and his family were exiled to Mecca, where he died a few years later. The era of the great 19th century Kurdish feudal revolts had come to an end.

The Pan-Islamic and Assimilationist Policies of Abdulhamid II, the Red Sultan

After the great feudal revolts of the 19th century, the Ottoman dynasty changed its approach and sought an accommodation with the Kurdish ruling classes, hoping to integrate them into the system by allowing them to share in

the advantages of power. Abdulhamid II, a very able sovereign, was extremely gentle with the Kurdish feudalists who had, until then, been revolting
against his authority.

The Ottoman sovereign made great use of a pan-Islamicist appeal and
skilfully dispensed decorations and pensions, which the Kurdish chieftains
took to mean that their personal merits were being recognized. Bahri Bey,
one of Bedir Khan's sons, was appointed aide-de-camp to the Sultan himself.
The descendants of Abdurrahman Pasha Baban obtained senior posts in the
administration and the university. Sheikh Abdul Qadyr, Obeidullah's son,
became President of the Ottoman Senate in 1908 and was later appointed
President of the Council of State. The gates of the imperial palace were kept
wide open for the exiled Kurdish leaders. Simple clan chieftains and notables
also benefited from the imperial magnanimity, receiving honors and titles to
land.

Abdulhamid II saw the incorporation of the Kurdish feudal lords into the
system as the last important stage in the centralization of an Ottoman state
geared to secure the Ottoman aristocracy's domination. This policy of centralization, based on the integration of the Kurdish leaders, enabled the Empire
to make good use of the Kurdish people's warlike qualities, partly as backing
for an eventual conflict with the Russians but mainly as a means of repressing
the national movements of the various peoples struggling against Ottoman
rule, such as the Armenians, the Arabs, the Albanians and even the Kurds
themselves.

Towards the end of November 1890, the Istanbul papers carried an
imperial *iradeh* announcing the creation of a special Kurdish cavalry force to
be known as the Hamidieh. The Hamidieh regiments were originally set up
in areas bordering on the Russian Caucasus (Erzurum and the northern
districts of Bitlis and Van), where the Kurds had not systematically rebelled
against the Porte. The region was also inhabited by an important section of
the Armenian people, whose liberation movement was in full swing. The
iradeh required each household in the areas concerned to provide one horse-
man, with his own horse, or an infantryman who would serve in the Nizamis,
the regular armed forces. The Hamidieh were formed on a tribal basis.

These cavalry units were armed by the government and had to do a specific
period of military service under Turkish officers each year. At the end of the
period they were supposed to hand in their arms and, although the clause was
never enforced, it did indicate that the authorities did not entirely trust them.
In wartime, these regiments of irregulars were to respond immediately to the
Sultan's call. The tribal chiefs were pampered, well paid, often promoted to
posts as officers or as Pashas. Their grip on the peasant masses was significantly reinforced, and their authority became even more absolute, since it was
now apparent that even the state and the Caliph were behind them. In
exchange, they were totally faithful to their "benefactor," Abdulhamid.

Serving under Turkish officers, notably the sinister Zeki Pasha, their
commander-in-chief and organizer, the Hamidieh went into battle for the
first time during the repression of the Armenian movement (1894–96) which
ended in a series of massacres in which tens of thousands of people were

killed. Later, these same "cossacks" were used against the Kurds of Dersim and southern Kurdistan who had risen up against the tyranny of the Sultan. They also went into action under Ibrahim Pasha against Arab nationalists.

These regiments survived the Young Turk "Revolution." Despite popular demands for their dissolution, the authorities kept them on under the new name "tribal regiments of light cavalry" (*achiret hafif suvari alaylari*), partly because they did not wish to anger the tribal chiefs, but mainly because they had every intention of using them again.

Having set up the Hamidieh and arranged for the integration of most of the Kurdish feudalists, Abdulhamid also took care to establish, in 1892, two tribal schools (*achiret mektebleri*) in Baghdad and Istanbul, whose purpose was to inculcate the principles of devotion to the Sultan-Caliph amongst the children of the chieftains of Kurdish and Arab tribes. Although these schools proved short-lived, they were certainly effective, since most of the Kurdish intellectuals formed in these schools evinced a measure of attachment to the Sultan and to the Caliphate right up until the early 1920s.

On the whole, Abdulhamid's Kurdish policy was crowned with success. Sheikh Obeidullah's was the last major Kurdish insurrection (the Dersim and Mosul revolts were purely local). Kurdish nationalism, which could easily have flourished during this period, remained confined to a few intellectual circles. The people themselves blamed their woes not on the "good and pious patriarch Hamid Baba" but on the worthless officials who failed to carry out his orders.

The First Kurdish National Organizations

The Kurdish revolts of the 19th century had no political organization or clearly defined political program. In the Islamic world, as in many parts elsewhere, the idea of creating a political party to organize and lead mass action was imported from the developed countries of Europe by intellectuals who had been formed in European schools. Kurdistan's modern intelligentsia began to emerge only towards the end of the 19th century. The first Kurdish intellectuals nearly all had aristocratic backgrounds: sons of princes exiled to Istanbul, or heirs to tribal chieftains educated in the tribal schools or in the Empire's military academies, which had, in 1870, also thrown open their gates to young Kurds.

In the Istanbul of the turn of the century, a city bubbling with revolutionary and nationalist agitation, these privileged few became familiar with European bourgeois ideas and became, in their turn, modern Kurdish nationalists. Like the intellectuals of other nations, they launched journals and associations, both clandestine and legal.

Until the Young Turk "Revolution," the pioneers of the Kurdish national movement were scattered in disparate circles and groups. A few were active members of Union and Progress.[21] In April 1898, Midhad Bedir Khan Bey founded the first Kurdish journal, *Kurdistan*. This bilingual Kurdo-Turkish publication was mainly cultural and educational in tone. But it also set out to act as a catalyst for the Kurdish national movement, and its pages provided a platform for all Kurdish patriots. Abdurrahman Bey eventually succeeded his brother, Midhad Bey, as editor. As the political circumstances and activities of its editors evolved, the journal was forced to emigrate, first to Geneva, then to London, then to Folkestone. After the Young Turk "Revolution" it reappeared in Istanbul, edited by Soureya Bedir Khan Bey. During the First World War it was once again uprooted, this time to Cairo, where it came out every fortnight.[22]

The first outline of an organization emerged in the period following the Young Turk seizure of power. The Kurdish leaders supported the new regime actively, in the hope that the national demands of the Kurdish people would be met. Taking advantage of the relatively liberal climate during the "Young Turk spring," Emir Ali Bedir Khan Bey, General Sherif Pasha and Sheikh Abdul Qadyr (Obeidullah's son, who was President of the Ottoman Senate), founded an association called *Taali we Terakii Kurdistan* (Recovery and Progress of Kurdistan) which published a Turkish language journal, *Kurt Teavun we Terakki Gazetesi* (Kurdish Mutual Aid and Progress Gazette) edited by Djemil Bey. The *Gazette*, the first legal publicly circulated Kurdish journal, was the focus for a massive debate on the problems of Kurdish culture, language and national unity, and thus very quickly became extremely popular amongst all Istanbul's Kurdish emigrés.

At about the same time (in the fall of 1908) a Kurdish Committee for the Diffusion of Learning (*Kurt Nechri Maarif Djemiyeti*), which seems to have been a subsidiary of the association mentioned above, started a Kurdish school in the Tshenberli quarter of Istanbul.

This association was, properly speaking, not yet a political organization with a well defined structure, program and strategy. It brought together a range of Kurdish emigré intellectuals and patriots whose ideas and ambitions were quite heterogeneous. Its socio-cultural and welfare activities (bringing the light of learning to the darkened minds of the Kurdish street porters) were supposed to prepare the ground for later Kurdish political movements. After an encouraging beginning, and perhaps because of the enthusiasm which made this rapid success possible, quarrels over supremacy broke out amongst the leadership (the Bedirkhanites against Sheikh Abdul Qadyr and his clan of Nehri Seyyeds): old rivalries re-emerged and the Kurdish feudal leaders denounced each other as traitors.[23] The Sheikh left to launch his own journal *Hetawe Kurd* (The Kurdish Sun). These divisions weakened the movement considerably.

While Kurdish activities marked time in Istanbul, Kurdistan itself was beginning to awaken to modern political life. Young militants and intellectuals set up Kurdish clubs (*Kurt Kulupleri*) in the main urban centers, notably Bitlis, Diyarbekir, Mus, Erzurum and Mosul. The Mus club, for example, had established contact with the main tribes of the Vilayet.[24] When it opened at the end of 1908, the Bitlis club had 700 names on its register. Within a few months, it had a membership of several thousand.[25] The clubs were organized on semi-military lines derived from the Young Turks, who had themselves drawn on the model of the Italian Carbonari. These clubs indubitably signaled the start of an organized political struggle in Kurdistan and clearly constituted a first attempt at setting up a modern political organization.

Following the March 1909 mutiny and overthrow of Abdulhamid II, the Young Turks, feeling they could do without non-Turkish intellectuals, threw themselves into their ultra-nationalist adventure. All non-Turkish schools, associations and publications were banned, their leading figures imprisoned or executed. The Kurdish association, the *Gazette*, the Tshenberli schools and the Kurdish clubs were amongst them. The most prominent Kurdish militants were given long prison sentences; some went underground, others, including most of the Bedirkhanites, went into exile once again.

Even during the "Young Turk spring," there had been revolts in Kurdistan; in Dersim, where the rising lasted until the end of 1909, but especially in Mosul, where Sheikh Mahmoud Berezendji — who, ten years later, was to declare himself "King of Kurdistan" and become a serious problem for the British colonialists — supported by the population, the Barzani and Zibari tribes, demanded nothing less than the complete withdrawal of all Ottoman military and administrative personnel from this area of Kurdistan, which he intended to rule as sovereign. The IVth and VIth corps of the Ottoman Army were sent in and sacked about forty villages but did not succeed in reducing Mustafa Berezendji's forces. A shaky compromise, the appointment of one of the Sheikh's relatives as Governor of Suleimanieh, brought only a brief respite in the hostilities. A few months after the ban on the activities of Kurdish patriots, the Barzani took up arms again, this time under the leadership of another Sheikh, Abdusselam. The Ottoman forces sent to quell this new uprising were defeated. In early 1910, the revolt spread throughout southern Kurdistan. An uprising broke out in Bitlis, led by Selim Ali (Khalifeh) and Moussa Bey. But once the Barzani had thrown the Turkish administrators and military out of their territory, they did not seek to extend the range of their activities. Isolated, the revolt in Bitlis was successfully repressed.

During this period of enforced clandestinity, links were formed between Kurdish militants and Armenian and Arab patriots, in the common struggle against the Unionist dictatorship. The Kurdish nationalists had manifested their sympathy for the Arab revolts which broke out during this critical period in Yemen, Iraq-i arab (Baghdad and Basra), and in Djebel and Djazira (Syria). Emissaries from Imam Yabya Sheikh Said, the leader of the Yemenite insurgents, had moved around Kurdistan collecting money for the movement.[26]

Faced with an alliance of the non-Turkish national movements, the Unionists were forced to adopt a more flexible policy. In 1912, the secret society *Kiviya Kurd* (Kurdish Hope), created in 1910 by a group of Kurdish students and intellectuals, was officially legalized. This society, which seems to have been the first centralized and structured Kurdish political organization, was led by a member of the Ottoman Parliament, Khalil Hassan Motki. Every Kurdish intellectual who was not in exile or in prison was a member. Its main ideologue was Dr. Chukru Mehmed Sekban, who later became an advocate of assimilation of the Kurds by the Turks.[27] From 1913 onwards, the society published a bilingual Turkish-Kurdish daily paper *Roja Kurd* (Kurdish Day), renamed *Hetawe Kurd* (Kurdish Sun) in 1914; its aim was to reform the Kurdish alphabet, propagate nationalist ideas and educate the Kurdish people.

The society concentrated mainly on work amongst Kurdish workers and young people, who financed its activities to a considerable extent. Eventually, it extended its network to the various towns of Kurdistan and to the groups of Kurdish emigrés in Europe. But then came the First World War. All the society's activists were mobilized and its promising and fruitful activities were suddenly interrupted.

Towards the end of 1912, an Association of the Friends of Kurdistan (*Kurdistan Mahibbur Djemiyeti*) had been formed in Instanbul to inform public opinion about the Kurdish question. There was also the *Mudjedded* (Renewal) Party, created by the Kurdish deputy Lutfi Fikri in late 1912 as a breakaway from the Unionists. Its program envisaged the secularization of the Ottoman Empire (separation of the state from religion), latinization of the alphabet, equal rights for women, etc. This body of reforms, which were very advanced for their time, only attracted a handful of intellectuals, not many of whom were Kurds, although the editor of *Idjtibat* (Opinion), the journal in which the Party presented its avant-garde notions, was Abdullah Cevolet, a noted Kurdish intellectual. Fifteen years later, Mustafa Kemal was to put these ideas into practice.

Generally speaking, this pre-1914 period was a short-lived political apprenticeship for an emerging Kurdish intelligentsia which was only just beginning to feel its way. This hard-won potential was to be largely dissipated by the outbreak of war.

The First World War

> The Turkish homeland is neither Turkey
> nor Turkestan
> Our homeland is an immense and
> eternal country: Turan!
> *Zia Gokalp*

The Unionist Triumvirate (Enver, Talat and Djemal) dragged the Ottoman Empire into the war in the hope of finally conquering this "Turan" which Gokalp had glorified.

In the pursuit of its Turanian utopia, and under cover of the war, the Triumvirate proceeded to massacre more than a million Armenians and 700,000 Kurds. The Turkish peasantry, which was mobilized *en masse* and packed off to the fronts of what Sultan-Caliph Rechad had declared to be a holy war, also paid a very high price.

What was the attitude of the Kurds during these four years of conflict? Mostly, they responded to the Caliph's religious arguments and his call to arms. However, some sections of the population, notably the tribes of southern Kurdistan and the inhabitants of Dersim, refused to take part. A few northern tribes actually fought alongside the Russian Army against the

Ottomans. A few rich intellectuals found means of avoiding conscription. Others vainly sought safety for themselves and their people in nearby Russia.

While promising the Kurdish national movement a major influx of material aid, Czarist Russia was actually preparing for the outright annexation of Kurdistan.[28] The Russians manipulated these Kurds just as other imperialist powers such as Britain and France used Kurdish, Turkish, Arab and Armenian notables in their own efforts at conquest and colonization.

Throughout the war, the Entente powers debated the sharing out of the spoils that would accrue from the fall of the Ottoman Empire. The Arab Middle East and the Armenian and Kurdish territories were the very nub of these discussions amongst the Allies.

In mid-May 1916 the Foreign Ministers of Britain and France signed an Agreement. The Russian government approved it a little later, on September 1, 1916. In a slightly modified form, this Agreement, known as Sykes-Picot, was to be the basis for the Sèvres Treaty in which Britain and France divided up the Middle East between themselves.[29]

The Post-War Years

The Mudros armistice (October 30, 1918) brought the hostilities to a close and confirmed the Ottoman Empire's capitulation to the Allied powers. The nationalist ravings which had incited the Turkish people to conquer the whole of Turan had almost lost them even their native Turkey. The British fleet patrolled the Bosphorus. British, French, Italian and Greek troops had occupied three-quarters of the Turkish territories, ignoring only the arid steppes of central Anatolia and part of the Black Sea coast.

The period from October 1918 to June 1919 presented the Kurdish people with their best ever opportunity to set up their own national state. From June 1919 to the end of 1921, it would still have been possible. There was a total political vacuum; the Unionists had fled and the authority of the Sultan and his government barely extended beyond the limits of the Ottoman capital. The remains of what had been the Ottoman Army were disintegrating; the bewildered officers were mainly concerned with their own personal fate as the army itself was due to be dissolved and replaced by a purely symbolic Imperial Guard. Russia, to whom the Sykes-Picot Agreement had allocated most of Kurdistan, had fallen to the Soviets and no longer had territorial designs upon neighboring countries. The Persian Army was in as wretched a state as its Ottoman equivalent.

Never had there been circumstances so favorable to the liberation of the whole of Kurdistan from the foreign yoke and for the creation of an independent national state. Even if one assumes that Britain and France would not have welcomed the emergence of such a state, they did not have available the means to prevent it, as was clearly shown by their withdrawal from Urfa and Aintab. Confronted with a *fait accompli*, the two powers would have made the best of it and would probably have adopted a conciliatory attitude in the hope of obtaining oil concessions. As it happens, Britain, for its own reasons, would not have been displeased had a Kurdish state been created. But this historic opportunity slipped through the hands of the Kurdish people. They were unfortunately still at a stage of development in which the only leadership to emerge was far more susceptible to clerical and feudal influences than to any "modernist" tendencies.

Torn as it was by the conflict between traditionalists and modernists, and divided into half a dozen parties and committees, this leadership could not rise to the occasion. The task of building a national state was beyond its capacities: it lacked the necessary historical and political intelligence. Those whom one could consider as the "radicals" of their time were in fact *Ottoman* intellectuals, products of Ottoman culture, with all that that implies in terms of a philosophical and political conception of the world.

The main point about the Ottoman intellectuals was that they were colonized intellectuals who, because of their lifestyle and "westernization," had become strangers to their own people. They had assimilated enough European culture to be aware of their people's backwardness, but not enough to understand the historical and economic mechanisms underlying this underdevelopment. Dependent and fatalistic (yesterday it was divine providence which ruled the affairs of this world; now it was the European powers!), always chasing the illusion that liberation would come without a struggle, they imagined that the only hope for themselves and their people lay under the protective wing of a "civilized power." This was the type of intellectual who developed and proliferated at the heart of a semi-colonized Empire, where the only road to success ran through the embassies of the great powers, and where one only became a Minister or a Pasha if one enjoyed the support of this or that European ambassador.

For the Kurdish Ottoman intellectuals who came out of this school, Kurdistan's salvation rested entirely in the hands of Britain and France, especially the former. Not surprisingly, a good number of such Kurdish intellectuals were amongst the founding members of the British Friendship Society, whose President was none other than the Sultan-Caliph himself.

In Kurdistan itself, things had changed considerably. Ever since the principalities had ceased to be independent, local political authority had fragmented even further, down to the level of the tribal chief. No traditional leader could mobilize even half the forces that Bedir Khan or Yezdan Sher had raised a few decades before.

The states of the Middle East (Iraq, Syria, Lebanon, Jordan, etc.) were not created out of the struggles of bourgeois or revolutionary vanguards. On the contrary, they were set up by British and French imperialism, to serve their own ends and in accordance with their own immediate needs. If Anglo-French imperialism had required an independent Kurdistan, they would have set one up, of their own accord, since the Kurdish leadership was at about the same stage of underdevelopment as its equivalent in many Arab countries. Indeed the British did at one time envisage the creation of a Kurdish state, as we shall see later.

First, let us mention the various Kurdish organizations set up after the Mudros armistice. The earliest was *Istiqlal-i Kurdistan* (Liberation of Kurdistan), set up by Seyid Abdullah, the son of Sheikh Abdul Qadyr. Its only activity seems to have been pleading for the Kurdish cause in diplomatic circles. The Committee for Kurdish Independence (*Kurt Istiqlal Djemiyeti*), founded in Cairo by Soureya Bedir Khan Bey, was to play a prominent part in the first Kurdish uprising in republican Turkey. But the most important of these organizations was indubitably *Kurdistan Taali Djemiyeti* (Society for the Recovery of Kurdistan) founded by Mullah Sait and Khalil Hayali of Motki, and Hamza Bey of Mukus.[30] This political association sought to secure for the Kurdish people the benefits of the Wilsonian principles concerning the self-determination of subject nations. Most of Istanbul's Kurdish emigrés were members. At its first congress, Sheikh Abdul Qadyr, back from exile in Mecca, was elected President. Emin Ali Bey, the son of Bedir Khan, and General Fuad Pasha became its Vice-Presidents and another General, Hamdi Pasha, was elected General Secretary.

After the congress, a delegation made up of the association's main leaders visited the American, British and French Commissions in the Ottoman capital to make their objectives known.

The question of the independence of Kurdistan gave rise to stormy debates within the association. The split was between the "radical" young militants who supported the idea of a totally independent Kurdistan, and the notables, led by Sheikh Abdul Qadyr, president of both the association and of the Ottoman State Council, who defended the idea of autonomy within an Ottoman framework, a framework which no longer existed but which could be rebuilt through struggle alongside the Turks. As Abdul Qadyr put it, "to desert the Turks in their hour of need and to deal them a fatal blow by proclaiming the independence of Kurdistan would be unworthy of our honor as Kurds. I insist that we must help them now. Furthermore, you are aware that the Turks have agreed to our intention of creating an autonomous Kurdistan enfeoffed to the Sultan. You also know that, should the Turks break their promises, the Kurdish nation will be able to obtain its rights by force." A few years later the Turkish rulers did indeed go back on their promises, the Kurds were defeated in their attempt to defend their rights by force of arms and Mustafa Kemal sent the excessively magnanimous Sheikh Abdul Qadyr to the gallows. The younger and more fervent members of the organization went back to Kurdistan to set up local branches and establish links with the population. A few managed, some months later, to mobilize the tribes of the area between Sivas and Malatya. A vast region around Kotchguiri was organized as the core of an independent Kurdistan by the middle of 1919. But the movement remained isolated from the rest of Kurdistan and was finally crushed by Kemalist troops in late March 1921. One hundred ten people were condemned to death; Mustapha Kemal pardoned them, to comply with a request from the Dersim tribes and so as not to antagonize the Kurdish chiefs at a time when his power was still very shaky.

The differences between the "autonomists" and the supporters of independence eventually caused a split. The latter group organized themselves to form a Kurdish Social Committee (*Kurt Teschkilat-i Itchtimaiye Djemiyeti*). During the same period there also emerged a *Kurd Millet Firkasi* (Kurdish

National Party) about which we know very little. On the other hand, the activities of the Kurdish club of Diyarbekir, which was started up again by the Djemilpachazade towards the end of 1918, are fairly well documented. The club, which adopted a position close to that of the Committee for Kurdish Independence, had several hundred members including about twenty intellectuals. At first, it mainly concentrated on cultural activities. By the time the club was thinking of setting up a military section, the Kemalists had acquired sufficient strength to dissuade them.

The Treaty of Sèvres (August 10, 1920)

"There could be no question of a peace conference until we had conquered Iraq and Syria," wrote Lloyd George, the British Prime Minister of the time, in his *War Memoirs*.[31] One of the key stages in this conquest was the occupation of the Vilayet of Mosul (Iraqi Kurdistan) four days after the conclusion of the armistice, despite the fact that according to the Sykes-Picot Agreement it should have gone to France. Britain had carried out many studies and investigations in this Kurdish territory and was well aware that it was rich in oil. Foreseeing difficulties in the negotiations, Britain sought to secure the support of the local population. Right from early 1918, the British set about establishing contacts with Kurdish leaders. In his quest for Kurdish interlocutors, Sir Percy Cox, later British High Commissioner in Iraq, went to Marseilles in July 1918 to meet General Sherif Pasha, the future head of the Kurdish delegation at the Peace Conference, in order to discuss the creation of an autonomous or independent Kurdistan.[32]

On December 3, 1917 Soviet Russia had proclaimed to the peoples of the East that it did not recognize the agreements signed by the Czarist government concerning the carve up of Iran and the Ottoman Empire. As a result, the "Russian zone" was open to the covetousness of the various other parties involved. Having contributed to the Allied victory, the Americans wanted their share of the spoils. The King Crane Commission's report to the Peace Conference recommended the setting up of an Armenian state in the major part of the area which was to have been annexed by Czarist Russia, a Turkish state with Istanbul as its capital in part of Anatolia, and later a Kurdistan covering about a quarter of the Kurdish territories. The report naturally suggested that all these states be placed under U.S. mandate.

At the conference table, despite some initial reservations, France finally gave its approval to the creation of a Kurdish state, as long as it did not include any of the Kurdish territories bordering on Syria or lying between "French" Cilicia and the western bank of the Euphrates, all of which had been granted to the French in the Sykes-Picot Agreement. The Kurdish and Armenian delegations had already settled their differences in an agreement signed in Paris on December 20, 1919 by General Sherif Pasha for the Kurds and Boghos Pasha for the Armenians.

The participants in the Sèvres Conference were Britain, the U.S. (observer), France, Italy, Japan, Armenia, Belgium, Greece, Hedjaz (today's Saudi Arabia), Poland, Portugal, Romania, the Serb-Croat-Slovene state (later to

be Yugoslavia), Czechoslovakia, Turkey and a Kurdish delegation acting as
an observer in the discussions concerning Kurdistan and Armenia. The
outcome was a long treaty of 433 articles, signed at Sèvres on August 10,
1920.[33]

Section III (Articles 62–64) dealt with Kurdistan and read as follows:

Article 62
A Commission, having its seat in Constantinople and made up of three members appointed by the Governments of Britain, France and Italy, will, during the
six months following the implementation of the present treaty, prepare for local
autonomy in those regions where the Kurdish element is preponderant lying east
of the Euphrates, to the south of a still-to-be established Armenian frontier and to
the north of the frontier between Turkey, Syria and Mesopotamia, as established in
Article 27 II (2 and 3).

Should agreement on any question not be unanimous, the members of the
commission will refer it back to their respective Governments. The plan must
provide complete guarantees as to the protection of the Assyro-Chaldeans and
other ethnic or religious minorities in the area. To this end a commission made up
of British, French, Italian, Persian and Kurdish representatives will visit the area so
as to determine what adjustments, if any, should be made to the Turkish frontier
wherever it coincides with the Persian frontier as laid down in this treaty.

Article 63
The Ottoman Government agrees as of now to accept and execute the decisions
of the two commissions envisaged in Article 62 within three months of being
notified of those decisions.

Article 64
If, after one year has elapsed since the implementation of the present treaty, the
Kurdish population of the areas designated in Article 62 calls on the Council of the
League of Nations and demonstrates that a majority of the population in these
areas wishes to become independent of Turkey, and if the Council then estimates
that the population in question is capable of such independence and recommends
that it be granted, then Turkey agrees, as of now, to comply with this recommendation and to renounce all rights and titles to the area. The details of this
renunciation will be the subject of a special convention between Turkey and the
main Allied powers.

If and when the said renunciation is made, no objection shall be raised by the
main Allied powers should the Kurds living in that part of Kurdistan at present
included in the Vilayet of Mosul seek to become citizens of the newly independent
Kurdish state.[34]

Before we go on to discuss the frontiers defined by Article 62 and to
highlight the composition of the hypothetical future Kurdistan envisaged in
the Treaty, it is worth noting that the fate of the Kurdish territory of Mosul
was not automatically linked to that of the rest of Kurdistan. The population
of the oil-rich Vilayet would be consulted as to whether they wanted to join
the independent Kurdish state only once the latter had become a reality. And
even if the "majority of the population of these areas" wished "to become
independent of Turkey," they could only do so if the Council estimated that
"they were capable of such independence." Failing which, the Council would
call on Britain to assume mandate powers over the area.

As for the frontiers of this hypothetical future Kurdistan, many territories
with an overwhelmingly Kurdish majority lying west of the Euphrates, such

as the districts of Adiyaman, Malatya, Elbistan, Darende and Divrik, were arbitrarily excluded. The Entente of August 10, 1920 between Britain, France and Italy stipulated that they were to become part of "the specifically French zone of interests." Article 27 (Section II, Clauses 2 and 3) allocated to the French Mandate of Syria not only the Kurd-Dagh (Kurdish Mountain) area and that part of the Djasireh plain now under Syrian sovereignty, but also the towns of Kilis, Aintab, Biredjik, Urfa, Mardin, Nusaybin and Djaziret ibn Omar (Cizre).[35] These two areas, which were to be directly or indirectly annexed by France, accounted for about a third of the territories of Ottoman Kurdistan.

The "still to be established Armenian frontier" had, in fact, already been determined by Article 89 (Section VI: Armenia) of the Treaty: "Turkey, Armenia and the other signatories agree that the frontier between Armenia and Turkey in the Vilayets of Erzurum, Trebizonde, Van and Bitlis be subject to the arbitration of the President of the United States. They agree to accept his decision and any measures he might recommend concerning Armenia's access to the sea and the demilitarization of any Ottoman territories adjacent to the said frontier."[36] President Wilson's verdict flew in the face of his own principles concerning the rights of peoples to self-determination. Without pausing to consult the local population or to determine its ethnic composition, he allocated to the Armenian state (which was to be placed under U.S. mandate) several territories whose population was mainly Kurdish, territories such as Mus, Erzincan, Bingol, Bitlis, Van, Karakilisa (Agri), Igdir and Erzurum: in other words a further third of Ottoman Kurdistan.

The "independent Kurdistan" envisaged by the Treaty was in fact, therefore, a country from which two-thirds of its territory had been lopped off, including its fertile areas and its traditional grazing grounds, not to mention Persian Kurdistan. The truncated state would have been left with the impoverished areas of Kharput, Dersin (Tunceli), Hakkari and Siirt, with Diyarbekir as its capital and the Vilayet of Mosul as its economic center. Britain would of course control the oil. Had the Treaty been implemented, the Kurdish territories would have been split into five parts, shared out between France in the west, Syria in the south, Persia in the east and Armenia in the north, leaving an independent Kurdistan only in the center. Given all this, it is somewhat surprising that entire generations of Kurdish nationalists have turned to this iniquitous Treaty and presented it as a recognition of the Kurdish cause in international law.

The Sèvres Treaty, which was quite methodically aimed at carving up the Turkish territories, was not only profoundly unjust and humiliating for the Turkish people, it was also an affront to the Kurds.

Following the fall and dismemberment of the Ottoman Empire, all its subject peoples were able to set up their own states. The only exception was the Kurdish people, largely because of the political incompetence and historical backwardness of its leaders. As a result, the Kurds of Ottoman Kurdistan were split amongst three newly created political entities — Turkey, Iraq and Syria.

Notes

1. For further details on this period during which the peoples under Ottoman domination first awakened to political life, see S. Mardin, *The Genesis of Young Ottoman Thought* (Princeton, 1962); E.E. Remshaw, *The Young Turks: Prelude to the Revolution of 1908* (Princeton, 1957); and especially Y.A. Petrosyan's comprehensive *The Young Turks* (in Russian), translated into Turkish and published by Bilgi Yayinevi, (Ankara, 1974).
2. Positivist philosophy had a very great influence first on the Unionists and later on Kemalism.
3. See Earl Turkey, *The Great Powers and the Baghdad Railway*, Macmillan (London, 1923).
4. "Eye witnesses have described the astounding scenes which took place in Saint Sophia Square and on the Galata Bridge. Greeks, Bulgarians, Kurds and Armenians embraced as brothers; Young Turk officers harangued the crowds, asserting that Jews, Christians and Muslims were no longer enemies and would now all work together to the greater glory of the Ottoman nation." Joan Haslip, *Le Sultan; la tragedie d'Abdulhamid*, Hachette (Paris, 1960), p. 241.
5. Curiously enough, Zia Gokalp, the main ideologue of pan-Turanianism was a young Kurdish pupil of Durkheim. Having carried out sociological and linguistic research on the Kurdish people (see *Kurt Asiretleri Hakkinda Istimai Tetkikler*, Ankara, 1975), he became a fervent convert who sought to hide his Kurdish origins and was adulated by the Turkish nationalists. He is now often cast as the "spiritual father of modern Turkey."
6. A program of Kurdish deportations had been worked out by Enver and Talat Pasha, the two Unionist leaders who were the main initiators of the massacre of the Armenian people. Ten articles of a law sanctioned by Sultan Mehmet Rashid V authorized mass deportations of Kurds to Anatolian Turkish villages where they would form less than 5% of the population, all in the name of "meeting the needs of the holy war." This program began to be applied during the war: 700,000 Kurds were deported to Anatolia. Cf. *Les Massacres Kurdes en Turquie*, Hoyboun Ligue Nationale Kurde (Cairo, 1928).
7. The following names of 17th century "Kurdish states" are cited in Professor Serafettin Turan's *Yuzyilda Osmanli Imperatorlugunun idari taksimati* (*Administrative Boundaries of the 17th Century Ottoman Empire*) Ataturk Universitesi, 1961, Yilligi, (Ankara, 1963), p. 205–207: Cizre, Hazro, Egil, Palu, Kigi, Gens, Bitlis, Hizan, Hakkari, Mahmudi, Sehrizor, Mihrivana, Imadiye, Asti, Tersil and Mihriban. Joseph von Hammer's *Histoire de l'Empire Ottoman* (Paris, 1836) only mentions the province of Diyarbekir which was "divided into eleven Ottoman sanjaks, eight Kurdish sanjaks and five hereditary fiefs (*hukumet*)."
8. Cf. Djalilie Djalil, *Kurdy Osmanskoj Imperii v pervoj polovine XIX veka* (*The Kurds of the Ottoman Empire in the First Half of the 20th Century*), (Moscow, 1973), p. 50.
9. A. Safrastian, *Kurds and Kurdistan*, Harvil Press (London, 1948), p. 52.
10. H. Von Moltke, *Lettres sur l'Orient* (Paris, 1872), p. 243.
11. The population of Kurdistan in Iran expressed its grievances to a British traveler in the area in these words: "We break our backs working all day but we still do not even manage to get enough bread to stave off our hunger. Men, women and children, we all go barefoot, in rags and starving." (H.C. Rawlinson, "Notes on a Journey from Tabriz through Persian Kurdistan to the Ruins of Takhti-Sleiman," *Journal of the Royal Geographical Society*, Vol. X, 1, 1840, p. 14.
12. *Sheref-Nameh*, Turkish edition, (Istanbul, 1975), p. 148.
13. In 1839, the Ottoman forces were defeated by Mehmet Ali's son, Ibrahim Pasha.
14. V. Dittel, "*Otchest Putechestvija po Vostoku C 1842 po 1845 g. Kurdy: Bedr-Khan-Bek*" ("*Notes on a Journey in the Orient from 1842 to 1845: the Kurds and Bedir Khan Bey*") in *Biblioteka dlja Tchtenija*, t.95, 1849, p. 205, quoted in N.A. Khalfin, *Borba za Kurdistan* (*The Struggle for Kurdistan*), (Moscow, 1963), p. 54.
15. N.A. Khalfin, ibid., p. 56.
16. D. Djalil, op. cit., p. 147.
17. N.A. Khalfin, op. cit., p. 74.
18. The message was received too late; Yezdan Sher's movement had already fallen. (Cf. Khalfin, op. cit.) Likhutin, the Russian commander has recorded Yezdan Sher's various propositions to the Russians for a common struggle against the Porte in *Ruskie v Aziatskoi Turtsii v 1854 i 1855 g. (The Russians in Asiatic Turkey in 1854 and 1855*); quoted in D. Djalil, op. cit., p. 168–9.
19. N.A. Khalfin, op. cit., p. 118, cites Russian foreign policy archives.
20. P.I. Averianov, *Kurdy v voinakh Rossii s Persii i Turtsiei v techenie XIX stoletia* (Tiflis, 1900), p. 288, quoted in N.A. Khalfin, op. cit., p. 126.
21. According to Israel Naamani, "the Kurdish militants participated in the 1907 Young Turk conference in Paris, at which all the political organizations representing the Ottoman Empire's non-Turkish peoples agreed to unite with the Young Turks in the struggle against Abdulhamid's tyranny" ("The Kurdish Drive for Self-Determination," *Middle East Journal*, No. 3, 1966, p. 280). Two Kurdish nationalist leaders, Abdurrahman Bedir Khan, editor of *Kurdistan*, and Hikmet Baban, also attended the 1902 Paris Congress.
22. Dr. Bletch Chirguh, *La Question Kurde* (Cairo, 1930), p. 50.
23. B. Nikitine, *Les Kurdes*, Imprimerie Nationale, Librairie C. Klincksieck (Paris, 1956).

24. M.C. Lazarev, *Kurdskij Vopros* (*The Kurdish Question*), (Moscow, 1972), p. 147, which draws on the Russian archives.
25. Ibid.
26. Ibid.
27. In a pamphlet published in 1933 by the Presses Universitaires de France, *La Question Kurde: Des Problèmes des Minorités*, Dr. Sekban states that: "Later events have shown that the emergence of an independent Kurdish state would have been a calamity, a disaster for the Kurdish people's real interests."
28. See Russian foreign policy archives quoted in M.C. Lazarev, op. cit., p. 159. (Cf. "Posolstovo v Konstantinopole," 1907–1913, d. 3572, 1.3, Sazonov-Tcharikov.)
29. For further details of the Sykes-Picot Agreement, see *Razdel Aziatskoj Turtsii, po seketnym dukumentam byvch. Ministerstva innostrannykh del, pod red. E.A. Adamova*, (Moskva, 1924). (*The Partition of Asiatic Turkey*, from the secret documents of the ex-Ministry of Foreign Affairs, published by the Soviet authorities).
30. Mullah Sait, later known as Bediuzzeman Said-i-Nursi, was the author of a series of philosophical and religious works entitled *Risale-i-Nur* (*Writings of Light*) and founded a fraternity, *Nurudju*, (*The Adepts of Light*) which today has several hundred thousand members, especially in Turkish Anatolia.
31. Quoted in M.C. Lazarev, op. cit., p. 338.
32. Dana Adams Schmidt, *Journey Among Brave Men* (Boston-Toronto, 1964), pp. 192–3.
33. For the text of the Treaty, see *Nouveau Recueil General des Traites* (Leipzig, 1924), t.XII, 3rd Series, pp. 664–779.
34. Ibid., pp. 677–8, my italics.
35. Ibid., pp. 668–9.
36. Ibid., pp. 683–4.

2

Kurdistan in Turkey

Kendal

General Overview

Territory and Population

Kurdistan in Turkey is the largest and most populous part of the Kurdish national territory. It stretches from the Gulf of Alexandria and the Anti-Taurus Mountains in the west, to the frontiers of Iran and the USSR in the east. To the north, it is bound by the Pontic Mountains, and to the south by the Turkish-Syrian and Turkish-Iraqi frontiers. Covering 80,000 square miles (30% of all Turkey) it makes up the eighteen counties (vilayets) of eastern and south-eastern Anatolia.[1]

Kurdistan in Turkey is a rugged mountainous country (Mount Ararat, 16,941 feet; Tchilo, 13,573 feet; Sipan and Djoudi, roughly 13,000 feet), and crossed by the great Arax, Tigris and Euphrates river systems. It has a continental climate and is thus subject to extreme fluctuations in temperature.[2] For half the year the southern part of the area is covered in snow. However, a more temperate and clement climate prevails in the plains of Urfa and Mardin, and in the Tigris valley.

The many rivers and waterways of this part of the Kurdish territory are fast flowing and seasonal, and are thus unsuitable for navigation. On the other hand, they do have a very high hydro-electric potential, estimated at over 90,000 million kWh.[3]

The once dense vegetation is now becoming sparse for lack of proper husbandry and reforestation. Oak, beech and walnut cover parts of the mountain slopes, while poplars, willows, Mediterranean fruit trees and vines are plentiful in the valleys and plains. The fauna is still abundant. Apart from the bears, foxes and wolves, familiar to the Kurdish peasant, there are also hyenas, wild boars, mountain goats, and so on.

According to the last general census, in 1970, the population of Kurdistan

38

in Turkey numbered 7,557,000 inhabitants[4] of whom 6,200,000 are Kurds, about 82% of the total. The remainder are made up of Turks (notably officials, military personnel and one time expatriates returned from Yugoslavia or Bulgaria and subsequently implanted in the most fertile parts of Kurdistan), Arabs (in the vilayets of Mardin, Siirt and Gazi Anteh) and about 8 to 9,000 Armenians, mainly in Diyarbekir and Kars.

These non-Kurdish peoples are scattered heterogeneously through the various provinces of Kurdistan. The population of the districts of Maras, Gazi Anteh, Malatya and Erzurum, which lie on the borders of Kurdistan and Anatolia, is mainly Turkish although many other ethnic groups live there. In the central and eastern regions, the population is almost entirely Kurdish.

Furthermore, any estimate of the number of Kurds in Turkey must also take into account the important concentrations of Kurds scattered in colonies throughout Anatolia (Cihanbeyli, Haymana, Kurtoghe, Tokat, Sankiri, etc.), and the hundreds of thousands of Kurdish emigrant workers in the country's main industrial centers. In Istanbul alone there are over half a million of them. This Kurdish community living away from Kurdistan numbered from two to two and a half million people in 1970.[5]

In short, there were about 8.5 million Kurdish speakers in 1970, which represents 23.8% of the population of the Republic of Turkey (total population 35.7 million in 1970). This figure of 8.5 million, which was reached on the basis of the 1970 census figures, is probably not very accurate. There are several conflicting estimates of the real number of Kurdish people in Turkey, ranging from 8 to 12 million. The Turkish authorities prefer to minimize the numbers, whilst some nationalist groups tend to exaggerate them.

It is also worth bearing in mind that a significant number of Kurds are still deeply marked by the brutalities of the past half-century of anti-Kurd repression and are very wary of declaring themselves as Kurds, as emerged clearly during the 1965 census in which I participated. When asked "What is your mother tongue?" destitute slum-dwellers who knew not a word of Turkish would answer heavily: "Better put Turkish, we don't want any trouble." The percentage of Kurds in the population is constantly increasing. From 1945 to 1965, the average rate of population growth in Kurdistan reached 2.88%, as against 2.65% in Turkey as a whole. The drop in mortality, and especially in infant mortality which fell from 2.25% in 1960 to 1.40% in 1970, has led to a sharp rise in annual population growth, which reached an average of 3.27% during 1965–70. Available data suggest that this trend has continued.

However, Kurdistan is still far from being one of the world's overpopulated areas. In 1970 there were only 20 people per square mile, as against 27 in Turkey overall. This population is very unevenly spread throughout the region: in the north and east, population density is low (6 inhabitants per square mile in Hakkari) whilst, in the western provinces of Kurdistan, it is often higher than the Turkish average.

Kurdish society is still mainly rural. In 1965, 27.8% of the population lived in the 146 Kurdish burgs (*ilse*) and 18 towns, seven of which have a population of over 100,000 (Gazi, Antep, Diyarbekir, Erzurum, Malatya, Elazig and Urfa). The remaining 72.2% live in 11,120 villages and 9,717 hamlets.[6] In 1965 there were still 70 to 80,000 semi-nomads. By 1980 there were barely 30,000.

In recent years urbanization has proceeded swiftly, due to the conjoined effects of population growth and the exodus from the land brought about by the constant and increasing mechanization of agriculture. But this urbanization has been rather anarchic, and has posed insoluble problems in terms of employment, housing, etc. The main Kurdish towns are now surrounded by slums and shanty towns.

Education and Culture

Illiteracy continues to be a major curse in Turkish Kurdistan, where, after half a century under a "democratic and secular" regime, 72% of people over six years of age still cannot read or write. The general illiteracy rate in Turkey is 51%, as opposed to 41.4% in the Turkish areas of the republic. In other words, there are almost twice as many illiterates in Kurdistan as in the Turkish parts of Turkey.

Even today, most Kurdish villages do not have a primary school. Where there is one, a single teacher is responsible for teaching Turkish to five classes. The same shortage of teaching staff is noticeable in Kurdistan's 50 or so secondary schools. Having completed secondary education under these conditions, Kurdish candidates present themselves for the same competitive university entrance exams as their more privileged colleagues from Istanbul or Izmir. It is thus hardly surprising to find that there are so few Kurdish students in higher education. In 1975, out of Turkey's 18 universities and 157 other seats of learning, Kurdistan had only one university (at Erzurum), one medical college (at Diyarbekir), and four engineering and teacher training colleges. Even in these, Kurdish students were in a minority.

The language of instruction is Turkish; Kurdish has been banned since 1925. The publication of books and magazines in Kurdish is also still illegal. Despite the rigors of repression, illicit Kurdish literary and political texts are secretly circulated. All such publications are printed in the Latin characters adapted for Kurdish by the Bedir Khan brothers in the thirties. This is in fact a new development; until recently, Kurdish intellectuals expressed themselves in Turkish. The writers and poets also used Turkish, not only to ensure legal distribution for their works but also because they were too unfamiliar with the forbidden literature and culture of their own people to have a real mastery of their own language. These Kurdish intellectuals, indeed, made a considerable contribution to Turkish culture. The most important novelist in the whole history of Turkish literature, Yacher Kemal, whose works include *The Pillar* and *Memed My Hawk*, both of which have been translated into 20 or more foreign languages, is a Kurd, as he never misses an occasion to stress. The poets, Cahit Sitki Taranci and Ahmet Arif, and the world famous film director, Yilmaz Guney, are also Kurds. Many of Guney's films have Kurdish themes and are set in Kurdistan. From Nesimi and Ruhi Su to Rahmi Saltuk, most of Turkey's famous singers are Kurds (often of the Shiite sect).

Since 1965 there has been a definite return to the roots. The urge to express themselves in Kurdish is becoming a driving force for more and more educated Kurds; the illiterates in any case speak only their mother tongue, knowing no other. This nationalism tinged with populism is laying the foundations for an important Kurdish cultural and literary revival.

Religion

Nearly all Kurds (99%) are Muslims. There are also about 30,000 Nestorian and Assyrian Christians, and 40 to 50,000 Yezidis, the misnamed "Devil worshippers."[7]

Most of the Kurdish Muslims are Shafeite Sunnis. The Shiites (Qizilbash or Alawi, followers of the Prophet's son-in-law, Ali) number only several hundred thousand, residing mainly in Dersim, Elazig and Maras. Many villages in Kurdistan have a Quranic school where the children learn, in Arabic, the rudiments of the religion. Some of the religious instructors (the mullahs) also teach their pupils the classics of Kurdish literature (Ehmede Khani, Melaye Jazari, Bateh, Teyran, Baba Tahir, Koyi, etc.) — without the knowledge of the Turkish authorities of course.

The mullahs play an important role in the social and cultural life of the Kurdish countryside. Only ten years ago, these village scholars survived on gifts in kind from the villagers and by the fruits of their own labor. Steeped in the people's poverty but aware of what was going on elsewhere, they clearly played a socially progressive role during the 1950s and 1960s when they often sided with the people against the authorities. This no doubt explains why from 1965 onwards the Ankara government had them replaced by a civil service priesthood formed in state schools. These new well-paid employees of the "secular" state often collaborate with the intelligence services (MIT) and serve to promote official ideology in the villages.

Religious fraternities (tariqaates) still operate throughout Kurdistan. They were severely repressed until the establishment of a multi-party system in 1926, but since then they have enjoyed official protection and have flourished. The influential sheikhs (spiritual leaders) of the Qadiri and Naqchebendi fraternities were respected for their ability to deliver large blocs of votes at election time and were courted by the authorities and the political parties. Some of these sheikhs eventually became members of parliament. The political authority they acquired, combined with their existing spiritual power and economic influence, which came from the fact that they were also large landowners, considerably reinforced their sway over the peasantry. But, as time went by, their authority began to crumble. Kurdish society was changing and the sheikhs were increasingly seen as the accomplices of the central authorities. Today their spiritual and economic power is being challenged. Similar structures can be found amongst the Shiites (Alawi). Their dignitaries are the dede, pir and seyyid, who play a similar role to the sheikhs.

Health

Despite the opportunities for making money quickly, few doctors seem attracted to the east (Kurdistan), which is officially recognized as an "underprivileged area" (mahrumiyet bolgesi). After three years of what the administrative jargon calls "Eastern Service" (*Sark Hizmeti*), young doctors fresh from medical school and the junior army doctors are invariably very eager to return to the incomparably higher level of comfort and culture of the big Turkish cities. As a result, medical personnel are very unevenly distributed in the Republic. In 1970, there were 4.3 doctors to every 10,000 inhabitants in Turkey, but in Kurdistan, there was only 1 per 10,000 inhabitants; in other words Turkey had 4.3 times more doctors per 10,000 people than Kurdistan.[8] This disequilibrium is growing. In 1965 Turkey only had 3.6 times as many doctors per 10,000 inhabitants as Kurdistan. The growing disparity is indicative of the different rates of development in the Turkish and Kurdish parts of the Republic.

Economic and Social Structures

Kurdish society is still mainly agrarian. As noted earlier, 72.2% of the people live in the countryside and make their living from agriculture and stock rearing. Industry provides jobs for only 5.5% of the active population. The rest of the urban population is engaged in trade, services and craft work.[9]

Traditional stock rearing remains a key sector. Indeed Kurdistan is the main source for cattle, sheep, goats and animal products in Turkey.

The techniques used in Kurdish agriculture have hardly changed since the Middle Ages and are far behind those practiced in the rest of Turkey. Kurdistan uses 39% of Turkey's carts, as opposed to only 3% of the country's agricultural machinery.[10] However, the constant growth in demand from the Turkish market, and the fact that some of the Kurdish minor nobles (*aghas*) have become capitalist farmers, has resulted in a sudden rush of mechanization. From 1965 to 1967 the number of tractors in use in Kurdistan went up by 46%.

Kurdish agricultural lands are also very unevenly distributed, as the following table illustrates.

Distribution of Lands in Turkish Kurdistan

Rural strata	Percentage of Rural Population	Percentage of Lands Controlled
Landless peasants	38.0	Nil
Small landowners (1–50 *dunam*)	45.4	27
Rich peasants (51–200 *dunam*)	14.2	40
Landlords, aghas, sheikhs, etc. (more than 200 *dunam*)	2.4	33

Note: A *dunam* is about a thousand square yards.

A bare sixth of landowners hold three-quarters of the land, whilst 38% of the rural population hold no land at all. Careful study of Turkish land registries reveals that these disparities have been increasing steadily ever since 1926 when Turkey adopted the Swiss legal code which stresses the importance of private property. The authorities turned a blind eye as the tribal chiefs, sheikhs and other notables gradually appropriated communal lands, state lands and lands belonging to the *Wafq* (public welfare organization). It is worth noting that, despite the various conflicts between the Ankara government and the Kurdish feudalists, the government never undertook any land reform program which would have undermined the authority of those through whom it sought to ensure its power over the Kurdish masses.

These disparities in property ownership have not as yet engendered any major conflicts between the mass of poor peasants (83.4% of the rural population) and the well-to-do section which supports and furthers the control of the central authorities. Blood ties, religious factors and the patriarchal tribal traditions, which still shape people's ideas despite the almost total collapse of the tribal structures themselves, all help to camouflage these contradictions. Banditry was, until very recently, the only expression through which they manifested themselves. It seems unlikely, however, that the demands and resentments formulated *vis-a-vis* the political authorities since the end of the sixties will leave the dominant Kurdish strata unscathed.

Although Kurdish agriculture seems archaic in its techniques and property relations, it is nonetheless well and truly oriented towards the outside world. It is now being integrated into the Turkish capitalist market. Cotton, sugar beet and tobacco, grown for both the Turkish market and for export, are tending to displace the traditional food crops.

But although capitalism is certainly penetrating the Kurdish countryside, capitalist relations of production are not yet the dominant ones. Kurdistan is one of those Third World countries living in several different centuries simultaneously. The peasant's biblical donkey shuffles alongside the feudal lord's latest model Mercedes. In economic terms, this means that the main forms of feudal exploitation (rent in kind and in labor) and even a few remaining practices of the primitive community survive alongside modern forms of capitalist exploitation. The peasants still supply the sheikhs and other religious dignitaries with what is effectively *corvée* labor. The disciples benevolently work in their master's field, harvest his crops, bring in his cereals, etc. And, as peasants, they pay substantial tithes to the petty nobles.

The surplus value accumulated through feudal exploitation is invested outside Kurdistan in the major Turkish urban centers. The Kurdish *aghas* and sheikhs acquire property, hotels and small factories in the big cities where profitability is higher.

In 1946, out of the 43,263 companies, factories and workshops registered under Turkish labor legislation, only 2,427 were in Kurdistan, representing 5.6% of the total.[11] Usually, these establishments are simple craft workshops producing soap, oil, carpets, etc. There are also a few sugar refineries (Elazig, Malatya), cement factories (Kars, Erzurum), tobacco processing plants (Bitlis, Malatya), and a textile factory at Diyarbekir. But most of the labor force is employed in the state controlled mining industries. The Kurdish sub-soil is rich in a variety of minerals, such as phosphates, lignite, copper, iron and chrome, and also there is some oil.

The chrome deposits mined at Maden, halfway between Diyarbekir and Elazig, are amongst the world's largest. An output of 915,000 tons in 1967 made Turkey the world's second largest producer of this mineral after the

USSR. The OECD report on Turkey noted that, in 1973, 2.2 million tons were produced, most of which was exported to the U.S.

The production of iron at Divrigi, a Kurdish area which has been attached to the predominantly Turkish-speaking province of Sivas because of its mineral wealth, reached about 1.6 million tons in 1967.[12] The ore extracted in Kurdistan is then transported to Eregli and Karabak on the Black Sea coast where the Turkish steel industry is based. And copper has been mined at Ergani, near Deyarbekir, for a long time now. Production reached nearly a million tons in 1970.

The known oil reserves in Turkish Kurdistan are insignificant compared to the fabulous oil wealth of those parts of Kurdistan presently located in Iraq and Iran. Shell, BP and Mobil, the main multinationals operating in this part of the world, used to maintain that there was not a drop of oil to be found in Turkey. It was only during the sixties, when the Turkish National Oil Company (TPAO) was able to prospect on its own account, that the Raman, Gazan (Siirt) and Diyarbekir oil fields were discovered. In 1971, production reached 4.4 million tons, most of which was reserved for domestic consumption.

Apart from mining, the state has also invested in the construction of strategic highways linking Turkey to Iran and Iraq and connecting the main military installations in Kurdistan. Erzurum, Diyarbekir, Malatya, Elazig and Van, the main garrison towns in Kurdistan, are also linked to the Turkish railway network through the Istanbul-Ankara-Malatya-Diyarbekir-Kurtalan, Malatya-Van and Ankara-Sivas-Erzurum lines. In addition, they are equipped with civil and military airports.

State investment has been mainly concentrated in the primary sector: mining and infrastructure projects. In 1968, only a negligible 1.93% of limited companies operating in Turkey had installations in Kurdistan.[13] Kurdistan, with its poor access to the ports, its small domestic market and its troubled political situation, is hardly attractive to private capital. What little private capital does flow in goes mainly into property speculation and the construction of modern buildings designed for Turkish military officers and civil officials as much as for the emerging Kurdish bourgeoisie.

As the primary and construction industries developed, a working class was formed. In 1980 it represented 5.5% of the active population of Kurdistan and 4% of the working class in Turkey. Because it enjoys such advantages as social security, guaranteed employment, paid holidays and the right to strike, this working class sees itself as privileged. However, in recent years, it appears to have developed a degree of class consciousness.

Most of the mountain villages and semi-nomadic (or semi-sedentary) tribes barter their animal products such as wool, goat's hair, butter and cheese for finished products such as sugar, tea, jewelry, toys, etc., or for certain fruits and vegetables itinerant traders bring from the plains by mule. But the big Diyarbekir and Erzurum merchants often deal directly with neighboring states such as the USSR and Iran. The agricultural chambers of commerce are very active.

The flow of trade between Kurdistan and Turkey is, on the whole, quite in keeping with metropole-colony relations in general, where the colony serves the metropole as a reservoir of raw materials and as a protected market for its products.

The big merchants, who help drain Kurdistan's wealth and channel it towards the Turkish metropole, are, with the big landowners, the main beneficiaries of bank credits. The banking system is, in any case, rather underdeveloped. In 1965 only 179 (0.9%) of Turkey's 1,981 bank branch offices were situated in Kurdistan. Savings are also at a very modest level, given the generalized poverty of the people. Again in 1965, savings deposits in Kurdistan amounted to only 479 million Turkish pounds, as against 15,202 million for Turkey as a whole.[14] The lack of any credit system worthy of the name hits mainly the small and medium producers and results in the emergence of a whole strata of usurers who lend at very high rates, up to 50 and 60% per annum.

Despite the considerable risks involved (the frontiers are mined) many poor peasants from frontier villages go in for smuggling. The usual consignments taken out are flocks of sheep (into Syria), medicines (to Iran and Iraq), tobacco and sometimes opium (again to Iran). The smugglers bring back Ceylon tea, which is cheap in the neighboring countries, Damascus cloth and a whole range of "Made in U.S.A." or "Made in Hong Kong" products which Turkey does not usually import. When they reach the towns, the smugglers take their modest cut and the products are sold at very high prices in the big department stores of Diyarbekir, Urfa, Antep and Ankara, where the authorities usually turn a blind eye.

Craft work and shopkeeping provide work for a significant proportion of the urban population in Kurdistan. The artisans of Diyarbekir, Mardin, Midyat and Erzurum make jewelry and other artifacts in gold, silver and crystal. Copper, especially inlay work, is a speciality of Diyarbekir.[15] And Siirt, Antep, Diyarbekir and Van are known for their carpets and cloth.

The administration employs about 1% of the active population of Kurdistan. Kurds occupy most of the subordinate positions.

Kurdistan under the Turkish Bourgeois Republic

Since the beginning of the 20th century, a chain of conflicts from Tripolitania and the Balkans to the First World War bled the Turkish people white. It also created a generation of military cadres who had become familiar the hard way with modern ways of thinking. At the end of World War I their country was exhausted and occupied by foreign troops. Patriotism demanded that they do something to help their people. It was this generation which produced Mustafa Kemal Pasha, Ismet Pasha, Ali Fuat Pasha, Kazim Karabekir Pasha, etc.

The situation in Anatolia was practically desperate. But, despite the occupation, the people showed no resistance and seemed to accept what was happening as if it was fated (*kismet*). Meanwhile, in Kurdistan, which was not occupied as yet, the Kurdish notables and religious leaders had become alarmed at the rumors suggesting that the "six vilayets" — Erzurum, Kars,

Bitlis, Erzincan, Mus and Van — were to be ceded to Armenia. Self-defense militias had been set up, mainly in response to the tales of persecution by the Armenian Republic which the Kurds of Kars were spreading.[16] Driven to hatred and excess by the centuries of oppression, massacre and deportation suffered under the Ottoman yoke, the Armenian militia had carried out reprisals of such violence that the Kurdish population was prepared to pay any price not to fall under Armenian sovereignty. The Kurdish notables had their own additional reasons for resisting such an outcome. When the Armenians had been deported, the Kurdish notables had seized their goods. Passing under Armenian domination would have meant dispossession, as well as persecution and servitude to a Christian regime. But did that mean that the Kurdish leaders were going to accept fighting for the liberation of the Turkish parts of Turkey, and creating a common state with the Turks, even though the Kurds had themselves been fighting for freedom from the Turkish yoke for over a century?

The Turkish nationalist leaders soon realized that their best recourse was to persuade the traditional Kurdish chieftains that the only way to escape domination by the Armenians was to fight alongside other Muslims for the creation of a Muslim state under the spiritual authority of the Caliph. A handful of these Turkish leaders, most notably Mustafa Kemal, were clear-sighted enough to understand that the independence of Turkey would not come through an American mandate or a British protectorate but through a war of liberation organized from Kurdistan.

The Turkish War of Independence (1919–23) and the Kurds

In May 1919, at the request of the British, the Grand Vizier, Ferit Pasha, sent one of the Sultan's most trusted servants, a general who had distinguished himself in the defense of the Dardanelles, on a mission to Anatolia. His task was to "help the Greeks of Trebizond set up a state on the Black Sea and to repress the *choura* (soviets) which were beginning to organize themselves in the north of Kurdistan" and which were being egged on by the Bolshevik inspired Kurdish Social Democrat Party.[17] The general in question was Mustafa Kemal. He had accepted the mission in the hope of finding a way of putting his plans for the liberation of Turkey into practice.

When he arrived in Kurdish territory, he immediately presented himself as the "savior of Kurdistan," the champion of a Caliph "imprisoned by the occupation forces" and the defender of "the Muslim lands soiled by the impious Christians." He appealed to "all Muslim elements," meaning Kurds and Turks, and called for "complete unity in the struggle to expel the invaders from the Muslim Fatherland."

At the time Mustafa Kemal was careful not to mention the Turkish nation. Instead, he stressed either the fraternity between Kurds and Turks, or the Ottoman nation in conflict with foreign occupation forces.

The first concrete political result of all this Kemalist activity in Kurdistan was the Congress of Eastern Vilayets which met from July 23 to August 6, 1919 in Erzurum. Fifty-four delegates came from the five Kurdish vilayets threatened with annexation by Armenia. (Kars, the sixth vilayet, was at the time part of the Western Caucasian Republic.) Conspicuous by their absence were representatives from the remaining Kurdish areas, such as Diyarbekir, Kharput, Dersim, Siirt, etc., which would remain unaffected by the threatened annexation. Obviously, these Kurds had decided that the Caliphate and Islam were not, in themselves, worth fighting for.

After long and often acrimonious debates, the Erzurum Congress decided to "do everything in its power to prevent Armenia annexing Muslim territories and to liberate the Muslim lands soiled by the *giaour* [infidels]." The Congress also acknowledged Mustafa Kemal's leadership in the struggle.

The Erzurum congress was Mustafa Kemal's first major political victory.[18] Kurdish forces organized and trained by Turkish officers under Kazim Karabekir Pasha's command engaged the troops of Menshevik Georgia and Dashnak Armenia. It was on this front that the first military victory of the Turkish War of Independence was won — by Kurdish forces; and it led directly to the Treaty of Gumru (today's Leninakan).[19] Having removed any threat on the eastern front, the Kurdish troops eventually went on to fight for the liberation of Anatolia and made a considerable contribution to the final victory.

A month after the Erzurum Congress, the Sivas Congress set up a committee for the defense of the rights of Anatolia and Thrace, charged with organizing popular resistance. The Congress, which ran from September 4–11, 1919, elected a General Representative Committee with Mustafa Kemal as its president. Furthermore, it was decided that, as Istanbul was still held by the occupying forces, all that was left of the Ottoman civil and military administration should come under the control of the said committee, which thus became the only legitimate seat of power.

On October 2, 1919, the existing civil and military administration broke off all links with the Istanbul government, which immediately fell as a consequence. The new cabinet opened negotiations with Mustafa Kemal which led to the signature of the (Amasya) Protocol. The Protocol envisaged the organization of elections for a legislature and pronounced on certain key issues of the day.

The vaguely phrased Article 1 accepted the principle of Kurdish autonomy, in that it "recognized the national and social rights of the Kurds." The main Kurdish leaders were informed of the fact. Mustafa Kemal's *Kuvvay-i Milliye* (National Forces) gained a large majority in the Ottoman Assembly following the elections. On January 28, 1920 this Assembly adopted a document known as the *Misak-i Milli* (National Pact) which reiterated the resolutions of the Sivas and Erzurum congresses and became the national charter of the new Turkey. It was a remarkably realistic document, based on a correct assessment of the regional and global balance of forces. The Turkish nationalists' pan-Turanian dream was giving way to a more concrete nationalism.

The reaction of the Allied Powers to the Ottoman Assembly's nationalist attitude was to occupy Istanbul officially and dissolve the legislature, on March 16, 1920. However, thanks to the Representative Committee, the

Assembly managed to meet in Ankara on April 28, 1920. Calling itself the Great National Assembly of Turkey (*Turkiye Buyuk Millet Meclesi*), it appointed a government which could claim to be the only legitimate holder of national executive power.

One of the first steps taken by this Assembly was to declare to the world that the legitimate authorities in Turkey would not recognize any agreement or treaty signed by the administration in occupied Istanbul. This was in no way a pointless act, given that the Treaty of Sèvres was due to be signed a few weeks later.

The Turkish War of Independence achieved its major military victory through the "great offensive" which culminated on September 9 in the rout of the Greek Army which had for three years been occupying parts of the Aegean and western Anatolia. The occupying forces had been armed and financed by British imperialism. The Treaty of Lausanne, negotiated two and a half months later, set the seal of international political and diplomatic recognition upon the Turkish victory.

Throughout the war, the Turkish officers who were directing its course were at pains to stamp out any emergent attempts at forming specifically Kurdish organizations or associations. The Kurdish movement in Kotchguiri was smothered in 1921. The Kurdish club in Diyarbekir had been closed as early as August 1919. The Kurds who fought both on the Georgian/Armenian front and against the Greek Army in the west thought they were going to build a state in which "Turks and Kurds would live as brothers and as equals," as Mustafa Kemal had promised. When the war came to an end, the Kurdish people found themselves devoid of any organized force; the only organized force of the time, the army, was firmly under the control of the Turkish nationalist military cadres. On November 1, 1922, a mere three months after definitive military victory had been achieved, Mustafa Kemal declared to the Assembly that "the state which we have just created is a Turkish state." Kurdistan had suffered the consequences of its own short-sightedness and lack of political leadership. The Kurdish people were quick to react, but once again they lacked organization; while there were constant revolts in Kurdistan, they were all finally crushed in 1939.

The Turkish War of Independence was strongly supported by the people, who sought to defend their lands against the savage violence wreaked upon the population by the Greek invaders. An economic congress gathered at Izmir in February 1923, before the Treaty of Lausanne had even been signed, determined the economic orientation of the new Turkey and consecrated the feudal-bourgeois alliance's domination over the new state. Overtures were made to foreign capital. The congress rejected motions proposed by a handful of proletarian delegates demanding recognition of the right to strike and the initiation of a land reform program.[20] The Allies, who for a while had feared that the movement led by Mustafa Kemal might be an offshoot of the Soviet Revolution, were effectively reassured.

The Kemalist Movement was in fact the final military phase of the Turkish bourgeois revolution which had been launched in 1908 with the Unionist coup d'etat. The fragments of the Union and Progress Committee had reunited and had gradually become the backbone of the Kemalist Movement. The principle of a "national economy led by the Turkish bourgeoisie," so dear to the Unionists, was henceforth the fundamental orientation of the Kemalist regime.

It is also worth noting that the 1917 Soviet Revolution played a significant part in the eventual Turkish victory. Despite the persecutions and assassinations suffered by the Turkish communists (notably the murder of the first Secretary of the Turkish Communist Party, Mustafa Suphi, and his comrades) Lenin's Russia gave the Kemalist Movement considerable support, at a time when Soviet Russia itself faced famine and the White armies.[21] In an effort to avoid being outflanked from the left, Mustafa Kemal went so far as to set up an entire pseudo Communist Party — whose delegates attended the Baku Congress — which he later dissolved, along with all other workers' organizations, in early 1925.

The Allies, fearing that Kemalist Turkey might tilt over into the Soviet camp, made the best of a bad thing and sought to come to terms with the fact of a politically independent Turkish state. Given the weakness of the Turkish bourgeoisie, such a state was bound to remain economically dependent on the West in any case, and might even act as a useful buffer between Soviet Russia and the West's colonies in the Middle East. In this regard it is highly significant that France signed a treaty geared "to re-establish friendly relations" with the Ankara government as early as October 2, 1921, a year *before* the Turkish military victory.

The Colonial Carve-Up of Kurdistan

The Treaty of Lausanne, signed by Britain, France, Italy, Japan, Greece, Romania, the Serbo-Croat-Slovene state and Turkey on July 24, 1923, gave international recognition to the Turkish state and carved up the national territory of the Kurdish people into four parts.[22] Sèvres had been humiliating for the Turkish people and deeply unjust to the Kurdish people. Lausanne, in contrast, was undeniably a victory for the Turks, but for the Kurds it marked the beginning of a new phase of servitude. Article 8 of the above mentioned Anglo-French Agreement had already given over the Kurdish territories of Djazireh and Kurd Dagh (south of Alexandrette) to the French mandated territory of Syria.

At Lausanne there was much talk about the Kurds, in their absence. Oil was a central topic in these discussions. Britain presented itself as the disinterested champion of the interests and freedom of the Kurdish people who "like all the other peoples of the region should enjoy national rights and have its own government." The Ankara delegation, on the other hand, asserted that "the Government of the Great National Assembly is the Government of both Turks and Kurds," that "the real representatives of the Kurds sit alongside the Turks in the Assembly," that "Turks and Kurds are equal partners in the Government of Turkey," and that "although Turks and Kurds may speak different languages, these two peoples are not significantly different and form a single bloc from the point of view of race, faith and custom."[23]

The Kurds in question, who enjoyed such solicitude and concern on the part of Britain and Turkey, the two main opposing parties at the Conference, were naturally enough the Kurds of the oil-rich area of Mosul, which both parties were eager to grab for themselves.

Following the occupation of Mosul by the British Army, Lloyd George and Clemenceau had met to settle the resulting controversy. France was persuaded to give up its rights to Mosul under the Sykes-Picot Agreement in exchange for Cilicia. Clemenceau was unaware that the territory was rich in oil, and accepted the British offer.

When France learnt of the Mosul oil reserves, the Clemenceau-Lloyd George agreement was immediately thrown into question. New negotiations culminated in the San Remo Pact, signed on April 24, 1920 and reformulated on December 23 of the same year. This laid down that "the British Government commits itself to grant the French Government, or parties designated by the latter, a 25% share, at current market prices, in the net production of crude oil which His Majesty's Government may procure from the Mesopotamian oil fields should these be exploited as a Government venture: should the exploitation of the Mesopotamian oil fields be carried out by a private company, the British Government undertakes to provide the French Government with a 25% share of said company."[24]

The Pact soon became the subject of a virulent press campaign in the U.S. The American government protested that its interests had been slighted by this "iniquitous carve-up." After laborious negotiations, the Americans obtained a 20% share in Turkish Petroleum, the company which held exclusive rights to the exploitation of the Mosul and Mesopotamian oil fields. The main shareholder in this company was none other than Lord Curzon,[25] the head of the British delegation of the Lausanne Conference. The American, French and British governments finally settled the distribution of shareholdings in Turkish Petroleum in May 1923.[26] The Turkish government had hoped to play on the rivalry between Britain, France and the U.S. to its own advantage, but faced with a settlement agreed by the great powers, it was forced to submit and to accept that the fate of Mosul would "ultimately be determined by the Council of the League of Nations."

The Council did indeed conduct an inquiry to determine the preferences of "the population concerned [the Kurds]." But on June 5, 1926, just as its verdict was to be announced, Mosul was attached to Iraq and came under British Mandate, despite the local population's desire for the establishment of an independent Kurdish state.[27]

On July 24, 1923, the parties involved in the Lausanne Conference signed a peace treaty. Most of the Kurdish territories were given over to Turkish sovereignty. The Treaty made no mention whatsoever of the Kurds, and granted them no national rights. It contained a few stipulations concerning the "protection of minorities" (Section III, Articles 37–44):

There will be no official restriction on any Turkish citizen's right to use any language he wishes, whether in private, in commercial dealings, in matters of religion, in print or at a public gathering.

Regardless of the existence of an official language, appropriate facilities will be provided for any non-Turkish-speaking citizen of Turkey to use his own language before the courts. (Article 39)[28]

Turkey commits itself to recognize the stipulations contained in Articles 38–44 as fundamental laws and to ensure that no law, no regulation and no official action will stand in contradiction or opposition to these stipulations, and that no law, regulation or official action shall prevail against them. (Article 37)

But Articles 40–45 specify that the minorities in question are "non-Muslim minorities" (Armenians, Greeks, etc.). Arguing that the Kurds governed Turkey as equal partners with the Turks, the Ankara nationalist authorities refused to include them amongst the minorities protected by the stipulations. A few years later, not only were the Kurdish people no longer accepted as "equal partners and allies," their very existence had ceased to be recognized. Before the First World War, Kurdistan had been divided between Persia and the Ottoman Empire. Following the colonial carve-up, it was split between Turkey, Iran, Iraq and Syria, the four most powerful political entities in Western Asia.

The Great Revolts of the Twenties and Thirties

Towards the end of 1922, a few Kurdish deputies, including Yusuf Zia, the deputy from Bitlis, and Colonel Halit Bey from Cebran, had founded a Committee for Kurdish Independence (*Kurt Istiqlal Djemiyeti*) in Erzurum, with links in the main towns of Kurdistan (Diyarbekir, Bitlis, Urfa, Siirt, Elazig, etc.). High-ranking officers like General Ihsan Novry Pasha, who had until then served the "National Forces" faithfully, swelled the ranks of this Committee — which already numbered many intellectuals, artisans and traders amongst its members. In Kurdistan itself, there were fears that the new Turkish government would adopt the Unionist policy on Kurdish matters. These fears had induced even sheikhs and religious leaders to join the Committee as early as 1923, as exemplified by the membership of Sheikh Said of Piran, Sheikh Sherif of Palu, Sheikh Abdullah of Melkan, etc.

Mustafa Kemal, a Unionist from way back who had played a major role in the July 1908 coup d'etat, was convinced, like all Unionists, that to forge a Turkish nation it was absolutely vital to liquidate the Armenians and then to assimilate the Kurds. Gokalp himself had laid down that the modern state was the political expression of a united and indivisible nation. On March 3, 1924, the very day the Caliphate was abolished, a decree banned all Kurdish schools, associations, publications, religious fraternities and *medressehs*. The break between Kemalism and the Kurds had become absolute.

From 1925 to 1939, the barbarities of the Turkish military forces in Kurdistan provoked constant revolts and peasant uprisings. In 1925 there was the major revolt led by Sheikh Said, then the revolts in Raman and Reschkoltan, halfway between Diyarbekir and Siirt. From 1926 to 1927 it was the turn of the populations of Hinis, Vorto, Solhan, Bingol and Gendj to rise up against the Turks. 1928 saw uprisings in Sassoun, Kozlouk and Perwari. From 1928 to 1932 an organized insurrection broke out in the

Ararat area. Finally, from 1936 to 1939 it was the inhabitants of the mountains of Dersim who were battling against the Turkish troops. Apart from the Ararat revolt and the one led by Sheikh Said, these were all local and spontaneous rebellions.

The Insurrection of 1925: The Committee for Kurdish Independence had been preparing for a general uprising ever since its foundation. Contacts had been established with religious and "feudal" leaders, and with Kurdish emigrés in Istanbul and Aleppo; 1923–24 was given over entirely to military preparations.

At the end of the summer of 1924, Yusuf Zia, the deputy from Bitlis, had gone to Istanbul to make contact with Turkish opponents of the Kemalist regime who had come together in the Progressive Republican Party (*Terrakiperver Cumhuriyet Firkasi*). A few days after his return to Erzurum, a rebellion broke out in the north of Bitlis. The Turkish government had got wind of Yusuf Zia's activities and had him arrested on the pretext that his brother was implicated in the revolt. The Turkish authorities were anxious to decapitate the general uprising which was in the offing. Yusuf Zia and Colonel Halid Bey, the military organizer of the Kurdish movement, as well as a number of other Kurdish leaders, were brought before a court martial in Bitlis in October 1924.

Meanwhile Sheikh Said of Piran, cast in the role of leader of the coming uprising by the absence of the other key figures, was ranging Elazig (Kharput), Diyarbekir, Gendj and Darhini in an effort to persuade the Kurdish peasants of the need to revolt against the Turkish yoke. Both the Sheikh and the Turkish authorities, who were following his movements closely, were well aware that a trial of strength was inevitable. The Turkish authorities launched a series of provocations in order to trigger off a premature uprising. A detachment of Turkish troops arrived in the village of Piran where the Sheikh was staying and announced that they had orders to arrest certain members of his entourage. According to N. Dersimi,[29] Sheikh Said "personally pleaded with the officer in charge of the detachment not to touch these Kurds, for fear of the inevitable consequences." The whole Turkish detachment was massacred by the over-excited villagers. The Sheikh fled north in an attempt to prevent this first skirmish developing into a premature general insurrection, but even before he arrived in Darhini, Kurds who had heard about the events at Piran had taken the town's Turkish officials and officers prisoner. The Sheikh no longer had any choice. A "law" promulgated on February 14, 1925 declared Darhini provisional capital of Kurdistan.[30] The Sheikh became "supreme commander of the Kurdish combatants." On February 26, his partisans occupied the important town of Kharput (Elazig) and disarmed its garrison.

Within a month, the Kurdish forces had seized control of vast areas of the country, embracing about a third of Kurdistan in Turkey, and were besieging Diyarbekir. At the same time other Kurdish units were liberating the region north of Lake Van and were advancing both towards the Ararat area and towards Bitlis. But before these forces came within sight of Bitlis,

Yusuf Zia, Colonel Halid Bey and their friends had been hung by the Turkish authorities.

Turkey decreed a partial mobilization and sent the bulk of its armed forces, 80,000 men, into the region. With the approval of the French government, fresh troops arriving from Anatolia traveled along the Northern Syrian railroad[31] and encircled the Kurdish forces besieging Diyarbekir, a well-fortified town defended by several batteries of Turkish artillery. The uprising was eventually quelled in mid-April. Some of its leaders were taken prisoner, others sought refuge amongst the followers of the powerful Kurdish chieftain Simko, in Iran, or amongst the Kurds of Iraq.

The insurrection had been a veritable tidal wave. It enjoyed mass popular support, as Turkish observers noted at the time. The repression which followed was, therefore, all the more terrible and bloody. On September 4, 1925, Sheikh Said and 52 of his followers were hung in Diyarbekir. Thousands of anonymous peasants were massacred, "to make sure the lesson stays learnt." Hundreds of villages were burnt to the ground. In the fall, four hundred Kurdish patriots were hung in Kharput, a hundred in Hinis, etc.

The wave of repression also took a heavy toll in the ranks of the Turkish opposition. A law concerning "the re-establishment of order" (*Takrir-i Sukum*) was promulgated during the Kurdish revolt. It granted the executive "all powers to officially ban any organization, movement, tendency or publication liable to endanger the country's stability and social order or to further reaction and rebellion." The executive made considerable use of these powers, not only to ban all pro-communist leftist organizations and publications but also workers' organizations and even the Progressive Republican Party, a bourgeois opposition movement. Many of the regime's generals were accused of treason, including Karabekir Pasha, who was accused of having corresponded with Sheikh Said. Some of them were hung, for all that they were veteran Unionists. According to H.C. Armstrong, ex-British military attaché in Turkey, the tribunals "instituted a reign of terror. A careless word or a whisper of criticism was enough to get one dragged before the bloody assizes."[32]

While it was sentencing and executing Kurds for having attempted to create an independent Kurdistan, the Kemalist regime was presenting the Kurdish movement to the outside world as a reactionary religious revolt geared to re-establish the Caliphate and the Ottoman dynasty. It was suggested that Britain had backed the Kurds in order to strangle the new Turkey. All this propaganda was fairly effective. But did it have any basis in reality? A few religious slogans were indeed used during the insurrection. But one should recall that Mustafa Kemal himself had not been above using religious slogans during the Turkish War of Independence. Is one therefore to conclude that he was only fighting for the Caliphate and that his was a religious struggle? Despite the fact that some of its key figures, such as Fevzi Pasha and Karabekir Pasha were devout Muslims, it should be clear that the movement led by Mustafa Kemal was in no way religious and had national independence as its primary goal. The same applies to the movement led by Sheikh Said. As it happened, the leader of the Kurdish movement was a religious figure rather than a general, but this in no way altered the movement's basic goal, the aspirations it expressed or the hope for liberation it aroused amongst the Kurdish masses.

Why, one may ask, did revolts similar to that led by Sheikh Said not break out in Turkish Anatolia? When a peasant uprising broke out in Menemen in 1931, its leader, a Turkish sheikh, was certainly not charged with having attempted to set up an independent Anatolia.

What were the aims of the movement led by Sheikh Said? The tribunal which condemned him was quite unequivocal on the subject: what was at issue was the creation of an independent Kurdish state.

As for the accusation concerning Britain's role in the birth of the movement, the Kemalists were never able to prove it. By contrast, there can be no doubt that Ankara enjoyed the support of French imperialism, which allowed the Turkish troops to travel along the North Syrian railroad during the repression of the Kurdish insurrection.

Nationalism was the core of the whole issue, as was quite clear to various lucid observers who would hardly qualify as agents of imperialism. Nehru, for example, wrote about how "the Turks, who had only recently had to fight for their own independence, crushed the Kurds, who were seeking theirs. How strange, that a defensive nationalism should turn into an aggressive one, and that a struggle for freedom should become a struggle to dominate others."[33]

The Mount Ararat Revolt: Following the defeat of the 1925 insurrection, warrior chieftains such as Yado of Palu or Aliye Unis of Sassoun took on the task of defending the civilian population against the repression carried out by the Kemalist troops. These chieftains managed to inflict heavy losses on the Turkish expeditionary corps.

The Turkish government was beginning to think that the only way to bring Kurdistan to heel was to denude it of population. During the winters from 1925 to 1928, almost a million people were deported.[34] Tens of thousands died on the way, for lack of food and supplies and because of the huge distances they were forced to cross in the middle of the harsh Anatolian winter.

The Kurds who had fled to Iran and Iraq after 1925 eventually began to regroup around Mount Ararat, in response to the efforts of *Hoyboun* (Independence), a National Kurdish League which had been formed not long before in Lebanon by some intellectuals and certain Kurdish chiefs.

Hoyboun's founding congress, held in August 1927 in the Lebanese town of Bihamdun, had brought together representatives of all the Kurdish parties, circles and political organizations (the Society for the Recovery of Kurdistan, Committee for Kurdish Independence, Kurdish Social Committee, etc.) They agreed to fuse.[35] It is worth noting that "as symbol of the alliance between Armenians and Kurds." Vahan Papazyan, an Armenian leader from the Dashnak Party, attended the conference. This alliance seemed essential to the Kurdish leaders who were very much on the look-out for possible sources of support and aid for their movement. Britain now held the Mosul oil fields. France was on excellent terms with Ankara. Nonetheless, these great powers continued to foster the myth that the civilized West might help the Kurds; what this really meant, of course, was that the Western powers would be able to use their influence on the Kurdish leaders as a bargaining counter in any eventual negotiation with the Turkish government. The Armenian Dashnak Party seems to have enjoyed more genuine Western support, perhaps because it was struggling not only for liberation of Turkish Armenia but also against Soviet control of Russian Armenia, from whence it had been expelled in 1920. In this sense its actions fitted in perfectly with the interests of the Soviet Union's opponents. In fact, the Dashnak Party no longer had a mass base in Kurdistan, whilst *Hoyboun*, the Kurdish National League, had massive popular support but no access to the material resources it needed to pursue its program.

It was as a result of this agreement between the Kurdish and Armenian nationalist leaders, and probably at the request of the latter, that the Ararat region, not far from Soviet Armenia, was chosen as the center for a new uprising. Another factor influencing this choice must have been the fact that from the Ararat area it would be easy to establish lines of communication with Iran, which had also promised to aid the Kurdish movement. The Shah had everything to gain: he would be weakening his rival, Kemalist Turkey, and his control over the insurrection would enable him to forestall the Kurdish revolt which was threatening to break out in Iran itself, under the leadership of Simko.

The Turkish government became worried by what it saw as an upsurge of "Kurdish-Armenian intrigue." It entered into negotiations with the Kurdish leader, who demanded that the exiled Kurdish chiefs be allowed to return to their homes. The Ankara government accepted this pre-condition; some of these chiefs then returned and joined the revolt, although others preferred to seek refuge in Syria. Then, in 1929, the forces that General Ihsan Noury Pasha had organized seized control of an area stretching from Mount Ararat to the northern parts of Van and Bitlis. The general prolonged the new talks with the Turkish emissaries for as long as he could. In the meantime he was systematically extending his zone of influence and a civil administration led by Ibrahim Pasha Haski Tello was being set up in all the liberated areas flying the Kurdish flag.

Ankara realized that time was working in favor of the Kurds and began to mass its troops in May 1930. Two army corps led by Salih Pasha launched the general offensive on June 11. After a month of combat, the Kurdish forces had taken 1,700 prisoners and seized 600 machine-guns and 24 cannons. They had also shot down twelve planes.

As was to be expected, Ankara managed to come to an agreement with Tehran. The Shah cut off his aid; the Turkish troops passed through Iranian territory and encircled the Kurdish *maquisards*. To legalize the situation, on January 23, 1932, Turkey and Iran signed an agreement in which Turkey gained certain Iranian territories around Mount Ararat and Iran received other territories around Van. The Kurdish revolt was surrounded and quelled at the end of the summer in 1930. Some of its leaders managed to flee. Others were captured and executed. L. Rambout reports that: "In Van a hundred intellectuals were sewn into sacks and thrown into the lake."

The blind violence which had been unleashed upon Kurdistan five years earlier redoubled in intensity. Planes were still burning Kurdish villages several months after the revolt had been crushed. A law published in the official Turkish journal announced that there would be no prosecutions for crimes or misdeeds committed during the repression of Kurdistan. This law, No. 1,850, read as follows:

> Murders and other actions committed individually or collectively, from June 20, 1930 to December 10, 1930, by the representatives of the state or the province, by the military or civil authorities, by the local authorities, by guards or militia-men, or by any civilian having helped the above or acted on their behalf, during the pursuit and extermination of the revolts which broke out in Ercis, Zilan, Agridag (Ararat) and the surrounding areas, including Pulumur in Erzincan province and the area of the First Inspectorate, will not be considered as crimes. (Article 1)

The area of the First Inspectorate covered all the provinces of Kurdistan; Diyarbekir, Elazig, Van, Bitlis, Mus, Hakkari, Mardin and Siirt. The Mount Ararat revolt, which had in any case not extended beyond a limited area, had been thoroughly quelled by the summer of 1930. This law is thus particularly revealing of the scale and savagery of the "pacification" of Kurdistan, a campaign during which the Kemalists devastated the Kurdish regions and killed thousands of inhabitants in areas which had not even been involved in the revolt.

In August 1930, when inaugurating the Sivas railroad, Ismet Pasha, the Turkish Prime Minister, announced that: "The revolution, fanned by foreign intrigue in our Eastern provinces, has lasted for five years, but today it loses half its strength. Only the Turkish nation is entitled to claim ethnic and national rights in this country. No other element has any such right."[36]

The Minister of Justice, Mahmut Esat Bozhurt, was quick to echo the point: "We live in a country called Turkey, the freest country in the world. As your deputy, I feel I can express my real convictions without reserve: I believe that the Turk must be the only lord, the only master of this country. Those who are not of pure Turkish stock can have only one right in this country, the right to be servants and slaves."[37]

Part of the blame for the butchery which followed the Mount Ararat revolt must be laid at the door of the Kurdish leadership, *Hoyboun*. They launched the revolt before the right material and political preparations had been made. Also, *Hoyboun*'s shortsightedness encouraged much closer Turko-Iranian and Turko-Soviet relations. But given that the "pacification" was carried out throughout Kurdistan and not just in the insurgent areas, it is probably fair to assume that Ararat was effectively only the pretext for Ankara to accelerate its assimilation program.

The Western press paid little attention to the events in Kurdistan, except when the Socialist International declared its position on the subject. Challenged by an Armenian representative of the Dashnak Party, the International adopted the following resolution on August 30, 1930:

> The executive of the IOS calls the world's attention to the massacres which are being committed by the Turkish government. Peaceful Kurdish populations who have not participated in the insurrection are being exterminated just as the Armenians were. The degree of repression extends far beyond containment of the Kurdish struggle for freedom. Yet capitalist public opinion has not in any way protested against this bloody savagery.[38]

The "bloody savagery" referred to by the Socialist International entered a new phase on May 5, 1932 when a law ordering the deportation and dispersion of the Kurds was passed:

> Four separate categories of inhabited zones will be recognized in Turkey, as will be indicated on a map established by the Minister of the Interior and approved by the other Ministers.
>
> No. 1 zones will include all those areas in which it is deemed desirable to increase the density of the culturally Turkish population. [This obviously referred to Kurdistan.]
>
> The No. 2 zones will include those areas in which it is deemed desirable to establish populations which must be assimilated into Turkish culture. [Ethnically Turkish Turkey.]
>
> The No. 3 zones will be territories in which culturally Turkish immigrants will be allowed to establish themselves, freely but without the assistance of the authorities. [The most fertile and habitable areas of Kurdistan were thus graciously offered to Turkish immigrants.]
>
> No. 4 zones will include all those territories which it has been decided should be evacuated and those which may be closed off for public health, material, cultural, political, strategic or security reasons. [This category included the more inaccessible areas of Kurdistan.][39]

A first draft of such a law had been drawn up and applied during the First World War. In its new version it envisaged the majority of the Kurdish people being deported and dispersed throughout Anatolia, whilst Kurdistan itself was to be partially repopulated by Turkish immigrants. Deported Kurds "established in burgs and towns should never be allowed to form more than one-tenth of the total population of a municipal district." Furthermore, "those who speak a mother tongue other than Turkish will be forbidden to form villages, quarters or groupings of artisans and employees." From the winter of 1932, several hundred thousand people were torn away from their lands and native villages, to be marched across the steppes of Anatolia under military escort. Only a shortage of material means prevented the Ankara government from deporting the whole Kurdish population.

Towards the end of 1935, the mass deportations were stopped, in response to the Dersim revolt. Dersim, during the thirties, was the last fortress of a Kurdistan which had been constantly at war since 1925. The confrontation was quite inevitable, since Dersim was part of Zone No. 4, the one which was due to be completely evacuated.

The Popular Resistance Movement in Dersim: Dersim was a veritable eyrie set high in the mountains, which had always retained its autonomy. Its inhabitants had not joined the Hamidieh and had refused to participate in the Russo-Turkish wars, the First World War, or the Turkish War of Independence, although they did have five deputies in the Assembly. The carefully prepared attack on this last pocket of Kurdish resistance was an integral part of the Ankara government's policy of piecemeal "pacification" of Kurdistan.

A state of siege was declared in 1936 and the new military Governor, General Alp Dogan, began to build military roads through the territory. He issued a communique demanding that the people of Dersim hand over 200,000 rifles to the authorities.

The people of Dersim had heard about the fate of the "pacified" regions of Kurdistan: the massive deportations, crushing taxes, summary executions, conscriptions into the labor corps to build military roads, etc. They were resolved to resist to the very end.

The government decreed a partial mobilization and the bulk of the Turkish troops were concentrated in the Dersim region. The Prime Minister, Ismet Pasha, came over specifically to inspect his forces. The trial of strength began in the spring of 1937. But this war was like no other which had been fought on Kurdish territory. There was no front, no battles between large military units. The people were convinced of the justice of their cause and knew their very survival was at stake. Guerrilla warfare became the order of the day throughout the region. By the end of the summer in 1937, despite massive use of poison gas, artillery and air bombardment, the Turkish Army had still to achieve any tangible military results.

Even though its leaders were treacherously assassinated, the revolt raged on more and more furiously. Throughout the middle of 1938, the Turkish government was forced to concentrate three Army divisions and most of its air force in this small area. Surrounded from 1936 onwards and cut off from all outside aid,[40] battered by artillery and grossly outmanned, the people of Dersim resisted with rare heroism till their ammunition ran out in late October 1938.

The Turkish Army had paid very dearly for its victory; the repression was even more violent than usual. People were shut up in caves and barns and burned alive by Turkish soldiers. Forests were encircled by troops and set alight, to exterminate those who had sought refuge there. There were also collective suicides; many Kurdish women and girls threw themselves into the River Monzour.[41] Dersim was entirely devastated.

The Turkish Communist Party has estimated that during these thirteen years of repression, struggle, revolt and deportation, "more than one and a half million Kurds were deported and massacred."[42] The whole affair reflected so badly on the "progressive Ankara regime" that "the entire area beyond the Euphrates" was declared out of bounds to foreigners until 1965 and was kept under a permanent state of siege till 1950. The use of the Kurdish language was banned. The very words "Kurd" and "Kurdistan" were crossed out of the dictionaries and history books. The Kurds were never even referred to except as "Mountain Turks."

Some Reflections on Kemalism

One may wonder, as Nehru did, how it came about that a defensive national-ism turned into an offensive nationalism. How was it that those who had only themselves so recently been humiliated and despised, who had won their liberty through a supreme effort, could in their turn become oppressors and tyrants?

At the beginning of the century, under the Empire, the term "Turk" had been a humiliating designation reserved for "rude peasants." Turkism was considered a dangerous and extremist current. The word "Turk" was ex-communicated, lest a nationalist consciousness prevail over Ottoman con-sciousness. It was this deep-seated contempt for Turks which provided the background for the emergence of an arrogant and aggressive "Greater Turkish" nationalism. Turkism only became respectable with the Kemalist victory, when it was set up as the official ideology of the new state. The contempt and humiliation which the Turks had suffered turned into a feeling of arrogant superiority and contempt for non-Turks. The nationalist leaders in Ankara proclaimed the Turks "the most valiant and noble race on earth." Mustafa Kemal's phrases. "A Turk is worth the whole universe" and "What a joy it is to be able to call oneself a Turk," are still prominently displayed in all schools and barracks throughout Turkey, as well as being inscribed on many public buildings.

From 1930 onwards, these chauvinistic proclamations were shored up by a mythical Turkish history. Having "demonstrated" that the Turks were descendants of the "Gray Wolves" from the Ergenekon Valley in Central Asia and belonged to the Aryan race (a frequent claim in the thirties), this "universal Turkish history" elaborated by the Institute of Turkish History "established" that the famous Sumerian, Egyptian, Babylonian, Lydian, Ionian and Hittite civilizations had all been created by Turks. Meanwhile, great stress was laid on the Turkish origins of Attila, Genghis Khan, Hulagu, etc. Today, throughout Turkey, this "universal Turkish history" is still taught in all schools and, apart from a few intellectuals, nobody questions its factual basis.

As for the Kurds, this "history" demonstrated that they also were of Turanian origin, in that they had come from Central Asia five thousand years ago. If they now spoke a "dialect," which was nothing but a "mixture of old Turkish, Persian, Arabic and Armenian," this was due to the fact that "lost in their inaccessible mountains, the Kurds ended up by forgetting their mother tongue and fell under the influence of their Persian neighbors." Tekin Alp, an official Turkish ideologue, makes it clear that right from the start Kemalism had Turkish nationalism as its only ideal. It was this fantastic, aggressive and exaggerated nationalism which confronted the Kurdish people. Since the Kurds were the only minority within the boundaries of Turkey, they were the only members of an "inferior race" in contrast to whom Greater Turkish nationalism could assert itself.

What better "proof" of the superiority and glory of the "Great Turkish nation" could there have been than these "brilliant victories" over "those who are not of pure Turkish origin"? What better way to illustrate the idea that the "Turkish people is great, civilized and valiant," than to invent a palpable antithesis, the "savage and backward Kurds," the only large non-Turkish minority in Turkey? What better means could the Ankara government find to flatter its people than the military exploits of its expeditionary corps in Kurdistan? Certainly not its successes in the arts and sciences; certainly not the economic situation, dominated as it was by a corrupt bourgeoisie and which condemned the mass of the Turkish people to vegetate in abject poverty under a growing burden of tithes, debts and taxes.

In this self-assertive phase, Turkish nationalism needed this militarism, a militarism which left so deep a mark during the years of the colonial campaigns in Kurdistan that it can still be felt at every level of Turkish political and social life today.

The Turkish nationalist rulers needed wars; but the neighboring countries were either British or French protectorates, or were powerful in themselves, like the USSR. So, instead, through provocation, deportation and attempted assimilation, wars were imposed upon the Kurdish people. These colonial-style wars also enabled the Ankara government to eliminate communist and liberal opposition. The exploits of the "Glorious Turkish Army" in "barbaric" Kurdistan were widely broadcast, which helped to intimidate the Turkish people and dissipate any tendencies they might have to revolt against the Ankara regime. These political interests and ideological circumstances were, I believe, largely responsible for the martyrdom suffered by the people of Turkish Kurdistan from 1925 to 1939.

Kemalism and its founder, Mustafa Kemal Ataturk, enjoy a general reputation abroad for being progressive, or even revolutionary. This legend is maintained by twenty or so rather mediocre books (the exceptions being Lord Kinross's *The Birth of a Nation* and Benoit Mechin's *Mustafa Kemal ou la mort d'un empire*). The legend is a useful model or archetype for the various Third World petty tyrants and potentates who "dislike socialism for being a foreign ideology" but who nonetheless need to present a "non-capitalist," "progressive" façade, the so-called "Third Road." Edouard Herriot, the one time President of France, was obviously taken in by this myth, as can be seen from his preface to the above mentioned work by Tekin Alp: "This Turkish revolution is particularly original in that it unfolded with the regularity of a logical plan. There were no unchained passions, no destruction of material wealth and no bloodthirsty hostility between parties or classes."

Let us take a closer look at Kemalism, its class nature and its political system. The Turkish war of independence relied largely on the notables, the landlords, merchants, factory owners and professional people who acted as intermediaries between the nationalist military cadres and the mass of the population. This emergent Turkish bourgeoisie was soon to seize control of the new state, at the Izmir Economic Congress in 1922. Kemalism was its smokescreen, its ideology.

None of the Turkish leaders disputed that capitalism was the right socio-economic system to adopt. They confined themselves to debating about how best to develop it, how to create a powerful Turkish bourgeoisie which

Turkish bourgeoisie

would in its turn lead the country towards progress. Some thought economic life should be left to private enterprise, and that the state should confine itself to promoting the growth of the private sector. Others suggested that, given the weakness of the Turkish bourgeoisie, it was not ready to be entrusted with the whole of the economy; a state sector was also necessary (Ismet Pasha). The outcome was that the first of these approaches was followed from 1923 to 1929, the second from 1930 to 1939.

During the period dominated by private enterprise, the generals and other dignitaries of the war of independence became directors of companies, bankers and importers. Along with a few other important notables, Mustafa Kemal himself created the Turkish Bank of Commerce, with a personal deposit of 250,000 Turkish pounds. This was by no means Ataturk's only commercial venture.[43] Following in their leader's footsteps the notables and all the civil and military bureaucrats who had emerged during the war of independence threw themselves into the frantic pursuit of wealth.

When the Great Depression of 1929 struck, there were both more rich people and more very poor people in Turkey than before. Statism was gradually introduced; the state began to build roads and factories. Kemalist Turkish intellectuals refer to this period of statism as the *Devrim*, which means both "reform" and "revolution." It was, in fact, a statism dedicated to the service of the private sector.

The main beneficiaries were those whom Ismail Cem has called the regime's "happy few": a coalition of big Istanbul merchants, Anatolian notables and landlords, the military cadres of the war of independence, the deputies and the senior bureaucrats. The so-called road building tax illustrates the point: each citizen, rich or poor, was called on to pay from 8 to 15 Turkish pounds each year. For a peasant family of five adults this represented an average contribution of 60 Turkish pounds, at a time when a metric ton of wheat was worth only 40 pounds. Many peasants could not afford to pay: they then had a choice between prison, banditry, or the labor corps (where their labor would be "set against their debts to the state").

The Kemalist regime claimed to "reject class and privilege," yet the fate of the Anatolian peasant — not to mention the martyred Kurds — was exactly as it was under Ottoman rule: no agrarian reform, no schools, heavy state taxes and the extortionate exactions of the landlords and moneylenders. The real scale of Ataturk's reforms, such as the importation of the Gregorian calendar, a new system of timekeeping, European dress, the Swiss Civil Code, the Italian Penal Code and French penal procedure, can only be measured against this background. All these reforms corresponded to the aspirations of an emergent Turkish bourgeoisie which felt humbled by the West and which sought to ape the way of life of the Western bourgeoisie down to the smallest details. If one couldn't emulate the Western bourgeoisie's spirit and know-how, one could at least present the right façade.

The suppression of the Caliphate in 1924 and the proclamation of the Republic were the most striking measures taken by the Kemalists. However, it is worth noting that, under the new republican regime, Mustafa Kemal had more personal power than any Ottoman Sultan since the early 19th century.

A regime which did nothing to improve the people's material conditions and which furthermore flew full in the face of their general traditions could hardly expect popular enthusiasm. The majority of the Turkish people manifested their opposition whenever the occasion arose. Mustafa Kemal was first and foremost the idol of the "civilized" notables and bureaucrats. The Liberal Party (*Serbest Firka*), founded in 1929 at Mustafa Kemal's instigation by one of his close associates, the ex-Prime Minister Fethi Okyar, and which had as its function to measure the depth of discontent in the country, proved so successful that it had to be banned a few months after being founded.

Many historians and observers have suggested that, on the political level, the Kemalist regime could be described as fascist. There are indeed some striking parallels.

From 1930 onwards, Mustafa Kemal Ataturk was known as the "Eternal Leader" (*Ebedi Sef*), which is not so different from "Fuhrer" or "Duce." His successor, Ismet Pasha, called himself the "National Leader" (*Milli Sef*). Successive governments were formed and dissolved at the whim of the "Leader," and were in any case only empowered to carry out his directives.

The People's Republican Party was the only party in a one party state. It claimed to represent "all the classes" but was actually entirely dedicated to the interests of the Turkish bourgeoisie and the higher ranks of the civil and military bureaucracy. It was quite inseparable from the state itself. From 1936 onwards, when Turkey was "flirting" more and more openly with the fascist powers, the President of the Republic, the "Leader," was also President of the Party, while the Republic's Vice-President was Vice-President of the Party and the Minister of the Interior was its General Secretary. In the towns the *Valis* (Prefects) presided over the Party's local sections.

There are further affinities with fascism. In June 1936 the Turkish government adopted Mussolini's form of labor legislation. Two other legal measures were also imported from Italy, in order to "protect the state's security and existence against subversive activities such as communism and anarchism": both strikes and trade unions were banned. Employers were authorized to make their workers work a thirteen hour day. Communists and workers' leaders were arrested. However, the petty bourgeoisie and middle classes, which usually make up fascism's social base, were not available to Kemalism. It remained a regime supported by the embryonic Turkish bourgeoisie and the higher reaches of the bureaucracy; essentially, it rested upon the army and the police, and was thus a fairly primitive militarist variant of bourgeois dictatorship.

The Quiet Years

After the fall of Dersim, there were no more major armed uprisings in Kurdistan. The massacres, the massive deportations, the militarization and systematic surveillance of the Kurdish territories had all had an undeniably intimidating effect on the population. Revolt ceased to be a credible avenue towards liberation.

As for the benefits of civilization introduced by the troops, a good account can be found in the report sent in by Osman Mete, a special correspondent for the Turkish paper *Son Posta*, who visited the area in 1948:

> I went to Tunc Eli, the old Dersim. The place was desolate. Tax collectors and policemen are still the only state officials the people have ever seen. I tried to meet people, to get to know their way of life, their spirit. But unfortunately very little remains from the period before the revolt. There are no more artisans, no more culture, no more trade. I met unoccupied people whose whole life now seemed to revolve around a flock of a hundred goats. No trace of civilization has yet penetrated the area. There are no schools, no doctors. The people do not even know what the word "medicine" means. If you speak to them of government, they translate it immediately as tax collectors and policemen. We give the people of Dersim nothing; we only take. We have no right to carry on treating them like this.[44]

Following the Second World War, in which Turkey did not take part, a wave of general discontent, exacerbated by famine and the draconian measures imposed from 1940 to 1945, forced the government of "National Leader" Ismet Inonu to liberalize the regime a little. The defeat of the major fascist powers was also a factor. The government was seeking a *rapprochement* with Britain and the U.S. in the hope of obtaining military and financial aid "to protect itself from Soviet Russia"; it therefore felt obliged to give the regime a certain democratic façade.

In 1946 several political parties were created, and for a while progressive publications were allowed. The Turkish Socialist Workers and Peasants Party (TSEKP) attracted several thousand members in a few months. This rapid success resulted in it being banned as early as December 1946.

In the 1950 elections, the first free general elections in Turkey's history, the Democratic Party was carried to power on a wave of popular support. The Party had been founded four years earlier by an important landlord, Adnan Menderes, and by Celal Bayar, a Prime Minister under Ataturk, who acted as spokesman for Turkish high finance; they were backed by a few breakaway bureaucrats. The people supported this Party not because they admired its program or its leaders, but as a reaction against the Kemalist reign of terror. The Democratic Party's victory was essentially a victory for the Turkish bourgeoisie which had become sufficiently powerful to do without the rigid *dirigiste* controls which the military bureaucracy still sought to impose upon it.

This institution of a multi-party parliamentary regime and the victory of the Democratic Party were undoubtedly a considerable move forwards for Turkey as a whole and even for Kurdistan, which was the Party's main stronghold. The police and military repression died down considerably. Both Turks and Kurds had become voters, and it was important not to antagonize them, for fear of losing electoral support. The exiled "feudal" Kurdish leaders were allowed to return home and recovered their goods and their lands. The Democrats were at pains to win them over: many were elected to parliament and some even became Ministers. Schools, roads and hospitals began to appear in Kurdistan.

American imperialism penetrated Turkey in 1948, under the Marshall

Plan. Menderes's Turkey ran up a considerable foreign debt. The Turkish bourgeoisie had neither the experience nor the technology nor the know-how necessary for development, and so had to call in foreign aid. As a result, by 1957 it was on the verge of bankruptcy.

In exchange for the American aid, Turkey sent thousands of Turkish soldiers (including many Kurds) to fight in Korea, joined NATO on February 18, 1952, turned itself into the advance post of imperialism below the southern flank of the USSR and, on February 26, 1954, authorized the U.S. to set up bases and listening posts throughout the country, Kurdistan included. In 1955, the Menderes regime signed the anti-communist and anti-Kurdish Baghdad Pact with Iraq, Iran and Pakistan. The new agreement replaced the old Saabad Pact signed by the same partners and for the same motives in 1937. On April 4, 1955, Britain joined the Pact. Although the Americans participated in all the Pact's activities and were in control of all its military decisions (a U.S. officer headed its military committee), they saw that it would be more useful to them politically if they themselves were not members. Following the July 1958 Revolution in Iraq and that country's withdrawal from the Pact, it adopted the name CENTO and was explicitly geared to provide "mutual military assistance in the event of Soviet aggression or internal revolts liable to threaten common security." The first concrete application was the repression of the Djiwanroji Kurdish uprising in Iran in 1956: both Iraqi and Iranian troops participated in the repression.

For the Kurds, this Democratic period marked the beginning of the disintegration of the feudal structures in the countryside. The Kurdish "feudalists" were figuring less and less as Kurds and more and more as landlords with access to an electoral clientele and capitalist privilege. Many tribal chieftains — aghas, beys and sheikhs — moved to the towns where they became entrepreneurs, wholesalers, city landlords and shareholders. Their children, who were educated in Turkish schools or American colleges, were later to provide the first wave of campaigners for what to be known as "Eastism" (*Doguculuk*), support for economic change and progress in "the East," as Kurdistan in Turkey is now officially known.

The beginnings of this ephemeral "Eastism" can be traced back to the aftermath of the July 1958 Revolution in Iraq, which for a short while actually called itself the Arab and Kurdish Republic. Radio Baghdad's Kurdish language broadcasts and previous broadcasts from Radio Cairo and Radio Erivan had inflamed popular feeling within Kurdistan in Turkey. It was clear that, in other countries, fellow Kurds lived as equal citizens. The great pall of silence which had descended after the massacres of the thirties was lifted at last.

The first group of "Eastists" (*Dogucu*) were based in Diyarbekir and published a daily broadsheet called *Ileri Yurt* (The Advanced Country) from the fall of 1958 onwards. The paper was written in Turkish and merely stressed the East's underdevelopment, its lack of hospitals, roads, schools, etc. It rapidly gained a large audience amongst Kurdish intellectuals.

In December 1959 the Menderes Cabinet arrested not only the paper's publishers, but all those whom the MIT, the political police, had classified as "Kurdists" (*Kurtsu*), about 50 people in all.

These arrests were partly intended as a diversion. The economic situation, the August 1958 devaluation of the Turkish currency by 220% and a very steep increase in prices, had caused considerable discontent, especially amongst bureaucrats on fixed salaries and in the army, which had lost much of its prestige and many of its old privileges under the new regime. The row over Cyprus, nationalistic declarations and the bogey of "Kurdish separatist subversion" were quite effective in temporarily distracting public opinion from the economy. Nonetheless, the army, which since 1950 had been gradually edged out of direct control over political life, was intensely resentful of its loss of influence and was carefully preparing a coup to "save democracy and restore the revolutionary norms of Kemalism."

The military coup d'etat on May 27, 1960 was the revenge taken by the Kemalist military and civil bureaucracy, who described themselves as "the enlightened" (*aydin*). A Committee of the National Front made up of the main participants in the coup governed the country for a year and half, then allowed a civilian government to take over following elections in 1961.

The putsch had not been particularly welcomed by the population, far from it. The Kurdish people especially feared a return of the old Kemalist militarism. One of the Committee's very first measures had been to intern 485 Kurdish intellectuals and notables in a military camp established at Sivas, where they were held for four months. Fifty-five of them, those the authorities deemed most influential amongst the Kurdish population, were exiled to the western cities of Turkey for two years. The general amnesty proclaimed after the coup did not cover the 49 Kurdish detainees. Another of the Committee's earliest decrees set out to ensure "the Turkicization of the names of Kurdish villages and towns." It also decided to set up "religious boarding schools" in Kurdistan, where Kurdish children, separated from their own milieu at a very young age, could be "Turkicized." (This effort at assimilation misfired completely; most of these educated Kurdish children eventually became Kurdish nationalists.) Half a dozen radio stations were set up in Kurdistan to broadcast in Turkish, in the hope that this would deter the population from listening to the Kurdish language broadcasts from neighboring countries.

A Committee decree on residence empowered the Cabinet to "transfer to another part of the national territory any persons convicted by official enquiry of having engaged in activities prejudicial to the national interest, along with members of their families, to the fourth degree, if it is judged necessary." The Kurds were the only "beneficiaries" of this decree.

On November 16, 1960, two months after the outbreak of the armed Kurdish uprising in Iraq led by Mustafa Barzani, General Gursel, the leader of the junta, issued a warning to any Kurds in Turkey who might be tempted to emulate their compatriots in neighboring countries. "If the mountain Turks do not keep quiet, the army will not hesitate to bomb their towns and villages into the ground. There will be such a bloodbath that they and their country will be washed away."

The new 1961 Constitution did grant a few democratic rights, however: freedom of thought and of the press, the right to form associations and independent trade unions, the right to attend public meetings and freedom from violations of a citizen's home or person. In 1963, a liberal interpretation of this Constitution led up to the recognition of the right to strike and to form collective agreements. But the ban on forming any regionalist associations which might divide the nation was maintained. Nonetheless, the Kurds did benefit to some extent from these democratic liberties.

An educated middle class had developed in Turkey and it now aspired to political power. The working class was also becoming more important both politically and numerically. The Menderes government's inflationist policy had threatened the petty bourgeoisie and forced it into the political arena. The Kurdish intelligentsia had developed a solid base in the cities. All these factors combined to ensure that the new Constitution was something more than a dead letter. In the second week of February 1961, three new political parties emerged, namely the Justice Party (AP), The New Turkey Party (YTP), and the Turkish Workers Party (TIP) which was founded by a handful of trade unionists.

In the 1961 elections no party obtained an overall majority, but the Justice Party led the polls and was thus confirmed as the successor to Menderes's Democratic Party. In Kurdistan, the votes were split mainly between the Justice Party and the New Turkey Party, one of whose leaders was a Kurd, Dr. Yusuf Azizoglu. A coalition government was formed, and the Army entrusted the presidency to one of their own, the now elderly Ismet Inonu.

In 1962 *Baris Dunyasi* (World of Peace), a liberal bourgeois Turkish journal, began to publish articles by the author, Musa Anter, on Kurdish language, literature and folklore. Since the editor, Ahmed Hamdi Basar, was famous as the founder and ex-president of the Union of Turkish Chambers of Industry and Commerce, also as the founder of the National Union of Turkish Businessmen and as a onetime close companion of Mustafa Kemal, publication of the journal was not suspended. Supposedly left-wing Kemalist intellectuals decried the "treason" and irresponsibility of the bourgeoisie and a lively polemic was engaged between *Baris Dunyasi* and the Kemalist journal *Yon*. In September of that year, a bilingual (Turkish and Kurdish) monthly magazine called *Dicle-Firat* (Tigris-Euphrates) appeared in Istanbul. Published by "Eastist" intellectuals close to Dr. Azizoglu, the magazine became very successful amongst the city's students and was consequently banned after a few issues. *Deng* (Voice) and *Riya Newe* (New Path), two other new publications, were also banned.

Following the breakdown of the first coalition government on June 25, 1962 due to the withdrawal of the Justice Party, a new cabinet was formed, with Inonu remaining as President. The Ministry of Health was entrusted to the deputy from Diyarbekir and leader of the New Turkey Party, Dr. Azizoglu. During his brief term of office, he had more hospitals and dispensaries built in Kurdistan than all previous governments put together, which gained him considerable popularity. He was eventually accused before the Assembly of "regionalism" and Kurdish nationalism by one of Inonu's straw men, H. O. Bekata, the Minister of the Interior, and was forced to hand in his resignation by the forces of the Kemalist bureaucracy.

"Eastism" was a transitory period in the rebirth of the Kurdish national movement. In the neighboring state of Iraq, Kurds were conducting a war of national liberation and broadcasts spoke constantly of Kurds and Kurdistan. Even the Turkish papers, to whom the Constitution had granted freedom of the press, were giving detailed accounts of "Barzani's Kurdish movement" in the hope of increasing circulation. Spurred on by the example of the Iraqi Kurdish movement and increasingly educated by the experiences of the growing democratic and socialist movement within Turkey, Kurdish militants were soon to become radicalized and to supply the big battalions of the Turkish left.

In 1966 the first Kurdish socialist journal, *Yeni Akis* (The New Current), appeared in Ankara under the editorship of Mehmet Ali Aslan, a lawyer from the Ararat region who was later to become president of the Turkish Workers Party. The journal published theoretical articles on the Kurdish question and defended the idea of an alliance between the Kurdish and Turkish working classes against the ruling classes, be they Turkish or Kurdish. It called for a socialist regime as the only means of bringing justice, equality and wellbeing to the Turkish and Kurdish people. *Yeni Akis* was the first publication to speak of "the Kurdish people" since the birth of the Turkish Republic. It was very successful amongst young people and intellectuals, and gave a new vigor to the Kurdish national movement. As a result, the Turkish bourgeoisie banned this bilingual monthly as soon as its fourth issue came out, on the grounds that the use of the term "Kurdish people" was harmful to national unity and encouraged separatism. The editor was imprisoned.

Freedom of the press clearly did not apply to the Kurds. However, certain judicial norms were more or less respected during this new era of "liberty." People were no longer sent to the gallows "for having claimed that the Kurds existed" as they were under Ataturk. Kurdish militants could now say and write what they wanted and get away with a few years in prison. Kemal Budilli, a lawyer and the deputy from Urfa, published his Kurdish Grammar (*Kurtce Grameri*); since he enjoyed parliamentary immunity, he was not prosecuted. Musa Anter, author of *Brina Res* (The Black Wound) and the *Ferhenga Kurdi-Tirki* (Kurdo-Turkish Dictionary), was repeatedly brought before a judge, as was Mehmed Emin Bozarslan who published a Kurdish ABC and Ehmede Khani's *Mem-o-Zin*. It is also worth noting the publication in Turkish — thanks to Dogan K. Sihhesenanli — of two English language works on the Kurds, *On the Origin of the Kurds* by McCarus and *The Kurdish Republic of 1946* (*Mahabad*) by W. Eagleton. Particularly significant was the publication of two works by the Turkish sociologist Ismail Besiksi: *Gocebe Alikan Asireti* (The Alikan Nomadic Tribe), his doctoral thesis, and *Dogu Anadolu'nun Duzeni* (literally The Order of Eastern Anatolia, which, given the sub-title, could be rendered as Socio-economic and Ethnic Structures of Eastern Anatolia). In 1971 these two works cost their author a twelve year prison sentence.

Such publications, and the militant actions of Kurdish youth and Kurdish intellectuals in the Turkish Workers Party, combined with the strength of the Kurdish nationalist movement in Iraq, seriously worried the Ankara government and the Kemalist military circles. In 1966 the Turkish government set up anti-guerrilla commando units to patrol Kurdistan in Turkey, to intimidate and terrorize the peasants, and to stamp out any tendencies they might have to imitate the Kurds of Iraq.

Originally inspired by intellectuals of bourgeois or feudal origins, the Kurdish national movement gradually began to attract a broader spectrum of students, as well as the urban and rural petty bourgeoisie. During the sixties, the poor and middle peasants, the urban lumpenproletariat and the agricultural laborers also began to listen carefully to those who spoke of the East's striking underdevelopment, of the inequality between Kurdish areas and western Anatolia, of chronic unemployment, etc. Given the authorities' inability to solve these problems satisfactorily, and bearing in mind the immense amount of ground covered since 1961, there was every reason to expect a rapid political radicalization of these strata in Kurdish society.

The Democratic and Socialist Movement in Turkey (1961–70)

Although external factors, such as the Iraqi Kurdish movement, Kurdish language broadcasts from neighboring countries and the growth of national liberation movements throughout the world certainly did play a very important role in the awakening of Kurdish national consciousness, it is clear that the political, ideological and social content of this consciousness came through contact with the democratic and socialist movement which grew up in Turkey from 1961 onwards. It was this movement which shaped the revolutionary and progressive Kurdish cadres.

Right up until 1968, the Turkish Workers Party (TWP) played a major role in organizing and leading the struggle against fascistic laws, against imperialism and for democracy. Founded by a dozen trade unionists, this Party, led by a notable progressive, Mehmet Ali Aybar, managed to channel all the progressive potential which Turkey had accumulated over the years. In its early days, the TWP was a workers party in name alone. The original membership was made up mainly of intellectuals with a liberal bourgeois, or even aristocratic background who had been educated abroad and spoke several foreign languages perfectly. Many had no precise notion of socialism and were merely opponents of the regime. These intellectuals brought with them a whole collection of manuscripts: political and philosophical works, progressive novels translated, sometimes years before, from French, English, German, Russian or Greek, none of which they had been able to release under the dictatorship, but which the new Constitution gave them the opportunity to publish.

In February 1963, Senator Niyazi Agirnasli joined the TWP and it became the first socialist-inspired party to be represented in Parliament since the foundation of Turkey. Under the new Constitution, the universities, the President, and any party represented in Parliament were empowered to call upon the Constitutional Court to judge upon the constitutionality of any law, new or old. Through its Senator, the TWP called for the abrogation of sixty-odd laws. Articles 141 and 142 of the Penal Code, laws which had been imported from Fascist Italy and frequently used against communists and "separatists," were cited as amongst the major obstacles to the development of a democratic movement. By 8 votes to 7, the Court rejected the demand that these Articles be abrogated, though it did restrict their application by stating that "Studying, teaching, explaining, publishing or researching into anarchism or communism cannot be counted as offenses under these laws." The duplicating machines began turning frenetically: Marx, Engels, Lenin, Hegel, Stalin, Mao, Castro, Ho Chi Minh, Nkrumah, Fanon, Guevara, Rosa Luxemburg, August Bebel, Brecht, Nazim, Hikmet, Gorky, Cholokhov, Mayakovsky, Giap, etc., all became available for the first time to the mass of the population, including many of the *aydin* (enlightened) who spoke no foreign language.

In the underdeveloped, largely illiterate, and malnourished Turkey of the sixties, a Turkey ridden by inflation and unemployment, those who could read, the students and intellectuals who had till then had only a few 19th century novels for intellectual sustenance, literally threw themselves upon these newly available works. From 1965 onwards, the universities barely managed to absorb one-fifth of the suitably qualified candidates who took the competitive university entrance exam. The rest, the vast majority of whom were from petty-bourgeois backgrounds, remained jobless. In this sense the high schools, even more than the universities, became a major force producing revolutionaries.

It was not long before every faculty had its own socialist club or debating society. These joined into a Federation of Debating Societies whose orientation was fairly close to that of the Turkish Workers Party. The Federation later evolved into the DEVGENC (Federation of Revolutionary Youth), which proved a veritable incubator for revolutionaries of every persuasion. Most of the student youth held the people as their supreme value; their ideal was to struggle to better the condition of the masses. However, this populism was not the choice of all young people. Some enrolled in the ranks of Colonel Turkes's Nationalist Action Party (MHP) which also decried the corruption of the system and promised a new era of order, discipline and greatness for the "great Turkish nation." The militia of this fascist party was to be one of the main forces used by the authorities against progressive youth. Yet another fraction of petty-bourgeois youth was attracted by pan-Islamist currents critical of the "capitalist and atheist regime."

In Kurdistan, thanks to the efforts of a few intellectuals, joined later by a number of artisans and small shopkeepers, several sections of the TWP were started. In practically every case, the opening of these sections was beset by violent incidents fomented by the political police or by Associations for the Struggle Against Communism, which had been set up throughout the country.

In the 1965 parliamentary elections, the TWP obtained 15 seats (out of 450) in the Assembly, which now became their platform.

The very development of the democratic and anti-imperialist movement was bound to lead to splits sooner or later.

Divisions over the analysis of the country's concrete situation and how to bring about a revolutionary situation soon emerged. By 1968, there was a clear differentiation between "Parliamentarists" and "Leninists," between those who supported a national democratic revolution and those who wanted a socialist revolution. The TWP continued to develop its program for a socialist revolution. Those who supported a national democratic revolution regrouped around Mihri Belli, and eventually split into several further factions, including two Maoist ones.

During this period the petty bourgeoisie increasingly came to dominate the socialist currents, and gradually eliminated the "bourgeois cadres" led by Aybar whom they deemed too soft and parliamentarist.

The working class was constantly referred to, but as yet had little weight in the party. It was only in 1967 that trade unionists close to the TWP split from the pro-American and pro-government Turk-Is trade union congress to form the DISK (Confederation of Revolutionary Workers Unions). Also in 1967, Kurdish militants close to the TWP organized mass meetings in the main towns of Kurdistan, protesting against injustice and national oppression, and demanding that the Kurdish people be allowed to exercise their democratic rights. In 1969, first in Ankara and Istanbul, then in the Kurdish towns, an Organization of Revolutionary Kurdish Youth (DDKO) set up Eastern Revolutionary Cultural Centers which played an important role in the Kurdish national movement. Their main militants were either members of the TWP, or very close to it.

From 1969 onwards, the TWP fell prey to its own internal contradictions and began to decline. Until then, it had achieved considerable advances on the ideological level within the overall Turkish context, as is shown by, amongst other things, a motion on the Kurdish question carried by its Fourth Congress in October 1970 — the resolution which led to the party itself being banned.

Although it was splintered, the revolutionary movement managed to conduct fairly large-scale anti-imperialist campaigns and was growing constantly. Since the authorities could do nothing to prevent this process, they tried to stamp it out by intimidation. The armed militias of Turkes's fascist party were given police protection and let loose; they occupied the "red faculties" and university halls of residence, brandished their firearms with impunity and assassinated noted militants in broad daylight. From 1969 to March 12, 1971, thirty-five people were murdered in this way, yet their killers, whose identity had been clearly established, were not brought to trial. The violence employed by the authorities and the apparent unlikelihood of any revolutionary change in the short term began to have an effect on certain sections of the youth. They started to train in the use of arms; some attended Palestinian training camps in secret. The result was two new groupings, Deniz Gezmis's Turkish Army of Popular Liberation (THKO) and Mahir Sayan's Turkish Popular Liberation Party (THKP), with its military organization, known as the Turkish Popular Liberation Front (THKC).

The development of working class struggles, the success of the Kurdish national movement and the radicalization of young people were all very worrying to the dominant classes and the upper echelons of the military. The "left" Kemalists expected a putsch by Army captains "of left-wing persuasion." In the end, to ensure that exceptional economic, political and legal measures, which would not have been accepted in normal circumstances, were put into effect — and to pre-empt a coup by the captains — the Army overthrew the Demirel government on March 12, 1971. A state of siege was imposed and the right to strike suspended. All student, teacher and youth organizations were dissolved, as was the TWP.

Thousands of people were arrested and tortured in counter-insurgency centers which had been set up by Turkish officers trained by the U.S. in Panama. In Kurdistan, more than a thousand people were arrested, herded into a military camp in Diyarbekir, then thrown into prison. Seventy-five per cent of those detained were from the countryside. Some were accused of belonging to the Democratic Party of Kurdistan in Turkey, others of having formed clandestine separatist organizations within the Organization of Revolutionary Kurdish Youth (DDKO). The peasants were charged with having sent supplies and money to Barzani. The trials were to last about two years; fifteen detainees were eventually sentenced to terms in excess of ten years, the rest got from six months to ten years.

While the jails were filling up with writers condemned to seven and a half years imprisonment for each subversive book, the fascist dictatorship blocked salary increases and raised prices steeply, to the great advantage of the industrial bourgeoisie and big retailers. The 1961 Constitution was stripped of all content.

Under the simultaneous pressure of intense popular anger and the generally hostile international reaction (notably in the European Community, membership of which the Turkish bourgeoisie aspired to), the junta was forced to organize parliamentary elections in October 1973. The great victor in these elections was Bulent Ecevit's People's Republican Party, which had publicly opposed the dictatorship.

Joining with the pan-Islamist Party of National Salvation (MSP), Ecevit formed a coalition government which decreed a general amnesty in July 1974. Following the invasion of Cyprus under the cover of a "peace-keeping operation," this coalition broke down over differences between the two parties in October 1974.

Demirel returned to power and commando operations started up with renewed intensity in Kurdistan. In the towns the state police and the fascist militias assassinated sixty people from March 31, 1975 to April 10, 1976.[45] However, as early as the fall of 1974, the left parties had managed to regroup and were issuing publications. Noteworthy amongst these was the bilingual monthly *Ozgurluk Yolu* (The Road to Freedom) published in Ankara after June 1975 by Kurdish Marxist intellectuals. This political and cultural journal covered the various aspects of the Kurdish question in Turkey and in the other parts of Kurdistan, as well as general Turkish issues concerning the left as a whole. In March 1976 another monthly review, *Rizgari* (Liberation), was issued. Its anti-Kemalist articles were so virulent that it was banned as soon as its second issue was brought out.

The Various Forms of National Oppression

Any historically constituted national entity which comes under the domination of another nation is a victim of national oppression. National oppression can be defined as the sum of the political, economic and cultural discrimination suffered by the dominated nation at the hands of the dominant nation. The essential function of such oppression is to maintain and perpetuate the domination of the oppressor nation, a domination motivated by the economic, political or ideological interests of the oppressors. It is exercised by means of a complex apparatus; the two main structures are, on the one hand, an ideological machine whose task it is systematically to negate and destroy the national identity of the oppressed; on the other, a powerful repressive force which can nullify any "troublemakers."

In the early days, the Turkish dominant classes' main motives for hanging on so desperately to Kurdistan were political. They aspired to create a great Turkish state endowed with the human and natural resources required to become a major power in the region. Today, however, their motive is more down to earth. Kurdistan is a colony which provides them with cheap and abundant labor, various minerals and agricultural products. It is also a "private hunting ground" for Turkish manufactured products. The Turkish government intends to hold on to it at any cost.

The economic exploitation of Kurdistan and the transfer of its wealth to the Turkish metropole is mainly carried out through state enterprises. Some leftist Turkish intellectuals suggest that, since Turkey is itself an underdeveloped country, it can by definition not have colonies. In asserting this, they blur all distinction between the concepts of imperialism and colonialism, two notions which refer to very different phenomena. They affect to be unaware that, although colonialism developed considerably during the imperialist era, it is by no means the mere product of imperialism. Both in the past and in the present, the colonization of other countries is not the exclusive prerogative of imperialist powers, in the sense given to the term by Lenin. For example, Portugal, a state which was just as underdeveloped and under imperialist domination as Turkey, certainly did have colonies in Angola, Mozambique and Guinea-Bissau until recently.

The other arguments often advanced to refute the suggestion that Kurdistan is a colony are based on the geographic contiguity of Turkish and Kurdish territory. But this is a very subsidiary feature, which is in any case fairly characteristic of colonialism. Were not the Caucasus and Kazakstan colonies of the Czarist Empire, for all that they were contiguous with Russia?

The essential and characteristic feature of the present status of Kurdistan is that its riches are being systematically drained away, to the advantage of the Turkish metropole. A growing gap between levels of development in the two areas manifests itself very concretely in the enormous divergences between the average standards of living in the Kurdish and Turkish parts of the Republic. These divergences are on a far greater scale than can be accounted for by the disparities which the unequal development of capitalism within a state can generate. They are the direct expression of metropole-colony relations. The Turkish Republic set up its apparatus for the repression of the

Kurdish people very soon after it had been founded. Following the War of Independence, during which they had been acclaimed as "equal partners" and as a "sister nation," the Kurdish people found that their very existence was being denied. The authorities then sought systematically to destroy everything which might suggest a specifically Kurdish identity. A whole scaffolding of linguistic and historical pseudo-theories, which supposedly "proved" the Turkishness of the Kurds, was to serve as a justification for the destruction of the Kurdish entity. These theories were erected into an official doctrine which was taught, inculcated and propagated by the schools, the universities, the barracks, the newpapers, the radio and publications of all sorts.

In order to ensure that official ideology would have a monopoly on the subject, Ankara banned any non-official publication which sought to discuss it. Historical or literary works, even travelers' tales published long previously in Turkish or in other languages, were removed from public and private libraries and for the most part destroyed if they contained any reference to the Kurdish people, their history or their country. Any attempts to question the official ideology even slightly were very severely repressed. In any case, Turkish intellectual circles did not make many such attempts.

During half a century in which the Kurdish people were quarantined, the Ankara government implemented a policy of terror and ideological conditioning which, in the words of the Turkish sociologist Ismail Besiksi, managed to "make people believe that he who announced 'I am Kurdish' was committing a crime so heinous that he deserved the death penalty."

The oppression resulting from this policy of terror affected the Kurdish people as a whole and manifested itself mainly in cultural and political affairs.

Cultural Oppression

The forms of discrimination which result when a people are prevented from expressing their identity culturally are often more difficult to bear than material poverty and economic exploitation. In Turkish Kurdistan, this oppression covers every aspect of cultural life and is particularly brutal in the domain of language. In this respect, the Kurd is treated as a foreigner in his or her own country.

Language is the cement of a national community and is thus a favorite target for those who seek to destroy that community. Many procedures are available to authorities who intend the gradual suffocation of a dominated people's language; some are direct, such as banning the written or spoken use of the language and generally putting obstacles in the path of its development, others are indirect, such as ensuring that education, information and social advancement are only accessible to speakers of the dominant language.

In Turkey under Kemalism, the authorities banned even the spoken use of Kurdish, at a time when only a tiny minority (3 to 4%) of Kurds spoke any Turkish at all.

Special government officials were charged with enforcing this ban in the Kurdish urban centers. The main victims were peasants bringing their surplus to market. They could not speak Turkish, yet for every word of Kurdish they uttered, they were liable — if caught — to a fine of five piastres.[46] At the time a sheep was worth about fifty piastres. The peasants were thus forced to use Turkish-speaking intermediaries of sometimes doubtful honesty. At each visit to the town they incurred fines which sometimes exceeded any profit they might have made from the sale of their goods. As a result, they started to stay away.

There were other good reasons for not going to town more often than was strictly necessary. The regime prided itself on its "accelerated Westernization" of the country; part of this program was a law which stipulated that every-body had to wear the "Republican cap." Should a peasant forget to remove his traditional headgear on approaching the town, he might be heavily fined by officials for this "serious offense." The possession of a few strands of smuggled tobacco could also cost him dearly.[47]

These various repressive measures, especially the ban on speaking Kurdish, turned the Kurdish peasants into a race of outlaws permanently at odds with the officials.

It seems highly unlikely that anybody endowed with even vestigial com-mon sense can really believe that one can eliminate a language used by millions of people merely by imposing police controls. Indeed it appears that the dignitaries of the regime had little faith in the enterprise's chances of success. Nonetheless, both the political leadership and the administrators carried on with the charade, preferring fiction to reality and often tilting over into pure farce. For instance, every time any important figure, such as the General Inspector of the East, was due to visit a Kurdish area, the governor would summon all the local mayors and notables and instruct them to make sure that any of their people who did not speak Turkish would stay at home during the official visit. The outcome was that the visiting dignitary would always find himself in a civilized, albeit remarkably deserted, town where people spoke only Turkish.

The growth of schools in which the only language of instruction was Turkish would no doubt have helped considerably to propagate the official tongue throughout the Kurdish countryside. But the Turkish authorities seem to have been well aware that, even when schools teach only the official ideology, something else is always transmitted as well: in the long-term, schools produce those who eventually bury a colonial system.

Similarly, despite frequent and violent clashes with the traditional Kurdish chieftains, the Turkish authorities studiously avoided taking any economic measures which might lead to the disintegration of traditional structures in Kurdistan. They well understood that the best way of controlling the Kurd-ish masses was through the intermediary of traditional leaders whose sup-port could be obtained in exchange for privileges. Indeed the government pursued a particularly obscurantist cultural policy in the Kurdish areas. As Fevri Gakmak, Ataturk's right-hand man, once put it, "Setting up schools in the Eastern provinces would awaken the people of those provinces and open up pathways for separatist currents such as Kurdish nationalism."

From 1950, with the inauguration of the multi-party parliamentary regime, Turkish governments lightened these restrictions to some extent. The Kurdish language was now only semi-clandestine; its use in private was tolerated, although it was still illegal to publish anything in it. This semi-clandestinity has been maintained up to the present day. Despite all efforts, most of them coercive, by the late sixties more than three-quarters of the Kurds in Turkey still did not speak the official language of the state. In Mardin, 91% of the population spoke not a word of Turkish; in Siirt, the figure was 87%; in Hakkari 81%; in Diyarbekir 67%; in Bingol 68%; in Bitlis 66%, etc.[48] Such was the level of Turkicization in the main Kurdish provinces.

In the seventies, a number of Turkish journalists, trade unionists and politicians noted the fact that Kurdish was still prevalent in the "Eastern provinces." The usual reaction was one of indignation; how could it be that, in an area which is an integral part of the Turkish Republic, there were millions of citizens who still spoke no Turkish?

Logically, the next step would be to question the official ideology and the textbook version of the problem, to demand that the Kurds be granted democratic rights and that an end be put to the policy of oppression. Unfortunately, the usual reaction was in fact merely to call on the authorities to take more "scientific" and appropriate measures in order to finally bring about the Turkicization of these "neglected citizens."

Mental inertia, chauvinism and nationalist conditioning do not fully account for such an attitude. The politicians, in particular, see it as an essential part of the Kemalist ideological edifice, in which no cracks must be allowed to appear. In this view, official recognition of the existence of a Kurdish people as a distinct entity would inevitably lead to eventual demands for political independence. Hence the obstinate pursuit of assimilationist policies.

Kurds are forced to use a language they cannot speak in all their dealings with the courts, the administration, etc. In their own country they have to use an interpreter whenever they attempt any official transaction. Ignorance of the official language severely handicaps them at school and exposes them to humiliations and beatings in the barracks when they do their military service.

In Turkey there are colleges and universities where the teaching is in French or in German or in English — but there is not one school where teaching is carried out in Kurdish, the language spoken by about one-quarter of the population.

Newspapers, books and records are available in half a dozen non-Turkish languages, but the Kurdish people still cannot publish in their own tongue. The courageous authors and publishers of the dozen or so books written on the Kurds to date are constantly harassed and pursued by the Turkish courts. In a further effort to choke off Kurdish culture, the Ankara government has even forbidden "the introduction and diffusion within the Republic of any publication, record, tape, etc., produced in Kurdish abroad."[49]

Treated as foreigners in their own country, the Kurds increasingly find that their own land is becoming alien to them. The Turkish colonizers have systematically changed the names of all the Kurdish towns and villages, substituting Turkish names for the originals. The word "Kurdistan," which has designated the country of the Kurds since the 13th century, was the first to be banned, because it implied the unity of the scattered Kurdish people and was therefore subversive. In Turkey they call Kurdistan eastern Anatolia, just as other parts of Kurdistan are known as northern Iraq or western Iran.

A people's history is another area which colonization usually attempts to conceal. The logic of a colonial system demands on the one hand the destruction of everything which might evoke the colonized people's true history, and on the other the elaboration and propagation of the colonizer's own version of history, which effectively negates the colonized people's particular historical experience. Accordingly, the Turkish authorities systematically purged the libraries of any books dealing with Kurdish history. They destroyed the monuments and other works erected during the era of the independent Kurdish principalities, and often enough built barracks on the rubble. (This was the fate meted out to the Birca Belek, the "multicolored palace" built by the Bedirkhanites at Djezira Botan on the banks of the Tigris.)

All historical or sociological research into Kurdish society was forbidden. The authorities constructed a whole historical theory to show that the Kurds were originally Turks. Until 1970 no research which did not fit in with this theory could be published.[50] The young Kurd learns at school that, even if the negligence of the central authorities has resulted in his having forgotten the Turkish language, he is nonetheless a member of the "pure Turkish race" and is a descendant, like all other Turks, of the "gray wolves of the Central Asian steppes." (In Iran the Kurds are told that they are "the purest Aryans" and "brothers of the Persians.")

The Turkish bourgeoisie feigns to believe that the Kurds of Turkey are Turks like any other. If the Kurds of Turkey are Turks, then surely so are those of Iraq and elsewhere. In which case, why did the Turkish government adopt an actively hostile attitude to the liberation struggle mounted under Barzani's leadership by the Kurds of Iraq in the early seventies even though it did not hesitate to intervene militarily in Cyprus to "defend the national rights" of a few hundred thousand Turkish Cypriots? The truth is that the Turkish ruling classes themselves give no credence to their mystifying, mythical historical theories.

A stranger in their own country and to their own country, the Kurdish people are also strangers to the outside world. Most can understand nothing of the information broadcast or published in the official language which they do not speak. They remain unaware of what is going on elsewhere, which further aggravates their cultural backwardness.

Turkish nationals are free to slander the Kurdish people at will, even to the point of calling publicly for their physical extermination. But the Kurds have no right of reply.

In recent years the papers and magazines of the Turkish right and extreme right (*Milli Yol, Yeni Istanbul, Otuken*, etc.), have published at least twenty anti-Kurdish articles and have never been prosecuted for doing so. For example, the following extracts are taken from an article by Nihal Atsiz published in the June 1967 issue of the nationalist journal, *Otuken*.

> If they [the Kurds] want to carry on speaking a primitive language with vocabularies of only four or five thousand words, if they want to create their own state and publish what they like, let them go and do it somewhere else. We Turks have shed rivers of blood to take possession of these lands; we had to uproot Georgians, Armenians and Byzantine Greeks . . . Let them go off wherever they want, to Iran, to Pakistan, to India, or to join Barzani. Let them ask the United Nations to find them a homeland in Africa. The Turkish race is very patient, but when it is really angered it is like a roaring lion and nothing can stop it. Let them ask the Armenians who we are, and let them draw the appropriate conclusions.

Everybody knows that the Armenians were subjected to a veritable genocide. The author of the article can threaten the Kurds of Turkey in this way without worrying about official prosecution. But when Kurdish students published a tract demanding that incitement to racial hatred be made a punishable offence, they were dragged before the courts and charged with "having claimed that there was a Kurdish people, thereby undermining national unity."

As for the Kurdish intellectuals, they are expected to reject their own culture and language, to become Turkicized. A person from Kurdistan cannot be appointed to fill a post without the prior approval of the political police (MIT). The authorities try not to nominate Kurds for jobs in the Kurdish provinces, preferring to separate them from Kurdistan.

Political Oppression

In Lenin's words, "The denial of the right to set up an independent national state is precisely one of the main forms of national oppression."

The Turkish bourgeoisie has equipped itself with a judicial armory which makes it absolutely impossible for the Kurds to set up legal associations, trade unions or political parties of their own. Article 57 of the Turkish Constitution stipulates that "the programs, statutes and activities of a political party must be in keeping with the democratic and secular principles of our Republic, which is based on liberty, the rights of man and the indivisibility of the national homeland."

Article 89 of the Turkish law bearing on political parties and associations is quite unambiguous about this principle of "indivisibility": "No political party may concern itself with the defense, development, or diffusion of any non-Turkish language or culture; nor may they seek to create minorities within our frontiers or to destroy our national unity."

The legislature thus indirectly recognizes the existence of people of non-Turkish culture and language living in Turkey. Given that the Greeks, Armenians and Jews were protected by the minority rights specifically granted under the Treaty of Lausanne, the Kurds were left as the main target of this discrimination.

Other laws are also frequently used to condemn Kurdish militants who dare make the slightest cultural or political demand, particularly Articles 141 and 142 of the Turkish Penal Code[51] which "protect the fundamental economic and social institutions of the country" and which provide for 5 to 15 year sentences for all those who "seek to destroy the political and legal order of the state."

Physical Repression

Until the early fifties, Kurdistan was held down by terror. Since then the authorities have relied more extensively on the corruption and self-interest of the traditional Kurdish chieftains and notables. But as these leaders' authority begins to crumble, Ankara increasingly falls back on the old methods of terror and intimidation.

The Turkish government is convinced that any concession to even the most moderate national or social demand would be taken as a sign of weakness and would encourage the formulation of more ambitious demands. Strict maintenance of the status quo is therefore the order of the day.

The national liberation struggle waged by the Kurds of Iraq from 1961 onwards seriously worried the Turkish leaders. After an abortive attempt to launch a joint military intervention with Iran and Iraq (Operation Tigris), they took repressive measures of their own. From 1966 onwards, anti-guerrilla units known as commandos were set up under the direct command of the Ministry of the Interior. In 1969 these commandos, who had been trained by American specialists in counter-insurgency, launched a vast campaign, raking the Kurdish countryside under the pretext of a general "arms search." The general pattern of these operations was as follows: A village is surrounded by armored cars and helicopters move overhead; all the villagers are rounded up without any explanation, then herded into specially prepared camps. They are then called upon the surrender their weapons. Should a peasant declare that he has none, he is severely beaten and humiliated. The Turkish troops force both men and women to strip; often they rape the women. "Suspects" are hanged by their feet from a gallows. Sometimes strings are attached to the genitals of naked men whom the women are then forced to lead through the streets in this manner. Many die under torture.

On March 11, 1970, the Kurds and Iraqis signed an agreement which was supposed to bring the armed struggle to an end and recognize the autonomy of Kurdistan in Iraq. Immediately the Turkish commandos redoubled their efforts to terrorize and intimidate the population of Kurdistan in Turkey, in order to discourage them from following the example given by the Kurds of Iraq.

During the more or less fascist period which followed the military coup on March 12, 1971, the commandos' activities were considerably extended and became a real "Kurd-hunt." The troops raked through the Kurdish provinces one by one; several thousand peasants were pursued, arrested and tortured. The Diyarbekir military court sentenced more than a thousand "Kurdish separatists" between 1971 and 1973.

Even under the "democratic parliamentary regime" of the late seventies the commandos were still at work in Kurdistan. There were more than 10,000 of them patrolling the frontier province of Hakkari from October to December 1975.

The counter-insurgency units are just one more weapon in the Turkish state's arsenal of repression. In the last resort, the task of ensuring order in the East is always turned over to the army. The present military occupation of the Kurdish territories is so pronounced that even the most unaware tourist cannot help but notice it.

Barracks, garrisons, military airports and armored units guard the entrance and exit of the main Kurdish towns. Every day there is a military parade to raise the flag in the town's central square, which is usually graced with a statue or bust of Ataturk; as a result, the Kurdish inhabitants are constantly reminded of the presence and power of the army. The schools, barracks, and press do everything in their power to inculcate and maintain the myth of the heroic Turkish Army's invincibility. No effort is spared to persuade the Kurds that any attempt to liberate themselves is bound to fail, and that "separatism" can only lead to disaster.

The Kurdish National Movement in Turkey through 1980

Changes in Kurdish Society

During the years 1960–1980, Kurdish society underwent profound changes which considerably altered its traditional structures. Feudalism broke down, nomadism disappeared and even semi-nomadism became the practice of only a few thousand people. As agriculture gradually mechanized, the countryside become increasingly depopulated; hundreds of thousands of peasants poured into the Kurdish towns and the big Turkish industrial cities.

The newly urbanized peasants lived piled up on top of each other in the local shantytowns. Most were unemployed or could only find occasional work. There were more and more agricultural laborers, as industrial cultivation of cotton, tobacco and sugar-beet spread in Kurdistan. These laborers, along with the petty bourgeoisie, were the most dynamic and responsive sectors of Kurdish society. Contact with the world of the proletarians and with progressive intellectuals politicized them very rapidly.

Changes in Kurdish Nationalism

Kurdish nationalism began to renew itself and change. For a long time it was led by traditional chieftains, who shaped it according to their own vision of the world and of politics. Then it became a bourgeois movement. Eventually the urban and rural petty bourgeoisie came to animate it. The Kurdish "feudalists" who in the past were often at the forefront of the national liberation struggle gradually became an intermediary for Turkish colonialism. After they were integrated into the system, and enjoyed the political and economic advantages if conferred upon them, their authority faded. Even so, they could still be a barrier to the development of the Kurdish national movement.

As for the Kurdish bourgeoisie, which began to fill out towards the end of the 1970s, it had no serious economic conflict with the existing authorities. It served as a regional intermediary for the Turkish commercial network, so there was no problem of competition with the Turkish bourgeoisie. Furthermore, this Kurdish bourgeoisie was not without representation in the Turkish political parties, which no doubt partly explains its very reserved, if not actually hostile, attitude towards Kurdish nationalism.

The fact that such attitudes became prevalent amongst the members of these two social categories, who were once so influential on the Kurdish political scene, does not mean of course that some of them might not remember their "national honor," set aside their economic interests, and side with the national movement.

In Turkish Kurdistan at the end of the 1970s, as has indeed often been the case in other colonized countries, the national movement was led by a petty bourgeoisie which was well aware of national oppression and faced a precarious economic situation. They had everything to gain from liberation.

A Movement in Full Swing

For generations of Kurdish nationalists, the only way to struggle against the authorities was to take up arms and engage in military struggle. The Kurdish elites later discovered that, although armed insurrection remained the highest stage of the conflict with the general authorities, it was not the only possible form of struggle. It became apparent that a successful campaign required careful political work, building up an organization, persuading people and drawing on experience acquired during political struggle conducted by peaceful means. This realization came gradually and was closely linked to the development of the democratic movement in Turkey, just as the upsurge of Kurdish national consciousness in the 1970s owed much to the struggle of the Kurdish people in Iraq.

From the spring of 1963 onwards, when a first meeting to protest against underdevelopment was held in Silvan, several meetings, marches and demonstrations were organized each year in all the towns in Kurdistan; protests against poverty, unemployment, rising prices, the commando operations, etc.

After a pause during the period of "parliamentary fascism" (March 1971–December 1973) these activities took off again, on a larger scale and with an increasingly radical and national content. Despite the virulence of the repression, national demands were formulated in speeches and displayed on placards, some of which were written in Kurdish. Slogans such as "Freedom for the Kurds," "Freedom for the peoples of Turkey," "No to national oppression" were inscribed on the walls of Kurdish towns and Turkish cities.

This assertion of Kurdish identity was not restricted to meetings and demonstrations organized by Kurds. It was also made by the audience during meetings organized by all the various Turkish political organizations. After 1974, whenever one of these parties held a meeting in a Kurdish town, the crowd would chant. "Freedom for the Kurds" and often disrupted the meeting completely.[52]

In parallel with the great strides made by these mass movements in the towns, related actions developed in the countryside, announcing the growth of a new awareness. The contradictions of the agrarian world, which were contained and camouflaged for so long by the patriarchal and religious ideology, began to manifest themselves more clearly and sometimes violently. Here and there, peasants occupied land belonging to the aghas (petty nobles) and demanded that it be redistributed; often they did not hesitate to confront the troops called in by the owner. This phenomenon remained at a very early stage, but each local success encouraged the landless peasants.

Efforts Towards Organization

The irruption on to the political scene of the petty bourgeoisie not only resulted in new methods and forms of political struggle, it also introduced a modern conception of political organization. The very idea that organization and the political education of the popular masses is a necessary precondition for the success of a national liberation struggle was itself a new element in the Kurdish context.

Through 1980 the Kurdish petty bourgeoisie was only able to apply this modern conception of organization on a limited scale, through what are conventionally known as "democratic mass organizations," such as youth movements, teachers associations, etc. People were still feeling their way when it came to the political field proper. The central question facing Kurdish militants in Turkey was whether they should organize within an existing legal party of the Turkish left or whether it would be better to start setting up a necessarily illegal Kurdish national party.

Any democratization of Turkey's public life, of the prevailing political structures and attitudes, is a step forwards for the Kurdish people. It was because the Turkish Workers Party, the only legal progressive organization throughout the sixties, was in the forefront of the struggle for democracy and socialism that most Kurdish militants decided to join it. As members, they came into close contact with the most advanced sector of the Turkish intelligentsia and came to know its possibilities and its limitations. Thanks to the legal framework of the TWP, they were able to re-open the dialogue with their own people.

Those Kurds who had decided to launch national parties were also able to put their ideas into practice. Half a dozen strictly Kurdish organizations surfaced in the 1970s. Often ephemeral, always short of resources and political cadres and faced with the inherent problems of illegality, they struggled to attract mass support. Only the Democratic Party of Turkish Kurdistan survived through 1978. It was founded in 1965 by two men: Faik Bacak, a lawyer from Urfa whom the Turkish political police murdered in July 1966, and Sait Elci, an accountant from Diyarbekir, whose killing in 1970 in Iraqi Kurdistan is still something of a mystery. Their organization based itself on the Kurdish nationalist parties of Iraq and Syria; it drew its members mainly from the more literate villagers and certain fringes of the petty bourgeoisie. In 1969 it went through a serious internal crisis. Some of its cadres, led by Dr. Divan, left to form a rival organization called the Democratic Party of Kurdistan in Turkey, which professed a more leftist position and support for the total independence of Kurdistan.

Apart from these clandestine Kurdish groups, one should also mention the Organization of Revolutionary Kurdish Youth (DDKO), a legal federally structured youth organization which was, in principle, non-political but which played an important role in Kurdish circles during the brief period (spring 1969–late 1970) its existence was tolerated by the authorities.

As a "cultural" organization, the DDKO set out to inform public opinion as to the economic, social and cultural situation in the East. It organized press conferences and public briefings, published posters, leaflets, etc., and generally focussed people's attention on the repression which prevailed in the Kurdish areas. From 1970 onwards, it published a monthly ten page information bulletin with a print-run of 30,000 which was distributed amongst Turkish political, cultural and trade union circles as well as in the Kurdish towns and villages.[53]

The vast information campaigns, the press conferences and the personal accounts concerning the nature and scale of the commando operations finally filtered through the press to the public. Liberal and democratic Turkish opinion began to react. Turkish student associations, industrial trade unions, teaching staff and the TWP protested against the repression suffered by the "people of the East."

During their investigations into conditions in the countryside, DDKO militants also strove to inform the peasants of their rights as citizens under the Constitution and encouraged them to organize themselves.

The Turkish government became worried by these activities; in October 1970, six months *before* the military coup, it had the main DDKO leaders arrested.

After 1975 new youth organizations, generally known as the People's Cultural Associations (HKD), formed in the Kurdish townships. They concentrated on educating their members and tried to help peasants and workers who came into conflict with the authorities or the petty nobles.

The progressive Turkish trade unions, the DISK and the TOB–DER, were the other main foci around which Kurdish workers, teachers, artisans and some small traders organized themselves. Peasant trade unionism was still virtually non-existent.

On the political level, most Kurdish militants opted for membership of the People's Republican Party, a social democratic party which they saw as the most effective instrument in the struggle for democracy under prevailing conditions. Given the fragmentation of the Turkish Marxist left (each splinter of which had a significant Kurdish membership) and its consequent lack of political weight, there appeared to be no satisfactory legal alternative available.

The Turkish Political Parties and the Kurdish Question

In 1976 there were over 20 legal and illegal political parties and groups on the Turkish political scene. We will indicate merely the general positions adopted by the main Turkish political forces *vis-a-vis* the Kurdish national question in Turkey.

Although a simplification, Turkish political groups and parties can be said to fall into four categories; bourgeois liberal, bourgeois nationalist, pan-Turanian (extreme right), socialist or communist.

1) The Attitude of the Bourgeois Liberal Parties: The main characteristic of these parties was their faith in free enterprise and their distrust of state *dirigisme*. Their support for Kemalism was essentially tactical and served to stave off the disapproval of the army. It is this group, in particular, which sought an alliance with the Kurdish property owning classes so as to integrate them into the Turkish political system and promote the penetration of capitalism into Kurdistan.

Menderes's Democratic Party: When it came to power in 1950, this party concluded a real alliance with the Kurdish notables, merchants and tradition-al chieftains. It accelerated the integration of Kurdistan into the capitalist market and thereby considerably improved on the Kurdish policy defined and followed by previous governments. The Democratic government's program of relative democratization of Turkey brought the mass deportations and military repression in Kurdistan to an end and significantly reduced the arbitrary powers of the administration. Although the government did not recognize the Kurds' cultural rights, although it was not averse to evoking the bogey of "separatism" in times of political crisis, and although it signed a pact (in Baghdad) with the other powers having a stake in Kurdistan so as to co-ordinate the repression of an eventual Kurdish insurrection, it did tacitly authorize the spoken use of Kurdish.

The Justice Party: The Justice Party (*Adalet Partisi*) was founded in 1961 to continue in the line of Menderes's Democratic Party, which was overthrown by the "neo-Kemalist" coup on May 27, 1960. Apart from the period, March 1971–October 1974, it was in power from 1965 and presented itself as the champion of liberal democracy. The party acted as a spokesperson for those Turkish financial and cultural circles closely linked to the multinationals and also established alliances with the major Kurdish businessmen and the petty nobles. It repressed any manifestation of Kurdish nationalism, but retained some support amongst the Kurdish population through a program of invest-ment in infrastructure projects geared to "develop the East which was neg-lected for so long by the bureaucratic governments." In fact the Justice Party and its President, Demirel, were very successful in Kurdistan at the 1965 elections; after that their support waned considerably.[54] The party line was that everybody who lived in Turkey was a Turk. As Demirel put it in a speech given in 1967 in the Kurdish town of Mardin: "Anybody who does not feel Turkish, or who feels unhappy in Turkey, is free to go elsewhere: the frontiers are wide open."

Having lost a great deal of support after 1970, the Justice Party was no longer in a position to govern alone. After late 1974 it held office as the main member of a heterogeneous coalition known as the "Nationalist" Front — in contrast to the left, whom they labeled "allies of international communism."[55]

Bozbeyli's Democratic Party and the Party of National Salvation: The Democratic Party (*Demokratik Parti*), which emerged from a split within the Justice Party, presented itself as the voice of the middle classes. In the late seventies it was in opposition; in the October 1973 elections it won 40 seats, but after that, as Turkish political life became increasingly polarized, it lost a great deal of ground to the Justice Party.

The Democratic Party never publicly announced its position on the Kurdish question and its electoral base in Kurdistan was negligible. In practice, this amounted to support for the existing status quo, characterized by the outright negation of the Kurdish nation's existence.

As for the PNS, which was, in 1976, the third largest party, with 49 seats in the Assembly, its message was one of "brotherhood between Muslims." It condemned the use of such categories as Turks, Kurds, etc. In other words, it did nothing to challenge the primacy of the Turks and the continued oppression of the Kurdish people.

2) *The Attitude of the Bourgeois Nationalist Parties*:

The People's Republican Party: This party (*Cumhuriyet Halk Partisi*) was the main member of a family of nationalist groupings descended from the Young Turks' Union and Progress Committee. Their ideal focussed around a national economy, Turkish national capitalism, although their intentions were by no means restricted to the economic sphere. It was in the name of this nationalism that the genocide of the Armenian people and the massacre and systematic destruction of the Kurdish people was carried out.

The PRP was created in 1923 by Mustafa Kemal Ataturk, and held a monopoly of political power till 1950, during which time it conceived and implemented the anti-Kurdish policy described earlier. Once in opposition, it sought to win support in the Kurdish towns, although it never changed its attitude in matters bearing on national unity.

In order to adapt to its new circumstances, this old party, which was for so long the main political instrument of certain sectors of the Turkish bourgeoisie and of the military and civil bureaucracy, was forced to renovate its ideology. A center-left current (*Ortanin Solu*) led by young militants grouped around Bulent Ecevit began to develop in 1963 and eventually imposed itself upon the rest of the party. Ecevit's refusal to collaborate with the civilian and military advocates of a "strong state" during the period of "parliamentary fascism" and his struggle for a return to democracy gained him considerable popularity; the PRP emerged victorious from the October 1973 elections though it fell short of an absolute majority and could therefore not form a cabinet on its own.

In the seventies the PRP called itself a social democratic party and sought admission to the Socialist International. It declared its intention to guarantee freedom of opinion, to legalize the Turkish Communist Party and to democratize Turkey's economic and political structures. Its election manifesto, *Ak Gunler* (Radiant Days), promised that "appropriate measures will be taken to develop the East economically and to make up for the backwardness that has built up in this regard over the years." Nowhere was there any mention, however, of the eventual recognition of the Kurdish people's cultural rights. The invasion and the occupation of two-fifths of Cyprus, supposedly to defend the rights of the Turkish Cypriots, was an apt reminder that the PRP might have been tinged with social democracy but remained fundamentally a *nationalist* party. Nonetheless, in the aftermath of the armed resistance of the Iraqi Kurds, it was the PRP that was principally responsible for the defeat of a motion before the Turkish parliament to declare a state of siege in the Eastern provinces. This party's parliamentary representatives, including several Kurdish members of the Assembly who joined around 1973, even called on the authorities to open up the frontiers and facilitate the settlement in Turkey of Kurds fleeing from the repression in Iraq. Even if such an attitude was partly motivated by the need to win Kurdish votes, it was nonetheless in sharp contrast to the virulent anti-Kurdism displayed by the party until the early seventies.

The Republican Confidence Party: Although much less important political-ly, the Republican Confidence Party also claimed to represent the nationalist approach. Composed of right-wing ex-members of the PRP, who defected when the party moved leftwards, it achieved notoriety by agreeing to serve as a servile "democratic facade" for the army and the MIT during the period of "parliamentary fascism." The RCP consistently expressed fanatical hostility to any manifestations of Kurdish identity, on the grounds that they threatened "the integrity of the Republic."

The "left" Kemalists: Although they did not have a significant political presence in parliament, the "left" Kemalists were nonetheless a force in Turkish political life. They presented themselves as hostile to both capitalism and communism. "Only a team of the most advanced cadres free from all particular and local ties and pressures can use the power of the state to implement the economic and social reforms necessary to the development of the country." For a detailed exposé of this group's doctrine, see *Turkiyenin Duzeni*, by its chief spokesman, D. Avciogla (Bilgi Yayinevi, Ankara: p. 589–740).

3) *The Attitude of the Pan-Turanian Extreme Right*: Despite the collapse of the pan-Turanian project, launched by the Union and Progress Committee during the First World War, this right-wing tendency within Turkish nationalism retained considerable support, especially within the army. Although its supporters no longer formed an organized political force, their ideas continued to be expressed in a great many papers, journals, books, etc.

From 1965 onwards, Colonel Alparslan Turkes began to weld this tenden-cy into an organized legal political party. Although he was well known for his fascist sympathies and had even been court-martialled in 1946 for "fascist and racist activities," Turkes was allowed to continue his career in the army. During the May 1960 military coup, in which he played an active part, he was head of the Turkish General Staff's NATO department. Having become a member of the National Unity Committee (MBK) and adviser to the Prime Minister, he then attempted to seize power with a dozen or so accomplices.

When the conspiracy failed, Turkes and his friends were expelled from the Committee and sent into exile as ambassadors to faraway countries (September 1960).

In 1963, having only just returned to Turkey, Turkes participated in another attempted coup, as a result of which he was briefly incarcerated. Following this defeat, he decided to found a political party modeled on the European fascist parties. On his recommendation, his supporters infiltrated the National Republican Agrarian Party (CKMP) and within a few months managed to do away with this party's leadership and to call an extraordinary party conference which elected Turkes as president. As soon as he had become leader of this venerable old legitimate party, he changed its name to the Nationalist Action Party (*Milliyetci Hareket Partisi*).

The good Colonel presented himself as the "liberator of the enslaved Turkish nation in Russia and China" and as the last rampart of the independent Turkish national state against "communism and Kurdish separatism."

After 1967 the NAP's young militants were organized in armed militias. Despite Article 2 of the Turkish law forbidding parties or associations to put their members through any form of military training, the authorities turned a blind eye to the fact that each year the NAP quite overtly trained hundreds of young people in the use of firearms.

The authorities' indulgence *vis-a-vis* these paramilitary activities was naturally not disinterested. The armed gangs carried out tasks which the police could not legally accomplish, such as intimidating progressive youth movements and orchestrating a series of provocations which contribute to a general climate of instability, thereby helping to justify an eventual declaration of a state of siege. These so-called Gray Wolves (*Bozkurt*) regularly invaded university residences and faculties; between 1969 and 1976 they murdered more than 200 Turkish and Kurdish progressive students, often right in front of contingents of the official police force. This party only had two seats in the Turkish parliament; but its influence on Turkish political life and its strength in the state apparatus exceeded its electoral support by far.

The NAP was violently and militantly anti-Kurdish. It only recognized the existence of Kurds in order to insist on "the need to Turkicize these inalienable regions of the Turkish nation." The liquidation of the Kurds was thus an integral part of their agenda.

4) The Attitude of the "Socialist" Parties and Groups: Until about 1960, socialism was a taboo word in Turkey. By the mid-seventies it had become an eminently fashionable designation to which everybody, from the petty-bourgeois radicals and the liberal bourgeoisie to the "left nationalists," laid claim. There were five legal parties by 1976, two illegal ones and a dozen or so "fronts," "armies," and "movements," who presented themselves as the legitimate heirs of Marx's thought. Each one published its own journal and many issued a daily paper and had their own publishing house; most of this literary output concentrated on denigrating rival organizations. Generally speaking, these groups had an exclusively student audience.

This variety mostly reflected divergences of opinion about foreign matters with little bearing on Turkey's concrete problems. When it came to a fundamental issue such as the Kurdish national question, the level of debate was usually rather mediocre. The threat of repression and the deep-rooted legacy of Greater Turkish chauvinism made the Kurds an issue to be avoided if possible; it was usually glossed over by stigmatizing those who asserted the Kurdish people's right to make their own decisions as "chauvinists" or "bourgeois nationalists." Others suggested that it was not the right time to divide the democratic and revolutionary forces by raising such questions since, in any case, the Kurdish people would regain its freedom and its rights when socialism triumphed in Turkey.

The Turkish Communist Party (TKP): The above was essentially the viewpoint of the TKP. Although it condemned anti-Kurdish repression and included the right of peoples to self-determination amongst its general principles as long ago as 1920, the Turkish CP never, during more than fifty years of existence, really tackled the Kurdish national question or demanded that the Kurdish people be allowed to take their own decisions. Fired by international solidarity, a communist intellectual like Nazim Hikmet could write poems of praise to the struggles of the Cuban, Indonesian or Indian peoples, but never once devoted a single line to the unremitting struggle of the Kurdish people, even though they fought the same enemy, the Turkish bourgeois regime.

The Turkish Workers Party: The TWP (*Turkiye Issi Partisi*), the only legal party of the Turkish left until 1971, played a major role in the spread of socialist ideas and the growth of the struggle for democracy in Turkey. The very dynamic of that struggle gradually led the TWP to an awareness of the situation faced by the Kurdish people and to a commitment to do something about it. However, this awareness of the Kurdish question did not come easily. It only emerged as a result of the hard struggle waged by Kurdish socialist militants within the TWP to change the attitudes of the left at a time when Turkish nationalist prejudices were still very prevalent.

This struggle bore fruit in November 1971, when the IVth Congress of the TWP adopted a resolution on the Kurdish issue which stated that: "There is a Kurdish people in the East of Turkey . . . The fascist authorities representing the ruling classes have subjected the Kurdish people to a policy of assimilation and intimidation which has often become a bloody repression."

Apart from the law of unequal development, one of the most fundamental reasons for the underdevelopment of the Kurdish areas, as compared to the other areas of Turkey, were the economic and social policies of the dominant classes who were very much aware that the region was inhabited by Kurds: "To consider the 'Eastern question' as merely a matter of regional development is, therefore, nothing but an extension of the nationalistic, and chauvinistic approach adopted by the ruling classes."

Furthermore, the Congress called on the Party to "support the Kurdish people's struggle for the exercise of the constitutional rights of all citizens and for the realization of all its democratic aspirations and demands."

Given the Turkish context this was a brave declaration. Never before had a legal political party represented in parliament recognized the existence of a Kurdish people in Turkey. In so doing, the TWP put its head on the block. In

June, the party was dissolved for pro-Kurdish separatist activities by the "strong" government of Niḥat Erim which the army had installed. The TWP's main leaders were given sentences of as long as twelve years and only regained their freedom in July 1974, under the provisions of an amnesty.

In the fall of 1974, Ms. Behice Boran and a few of the old leaders of the TWP revived the party and kept the name. But the TWP was now no longer the only legal left-wing party in Turkey. Even before the TWP had been resuscitated, some of its pre-1971 cadres who were close to the Turkish Communist Party had set up a Turkish Socialist Workers Party (TSWP); others had founded the Socialist Party (SP). In 1976 the TWP only had a solid base in a few big towns; it lost much of its once considerable influence in industrial and teaching unions to the Turkish CP.

The new leadership of the TWP was extremely cautious in its approach to the Kurdish question. Ms. Boran and the other leaders of the TWP referred to the need to "subordinate any movement or current, however progressive, democratic or legitimate it may seem when taken in isolation, to the imperatives of the struggle for socialism presently being waged by the working class and its allies."[56] Kurdish socialist militants left the TWP in droves.

The Socialist Party: Created in 1974 by Mehmet Ali Aybar and his liberal socialist associates, the SP (*Sosyalist Partisi*) did not claim to be a strictly Marxist party. It drew its members from the ranks of the liberal intelligentsia and apparently enjoyed the support of certain trade unionists. Despite the personality of Aybar, who consistently defended democratic freedoms from the forties onwards, the SP only had a very limited audience. Keeping strictly within the bounds of legality, the SP took no position on the Kurdish question, although it protested systematically against "repression by the commandos in the East."

The Turkish Socialist Workers Party: Founded in 1974 with the aim of "rallying the various existing revolutionary factions and circles," the TSWP (*Turkiye Sosyalist Isci Partisi*) had a hard time surviving. With a real base in only half a dozen Turkish towns, this legal group, which set out to be to the left of the TWP, attracted only a few industrial trade unionists as well as a number of intellectuals. Its journals, *Ilke* (The Principle) and *Kitle* (The Masses), which were quite eloquent on most issues, did not devote a single article to the Kurdish question.[57]

The "Maoist" groups: Under this heading come a number of groups and parties who declared themselves to be followers of "Mao Tse-Tung's thought." They indulged in endless faction fights and often struggled against the other sections of the Turkish left, the "counter-revolutionary revisionist social fascists," with as much virulence and sometimes by the same means as the extreme right did. Their audience consisted almost entirely of students.

The Turkish Labor Party, the only legal "Maoist" grouping, was founded in 1974 by Mihri Belli who, from the mid sixties, consistently defended the idea of a "national democratic revolution," as opposed to the TWP's "socialist revolution." In the late sixties, this approach enjoyed considerable support amongst young people. After that, however, its supporters split again and again into a multitude of tiny groups.

As a justification for his refusal to recognize the Kurdish people's right to self-determination, Belli argued that "first they must join with us in making the revolution; then we will grant them cultural rights. This is the Marxist solution to the problem."

The other Maoist formation was the illegal Turkish Workers and Peasants Revolutionary Party (TIIKP) led by Dogu Perincek, who edited a journal called *P.D. Aydinlik* (Revolutionary Proletarian Clarity). The TIIKP, which was a little more influential than Mihri Belli's TLP, spent most of its time fighting the progressive teaching and industrial trade unions (DISK, TOB– DER) as well as the other democratic or socialist parties and organizations.

On the Kurdish question, this party expressed a position which was bursting with contradictions and which was probably essentially geared to the Party's immediate tactical requirements. According to its program, the TIIKP "recognizes the Kurdish nation's right to self-determination and to set up its own state if it so wishes" (Art. 52).[58] However, the TIIKP set itself up as "the vanguard of the workers and people of Turkey's two nationalities"[59] (Kurdish and Turkish) and proposed that the Kurdish national question be resolved "within the framework of a popular democratic republic which will bring the two fraternal peoples together on an equal basis."[60] This promise remained rather theoretical, especially as in practice this party violently attacked any attempt to set up Kurdish political organizations or trade unions. In the name of defending Turkey against "the threat of social im- perialism," its members called for an intensification of the Turkish military occupation in Kurdistan.

And the others: Notable amongst the great many other clandestine or semi-clandestine groups was the Turkish Popular Liberation Army (THKO) led by Deniz Gezmis (until his execution in 1972) which advocated urban guerrilla warfare. It fought to free Turkey from imperialist domination. In this phase of the struggle, the "immediate political task" was for the peoples of Turkey to join in a united front. Although it recognized the existence of a Kurdish people in Turkey and admitted that their national struggle was legitimate, the THKO argued that the problem could only be solved after the revolution. The organization drew most of its recruits from student youth and attracted a great many young Kurds, not least of which Deniz Gezmis himself.

As for the Turkish Popular Liberation Front, the military organization of the Party of the same name, it recommended encircling the cities from the countryside. Originally founded by Mahir Sayan, who was executed in 1971 during a military operation, this clandestine organization appeared to have some supporters amongst young army officers as well as amongst students. Liberation from imperialist domination and the defense of Turkey's inde- pendence in the face of "the ambitions of social-imperialism" were the immediate revolutionary tasks it set itself. The TPLF occasionally issued leaflets in Kurdish but made no declaration concerning the rights of the Kurdish people or the solution to the Kurdish question in Turkey.[61]

Despite considerable progress, the Turkish socialist and democratic movement remained essentially restricted to the intelligentsia, part of the petty bourgeoisie and a few small sections of the industrial proletariat. Even greater efforts, more research and more challenges to established thought would be necessary before it could begin to make a major impact on the country.

This lack of maturity manifested itself particularly sharply in the attitude to the Kurdish question adopted by nearly all the Turkish left groups, an attitude which was still imbued with nationalistic and chauvinistic conceptions inherited from the ideology of the Turkish ruling classes.

Because the development of class consciousness amongst the Kurdish people, who still lived under an occupation, was slow compared to the growth of their national consciousness, the Turkish left came to denigrate the latter type of consciousness. But fighting the "nationalist tendencies" of the oppressed nation in the name of the urgent need to develop the struggle for socialism is in practice quite self-defeating.

Far from worrying about the development of a national consciousness amongst the Kurdish masses, who had been kept at a medieval level of cultural development, those who cared about the liberation of peoples should have rejoiced at this awakening to political life. The birth of a national consciousness amongst an oppressed people, the emergence of a desire to free themselves from cultural oppression as well as from economic and political oppression was in itself a considerable step forwards.

Indeed the lack of understanding displayed in this regard by a would-be Marxist Turkish left was particularly surprising. It is surely a peculiar version of Marxism which hurls accusations of "bourgeois nationalism" and "chauvinism" at Kurdish revolutionaries, who call and work for unity in action between the Turkish and Kurdish people, simply because these revolutionaries insist on their own people's right to self-determination and refuse to subordinate their national struggle by putting it off indefinitely.

Any party which claims to follow Marxist principles owes it to itself to defend the right of an oppressed people to set up their own national state and organize their own national life freely. Even apart from questions of respect for doctrinal principles, there are simple tactical considerations which should encourage the "Marxist" left to support anything which might weaken its "deadly enemy," the Turkish bourgeoisie, and to form alliances with all the opponents of this bourgeoisie's domination. It is quite indubitable that the Kurdish people's liberation struggle inevitably undermines the economic, political, military and ideological support of the Turkish ruling classes and thereby contributes to the struggle for socialism. The struggle against the dominant nation's chauvinism and nationalism, against national oppression, and for the right to self-determination, cannot but be a healthy and invigorating contribution to the Turkish democratic and socialist movement as a whole.

Some Concluding Remarks

Mire Kor and Bedir Khan launched their people's struggle for independence at the same time as the Greeks and the Bulgarians, as Bolivar and San Martin.

Since then the Kurds' desire for independence has manifested itself in over a hundred revolts, first against the Shahs and Sultans, then against the states who carved up Kurdistan following World War One. The failure of these revolts was partly due to a variety of *external factors*. Kurdistan stands in the middle of one of the most avidly coveted regions of the world. It has no access to the sea and is surrounded by the reactionary states which occupy its territory. There were also *internal factors*. Until the early fifties the tribal consciousness was still predominant, there was no central authority and feudal quarrels divided the people. Kurdistan was cut off from the outside world and, because of the accumulated cultural backwardness of the Kurdish people, they lacked a modern intelligentsia capable of understanding contemporary events and drawing the appropriate lessons. However, even given these internal structures, had Kurdistan been a British or French colony, it would have won its independence long ago, and with far fewer sacrifices.

Eventually, with the disappearance of nomadism, the penetration of capitalism and the atrophy of traditional pastoralism, the "feudal" and tribal structures began to fall apart. Modern classes emerged. A revolutionary elite coalesced. In its turn the peasantry shook off its lethargy and began to take part in political life. As an inevitable consequence of this general awakening, the Kurdish population as a whole became increasingly aware of its situation as an oppressed, subject nation kept under a foreign yoke by force. Resentment of the Turkish authorities' oppressive practices grew. The armed struggle of the Kurds in Iraq advanced the Kurdish national consciousness considerably and reinforced aspirations to a united and independent Kurdistan. It seemed that at last all the conditions necessary for a modern revolutionary national liberation struggle were gathered in Turkish Kurdistan.

Given the balance of forces in the late seventies, the best a revolutionary Kurdish party could do was to form an alliance with progressive Turkish forces and lead the political struggle for democratization of the Turkish regime and the inauguration of a federal system. As the Kurdish people are not a small minority in Turkey, but rather a national community accounting for about a quarter of the Turkish state's population, the inauguration of a Turko-Kurdish federation might well prove acceptable. However, the Kurdish people's assent to such a solution would not be enough to bring it about. A federation is a free union between equal partners and requires the agreement of both parties. The Turkish people's assent to such a project would be thus also essential; given the deep-rooted nationalism and Greater Turkish chauvinism whose historical origins we have hopefully illustrated, this assent was unlikely to be forthcoming.

Whatever happens, the Kurdish people will reserve the right to determine their own fate and to organize their national life as they choose on the territory they have occupied for centuries. The effective exercise of these inalienable rights will depend first on their own strengh and then on the political, moral and material support of democratic and progressive forces throughout the world. Just as in the previous century the struggle for an independent Poland was a factor in the progress of Europe as a whole, so the struggle for a free, united, independent and socialist Kurdistan is a major force for progressive change throughout the Middle East, since it aims at a profound modification of the reactionary status quo which currently prevails in the area. In this sense, the Kurdish people's struggle for national independence is an integral part of the democratic struggle for freedom and independence waged by people throughout the world and a contributory factor in that struggle's eventual success.

In this last quarter of the 20th century, when the right to independence is being claimed for islands with only a few tens of thousands of inhabitants, the Kurdish people, whose numbers exceed those of the populations of most sovereign states on the planet, cannot remain the *only* human community of this size not to enjoy a national existence of its own. No political, ideological or economic motive can possibly justify the continuation of such inequity.

Notes

1. The eighteen vilayets have an area of 86,087 square miles, but I have included the mainly Kurdish adjoining territories which the administration has arbitrarily included in the vilayets of Sivas and Maras. The eighteen vilayets of Kurdistan in Turkey are: Adiyaman, Agri, Bingol, Bitlis, Diyarbekir, Elazig, Erzincan, Erzurum, Gazi Antep, Hakkari, Kars, Malatya, Mus, Mardin, Siirt, Tunceli, Urfa and Van.
2. Summer temperatures of 104°F have been recorded in Kars and Erzurum, where the thermometer often falls to −22°F during the winter.
3. The Keban Dam built across the Euphrates is the only major installation to make even partial use of this great potential.
4. Source: *1970 Genel Nufus Sayimi Sonuclari* (Results of the General Population Census, 1970) published by the Ankara National Institute of Statistics. The calculations here are based on the partial data presented in this census.
5. The size of the Kurdish "diaspora" can be explained both by the scale of the deportations in the twenties and thirties and by the endless exodus of Kurdish workers to the Turkish cities in search of jobs. During the First World War the Turkish authorities deported 700,000 people to Anatolia. Following the 1925 Kurdish revolt, the Kemalist regime deported about one million Kurdish men, women and children during the winters of 1926–28. Some of these people have since returned to their homes. Others were assimilated. Most have remained in Anatolia, but have jealously guarded their customs and their language.
6. Cf. the remarkable study by the Turkish sociologist Ismail Besikci, *Dogu Anadolu'nun Duzeni, sosyo-ekonomik ve etnik temeller* (Socioeconomic and Ethnic Foundations of the Structures of Eastern Anatolia) from which these data have been drawn, after comparison with official Turkish publications on the 1965 and 1970 censuses carried out by the National Institute of Statistics. Mr. Besikci was sentenced to twelve years imprisonment for his research into Kurdish society in Turkey.
7. The Yezidi doctrine, as formulated in *Mishefa Res* (The Black Bible), is a strange mixture of vestigial Mazdeism (the old religion of the Kurds and Persians professed by Zoroaster), Muslim ritual, Sufi mysticism, Brahmanism, etc. Cf. R. Lescot, *Enquete sur les Yezidis de Syrie et du Djebel-Sindjar* (Beirut, 1938).
8. The 1970 census (op. cit.) gives an overall figure of 1 doctor for every 2,300 inhabitants in Turkey as a whole and indicates the number of doctors per 1,000 inhabitants for every town. The figures given here for Kurdistan have been calculated on this basis.
9. Cf. I Besikci, op. cit. p. 63. Corresponding percentages for Turkey as a whole at the same time (1966) are unavailable. *The Third Five Year Plan, 1973–1977*, published by the National Planning Office (DPT), gives the following figures for 1972: agriculture accounts for 65% of the population, industry for 11% and services for 24%.
10. Cf. I Besikci, op. cit.
11. *Annual Statistics 1964* (in Turkish), ONS (DIE), Ankara.
12. Source: DPT (NPO), op. cit., p. 271.
13. DDKO, *Dava Dosyasi*, Komal Yayinlari (Ankara, 1975), p. 173.
14. Ibid.
15. "Copper inlay is an ancient Kurdish technique which was imported into Europe by Eastern craftsmen. Venice developed special workshops which produced many fine pieces notably during the 15th century and on a number of these one finds the signature of a certain Mahmud the Kurd." Thomas Bois, *Connaissance des Kurdes*, Khayats (Beirut, 1965), p. 30.
16. From 1916 to 1920 the Kars region changed hands four times, passing from Ottoman to Russian sovereignty and back. For more than a year it was part of the Western Caucasian Republic which

also included Batum and certain areas of Tiflis and Erivan.

17. Cf. Robert Dunn, *World Alive* (New York, 1956). These Soviets which emerged first in the province of Kars seemed very likely to spread the wildfire throughout the neighboring Kurdish territories.

18. For further details on the Turkish War of Independence, see Sabahattin Selek's very comprehensive *Anadolu Ihitali* (The Anatolian Revolution), (Istanbul, 1963), Vols. I and II.

19. Peace negotiations were opened on November 6, 1920 but, before they could be concluded, power changed hands in Armenia, moving from the Dashnak Party to the Armenian Marxists. The vilayet of Kars, which had been annexed by Russia in 1878, was handed back to Turkey and Gumru, a mainly Armenian area, was ceded to Armenia.

20. For details of the Conference, see Gunduz Okcun, *Turkiye Iktisat Kongres, 1923, Izmir* (The 1923 Izmir Turkish Economic Congress), (Ankara, 1968) and K.B. Harputlu's *La Turquie dans l'impasse*, Anthropos (Paris, 1975).

21. According to General Ali Fuat Cebesoy, Mustafa Kemal's Moscow envoy, the Soviet aid program consisted of ten million gold rubles or enough arms and munitions to equip three Turkish divisions. Russia would supposedly have also paid a million gold rubles to the Berlin government, in payment for the sale to the Turkish Army of spare parts needed for German weapons acquired during the Ottoman Empire.

22. For the text of the agreement, see *Nouveau Recueil General des Traites*, op. cit., Vol. XII, 3rd Series.

23. Cf. *Conference de Lausanne*, by the French Foreign Secretary. Ismet Pasha's speech to the January 23, 1923 session.

24. Cf. *Nouveau Recueil General des Traites*, op. cit., p. 580.

25. Lord Curzon was Viceroy of India before the First World War.

26. Shares in Turkish Petroleum (later known as the Iraq Petroleum Co.) were distributed as follows: 23.75% to Anglo-Saxon Petroleum Co. Ltd. (Shell); 23.75% to D'Arcy Exploration Co. Ltd. (Anglo-Persian); 23.75% to the French government; 23.75% to Near East Corporation (American); and 5% to Gulbenkian for services rendered in obtaining oil concessions in Mesopotamia for Turkish Petroleum from the Ottoman authorities. See C.P. Nicolesco, *Gisements Petroliferes de l'Irak*, Les Presses Modernes (Paris, 1933).

27. Cf. *La Question de Mossoul à la 35eme session de la S.D.N. (Geneve)*, (Lausanne), 1925.

28. Cf. Louis le Fur, *Recueil de textes de droit international public*, Dalloz (Paris, 1934), p. 762–3.

29. Dr. N. Dersimi, *Kurdistan Tarihinde Dersim* (Dersim in the History of Kurdistan), (Aleppo, 1952), p. 176.

30. Ibid.

31. L. Rambout, *Les Kurdes et le droit*, Ed. du Cerf (Paris, 1947), p. 26.

32. H.C. Armstrong, *The Grey Wolf.* Commenting on the teror which followed the insurrection, Armstrong wrote: "Kurdistan was devastated by fire and set to the sword. The men were tortured and killed, the villages were burned, the harvests were torn up, the women and children were abducted or murdered. Mustafa Kemal's Turks massacred the Kurds as ferociously as the Sultan's Turks had massacred the Greeks, Armenians and Bulgars."

33. Jawaharlal L. Nehru, *Glimpses of World History* (Allahabad, 1935), Vol. 2, p. 1, 108.

34. L. Rambout, op. cit., p. 29.

35. The main leaders of *Hoyboun* were members of the most famous Kurdish feudal families. Many Kurdish intellectuals also joined this league whose program was the liberation of Kurdistan in Turkey. The main leaders of *Hoyboun* were Qadry Djemil Pasha, Djeladet Ali Bedir Khan Bey, Hassan Agha Hadjo, Ihsan Nuri Pasha, Ekrem Djemil Pasha, Memdouh Selim and Arif Abbas. Djeladet Ali Bedir Khan Bey and his brother, Kamouran A. Bedir Khan Bey, started an important Kurdish cultural movement whose activities included the publication of Kurdish journals (*Hawar*, *Ronahi*) and newspapers (*Roja-nu*, *Ster*) in Damascus and Beirut, as well as various literary works. They were also the originators of the latinized Kurdish alphabet.

36. See *Milliyet*, No. 1636, August 31, 1930.

37. *Milliyet*, No. 1655, September 16, 1930.

38. Quoted in L. Rambout, op. cit., p. 31.

39. For the full text of this law, see *De la question Kurde, la loi de deportation et de dispersion des Kurdes*, issue no. 8 of the Kurdish journal, *Hawar*, (Damascus, 1934).

40. At the time the Turkish government claimed that Dersim was only able to resist for so long because it was being aided by the Soviet Union!

41. See Dr. N. Dersimi, op. cit., for details of the carnage.

42. *T.K.P. Dogusu, kurulusu, gelisme yollari* (The Communist Party of Turkey: Birth, Organization and Avenues of Development), p. 21.

43. Ismail Cem, in *Turkiyede Gerikalmiz ligin olusumu* (Istanbul, 1973), lists Ataturk's personal holdings: 38,216 acres of cultivated land, a brewery, two dairies with a daily output of 64,000 pints of milk, two yogurt factories, a winery (170,000 pints of wine a year), restaurants, casinos, night clubs, fifty or so buildings, etc. All of which sheds a certain light on the slogan launched by Mustafa Kemal and constantly proclaimed ever since by the Turkish ruling classes: "We are a people without classes or privilege."

94   A People Without a Country

44. *Son Posta*, April 1948.
45. *Le Monde*, April 10, 1976.
46. Cf. *Erzincan 1932* by Ali Kemali, the Turkish governor of this Kurdish province. Despite the author's paternalism the book is informative as to the miserable situation of the peasantry in the thirties.
47. Under the pretext of preventing contraband and enforcing the state monopoly on the sale of tobacco and cigarettes, the Turkish government forced the Kurdish producers to sell their tobacco crops to the National Tobacco Office at fixed prices. The producers were not even allowed to retain part of their own crop for personal consumption; any Kurd caught with a personal stock of tobacco was severely punished. Later the Turkish tobacco growers of the Aegean and Black Sea Coasts were allowed to sell their crops either to the Office or to private dealers, but their Kurdish colleagues still had to sell only to the Office, and still at fixed prices.
48. *Cumhuriyet*, July 31, 1966.
49. Government decree, January 25, 1967, in *The Official Gazette of the Republic of Turkey (T.C. Resmi Gazete)*, February 14, 1967.
50. Two works on the Kurdish question recently appeared in Turkey: *Her Bakimdan Turk Olan Kurtlerin Mensei* (The Origin of the Kurds, Who Are Turks in Every Respect) by Fahrettin Kiziloglu, published by the Ministry of Education; and *Dogu illeri ve Varto Tarihi* (A History of Varto and Its Provinces in the East) by Serif Firat.
51. These Articles, which were used against both Kurdish and Turkish progressive militants, were taken from the Penal Code of Mussolini's Italy.
    Article 141 of the Turkish Penal Code: "Anyone creating, leading or inspiring associations, whatever their designation, which seek to ensure the domination of a particular social class or to overthrow the country's existing social and economic institutions, is liable to a period of imprisonment running from eight to fifteen years."
    Article 142: "Anyone spreading propaganda of any type which seeks to ensure the domination of one social class over another or seeks to overthrow any of the country's existing fundamental institutions, or aims to destroy the social and legal order of the state, will be liable to five to fifteen years imprisonment."
52. In June 1975, Colonel Turkes, leader of the extreme right Nationalist Action Party and vice-premier, sought to hold an election meeting in Diyarbekir, the historic capital of Kurdistan and a stronghold of Kurdish nationalism. Despite the arrival of several thousand of his partisans and a massive deployment of police and armored vehicles, the meeting was forced to close prematurely.
53. For the full text of the nine issues of this bulletin and other works by the DDKO, see *D.D.K.O. Dossier (D.D.K.O. dava dosyasi)*, (Ankara, 1975).
54. The decline in the JP's support is appreciable throughout Turkey. In the 1965 elections this party won 53% of votes cast and 260 (out of 450) seats in the Assembly. It maintained its position in the October 1969 elections, with 256 seats. But in October 1973, it suffered a hefty defeat and was displaced as the country's most important political party by Bulent Ecevit's PRP, winning only 170 seats in the Assembly.
55. The coalition also included Prof. Erbakan's religiously oriented National Salvation Party, Prof. Feyzioglu's right-wing Republican Confidence Party and Colonel Turkes's Nationalist Action Party.
56. Cf. *Yuruyu* (The March), the TWP's weekly, No. 52.
57. This is also true of the predominantly religious (Shi'ite) Union Party which presented itself as socialist in the seventies.
58. Cf. *T.I.I.K.P. Davasi Savunma* (Istanbul, 1975), p. 370.
59. Ibid., p. 373.
60. Ibid., p. 378–9.
61. There are also two Trotskyist groups, each with its own publishing house (*Suda* and *Koz*). As of 1976 they had no known position on the Kurdish national question in Turkey.

3

Kurdistan in Iran

A. R. Ghassemlou

The Kurds of Iran

A Geographical Overview

Kurdistan in Iran covers an area of about 50,000 square miles. It reaches from Mount Ararat in the north to the other side of the Zagros Mountains. To the west it is bound by the Iraqi-Iranian and Turkish-Iranian borders, to the east by Lake Urmiah (Rezaiyeh). Even the cities are situated at altitudes of over 3,500 feet in this mountainous region.

The climate is continental and the annual rainfall rarely exceeds 8 inches although in the fertile valleys below it reaches 40–60 inches. The variation in temperature between the summer high and the winter low is about 100°F. In Saqqez, the temperature sometimes drops to 22°F during the winter; in Kermanshah it reaches as high as 110°F in the summer. The shortage of water is not as acute as in most parts of Iran; there are many rivers, such as the Kizil Uzen (Sefidrud), the little Zab (a branch of the Tigris), the Jaghatou and the Tataou. Lake Urmiah, with a surface area of 2,500 square miles, and Lake Zrever are the largest bodies of water in this part of Kurdistan.

The mountains are well wooded. From Lake Urmiah to Luristan there are more than ten million acres of forest, mostly oak, from which fourteen different products are obtained. But the forests are not very dense because the mountain people, having no other source of fuel, use a great deal of wood and are thus exhausting an irreplaceable resource.

The as yet unexploited sub-soil of Kurdistan in Iran is rich in minerals. Oil is extracted in the Kermanshah region, where the government and the oil multinationals have set up installations, but production goes to meet local demand and does not exceed a million tons a year.

The Iranian administration has divided Kurdistan in Iran into three provinces, but only the central area, Sina (Sanandaj), is officially referred to as

Kurdistan. The north is called Western Azerbaijan and the south is known as Kermanshah. Ethnically speaking, one should also include Luristan itself, with its capital, Khuramabad.

The Population

Given the chauvinism of the governments who administer the areas inhabited by Kurds, it is by no means easy to find undoctored figures for the Kurdish population. The Iranian government has always claimed the Kurds as "pure Iranians" and has carefully avoided any distinction between "Iranians" and "Persians," so no statistics on the national composition of the population have ever been made available. But it is clear that the overwhelming majority of the population of Kurdistan in Iran is Kurdish. The following figures give some idea of its importance.

Table 1
The Kurdish Population in Iran

Years	Iran (total)	Kurdistan in Iran	Kurds in Iran	% of Kurds in the Iranian Population
1970	28,258,800	4,803,860	4,521,280	16
1975[1]	32,440,000	5,514,800	5,190,400	16

Sources: *National Census of Population and Housing*, November 1966, Tehran; *Monthly Bulletin of Statistics*, November 1971, UN, New York.

Of the people living in Iranian Kurdistan, 12.8% are Azerbaijanis (470,000) and Persians (235,000). On the other hand, there is a tight community of 400,000 Kurds in the Province of Khorassan, notably in Gutshan and Dorgaz.[2]

The population density of Kurdistan in Iran is twice that of the rest of the country, as Table 2 shows. Kurdistan in Iran occupies 7.6% of Iranian territory and is the home of 17% of the Iranian population.

Table 2
Population Density in Iranian Kurdistan

	Area (m^2)	Area (%)	Inhabitants per m^2 1970	1975
Iran	640,000	100	44	50
Kurdistan in Iran	49,000	7.6	98	112

Table 3
Distribution of Population in the Four Provinces of Kurdistan in Iran, 1966

Area	Urban (%)	Rural (%)
Mahabad	25	75
Saqqez	19	81
Sanandadj	27	73

Kermanshah	49	51
Iranian Kurdistan*	30	70
Iran*	50	50

*1975 estimates.
Sources: *National Census of Population and Housing*, November 1966,
Tehran; *Monthly Bulletin of Statistics*, November 1971, UN, New York.

Urbanization has proceeded apace. The figures in Table 4 are for the four
main towns.

Table 4
Growth of the Urban Population in Iranian Kurdistan

Town	1956	1966	1976*	% Growth (1956–76)
Mahabad	20,332	28,610	42,000	208
Saqqez	12,725	17,834	26,000	204
Sanandadj	40,641	54,587	76,000	187
Kermanshah	125,439	187,930	300,000	239

*Author's estimate.

Large families are still the rule in Iranian Kurdistan, with, on average, five
members per household in the towns and six in the countryside.

The disintegration of the tribal structure began at the turn of the century
and entered its final phase in the seventies. The rapid growth of the domestic
market as capitalism developed, the agrarian reform (even if it was fairly
limited in Kurdistan), and massive migration to the towns, as well as other
cultural and social changes, all contributed to the elimination of tribal society
in Iranian Kurdistan. Naturally, some tribal ties continued to survive, but the
classical tribal structure dominated by a Mir, Beg or Agha and bound
together by hierarchical relations, was collapsing.

If Kurdish society in Iran can no longer be considered as a tribal society,
then *a fortiori* there can be no grounds for treating it as a society of tribal
nomads. There are no more nomadic tribes in Kurdistan although a few
semi-nomadic tribes still spend the winter in their villages and go off to graze
their herds in the mountains in the spring.

Religion

The population of Iranian Kurdistan is 98% Muslim. The remaining 2% is
made up of Armenian and Assyrian Christians and some Jews. Most of the
Muslims are Sunnis (75%); the Shiites are mainly concentrated in Kermanshah and Luristan.

The sheikhs, the Sunni religious dignitaries, still exercise considerable
influence in Iranian Kurdistan. The two main sects (*tariquates*) are the Qadiri
and Naqchebendi. The sheikhs' followers are known as *murids, dervishes* and

sufis. Each *murid* must see his sheikh once a year, bring him a present and receive his benediction. Apart from this, there is no other form of religious hierarchy amongst the Sunni Kurds. A young Kurdish priest (*mullah*) will receive his diploma from a renowned religious dignitary and will then be sent to a village, where his income will depend entirely on presents from his parishioners. Since most of the peasants are poor, the young *mullah* usually has to participate in agriculture and stockrearing. Living in close contact with the rural population, well aware of their poverty and their deplorable living conditions, such young "intellectuals," who are often the only literate people in their villages, usually become active participants in the national liberation struggle. Consequently, the Iranian authorities tried to "re-organize" the Sunni hierarchy by granting the *mullahs* a monthly stipend, in the hope of bringing them round to serve the interests of the state.

Language and Literature

Kurdish is an Indo-European language of the Iranian type. Despite this affinity, and despite the supremacy of Persian which is the only language in which teaching is allowed in Iran, the Kurdish language and literature have retained their originality, have developed and have contributed to the consolidation of national feeling. This development surged forward particularly during the short life of the independent Kurdish Mahabad Republic in 1945–46. Kurdish has been banned in Iran since the 1940s. In the interim, the Kurds of Iran have drawn upon the publications of the Kurds of Iraq, where the Kurdish language and literature have progressed enormously since the Revolution of 1958.

Unfortunately, there has been practically no exchange of literature between the Kurds of Turkey and those of Iran, since the alphabets used in the schools of these two countries are quite different. In Iran all teaching is in Persian, which is written in Arabic script; in Turkey all teaching is in Turkish, which uses the Roman alphabet. The huge majority of Kurds in Turkey, and certainly all the young people, no longer know the Arabic alphabet and cannot read Kurdish texts published in Iran or Iraq. Similarly, only the tiny minority of Kurds in Iran who have been through secondary or higher education can read Kurdish texts in Roman script. The situation is quite different, however, when it comes to the exchange of Kurdish publications between the Kurds of Iran and Iraq; both countries teach the Arabic alphabet and, furthermore, most Kurds in Iran and Iraq speak Sorani, the dialect of Southern Kurdistan.

In the sixties and seventies many books, pamphlets and periodicals in Kurdish were published clandestinely in Iranian Kurdistan. The purity and richness of the language used in these texts is often striking, which is rarely the case in the publications of the Iraqi Kurds, despite the number of Kurdish books and periodicals which are published there.

Another element also influenced the development of Kurdish language and literature in Iran: although the Kurdish language was officially banned and there was not a single Kurdish school in the whole country, many radio stations did broadcast programs in Kurdish, most notably the Kermanshah station. The role of these Kurdish broadcasts by Iranian stations was fairly ambiguous. The Iranian government was pursuing two distinct goals: on the one hand, the broadcasts, which were listened to by Kurds in Turkey as well as in Iran, served as propaganda for the Shah's policies; on the other, they methodically played down any originality in the Kurdish language and presented it as a dialect of Persian. However, reading Kurdish poems and singing Kurdish folksongs over the radio helped further the diffusion of Kurdish literature and consolidate Kurdish national awareness.

Given that Kurdish is banned and that Persian is the sole official language, many Kurdish intellectuals write and publish in Persian. The best received Persian language novel of the seventies, *Mrs. Ahou's Husband*, was written by a Kurd from Kermanshah while he was in prison for a political offense. The action of the book takes place entirely in Kurdistan and the whole novel is an analysis of pre-war Kurdish society.

The verses of many young writers were published and read secretly but the greatest contemporary Kurdish poet was undoubtedly Hemin, whose *Clarity and Darkness*, published in 1974, was acclaimed as an unparalleled success.

Modern Kurdish prose in Iran was also developing. In the seventies it consisted predominantly of underground political literature, mainly newspapers and magazines. After 1970 a few books and pamphlets on the most burning political issues of the day began to be clandestinely published in Kurdish. However, the distribution of these Kurdish texts immediately ran foul of the Iranian regime's repressive policies. Savak (the secret police) tortured and imprisoned several people merely for being in possession of a single Kurdish publication.

Education

Since all teaching in Kurdish in the Shah's Iran was forbidden, Kurdish schoolchildren were forced to study in Persian, a language which they had to learn at school. The schools were ill equipped and there were by no means enough of them. The average class had over forty pupils. In many villages there was only one teacher, who had to cope with 250 to 300 children. In several towns and especially in the villages, tens of thousands of school-age children never saw the inside of a schoolroom. Table 5 shows the percentage of illiterates. More than 70% of the total population and more than 80% of women were illiterate in 1975. Even more seriously, two out of five girls and one out of four boys between the ages of seven and fifteen were not attending school at all. Table 5 clearly presents an interesting contrast with the Shah's slogans. Is this the "Great Civilization" and the emancipation of women which the regime's mass media boasted about night and day?

Table 5
Percentage of Illiterates Aged Ten or Over, 1966

Province	Province as a whole		Urban Population		Rural Population	
	Total	Women	Total	Women	Total	Women
Mahabad	85.6	94.5	62.5	81.6	94	99.1
Saqqez	86.9	95.3	62.6	81.4	93.1	98.7
Sanandadj	82.4	90.5	55.7	69.1	92.9	98.8
Kermanshah	70.7	81.8	53.2	66	89.2	98.3
Kurdistan in Iran						
(1975 estimate)	70	80	40	60	85	95

Source: *National Census of Population and Housing*, November 1966, Tehran.

Health

Medical care was inadequate in the towns and practically non-existent in the countryside. In 1966 there was one doctor for every 4,800 inhabitants and in several regions with over 20,000 inhabitants there was no doctor at all. (The average in Europe is one doctor per 500 inhabitants.) In the seventies there was little change. Despite a favorable climate and a relatively good supply of drinking water, trachoma, malaria and tuberculosis were all widespread in Iranian Kurdistan.

Economic Conditions

Although capitalist relations of production were introduced in the period between the two world wars and became more and more prevalent in the 1970s, Kurdistan in the Shah's Iran was still an agricultural region. Most of the active population worked in agriculture, which remained the most important source of income. Table 6 shows how the population was distributed amongst the main sectors of the economy.

Table 6
Distribution of the Active Population By Economic Sector, 1966 (%)

Province	Agriculture & Mines	Industry & Building	Services
Mahabad	67.8	10.7	21.5
Saqqez	70.5	8.8	20.7
Sanandadj	63.1	11.4	25.5
Kermanshah	46.9	16.9	36.2
Iranian Kurdistan			
(1975 estimate)	65–70	10	20–25

These figures call for a little elucidation. Apart from the oil industry in Kermanshah, there was practically no extractive industry in Iranian Kurdistan. Furthermore, construction was largely responsible for the figures under "Industry and Building"; indeed modern industry employed less than 5% of the active population.

Agricultural production supplied 80% of the national income, 45% from livestock and dairy production, 35% from crop farming. The annual *per capita* income in Iranian Kurdistan rose from $80 in 1960 to $150 in 1975. According to official sources, the annual *per capita* income for 1975 in Iran as a whole was $1,340.

Most of the increase in Iran's national income was due to the rapid growth in oil production and, in the 1970s, to the sharp increase in oil prices. Iranian Kurdistan's share of this multi-billion dollar influx of oil revenue was minimal. Not one of Iran's many large-scale industries set up a plant in Kurdistan. Apart from the strategic railroad that joins Iran to Turkey, there was not a single mile of railway track in Kurdistan, nor did the government intend to lay any. A single asphalt road — again for strategic purposes — was being built along the Iraqi frontier, to link Southern and Northern Kurdistan.

The standard of living in Kurdistan remained very low. According to 1966 statistics, more than 50% of families (average size about five or six people) lived in a single room.[3] 80% of all dwellings were built of cob. Most dwellings did not have running water or electricity. The average working week in the cities was 54 hours long.

In the seventies, as capitalism developed in Iran, Iranian Kurdistan's economy, which has been dependent on the Iranian economy since the beginning of the century, became an integral part of the Iranian economy. If Iran remained an underdeveloped country despite all the changes that had taken place, Kurdistan in Iran was certainly one of the most underdeveloped areas of the whole periphery.

The Kurdish Tribe and its Development

Although tribalism had disintegrated both socially and economically by the end of the seventies, it is worth looking back on the development of the Kurdish tribe. Rural society remained profoundly marked by tribal relations.

In the middle of the 19th century, the nomadic tribes accounted for one-third of the population of Kurdistan. They held their lands collectively from the sovereign, and were under his protection. The tribe (*ashirat*) in Kurdistan was made up of clans (*taife, bar, tira*) which were themselves divided into sub-groups: *hoz, khel* or *bnamal*. Both the Beg, the leader of the tribe, and the Aghas, the clan chieftains, enjoyed complete legal administrative authority. The Beg's decision was final in all cases; however, the *eshevins*, so-called "white beards," had a major influence on his decisions. When the Beg died his eldest son succeeded him, or, if there was no male descendant, the "white beards" elected a new leader. In a few rare cases a woman could even become the tribal chief.[4] The chief settled all litigation and gave consent for marriages, etc. Although he owned neither the tribe's land nor grazing grounds, the chief was always *primus inter pares*, and did enjoy certain privileges; the peasants regularly presented him with agricultural products and quantities of wool.

Within each tribe, we can distinguish three groups; first, there was the chief and his family, who were the privileged members of the tribe; second, there were the servants (*khulams*) who filled a variety of functions; finally, there was the main body of ordinary members of the tribe. Each tribe also had its clergy, which was composed of sheikhs (representatives of the various sects), priests (*mullahs*) and *seyyids* ("descendants" of the Prophet). The clergy also enjoyed certain privileges. There were considerable economic disparities between members of a tribe, based on unequal ownership of livestock. Even in cases where private property did not exist, these disparities played an important role. Some members of the tribe would have only a few sheep whilst the chief and other dignitaries would have large flocks of sheep and goats.

Exchange between the nomadic and semi-nomadic tribes developed to a fairly high point, mainly because these pastoral tribes had hides, wool and goat-hair to offer, as well as more milk, dairy products and meat. Within the tribes various trades such as carpentry, metal-working and the weaving of carpets, tents and clothing developed. Exchange enabled each tribe to establish its own summer and winter quarters, the *hevar* and *germian*. All along the road between these, the tribe was entitled to sell its products and supply its needs by trade. By the beginning of the 20th century, the use of currency had spread amongst the Kurds and the chief's wealth was evaluated in terms of his gold and money holdings as well as by the size of his herds.

The advance of exchange relations and the subdivision of the grazing grounds came about gradually, as the nomad tribes became more and more sedentary during the end of the 19th and the beginning of the 20th century.

Between the two world wars, the Iranian government used the army to sedentarize the Kurds, with disastrous consequences; often whole tribes were completely exterminated. Out of the 10,000 members of the Jalali tribe who lived on the frontiers between Iran, Turkey and the Soviet Union only a few hundred survived deportation to Central Iran and returned to their own territory in 1941. General Ahmed Agha Khan became so notorious for his liquidation of the Lurs that he was nicknamed "the butcher of Luristan." The same treatment was meted out to the members of the Galbaghi tribe: they were deported to Hamadan and Isfahan and their lands occupied by Turkish-speaking peoples. "The constraints imposed upon them during the move were so severe that many chose to go into the hills and fight like rebels for several months."[5]

These forced migrations suited the interests of the Iranian bourgeoisie, which needed a settled population to form a significant and dependable market. The ban on trade across the frontiers and the Iranian government's program of centralization forced the tribes to obtain their supplies from within the country. Sedentarization was very much to the advantage of both the Kurdish and Iranian landowners who were able to exploit the peasants and buy their lands. It was also much easier for the tax collectors to extract payment in the villages than to have to go chasing after the tribes in the mountains of Kurdistan. This increased state revenue, as did the ban on frontier trading and the improved control over contraband after the tribes' migrations were restricted. Furthermore, a sedentary population made it much easier to register and enroll young people for the newly established military service.

Following the partition of Kurdistan, the new frontiers, especially that between Turkey and Iran, prevented the traditional summer and winter migrations. The semi-nomads were stripped of the right to cross the frontiers. In some cases the lines of the frontier cut tribes into two or even three groups, as happened to the Chikak tribe (split between Iran and Turkey) and the Herki tribe (split between Iran, Iraq and Turkey). Certain factors did delay the sedentarization of the Kurdish nomads: the climate was favorable to stockrearing and the grazing was good, there was a shortage of irrigated land, and the tribes preferred to live an independent life without any obligations to the state. But eventually, as the state consolidated the centralization, nomadism faded out.

There were practically no nomads left by the 1970s. As Table 7 shows, there has been a very rapid increase in the number of villages and in the village population over the last century.

Table 7
Number of Villages and Size of Population

Area	Number of Villages			Size of Population		
	1851	1951	1967	1851	1951	1967
Bareh	8	161	203	1,125	15,000	28,080
Marivan	14	111)		1,040	17,800)	
			) 290			) 84,177
Hauraman	9	121)		605	29,500)	

In the late seventies there were over 7,500 villages in Iranian Kurdistan; many were very small, only 5 or 10 families, others were much larger, with 1,000 or 2,000 families. The average village was made up of 50 to 100 families. Statistics show that 90% of the rural population of Kurdistan in Iran was sedentary.

During the second quarter of this century, the chiefs seized both the grazing and the arable land, and thereby became "feudalists." The land which was originally assigned to the whole tribe by the sovereign gradually became the private property of the chief.

Following the agrarian reform implemented during the sixties and seventies, "feudalism" as such ceased to exist. Capitalism and the market economy became dominant features in Kurdish society in Iran, and the traditional social structure was replaced by one which changed the society in many ways. However, although the economic infrastructure was altered fairly fundamentally in a short space of time, the people's traditions and mentality did not change much.

The Social Structure

The impact of the agrarian reform on the structure of Kurdish rural society can be seen from Table 8.

Table 8
Social Structure in the Kurdish Countryside

Group	% of Rural Population		Landholding of each Family
	1960	*1975 (est.)*	*(in acres)*
Big Landlords	0.3	–	Over 750
Medium Landlords	0.6	0.8	75–125
Small Landlords	1.5	2.5	12–50
Middle Peasants	3	32	1–7
Landless Peasants	72	24–26	–
Agricultural Laborers	10	23–26	–
Others	12.6	14.7	–

Although one should remember that the 1975 figures are approximations since there is a lack of statistics on the results of the agrarian reform, the broad trend emerges clearly. The big landlords, who used to own more than 60% of the land, disappeared from the scene. The medium landlords very often managed to hang on to their lands by avoiding the agrarian reform law; because of the political situation in Kurdistan, the government did not press them too hard. But the redistribution of the big landholdings swelled the ranks of the small landlords and even more those of the middle peasants who became the largest group within the rural population.

Since there was no major investment in the area, the industrial proletariat in Iranian Kurdistan did not grow very much. On the contrary, an unprecedented level of unemployment was typical of the Kurdish towns and was constantly aggravated by migration from the countryside. The massive industrialization which took place in many parts of Iran hardly touched Kurdistan.

The Kurdish industrial bourgeoisie was, therefore, also very weak. As the towns grew, the Kurdish middle classes associated with local administration or the fast growing service sector became an important economic and political force. This petty bourgeoisie acted as the main relay for capitalism in Kurdistan and formed the Shah's regime's social base in Kurdish society.

An Historical Overview

From the Battle of Chaldiran to the Second World War

On August 23, 1514, with the help of the Kurds, Sultan Selim's army defeated the forces of Shah Ismail Safavid at Chaldiran, north-west of Lake Urmiah. This date marks the first division of Kurdish territory between Iran and the Ottoman Empire.

After the Battle of Chaldiran, throughout the 16th century, both countries set about the consolidation of centralized states. This centralizing tendency ran into opposition from the Kurdish principalities. In 1608 the heroic and now legendary resistance of Amir Khan Bradost in the fortress of Dymdym was crushed by the forces of Shah Abbas Safavid. The Kizilbache Army proceeded to massacre the Kurdish inhabitants of the area west of Lake Urmiah. In 1639 Shah Abbas signed a treaty with Sultan Murad which formalized the partition of Kurdistan; the frontiers through this part of Kurdistan have changed little since. Over the 500 years since Chaldiran, the Kurds of Iran have struggled constantly against the hegemony of Isfahan (the old Iranian capital) and Tehran. The Kurdish principality of Ardelan in the Province of Sina was the last to fall and managed to keep its autonomy until 1865.

One of the greatest of the Kurdish revolts during the 19th century broke out in 1880. Under the leadership of Sheikh Obeidullah, this revolt liberated the whole region between Lake Urmiah and Lake Van. It was the first Kurdish movement aimed at unification and independence for Kurdistan as a whole. The revolt was crushed by the combined forces of the Ottoman and Persian Armies.

During the First World War, Kurdistan in Iran became a battlefield for the Turkish and Russian Armies. To weaken Kurdish national feelings, the Turks fanned religious hatred against non-Muslims, notably Armenians.

The disintegration of the Ottoman Empire intensified the struggle waged by the Kurds of Turkey for recognition and independence. In Iran, the repercussions of the 1920 Treaty of Sèvres, the revolt of the Kurds of Iraq under Sheikh Mahmud and the weakness of the Tehran government all encouraged the northern Kurds to revolt. Between 1920 and 1925 Simko (Ismail Agha), chief of the Shikak tribe, managed to hold the entire region west of Lake Urmiah and called for the independence of all Kurdistan.

In 1923, Simko went to Suleimanieh to discuss the co-ordination of their two movements with Sheikh Mahmud. British agents were sent in to lure Simko with false promises, and he committed the tragic error of killing Mar Shimun, the Assyrian leader. His position was substantially weakened as a result.

In 1925 Reza Khan, later Reza Shah, came to power in Iran through a coup backed by the British, and attempted to create a centralized state. On June 21, 1930, Simko was invited to attend negotiations with the Iranian military at Uchnu, where he was assassinated. A few years later, in 1931, another revolt broke out, this time in the south of Kurdistan in Iran, under the leadership of Jafar Sultan.

The Kurdish Republic of Mahabad

On August 20, 1941, the Soviet, British and American Allied Armies entered Iran. Reza Shah's dictatorship was replaced with a weak government, based in Tehran and with no control over the south of the country, which was under British and American occupation, or the north, which was occupied by the Soviet Union. Various democratic rights were granted to the growing number of political parties in the country.

The Mahabad area was occupied neither by Britain or America nor by the Soviet Union. It was an area with a long tradition of Kurdish nationalism. In September 1942, seizing an exceptionally favorable opportunity, the Kurds of Mahabad launched the first Kurdish political movement, the Komala JK (*Jiani Kurdistan*, Rebirth of Kurdistan).

The strictly nationalist Komala, led by urban middle class intellectuals, soon attracted mass support in the towns and countryside. Despite its semi-legal status, Komala had no carefully defined political program and no solid organizational framework. A new leadership was elected in 1943.

The democratic movement in Kurdistan soon outgrew the Komala structure. There was a manifest need for cadres with a broader political outlook, for a political program in keeping with the times and for an organization capable of leading tens of thousands of members. A new party was founded in 1945, the Kurdish Democratic Party, which all the members of Komala joined. An eminent intellectual and respected political and religious figure, Qazi Mohammed, played a large part in its foundation. The KDP presented a program which contained eight key points:

1) The Kurdish people in Iran must manage their own local affairs and be granted autonomy within Iran's frontiers.
2) They must be allowed to study in their mother tongue. The official administrative language in the Kurdish territories must be Kurdish.
3) The country's Constitution should guarantee that district councilors for Kurdistan be elected to take charge of all social and administrative matters.
4) State officials must be chosen from the local population.
5) A general law should provide the basis for agreements between peasants and landowners so as to safeguard both sides' future.
6) The KDP struggles for complete fraternity and unity with the Azerbaijani people and with the minorities resident in Azerbaijan (Assyrians, Armenians, etc.).
7) The KDP is committed to progress in agriculture and trade; to developing education and sanitation; to furthering the spiritual and material well-being of the Kurdish people and to the best use of the natural resources of Kurdistan.
8) The KDP demands freedom of political action for all the people of Iran so that the whole country may rejoice in progress.

Because this program reflected the Kurdish people's aspirations, it rapidly won the support of most of the population. The specific conditions of the times in both Kurdistan and in Iran generally encouraged the democratic forces to go on the offensive. On January 24, 1946, during a mass meeting attended by delegates from all the areas around Saqqez, the first Kurdish Republic was proclaimed and Qazi Mohammed, the leader of the KDP, was elected President.

This Republic lasted less than a year, but it was endowed with a remarkable dynamism and managed to achieve several of the goals formulated in the KDP program. Kurdish became the official language in the administration and in the schools. Several Kurdish periodicals appeared regularly, notably *Kurdistan*, the KDP organ, *Halala* (The Tulip), a paper for women, and *Grougali Mindalan* (The Children's Babil), a children's magazine. The first Kurdish theater was founded. Kurdish women began to play an active part in social and political life for the first time. Thanks to the rapid development of direct trade with the USSR, the economy also began to improve. The lands of the landowners who had fled Kurdistan and gone to collaborate with the Tehran government were distributed to the Kurdish peasants and to the Barzani families who had found refuge in Mahabad from the persecutions of the Iraqi government. However, there was no agrarian reform similar to that implemented in neighboring Iranian Azerbaijan. As the KDP program indicates, the authorities in the Republic strove to reconcile the interests of the peasants and "feudalists."

The top jobs in the administration, which had until then been held only by Persians and Azerbaijanis, were given to Kurds. The Imperial Iranian Army and police were dissolved and replaced by a National Army and *Peshmerga* forces.[6]

The Republic's red, white and green flag was emblazoned with a sun surrounded by corns of wheat with a quill in the middle; the sun for freedom, the quill to underline the importance of education. A well-known Kurdish song became the national anthem:

> O Enemy, the Kurdish-speaking people still exist
> Let no one say the Kurds are no more
> The Kurds live on, our flag shall never fall.

The cabinet was composed of thirteen ministers, including a War Minister and Foreign Secretary. As no parliament had been elected yet, there was no legislative assembly, so laws were issued by presidential decree. But all judicial tasks were assumed by the Supreme Court and the Ministry of Justice. The authorities began to set up a local administration for the Republic. The precise status of the new government was still indeterminate: was it an autonomous regional government or a fully independent republic? The official designation for the new body was the "State of the Kurdish Republic," (*Dawlati Djumhouri Kurdistan*), but it was also known as the "National Government of Kurdistan" (*Houkoumati Milli Kurdistan*), as in Azerbaijan. The Kurdish government in Mahabad had not yet defined its own ambitions.

On April 23, 1946, the governments of Azerbaijan and Kurdistan signed a treaty of friendship. It had seven articles:

1) The representatives of the two governments will be accredited in each other's territory whenever they consider it necessary.
2) In Azerbaijani territory with a majority Kurdish population, Kurdish administrators will be appointed, and vice versa.
3) The two governments will set up a commission to deal with economic

questions and this commission shall be responsible to the leaders of the two governments.

4) Whenever necessary, Azerbaijan and Kurdistan will form a military alliance providing for mutual support.

5) Any negotiations with the Tehran government must have the approval of the two governments.

6) The government of Azerbaijan will take measures to contribute to the development of the Kurdish language and culture amongst the Kurds living in Azerbaijani territory, and vice versa.

7) Whoever tries to undermine the historic friendship, the democratic unity or the alliance between the two peoples shall be punished conjointly by the two governments.

Having said all this, the fact remained that the two governments had a different approach to internal policy. In Azerbaijan the authorities took the peasants' and workers' demands into consideration and embarked on a large-scale program of economic and social reforms, whereas in Kurdistan the order of the day was national unity with no bias in favor of the popular strata of society. As Kurdish society was more backward socially and economically, the goals proclaimed were much more modest.

There was still the problem of drawing up the frontiers between the two governments. Extensive discussion was needed to settle the status of the region west of Lake Urmiah, notably the towns of Khoy, Salmus (Chalpur), Urmiah (Rezaiyeh) and Miandouad. But in the spring of 1946 these differences were secondary. The main priority was the defense of the two states' very existence against the threats posed by the American and British-backed Tehran government. The treaty between the Kurds and Azerbaijanis had enormous implications for the two peoples and was, not surprisingly, very badly received in Tehran.

The KDP was one of the founders of a front which also included the Tudeh Party and the Democratic Party of Azerbaijan, as well as three other progressive parties. Iranian Kurdistan had thus become a base for all the democratic forces in Iran.

The Republic of Kurdistan was also a center for co-operation and solidarity between all the various parts of Kurdistan throughout the Middle East. Kurdish patriots were warmly welcomed: thousands of Barzanis and representatives from the Kurds of Turkey, Iraq and Syria were cordially received in Mahabad. The whole Kurdish nation saw the Mahabad Republic as a symbol of their aspirations and hoped that it would become the core of a struggle for the liberation of all Kurdistan. However, at the time, the political situation in Iran, notably the status quo guaranteed by the Anglo-American occupation of the area south of Saqqez, prevented the Kurdish Republic from liberating Saqqez, Sanandaj and Kermanshah. The Republic's sovereignty extended northwards from Saqqez over the whole northern part of Iranian Kurdistan, an area with an estimated population of one million.

In keeping with the Tehran Agreements, the Allied forces began to leave Iran six months after the end of the war. The Soviet forces moved out of the northern areas of the country a few months after the Anglo-American troops departure. Before long the Iranian and Soviet governments signed an agreement which allowed for Soviet participation in the exploitation of oil in the north of Iran. By late May 1946, no Soviet troops were left on Iranian territory.

In the fall of 1946, the Tehran government launched a campaign to organize elections throughout the country; these "free" elections supposedly required the presence of Iranian government troops in Kurdistan and in Azerbaijan to supervise the proceedings.

In December, the Imperial Army advanced on Azerbaijan. The Azerbaijani movement collapsed almost without resistance, and its leaders sought refuge in the USSR. The National Government of Azerbaijan fell on December 17, 1946 and soon afterwards the Iranian troops also entered Mahabad. Again the Imperial Army encountered no armed resistance. But the leaders of the Republic, headed by Qazi Mohammed, remained on the spot. Only the Barzani withdrew, to Naqadeh and Uchnu.

In Azerbaijan thousands of democrats were massacred by armed irregulars while the Shah's generals turned a blind eye, but in Kurdistan the Iranian Army decided to temporize. As for the Barzani, they were still awaiting the outcome of the negotiations being conducted in Tehran by a delegation headed by Mullah Mustafa. However, this lull did not last long. In late December Qazi and several other Republican leaders were arrested. Mustafa Barzani's negotiations broke down: on February 22, 1947 the Iranian Army advanced on Naqadeh. The Barzani withdrew towards the Iranian-Iraqi frontier and successfully warded off the attacks of the Imperial forces, who suffered heavy casualties. Many Imperial soldiers and officers were taken prisoner. On April 13, the Barzani passed into Iraq.

Meanwhile the Iranian Armed Forces were disarming the supporters of the Republic; only those tribes who had collaborated with the Tehran government and helped fight against the Barzani were allowed to keep their weapons. After a formal trial before a military tribunal, Qazi Mohammed, his brother Sadr Qazi, and his cousin Seif Qazi were condemned to death. Because of the popularity of the Qazis, the Iranian authorities hesitated for some time before carrying out the military tribunal's sentence, but eventually, on March 30, 1947 at dawn, Qazi and his two companions were taken to Mahabad's Tchouar Tchra Square by a large force of Iranian troops and hanged. Mass executions followed soon after in the other towns of Iranian Kurdistan.

Under Sheikh Ahmed, their spiritual leader, most of the Barzani, particularly the women and children, escaped to Iraq. But Mustafa Barzani had little faith in the Baghdad government; so on May 27, he led 500 men across the Turkish border and re-entered Iran two days later. Ten thousand troops were sent against them. The battle went on for three weeks, until on June 18, 1947, having traveled over 200 miles, Barzani's forces crossed the River Arax and entered Soviet territory.

A thorough analysis of why the Kurdish democratic movement failed is beyond the scope of this essay. However, we can highlight some general weaknesses, notably in its leadership. It had been impossible to form enough capable and dedicated political and military cadres in the eleven months of the Republic's existence, and this shortage manifested itself in every sphere. However, external factors also played an important role. The Tehran government which was determined to repress the progressive movements in Azerbaijan and Kurdistan enjoyed the backing of the Anglo-Saxon powers, especially the U.S. Furthermore, the Tehran regime encountered little difficulty in neutralizing Soviet policy in Iran. However, given the political and military fragility of the Tehran government and the great popularity of the Republic of Kurdistan, the Kurdish forces could have put up an effective resistance which, as the Barzanis' experience showed, might well have been successful.

The Vicissitudes of Twenty Years of History

Following the fall of the Republic, a period of general political depression began. Most of the KDP's militants and the Republic's cadres were either executed or imprisoned. But the young people were not quiescent for long. Right from 1948, clandestine Kurdish publications were being circulated in the Mahabad area.

On February 4, 1949, there was an attempt upon the Shah's life at the University of Tehran. Encouraged by the Anglo-Iranian Oil Company, the government took advantage of the incident to crush the democratic movement throughout Iran, including Iranian Kurdistan where hundreds of KDP militants and sympathizers were arrested and sentenced to several years imprisonment.

However, when Dr. Mossadegh came to power in Tehran, there was a great revival of clandestine progressive party political activity. At the 1952 elections, six years after the fall of the Republic, the KDP candidate received between 80 and 99% of the votes in Mahabad and the surrounding areas. As a result, the elections were declared null and void and the government appointed a Tehran religious figure as the representative for Mahabad.

During the course of the same year, the peasants of Bokan rose up against the tyranny of the "feudalists" and the police. Led by the KDP, the movement rapidly spread to the area between Bokan and Mahabad. But by order of the Shah, the Iranian Army was sent in to help the Kurdish "feudalists" crush the peasant revolt.

During the Mossadegh government's campaign to nationalize the oil industry, which was still controlled by the Anglo-Iranian Oil Company, Iranian Kurdistan was solidly behind Mossadegh, and continued to be so after the nationalization. In the August 13, 1953 national referendum, the Kurdish people voted unanimously to limit the Shah's powers. In Mahabad itself, out of 5,000 voters, only two voted for the monarchy.

A few days later, on August 19, 1953, a coup organized by the CIA overthrew the Mossadegh government.

The hesitancy of the Mossadegh government, the conservatism, flabbiness and errors of the main democratic force in Iran, the Tudeh Party, and the passivity of the patriotic elements on the day of the coup gave the conspirators an easy victory. When the police uncovered the organization of the Tudeh officers, the defeats of the national and democratic forces followed one upon the other.

The counter-revolutionary coup was organized and led by the CIA in order to re-establish a reactionary and pro-imperialist regime in Iran. The nationalization of oil, which symbolized the Iranian people's long struggle, was revoked. All national and democratic organizations were suppressed, thousands of democrats and patriots were imprisoned, hundreds of militants, representing the whole spectrum of opposition politics, were executed. Tyranny and militarism became the prevailing order in Iran.

On February 23, 1955, Iran, Iraq, Turkey and Pakistan signed the Baghdad Pact. Britain joined soon afterwards, on April 4. Although the United States was not a member, it contributed regularly to the work of the various Pact committees. Amongst other things, this Pact, like the 1937 Saabad Agreement, was directed against the Kurdish movement.

Even in the period after the August 19 coup, the Juanro, a Kurdish tribe based to the north of Kermanshah near the Iraqi frontier, had managed to retain a measure of local autonomy. Their inaccessible mountain fastness had enabled them to defend their country. On February 4, 1956, encouraged by the rout of the democratic movement and assured of the backing of other Baghdad Pact signatories, the Shah's regime launched a major attack on this last stronghold of the Kurds in Iran. Thousands of soldiers, tanks and planes were sent against the Kurdish villages. Noury Said's government hastened to help the Imperial Army. The Juanro resisted heroically, but the struggle was too uneven. They were surrounded and had to abandon their villages and flee to the mountains. The famous Juanro Fortress, the symbol of their freedom, was bombed into the ground.

On July 14, 1958, a revolution in Iraq destroyed one of imperialism's most secure bases. It also opened up new avenues for the democratic forces and Kurdish organizations. The revolution inevitably had serious repercussions in Iran, and especially in Iranian Kurdistan: the Kurdish movement in Iran began to develop rapidly once more.

In the fall of 1959, frightened by the growth of the Kurdish democratic movement, the Tehran government tried again to clamp down on dissent. Both in the towns and in the countryside, hundreds of workers, peasants, teachers and religious figures were arrested. Four militants, three of whom were members of the KDP's Central Committee, were condemned to death. Thanks to the solidarity manifested by public opinion in Europe, throughout the Middle East and especially in Iraq, the Shah was forced to commute the sentences to life imprisonment.

The Armed Struggle of 1967–68

In September 1961 an armed insurrection broke out in Iraqi Kurdistan and, although the movement lacked a coherent program, it soon attracted the support of the Iraqi Kurds and the sympathy of the Kurds in Iran. This sympathy found concrete expression in the form of substantial material aid.

Supplies, money, clothing and ammunition bought from Iranian Army officers were sent to Iraqi Kurdistan. Until 1966 this assistance, organized by the KDP in Iran, made a major contribution to the survival of the movement led by Mustafa Barzani.

It was not long, however, before the Shah offered Barzani direct aid, in the hope of weakening the Baghdad government whom he had never forgiven for having overthrown the Hashemite monarchy. The Shah also intended this aid as a means to secure some direct influence within the Kurdish national movement. The idea was to make Barzani's movement dependent upon the aid and to increase that aid as the movement grew, so that eventually the Kurdish movement's very survival would depend upon it.

The Tehran government calculated that, by helping Barzani, it might neutralize the Kurdish movement in Iran or even break the solidarity between the Kurds of Iran and Iraq. Once the Shah had increased his aid, he demanded that Barzani collaborate with the Iranian authorities in restraining any political activity by the Kurds of Iran. The result was the famous "thesis" propagated by the Kurdish national movement calling on the Iranian KDP to "freeze" all its activities. According to this thesis, the only correct course for members of the Iranian KDP was to remain "calm" and do nothing to provoke the Tehran government into carrying out its threat to cut off all Barzani's aid. Any KDP militant who refused to accept this thesis was *persona non grata* in Iraqi Kurdistan and every serious Iranian KDP action against the Shah's regime was considered as a hostile act towards the "Kurdish revolution." This, at a time when hundreds of Iranian Kurdish militants had joined the ranks of the *Peshmerga* to fight against the forces of the Baghdad government.

In early 1967 several Iranian KDP leaders and militants concluded that they could no longer support the policy of co-operation between Barzani and the Tehran government; they left Iraq and returned to Iran. Even before they returned, there had been several clashes between Kurdish peasants in Iran and the Shah's police. The militants' arrival encouraged those who had been waiting for a long time to take up arms. The nexus of an insurrection developed very quickly in the region between Mahabad, Baneh and Sardacht. A KDP Revolutionary Committee was set up to lead the movement. The guerrilla struggle that ensued in the winter of 1967 lasted 18 months. Trapped between the Iranian forces and those of Barzani and finding themselves quite friendless, the young and inexperienced leaders of the struggle fought on bravely but were finally decimated. Sharif Zadeh, an electrical engineer, Abdullah Muini, a student and Mala Avara, a priest and member of the Revolutionary Committee were all killed in battles with the Iranian Army. In the spring of 1968, when Suleiman Muini, Abdullah's elder brother, tried to cross over into Iran, he was arrested by order of Barzani and executed. His body was handed over to the Iranian authorities who exposed it in several Kurdish towns in Iran.

Having lost its leaders, the movement collapsed. Some of the militants fled Iraq, where they had to go into hiding to escape the attentions of Barzani's *Peshmergas*. More than 40 Iranian KDP militants were either killed or arrested and turned over to the Iranian authorities by Barzani's men.

Kurdistan in Iran and the Kurdish National Movement in Iraq (1961–75)

The leadership of the Kurdish movement in Iraq continued with its policy of blocking the Iranian Kurdish democratic movement from 1966 right up to the time of the March 11, 1970 agreement with Iraq which recognized the autonomy of Iraqi Kurdistan. From then on, however, the leaders of the Iraqi KDP provided a more friendly welcome for Iranian KDP militants. Relations between the two parties improved over the following four years, but there was still no question of the Iranian Kurds taking any major political initiative in Iranian Kurdistan, let alone organizing a new guerrilla war. The KDP in Iraq continued to consider the Shah's government, the worst enemy of the Iranian Kurds, as its closest ally.

The Shah's regime kept the Kurds of Iraq supplied with war materials and food but brutally repressed any Kurdish demands or actions inside Iran. Hundreds of Iranian KDP members languished in the Shah's jails. Two leaders of the KDP each spent twenty years in prison.

On December 19, 1972 five Kurdish patriots were executed in Sanandaj. On March 22, as he was leaving a Party meeting, Qadir Wirdy, a member of the central committee of the Iranian KDP, was killed in broad daylight by the police in Baneh. On April 15, 1972, two members of the Iranian KDP were shot in Sannandaj; in May 1972 in the same town, a boy of 17 was executed for political offenses.

The sad end of the movement led by Barzani in Iraq showed how dangerous and even tragic it could be to adopt Machiavellianism as one's political credo and to sacrifice the very principles of national liberation for ephemeral tactical advantages.

Kurdistan in Iran Before the Fall of the Shah

The Shah's Policy in Iranian Kurdistan

During the third quarter of this century, Iran underwent many economic, social and political changes. The rapid economic growth so often boasted about by the regime's spokesmen profited only the ruling classes, particularly a rising bourgeoisie, linked to foreign capital, and the Pahlavi family, who controlled all the key sectors of the national economy. The mass of people, notably the workers in the towns and countryside, continued to live in poverty. A large part of the population remained illiterate and had no access to medical facilities of any kind. The whole philosophy of the Shah's American-inspired "White Revolution" was to open up avenues for capitalist development in the towns and countryside so as to broaden the domestic market and establish a solid base for the regime by creating a large petty bourgeoisie, notably in the rural areas. This kind of development reduced the danger of social explosion in a country where, before the land reform, the huge majority of peasants were landless.

The rapid growth of capitalism generated several contradictions within Iranian society. The advance of the so-called national bourgeoisie was held back by the privileged position which the Shah had granted to foreign capital. In the seventies, oil revenues alone exceeded $20 billion per annum. Since Iran is also rich in natural gas, copper, etc., the country hardly lacked financial resources. However, the 1977–78 budget went at least one billion rials into the red.

Far from solving the social problems of the countryside, the agrarian reform created new economic problems. In 1950, Iran was a net exporter of agricultural products. But Iranian agriculture remained chronically stagnant. When demographic growth and the rising standard of living provided for part of the middle classes by the oil revenues increased the level of food consumption, Iran became an importer of foodstuffs.

The disintegration of rural society and the increasing mechanization of agricultural work in several areas of the country resulted in a massive peasant exodus to the towns. Urban unemployment increased steadily and city life became harder, both socially and economically. Despite all these social and economic upheavals, there were no corresponding political changes. The bourgeoisie and the middle classes acquired considerable economic power and broadened their social base; the working class, with its one million industrial workers, also became a force to be reckoned with; nonetheless, the Shah continued to monopolize political power. Legislation, justice and executive power were all firmly in his hands. He exercised direct control over the three bodies which effectively governed the country, namely the army, the police and the Savak (secret police).

The Shah's regime increasingly played the part of policeman in the Middle East, as was demonstrated by the intervention of the Iranian Army in Dhofar which is situated at the southern extremity of the Arabian Peninsula. Iran was linked to the U.S. by a bilateral military pact as well as through CENTO. Thousands of U.S. advisers were sent to train the Iranian army, police force and security police.

The Shah attempted to build up the most powerful army in Western Asia. Iran became the main customer for U.S. arms. According to a report presented to the U.S. Senate in 1976, Iran paid $10,400 million to the U.S. in the five years 1972 to 1976.[7] In 1972 there were between 15,000 to 16,000 American military advisers in Iran; there were 24,000 by 1977.[8] In the same report, American experts outlined the three reasons underlying U.S. interest in Iran: first, the country's geographical position; second, Iran's ability to guarantee the West a continuous flow of oil from the Persian Gulf; third, the growing opportunities for investment in the country and Iran's sizable trade with the U.S.

The Shah's dictatorship had reached its apogee by the mid-seventies. Nothing remained of democracy and liberty. All the political organizations, trade unions, professional and even religious associations were banned. There was absolutely no freedom of the press. Members of Parliament and the Senate were personally appointed by the Shah. All the functions of state were under his orders. Only he could limit or extend the enormous powers of Savak.

All these traits applied to Iran as a whole, including Iranian Kurdistan where the situation was in many ways worse. Kurdistan was more extensively militarized than any other part of Iran. The army, the police and especially Savak exercised complete authority. The movements of the population were strictly controlled: each Kurdish peasant traveling from one village to another had to inform the mayors of both villages, who, in turn, were obliged to inform the security police. Following the agreement signed between Iran and Iraq on May 6, 1975 in Algeria and the resulting collapse of Barzani's movement, the Iranian frontiers populated by Kurds were kept under the closest possible surveillance.

National oppression weighed heavily throughout Iranian Kurdistan. The Shah's regime absolutely refused to recognize the existence of a non-Persian Kurdish people whose nation extended beyond the Iranian frontiers. Even the most minimal demand for national rights was very severely repressed. The assimilation policy launched by Reza Shah sought to crush all Kurdish opposition in Iran.

To a greater or lesser extent this policy of national oppression also applied to the regions inhabited by Arabs, Baluchis or Azerbaijanis. Although non-Persian nationalities account for more than half the Iranian population, the Shah's regime recognized no national rights. But the national question cannot be resolved by simply pretending it does not exist.

The Positions Taken on the Kurdish Question by the Various Forces of the Political Opposition in Iran

Kurdistan in Turkey is the most underdeveloped area in that country. Kurdistan in Iraq used to be considered the most developed region of Iraq, thanks to favorable natural conditions and the oil industry. But in the seventies it was Kurdistan in Iran which became the most dynamic part of Kurdistan, for all that it had been racked by wars and inherited a disorganized economy.

The abolition of "feudalism," the introduction of capitalist relations of production and the changes in the social structure led to a disintegration of the essentially stagnant traditional society. The economy of Kurdistan was no longer on the margins of the Iranian economy, but became fully integrated. After the traditional social structures disappeared, there was a rapid transformation. Although Kurdistan in Iran remained one of the most underdeveloped parts of Iran, it was the most developed part of all Kurdistan.

In Turkey and Iraq, the Kurds are the only sizable oppressed national group, whilst Iran is a country inhabited by several nations — Baluchis, Arabs and Azerbaijanis as well as by Kurds and Persians. In terms of numbers, the Kurds are only the second largest oppressed nationality, after the Azerbaijanis, of whom there are nearly ten million. However, since the Azerbaijani bourgeoisie was largely integrated into the central state apparatus of the Shah's regime, national sentiment ran highest amongst the Kurds, who were thus considered the most dangerous nationality by the Shah's regime.

Although the percentage of the population that is Kurdish, and the extent of the Kurdish territories, are smaller in Iran than in Iraq or Turkey, the fact that non-Persian nationalities make up more than half of the Iranian population meant that the national question was particularly crucial as the Shah's regime neared its end. It is in this context that one must understand the way the various opposition parties and organizations in Iran approached the national question in general and the Kurdish question in particular.

The Position of the Tudeh Party: The Marxist-inclined Tudeh Party was founded in 1941, with the aim of becoming a mass party representing all sections of the population; but it never took an unequivocal position on the national question. It is true that in 1945–46 the Tudeh defended the national and democratic movements in Azerbaijan and in Kurdistan. From then onwards, however, the Tudeh became more conservative, despite having formally proclaimed itself as a Marxist-Leninist party.

Its program, published in 1975, devoted only two paragraphs to the national question. At the end of the section dealing with ruling class policy, it argued that:

> National oppression against the peoples living in Iran is another aspect of the Iranian ruling classes' anti-democratic policy. Iran is a multi-national country and different ties link the various peoples who live here. For centuries these peoples have shared a common fate and have collaborated to create a rich and worthy Iranian culture. Side by side they have made innumerable sacrifices in the struggle for independence and freedom. The essential interests of the Iranian peoples merged in the fight against imperialism and reaction. However, because of national oppression, some of these peoples were denied the rights they were entitled to. National oppression has become an obstacle to the realization of the deep unity between the peoples and a barrier to the country's political, economic and cultural progress.[9]

No mention is made of the fact that the Persian people suffered no national oppression. One might think that in terms of national rights the Persians found themselves in the same situation as the Baluchis and the Kurds. The program claimed that the peoples of Iran share a common destiny. But was this common destiny chosen by the oppressed peoples of Iran or was it imposed upon them by force? The present frontiers of Iran are the outcome of many struggles. Can they be considered as national frontiers when they have bisected the Azerbaijani, Kurdish, Baluchi and Arab national entities? Finally, whose culture are we speaking of? Culture as it was recognized in the Shah's Iran was the culture of the dominant nation, it was Persian culture. Not only did this culture not belong to the Kurds and other peoples, their own national culture was trampled underfoot, their history falsified and their cultural heritage actually attributed to the Persians.

In a second paragraph, the Tudeh Party presented its proposed solution to the national question:

> The Government of the national and democratic Republic of Iran is in favor of a voluntarily conceived unity of the peoples of Iran and feels that in order to create true unity between the peoples of Iran on a basis of equality and friendship, national oppression must be eliminated. Therefore, the said Government will adopt the following principles in its effort to resolve the national question: (a) All peoples living in Iran must enjoy the exercise of their right to self-determination; (b) The rights of the national minorities must be recognized by granting them full national, social and cultural rights.

Compared to the other documents and declarations of the Tudeh Party on the national question, this program was a big step forward in that it included the demand for the right to self-determination. However, at no point in the program was there any mention of the oppressed *nationalities* in Iran. The underlying implication was that the oppressed peoples of Iran had not yet become nations. The program spoke of a right to self-determination, not of a right to separation.

The program quite unequivocally limited the right to self-determination. In a paragraph dealing with the consolidation of national sovereignty, the first task, according to the Tudeh, is to "defend the country's *territorial integrity* and to ensure and consolidate its political and economic independence." How can one demand a realization of the right to self-determination while at the same time struggling to retain territorial integrity? What would be the attitude of the Tudeh to one of the oppressed peoples of Iran using its right to self-determination to separate from Iran and found its own state? Which article of its program would the Tudeh drop?

The National Front: Founded in 1950 by Dr. Mossadegh, this party was popular with the Iranian middle classes. The three foreign-based sections of the National Front (conservatives in America, moderates in Europe and Marxist-oriented radicals in the Middle East) never recognized the existence of the national question in Iran. In its program, published in 1972, the National Front made no mention whatsoever of national oppression. Its approach to the national question differed from the Shah's on only one point: while official propaganda spoke of the "Iranian nation" to stress that there was only one nation in Iran, the National Front's publications referred to the "peoples of Iran."

The Mujahedeen e Khalq: This organization was formed in 1970 and conducted a guerrilla offensive in Iran's main towns, especially in Tehran. Starting out as a Muslim organization, it went through a phase in which Muslims and Marxists fought side by side, then finally split into two organizations, the one Marxist and the other Muslim.

Having opted for armed struggle, this organization was naturally interested in the oppressed peoples of Iran, especially the Kurds, who, given their specific national and geographical situation, represented an important potential force in any armed struggle against the Shah's regime. The Mujahedeen were thus sympathetic to the movements of the oppressed peoples of Iran although they failed to elaborate a clear and precise program.

The Organization of Iranian People's Fedai Guerrillas: In February 1971 a guerrilla offensive was launched in the Siakal area of northern Iran; when this offensive failed in the countryside, Marxist guerrillas regrouped in the cities and founded the Fedayeen organization. Right from the start the leaders and theoreticians of this organization paid particular attention to the national question. In his essay entitled "What a Revolutionary Needs to Know," published in 1970, A.S. Farahani, one of the founders of the Fedayeen,[10] stated that the national question had to be faced head-on and that: "Kurdistan has its own characteristic traits. The Kurds should be able to gain their autonomy through a referendum."

The second issue of an interesting analytical magazine, *19 Bahman*, was mainly concerned with the question of "How to win mass popular support for the armed struggle," and tried to provide a definition of national oppression. In an essay on the armed struggles of the oppressed people and on "the situation of the Kurdish people," one author put forward views which were radically new to Marxist literature in Iran:[11]

> The frontiers have divided the Kurds and the other oppressed peoples of Iran. Their movement is linked with movements operating across the Iranian frontiers. During the last several decades, these people have risen up many times against the central government. The importance for the revolutionary movement of the Kurdish people, is reflected in the following considerations: (1) These movements are confronting a regime linked to imperialism; they are therefore anti-imperialist in character. They can be won over to the revolutionary movement by reinforcing their progressive character and inducing them to join with the oppressed masses in a united front against the regime. (2) These movements enjoy the support of the oppressed masses (of their region) and therefore constitute an important force in the struggle against the enemy. (3) Because of their mass character and because of the support they receive from the other part of their people across the frontiers, these movements are very difficult to eradicate. Regional and international contradictions emerge very quickly in these conflicts and can give them a broader dimension which may absorb all the regime's forces. (4) The cornerstone of the unity and solidarity of the peoples of Iran in their quest for a free and democratic society is the struggle to unite the peoples of Iran against the common enemy by doing away with all bourgeois and petty bourgeois narrow-mindedness concerning the national question. The revolutionary movement thus has a duty to further this unity.
>
> Militants associated with the Kurdish people and with the other oppressed peoples must take as their first priority the development of their national liberation movement, so as to ensure the unity of the liberation movement of all the peoples of Iran. These militants can play a much more useful role amongst their own people than in society at large (. . .) The growth of a progressive ideology amongst the Kurds is an important factor in the linkage between the armed revolutionary movement and the national movement of the Kurdish people. The armed revolutionary movement sees the armed national movements of the Kurdish people and the other oppressed peoples as a powerful force which will undeniably play a major role in determining the future of our country.

The Kurdish Democratic Party of Iran

The Iranian KDP was founded on August 16, 1945 in Mahabad. A year later, Kurdish intellectuals in Iraq who had been strongly influenced by the popularity of the Mahabad Republic, set up the Iraqi branch of the KDP. When the Republic was defeated, there was no longer any point in the Iraqi organization remaining a branch of the Iranian KDP. Both sections nonetheless kept the same name without having a common program or a unified organization.

However, during the years immediately preceding the March 11, 1970 Agreement, the Iranian KDP had dropped its progressive orientation to become a purely nationalist party and placed itself under Barzani's authority. During this period the Party's activity in Iran was "frozen" and the few publications issued by its Central Committee dealt only with the problems of Iraqi Kurdistan and paid no attention to socio-political questions affecting Iran as a whole. The Party's Second Congress in 1964 did not go beyond this narrow brief. Indeed several delegates were refused the right to participate in the work of the Congress by Barzani's associates.

After March 1970 things were very different. In June 1971 the Third Party Congress elected a new Central Committee and adopted a new program and new Party statutes. The Fourth Congress, held in September 1973, marked a turning point in the Iranian KDP's history. After introducing a few amendments, the Congress approved the program and statutes adopted at the previous conference. Forty-nine delegates representing Party organizations both within the country and outside participated in the work of the Congress. The participants included the founders of the Party and many young people. The Congress discussed and unanimously approved the Central Committee's report which reviewed the various stages of the Party's history and sketched the broad lines of its perspectives on the future. Finally a secret ballot was held to elect the new members of the Central Committee and its candidate members. The Iranian KDP was in fact the only opposition political organization which continued to be active in Iranian Kurdistan. With roots going back for over thirty years, the Party was well respected by all the major organizations of the Iranian left. It was thus to be expected that Mr. Hoveida, the Shah's Prime Minister, considered it to be a party "manipulated from abroad." The following are extracts from the Iranian KDP's Program:

The Kurdish Democratic Party is the vanguard of the Kurdish people in Iranian Kurdistan. Alongside the progressive forces of all the peoples of Iran, the KDP struggles against imperialism and the reactionary monarchical regime. Our fight is for the liberation of all Iran as well as for the Kurdish People's right to self-determination . . .

The KDP's strategy aims to ensure the autonomy of Iranian Kurdistan in the framework of a democratic Iran. The autonomous Government of Iran will administer the entire territory of Iranian Kurdistan; the frontiers of Kurdistan in Iran will be determined in terms of historical, geographical and economic factors corresponding to the wishes of the vast majority of the population in this area. All decisions on matters of foreign policy, national defense and long-term economic plans affecting Iran as a whole will remain the prerogative of the Government of Iran. In all other matters, the autonomous national Government of Kurdistan will assume full responsibility; representatives of the autonomous national Government of Kurdistan will participate in the proceedings of the Central Government. The official language of the national autonomous Government of Kurdistan will be Kurdish. Teaching at every level will be carried out in Kurdish, as will all local government proceedings. Persian will also be considered as an official language in the autonomous national Government of Kurdistan, and will be taught in the schools along with Kurdish, starting in the fourth year of primary education. National minorities resident in Kurdistan will have equal rights with Kurdish citizens. They will enjoy their own cultural rights and their children will learn their respective national languages in the primary schools. All minorities will be entitled to publish journals and books in their respective languages. Religion and the state will be kept separate: freedom of belief will be guaranteed for all religions. Racial and religious discrimination will be made illegal.

The Preconditions for Success

The Kurds are probably the only people of over 15 million individuals not to have attained a national existence till today. They have repeatedly come close to victory but each time the attempt has failed, for one reason or another. Some of these reasons are still relevant: the Kurds have no access to the sea and have remained in their mountains surrounded by other peoples since the Middle Ages. They have had little contact with the fruits of civilization. Kurdish society is still backward compared to that of the neighboring peoples. Geographically divided between the Iranian and Turkish giants, and then, after the First World War, between four different states, all the areas of Kurdistan are peripheral and underdeveloped. How can a small and divided people rise up against several governments at once? Have not various Kurdish uprisings been crushed by the joint action of these governments? Defeat piled upon defeat have given rise to a legend which says that the Kurds have no friends. The truth is the Kurds have many friends but to find them they must seek them out, especially in the country they live in. In every part of Kurdistan, and particularly in Iranian Kurdistan, historical experience has shown that the Kurdish people's struggle cannot succeed if it is isolated from the rest of the country's population. Since the Kurds of Iran operate within an Iranian political context, their struggle is organically linked to that of the other peoples of Iran. And it must be said that, in the Kurds' struggle against the Shah's regime, the democratic forces of Iran were more reliable and significant allies than even our fellow Kurds of Iraq or Turkey. The common enemy united these forces into a united front. True, the Iranian left (just like the Iraqi or Turkish left) did not always share the Kurdish movement's point of view on every aspect of the national question, but the progressive movement quite simply had no other allies in Iran. The same is true in Turkey, Iraq and Syria. The Persian, Turkish and Arab peoples are friends not enemies of the Kurdish people.

After detailed analysis, the Iranian KDP opted for armed struggle as the only means to attain its goals. This form of struggle was imposed by the Shah's dictatorial regime. No alternative could bring about revolutionary change, and under the Shah there was no room for democracy or for the national rights of oppressed peoples. To unite one must also have a minimum common program. The Iranian KDP proposed the following as a starting point:

1. The overthrow of the dictatorial pro-imperialist regime.
2. The setting up of a democratic and patriotic government.
3. A guarantee of democratic liberties for all the peoples of Iran.
4. Recognition of the oppressed peoples' right to self-determination within Iranian frontiers.
5. Support for all the national liberation movements and for the right of all peoples to self-determination.
6. The creation of a democratic and patriotic government, based on mutual respect, recognition of national sovereignty and non-intervention in inter-

nal affairs, which would establish close and friendly relations with all socialist and anti-imperialist states.

All democrats, all those who defend human rights are our friends. The national liberation movements and the liberated countries of the Third World, the socialist countries and world public opinion owe it to themselves to support the Kurdish people's right to self-determination.

Notes

Publisher's Note: This chapter was written before the overthrow of the Shah in Iran.
1. The 1975 estimates are extrapolations from the average rate of population growth nationally — viz., 2.8% per annum. The figure of 16% was derived from the Iranian government's 1966 Census results and the number of inhabitants in Kurdistan. This percentage does not in any way exaggerate the Kurdish population; on the contrary, since the Kurdish population has a lower rate of urbanization (30%, as opposed to 50% for Iran as a whole), the average growth rate in Kurdistan is probably higher than 2.8%.
2. These groups were installed by Shah Abbas Safavid at the beginning of the 17th century to defend the frontiers of Iran against the northern tribes.
3. Henri Binder, a French traveler, wrote in 1887: "I measured two of these rooms. One of them (10 feet long, 9 feet wide, 6 feet high) housed one man, two women and two donkeys. In the other (15 feet long, 9 feet wide, 6 feet high) there lived a man and his wife, his daughter, his son-in-law, two children, a pair of oxen, two donkeys and four sheep." H. Binder, *Au Kurdistan, en Mesopotamie et en Perse*, (Paris, 1887), p. 351. Eighty years later, things were little different.
4. For instance, Ms. Adila who led the important Jaf tribe before the First World War.
5. A. Lambton, *Landlord and Peasant in Persia*, (London, 1953), p. 285.
6. It was at Mahabad that the term *Peshmerga* was applied to the troops for the first time.
7. *U.S. Military Sales to Iran: A Staff Report to the U.S. Senate*, July 1976, p. 7.
8. Ibid.
9. *Program of the Iranian Tudeh Party*, December 1975, p. 18.
10. Savak announced his execution on March 15, 1971.
11. *19 Bahman*, a theoretical journal, January 1975, pp. 97–102.

4

The Kurdish Republic of Mahabad

Archie Roosevelt, Jr.

The dream of Kurdish nationalists, an independent Kurdistan, was realized on a miniature scale in Iran from December 1945 to December 1946. The origin of the little Kurdish Republic, its brief and stormy history, and its sudden collapse is one of the more illuminating stories of the contemporary Middle East. Its strangely discordant themes of tribal warfare, rival imperialisms and social systems, medieval chivalry and idealistic nationalism well illustrate the complexity of the Kurdish picture, involving as it does a people never united and now split among five nations, none of which is sympathetic to Kurdish nationalist aspirations.

In September 1941, the British and Soviet forces invaded Iran, toppling over the structure painfully erected by Reza Shah Pahlavi. As his soldiers scattered, they sold or surrendered their arms to the tribes which still roamed the desolate mountains of Iran, holding to their organization, mores, and way of life in spite of the old Shah's efforts to subdue them. Among those thus benefiting from the Iranian collapse were the Kurdish tribes occupying the mountains along the Iraqi and Turkish borders from Maku, in the shadow of Mount Ararat in the north, to Qasr-i-Shirin, on the Kermanshah-Baghdad road in the south.

In the north, the Kurdish tribes in the mountains west of Lake Urmieh found themselves contained by the strong Soviet garrisons in Rezaieh, Shahpur, Khoi, and Maku. In the absence of effective Iranian authority, the Soviets maintained direct relations with the tribes — the Jalali in the north, the Shikak in the mountains west of Shahpur, and the Herki west of Rezaieh. The chiefs of these tribes were allowed to manage their own affairs by the Soviets, who only required that they maintain security and provide grain for the Red Army. At the southern extreme of the Kurdish Area, near the Kermanshah-Baghdad road — one of the main supply links between the Western Allies and the Soviet Union — British troops kept the tribes quiet. It was in the large area between the British and Soviet forces, in the vacuum left by the fleeing Iranians, that the Kurds were able to regain their autonomy. At first the two main centers of disturbance were Merivan and the Avroman Mountains, where Mahmud Khan of Kani-Senan established a precarious hegemony; and Baneh, where Hama Rashid Khan, long in exile in Iraq, built up a principality which included Saqqiz and Sardasht. Both of these tribal chiefs were recognized for a time by the Iranian government as semi-official governors of their areas, but were then driven into Iraq by the reorganized Iranian Army. By the fall of 1945, all of Kurdistan south of the Saqqiz-Baneh-Sardasht line was again firmly in government hands. The vacuum was thus reduced to the small area between this line and the Soviet forces based in Rezaieh, in which there was only one town of any size — Mahabad, formerly known as Sauj Bulagh, a few miles south of Lake Urmieh.

Formation of the Komala

It was in this town of Mahabad, left to its own devices by the Allies, that the most recent of the Kurdish nationalist movements was born. On August 16, 1943, a dozen young Kurds, most of them small merchants and petty officials of the town, founded the *Komala-i-Zhian-i-Kurd*, or "Committee of Kurdish Youth." For purposes of secrecy, the membership of the new party was kept below 100 and was organized in cells; the semi-weekly meetings were never held in the same house twice in succession. The Constitution of the Komala was strongly nationalist and membership was restricted to persons of Kurdish descent on both sides of the family, the only exception being for those with an Assyrian mother — an indication of the close relations between Kurds and Assyrians.

The Komala spread rapidly, not only in Iran but in other countries as well, where Kurds saw in the new group a more vigorous force than in the traditional Kurdish nationalist parties. Chapters of the Komala were founded in the Iraqi towns of Mosul, Kirkuk, Erbil, Suleimanieh, Rowanduz, and Shaklawa; and there was a chapter functioning even in Turkey, where Kurdish nationalist activity was an offense punishable by death. The chiefs of the tribes in the vicinity of Mahabad also sent emissaries offering help. They were told that they were not needed then, but might be called on in the future.

It was inevitable that the two great powers primarily interested in the area should eventually hear of the Komala. The British, whose Kirkuk oil fields were located in Kurdish country, kept a watchful eye on developments. Their political adviser in Mosul sometimes ranged as far as Mahabad, while his subordinates were stationed in Rowanduz, Kirkuk, Erbil, and Suleimanieh. Yet the British could not encourage Kurdish aspirations without arousing Arab resentment, and so remained deaf to the overtures of the Kurdish nationalists.

The Kurdish Republic of Mahabad, 1946

Soviet Infiltration

With the Soviets it was a different story. At first they were evidently unprepared for active work among the Kurds, although they did once, in 1942, invite the leading aghas to Baku. In the spring of that year, when the Kurds raided some villages west of Lake Urmieh, the Soviets even brought back the Iranian Army and gendarmerie (though they rendered their possible services ineffective by constant interference). Yet the Soviets eventually realized the potentialities of the situation. The year 1944 saw Azerbaijan and Kurdistan filled with Soviet political officers and other agents, mostly Muslims from Soviet Azerbaijan. The work in Kurdistan centered around the Soviet Consulate in Rezaieh, attached to which was at least one of the Soviet Union's 100,000 Kurds, known as "Captain Jafarov," who wandered freely among the tribesmen and villagers in Kurdish dress.

Soviet activity in Mahabad dates from the time two of these agents, known as "Abdullahov" and "Hajiov," appeared, ostensibly to buy horses for the Red Army. Apparently a chance encounter first brought them into contact with the Kurdish nationalist movement. The story is that Abdullahov met a man dressed in Kurdish costume in an Armenian wine-shop in Mahabad and complimented him on wearing the national dress.[1] This attention aroused the interest of the Kurd, who happened to be one of the founders of the Komala. They fell into conversation, and finally the Kurd asked whether the Soviets would furnish arms if the Kurds were to form a nationalist party. Abdullahov parried with the question, "Who are you afraid of?" The Kurd said that they feared only their own khans. Abdullahov replied with an expression of contempt for the khans; the Kurd then brought him to a private home where he introduced him to the other leaders of the Komala. Further contacts with Soviet authorities were arranged and one of the Komala leaders who knew Russian became the party's liaison officer. From that time, although the party program called for appeals to each of the Big Three impartially, the Komala moved inevitably into the Soviet orbit.

During this period VOKS, the Soviet international propaganda organization, was starting a number of "Iranian-Soviet Cultural Relations Societies" in all sections of Iran. As the Komala had grown too big to continue meeting in private homes, its leaders now asked the Soviets to found a branch in Mahabad; they hoped thus to obtain a place to meet without attracting too much attention. The Soviets readily complied, and it was founded, not as a branch of the Iranian-Soviet Relations Cultural Society, but as the "Kurdistan-Soviet Cultural Relations Society" (*Anjoman-i-Farhangi-i-Kurdistan-u-Shuravi*). The clubhouse was soon crowded with Kurds, who showed their gratitude to their new patrons by sending ten cases of cigarettes made of Kurdish tobacco to the victors of Leningrad.

It was at a ceremony in the Society's clubhouse, in April 1945, that the Komala finally came into the open. The Soviet Consul from Rezaieh and the chief of VOKS in Azerbaijan were honored guests. The main feature of the program was an "opera" in which a woman called "Daik Nishteman" (Mother Native Land) was represented as abused by three ruffians, "Iraq,"

"Iran," and "Turkey," finally to be rescued by her stalwart sons. The audience, unused to dramatic representations, was deeply moved, and blood-feuds generations old were set aside as life-long enemies fell weeping on each other's shoulders and swore to avenge Kurdistan.

At this ceremony the future head of the Kurdish state, Qazi Mohammed, was finally admitted to the party, to the gratification of the Soviets, who had not liked the democratic organization of the Komala and had long been looking for someone on whom they could count to lead it according to their suggestions. At first the Soviets, realizing the strength of the tribes, had approached tribal chiefs with requests to lead the nationalist movement. But only three of them commanded sufficient prestige for the task — Qaranei Agha Rais-ol-Ashair, venerable chief of the Mamesh and the acknowledged leader of the federation of which they were a part; Amr Khan Sharifi, chief of the Shikak and "grand old man" of Kurdistan; and Amir Asad of the Dehbokri, die-hard conservative who, as honorary chief of the gendarmerie, had been made responsible for security of the area by the Iranian government. But Soviet overtures to each met only polite evasion.

Thus it was that the Soviets finally turned to Qazi Mohammed, hereditary judge and religious leader of Mahabad, and a member of its most respected family. They were frequent guests at his house and eventually helped him, through pressure on the Iranian government, to replace Amir Asad as government representative in the area, by his brother Seif Qazi, who took over the title of Commander of the Gendarmerie. Qazi Mohammed is said to have learned of the Komala only about a year after its formation, when he sent emissaries discreetly offering his adherence. Komala leaders had decided not to admit him, fearing that because of his strong and authoritarian character and also because of the deference which they themselves had been accustomed since childhood to show him and his family, he would eventually dominate the party and end its democratic character. When at Soviet insistence the Komala finally did admit him, there came about precisely the result they feared — one-man rule of the party.

Qazi's admission enabled the Soviets to draw the Kurds rapidly into line with Soviet policy, which, by the summer of 1945, began to reflect the growing aggressiveness shown by the Soviets elsewhere. Previously, the instrument of Soviet penetration in Iran had been the Tudeh Party, a popular front of Iranian left-wingers which, although successful in other parts of Iran, had never been able to take root in Kurdistan.[2] Now, however, the Soviets were considering a new and ambitious plan — the attachment of north-western Iran to the Soviet Union. Accordingly they formed an independence party to replace the Tudeh in Azerbaijan, a party which could then without embarrassing the Tudeh in other parts of Iran stage a revolution, declare the province independent, and possibly request incorporation in the Soviet Union. Obedient to Soviet orders, the Tudeh abolished itself and re-formed as the "Democratic Party of Azerbaijan," whereupon it began to use Azerbaijani Turkish as its official language and to demand separation from Iran.

The Kurds of Western Azerbaijan — which includes Mahabad — could hardly have been expected to join a party purportedly dedicated to Azerbaijani Turkish nationalism, so a new party had to be formed to fit them into the Soviet scheme. On September 12, Captain Namazaliev, Soviet Town Commandant in Miandoab, summoned the chiefs of the important Kurdish tribes, together with Qazi Mohammed and Seif Qazi, to Tabriz ostensibly to see the Soviet Consul. When they arrived, the bewildered Kurds were suddenly told to proceed to the railway station, where they were hustled onto a train and taken to Baku. For three days they lived in a villa outside the town and were entertained with tours, the theater, and the opera. On the fourth day they were ushered in to see Bagherov, President of the Azerbaijan SSR, who harangued them regarding the wrongs they had suffered under Reza Shah, and said that the Soviet government would help the new Democratic Party, which was dedicated to freedom for the oppressed and which he strongly urged them to join. He condemned both the Tudeh Party, which he characterized as a group of ineffective trouble-makers, and the Komala, which he said was started in Iraq under the auspices of British intelligence and was nothing but an instrument of British imperialism. Then, after a warning not to say anything about the trip, the Kurds were put on the train to Tabriz, where they were loaded into Red Army vehicles and driven off to their homes.

The Democratic Party of Kurdistan

The results of the expedition were soon apparent. Shortly after his return, Qazi Mohammed called a meeting of Kurdish notables to announce the formation of the Democratic Party of Kurdistan, which he urged all to join. Concluding from its name that the goal of the party was democracy on the American model, many responded enthusiastically. A manifesto, signed by Qazi Mohammed and 105 leading Kurds, was issued; it stated that the Kurdish people now wished "to take advantage of the liberation of the world from Fascism and to share in the promises of the Atlantic Charter." The declaration said that the Kurds wished nothing but the human and constitutional rights denied them by Reza Shah, and listed their aims as follows:

1. The Kurdish people in Iran should have freedom and self-government in the administration of their local affairs, and obtain autonomy within the limits of the Iranian State.
2. The Kurdish language should be used in education and be the official language in administrative affairs.
3. The provincial council of Kurdistan should be immediately elected according to constitutional law and should supervise and inspect all state and social matters.
4. All state officials must be of local origin.
5. A single law for both peasants and notables should be adopted and the future of both secured.
6. The Kurdish Democratic Party will make a special effort to establish unity and complete fraternity with the Azerbaijani people and the other peoples that live in Azerbaijan (Assyrians, Armenians, etc.) in their struggle.
7. The Kurdish Democratic Party will strive for the improvement of the

moral and economic state of the Kurdish people through the exploration of Kurdistan's many natural resources, the progress of agriculture and commerce, and the development of hygiene and education.

8. We desire that the peoples living in Iran be able to strive freely for the happiness and progress of their country.

The Manifesto ended in Soviet style with the words, "Long Live Kurdish Democratic Autonomy!"

The formation of the new party resulted in the dissolution of the Komala and the absorption of its members by the Democrats. Yet from the beginning the tribal chiefs, fearful of communism, were wary of the new party, though many signed a pledge of support presented them by a Soviet political officer touring the tribal areas. This underlying tribal opposition would have made Qazi Mohammed's position untenable had it not been for a fortuitous accession of strength which arrived from Iraq — Mullah Mustafa and his Barzanis.

The Barzanis had been even in Ottoman times one of the most troublesome of all the Kurdish tribes. In the 1920s Sheikh Ahmad of Barzan, considered a god by the Barzanis and neighboring tribes, frequently rebelled against the British, who several times were forced to call in the RAF. Finally Sheikh Ahmad, his younger brother Mullah Mustafa, and his principal followers were exiled, first in southern Iraq, then in Suleimanieh. On June 11, 1942, Mullah Mustafa, who had taken over the leadership from his brother, escaped to Barzan.

The story of Mullah Mustafa's subsequent struggle with the Iraqi government, of how he twice defeated the Iraqi army in 1945, and how by judicious use of funds the Iraqi Minister of Interior was able to enlist other Kurdish tribes against him and drive him from Barzan, must be told at another time. Suffice it to say that on October 11, 1945, Mullah Mustafa, Sheikh Ahmad, and about 1,000 armed Barzanis and their families entered Iran at a point north of Ushnuieh. With them were a number of Iraqi petty officials and schoolteachers of Kurdish descent, and Kurdish deserters from the Iraqi army and gendarmerie, including twelve army officers. The latter were men of high caliber, several of whom had been trained in England and had held positions on the Iraqi general staff.

Shortly after his arrival in Iran, the Mullah met a number of Soviet officers, including the general commanding Soviet forces in Western Azerbaijan. The Soviets told him to place himself under the orders of Qazi Mohammed, and ordered the local Kurds to feed and house the destitute Barzanis. By the end of October the Mullah's forces, swollen by refugees and adventurers from Iraq, numbered nearly 3,000 men armed with British rifles captured from the Iraqi Army, machine guns, and one field piece.

The Kurdish People's Government

In November and early December, Soviet agents circulated among the tribes, telling them to mobilize for the coming struggle for independence and ordering the chiefs to assemble in Mahabad. All co-operated with the exception of the Mamesh, the Mangur, and the Dehbokri. Meanwhile in the rest of Azerbaijan the position of the Iranian government was rapidly deteriorating. Armed "Democrats," many of them from Soviet Azerbaijan or the Caucasus, began to attack Iranian soldiers and gendarmes, who soon hardly dared leave their barracks. The whole province was in open rebellion, while the Red Army stopped relief columns sent north by the central government to reinforce its hard-pressed garrisons. Finally, on December 10 the Democrats attacked the garrison in Tabriz and forced it to surrender. All eastern Azerbaijan then fell under the control of the newly-formed "Azerbaijan People's Government."

The fall of Tabriz was the cue for Qazi Mohammed to declare his own area independent — which it had long been in fact. On December 15 at a meeting in Mahabad attended by tribal chiefs, the leaders of the new Kurdish Democratic Party, Mullah Mustafa, and three Soviet officers in a jeep and armed with machine guns, he solemnly inaugurated the Kurdish People's Government and raised the Kurdish flag. A national parliament of thirteen members was formed, and on January 22, 1946, Qazi Mohammed was elected president of the new republic. The Minister of War was his cousin, Mohammad Hosein Khan Seif Qazi, a merchant whose military reputation rested on his honorary rank of captain in the Iranian gendarmerie. Seif Qazi, Mullah Mustafa, Amr Khan Shikak, Hama Rashid Khan Banei (just returned from Iraq with his tribesmen), and Zero Beg Herki[3] received the rank of "marshal," and were provided with Soviet uniforms, complete with high boots, stiff shoulder-straps, and red-banded garrison caps.[4]

The new government, which controlled only a minute territory including the towns of Mahabad, Bokan, Naqadeh, and Ushnuieh, sent observers to the opening of the Azerbaijan National Parliament and even convoked a miniature parliament of its own. It also dispatched Mullah Mustafa south to fight the Iranian garrisons in Saqqiz, Baneh, and Sardasht, cut off from each other and their base in Senandaj by the heavy winter snows.

Relations with Tabriz and Tehran

Meanwhile in the north the capture of Rezaieh by the Azerbaijani Democrats brought new problems to the Kurdish government. Although the majority of the inhabitants of the plains west of Lake Urmieh, from Rezaieh north to Maku, are Azerbaijani Turks, the tribes of the hills commanding the plains are Kurds. The Miandoab area, south-east of the lake, also has a mixed population. These areas were claimed by both the Tabriz and the Mahabad governments and were a source of constant friction. Amr Khan and the tribes paid little attention to the Azerbaijani Democrats, and were continually encroaching on the villages and towns presumably under the control of Tabriz. In April 1946, the Soviets brought Qazi Mohammed to Tabriz in an attempt to settle the differences between the Azerbaijanis and the Kurds. It was essential at that time that the two new states form a united front, as negotiations were about to open between the Democrats and the Iranian government for a permanent settlement of the status of the province.

The final result of talks between Pishevari, leader of the Azerbaijani Democrats, Qazi Mohammed, and the Soviets was a treaty signed April 23, 1946, by the Kurdish and the Azerbaijani representatives. Publication of this treaty caused consternation in Tehran, as its clauses and indeed its very existence showed that the twin Democrat regimes considered themselves independent nations with the right to exchange representatives and make treaties. The text of the treaty was as follows:

1. The two signatory Governments will exchange representatives whenever it is deemed advisable.
2. In those areas of Azerbaijan where there are Kurdish minorities, Kurds will be appointed to government departments, and in those parts of Kurdistan where there are Azerbaijani minorities, Azerbaijanis will be appointed to government departments.
3. A joint economic commission will be formed to solve the economic problems of the signatory nations. Members of this commission will be appointed by the heads of the National Governments.
4. The military forces of the signatory nations will assist each other whenever necessary.
5. Any negotiations with the Tehran Government will be conducted in the joint interest of the Azerbaijan and Kurdish National Governments.
6. The Azerbaijan National Government will take the necessary steps to promote the use of the Kurdish language and the development of Kurdish culture among the Kurds of Azerbaijan, and the Kurdish National Government will take similar steps with regard to the Azerbaijanis living in Kurdistan.
7. Both signatory nations will take measures to punish any individual or group seeking to destroy the historic friendship and democratic brotherhood of the Azerbaijanis and the Kurds.[5]

The Azerbaijani Democrats next proceeded to negotiate a settlement in Tehran with the Iranian Premier, Ahmad Qavam. By its terms all Azerbaijan, including the Kurdish areas, became once more nominally part of Iran, while the Democrat leaders were "appointed" to posts in Azerbaijan Province corresponding to those they already held in the Democrat government. The Kurds reacted unfavorably to the agreement. Although they had been represented in at least some of the negotiations by Sadr Qazi, Qazi Mohammed's brother and a deputy in the last Iranian parliament, they felt that their wishes had been largely ignored. Whereas the Azerbaijani Democrats had legalized the positions they had seized, Qazi Mohammed's government now had no legal basis at all. The Kurds had progressed from the condition of a minority in the Iranian state to that of a minority in an Azerbaijani Turkish state.

Finally, Qazi Mohammed himself went to Tehran to voice his disapproval to Premier Qavam. He asked to be made governor of a new Kurdish province consisting of the Kurdish parts of Azerbaijan, combined with the much larger areas inhabited by Kurds still under Iranian control — a territory that would stretch from the Russian border to a point half way between Kermanshah and Senandaj.[6] This new province was to have a degree of local autonomy, with its provincial officials and its army garrison recruited entirely from the local population. The wily Iranian premier agreed to Qazi's proposal, but with the proviso that Qazi must also obtain the consent of Dr. Javid, the Democrat Governor of Azerbaijan. Dr. Javid indignantly rejected the plan, and friction continued between the Kurds and the Azerbaijani Democrats.

Although in the course of these conversations in Tehran a truce had been agreed upon by the central government on the one hand, and the Kurds and Azerbaijanis on the other, sniping and skirmishing continued, occasionally flaring up into open warfare. The Iranians, in view of the declared intention of the Soviets to evacuate Iran early in May,[7] now began to take more active military measures. The Kurdish front was held by the Iranian Fourth Division under the command of General Homayuni, recently transferred from Khuzistan, where he had carried out a vigorous disarmament program among the Arab tribes. In mid-April, Homayuni opened the roads and rushed reinforcements to Saqqiz, Baneh, and Sardasht.

The Soviets were said to have promised the Kurds planes, tanks and heavy weapons, and to have taken some fifty young Kurds to Baku for military and political training. For the present, however, Qazi Mohammed had to rely on tribal levies to oppose the Iranians. In the hills overlooking General Homayuni's forces was a formidable but divided force consisting principally of the Barzanis, but also including small Kurdish tribes always ready for fighting and looting, and Hama Rashid and his henchmen.[8]

As General Homayuni pulled more and more reinforcements into the area, Qazi Mohammed and the Soviets put pressure on Amr Khan of the Shikak and his allies, the Herki, to come down from the north and aid in the operations. At first Amr Khan demurred on the excuse that his horses were in pasture elsewhere and could not be moved, but at the beginning of May he reluctantly sent his tribesmen to the battle zone.

The month of May 1946 was marked by a number of fierce battles, all fought by small numbers and none of them followed through by decisive operations. In the beginning of the month the Kurds won a victory damaging to Iranian prestige when they surprised an army column on a road march near Saqqiz, killed twenty, and captured thirty-odd prisoners, two machine guns, and 4,000 rounds of ammunition. The Kurdish prisoners were conscripted in the Kurdish army, the rest were sent to Tabriz.

The Kurds were repulsed, however, in an attack on the Mahmudabad Pass near Saqqiz, designed to cut the Senandaj Road, and again later after they had seized the hills overlooking Saqqiz. The Iranian Army drove them off and erected round watch-towers of mud on the summits, each manned by thirty or forty soldiers. Finally a truce was effected whereby liaison officers were exchanged,[9] each side was to stay within its lines, and the Kurds were to have the right to inspect vehicles going from Saqqiz to Baneh and Sardasht and so stop arms and ammunition from reaching the Iranian garrisons there. The Shikak and the Herki returned to the north.

Character of Qazi Mohammed and the Kurdish Republic

After this period of conflict, Qazi Mohammed drew aside his iron curtain and gave non-Soviet observers a chance to look at his country. Although feeling against the British on account of the expulsion of the Barzanis from Iraq, Soviet-sponsored anti-British propaganda, and certain events in the past in which the Kurds considered they had been victims of British opportunism, was too strong to permit them to visit the tiny Kurdish Republic, at various times four Americans and one Frenchman were guests of Qazi Mohammed.

These observers found the Republic to be a going concern. Although without any legal basis, Qazi Mohammed's government continued as before, changing only the title of its ministers from *wazir* (minister) to *rais* (chief). He himself became merely leader of the party (*Pishwa-i-Hizb-i-Dimokrat-i-Kurd*). The villages were run by their old landlords and tribal leaders with the aid of a gendarmerie locally recruited and dressed in Kurdish costume, but commanded by officers from Mahabad with Soviet uniforms. Mahabad itself, from a typically drab Persian provincial town, had become picturesque and colorful, its streets thronging with Kurds in national costume, free for the moment of the hated Iranian soldiers and gendarmes.

Those who had an opportunity to meet Qazi Mohammed could not fail to be impressed with his personality, and easily understood how he had become a symbol for Kurdish nationalists everywhere. A short man of fifty, dressed in an old army overcoat, he had a lightly bearded, ascetic face, slightly yellowish in complexion from a stomach complaint. He neither smoked nor drank and ate very little. His voice was gentle and well-modulated, his gestures quiet but effective. Something of an internationalist, he was interested in all the peoples of the world and knew many languages, including Russian, a little English, and Esperanto. His desk was customarily littered with grammars and readers and literary works in foreign tongues.

He seemed to be a man of deep convictions, backed with a rare courage and self-sacrifice, but tempered with broad-mindedness and moderation. During the period in question, at least his demands were moderate: Kurdish autonomy within the Iranian state. He professed to share the view of many Kurds that, since they were members of the same Iranian racial family as the Persians proper, there was no reason why they could not form the same combination as did the ancient Medes and Persians. Qazi himself thought the Kurds were the descendants of the Medes, and liked to give his own etymology of Mahabad — "abode of the Medes."

Yet it would be impossible to deny that he and his followers also held pan-Kurdish aspirations and hoped to make Mahabad the center of Kurdish culture and the Kurdish nationalist movement, replacing Syria and Suleimanieh, its centers at that time. Great efforts were being made to put Kurdish education on a sound footing. At first Kurdish teachers had to translate from Persian textbooks orally in the classroom, but shortly before the fall of the Kurdish Republic, textbooks in Kurdish had been printed for the primary grades. In addition to a newspaper and a political monthly periodical, both called *Kurdistan*, there were published two primarily literary magazines,

Havar and *Hilal*.[10] All of these were printed on a press presented by the Red Army to the Democratic Party of Kurdistan. The importance Qazi Moham-med attached to literature and the Kurdish language may be adduced from the presence on his staff of two young poets, Hazhar and Hieman, whose poems were published in spite of the paper shortage.

Although these efforts did not suffice during the republic's short life to bring it anywhere near the standard of the other two centers of Kurdish culture where Kurdish has been freely written and taught for twenty-five years, politically at least Mahabad was the focal point toward which all Kurdish eyes now were turned. In intellectual Kurdish circles in Beirut, Istanbul and Baghdad, as well as among the wild mountains of Western Asia, all were watching to see whether Qazi Mohammed would succeed or fail. Couriers brought communications to him from groups of Kurds not only in Iraq but in Syria and Turkey as well. His movement appealed especially to the young people, who felt that the older nationalist parties had not accom-plished much. In Iraq, for instance, a new secret party, the leftist "Ruzgar," was formed of these elements.

Anti-Soviet Sentiment

The old nationalist parties, the Hewa in Iraq and the Khoybun in Syria, were not enthusiastic about Qazi Mohammed because of his Soviet connections. Fear and even hatred of the Soviets among the Kurds was strong for several reasons. In the first place, most Kurds are deeply religious and remained distrustful of the Soviet attitude toward religion. Furthermore, many of them met refugees fresh from the Soviet Union or talked to Muslims in the Red Army, few of whom painted a rosy picture of the lot of Oriental peoples under Soviet rule. It must also be remembered that the Russians have been traditional enemies of the Kurds since the days of the Czars. Russian troops in World War I fought over a large part of Kurdistan, leaving a trail of ruin and depopulation still traceable in many Kurdish valleys and villages. In Mahabad itself, Russian troops had been under orders for several days to shoot anyone appearing in the streets, and the town was looted and burned. None of this had been erased from the long memories of the Kurds, who still frightened their crying children into silence by threatening them with the word "Rus-sian."

The Soviets tried hard to counteract this unreceptive attitude. They played up "Kurdish autonomy" in the Soviet Union, and the brave deeds of one Samand Siamandov, Red Army colonel of Kurdish origin, "Hero of Lenin-grad." How much success they had is hard to judge, but certainly large sections of the population, as well as landlords, merchants, and religious leaders, continued to distrust them and to extend this distrust to Qazi Mohammed, whose connection with the Soviets was undeniable. The walls of the building in which his government was housed were plastered solidly with Soviet propaganda posters; his newspapers and magazines contained a large proportion of Soviet material translated word for word into Kurdish; and his poets composed panegyrics to Stalin and the Red Army.

Yet in contrast to the rest of Azerbaijan, Kurdistan was to outside appearances free of Soviet agents. Aside from a few Iran-Sovtrans truck drivers, who acted as observers for the Soviet and pro-Soviet governments, Soviet citizens were almost unknown in the area and Soviet agents kept under cover. There was said to be a Soviet representative in residence in Mahabad, though his presence was denied by Kurdish authorities.[11] Hashumov, Soviet Consul in Rezaieh, and his assistant Aliakbarov made occasional trips to Mahabad.

While terrorism reigned unchecked in Eastern Azerbaijan, in Kurdistan there were few if any political prisoners and only one or two cases of what may have been political assassination, though a number of Kurds not in sympathy with the regime did flee to Tehran. In the streets of Mahabad one could hear radio broadcasts from Ankara or London, while in Tabriz to listen to these brought the death penalty. Whether the reason for this freedom was the moderation and liberalism of Qazi and his cabinet, or the presence of the tribes who would not tolerate violent action against persons connected with them, the net result was to make the regime popular at least among the citizens of Mahabad, who enjoyed their respite from the exactions and oppression they considered to be characteristic of the central Iranian government.

Opposition of the Tribes

If the Soviets kept their overt interference to a minimum in order to reconcile the tribes to the regime, they were certainly unsuccessful. In addition to historical, social, and religious reasons for the tribes' opposition to the Soviet-supported government, there were strong economic ones. The Kurdish tribesmen depended largely on their tobacco crop for their livelihood, and now that their market in the rest of Iran was cut off they suffered considerable hardship. In certain areas food supplies already strained had to be shared with the destitute Barzanis, who had long outworn their welcome.

This tribal discontent was at its strongest in the south where the deceased Qaranei Agha's son, Mam Aziz, chief of the Mamesh, along with his ally, Bayazid Agha of the Mangur, so openly opposed Qazi Mohammed that the Soviet vice-consul finally came down from Rezaieh and threatened to have the Barzanis sent against them. When Mam Aziz continued to resist, the Barzanis did indeed attack him and he was forced to flee to Iraq with some of his tribesmen. From Rezaieh north, the tribes looked to the leadership of Amr Khan Shikak, who had resigned from his position in Qazi's government as Minister of War and for the time being was keeping aloof in Zindasht, his mountain capital south-west of Shahpur. The only tribes Qazi Mohammed could count on were the Gawrik of Mahabad, numbering less than a thousand armed men, and part of the small tribe of Zerza, in the Ushnuieh region. Even Mullah Mustafa and his Barzanis did not get on with Qazi Mohammed, who was no longer able to feed them.

Thus it was that Qazi Mohammed, in the face of the increasingly aggressive attitude of the Tehran government, found himself almost without support. Despite Soviet promises of aid and *materiel*, in the fall of 1946 Qazi

Mohammed was still without either heavy weapons or trained men, or indeed any effective army at all. As Iranian preparations became increasingly obvious, Qazi sent frantic messages to the tribes, his only hope, saying that the Soviets had promised the Kurds their support and demanding that the tribes come to the front to fight the Iranian Army. The tribes refused.

Re-establishment of Iranian Control

Meanwhile, events were moving rapidly. The Tehran government had been insisting that the Democrats surrender the district of Zenjan, which is not in the province of Azerbaijan. When the Iranians seemed about to back up this demand by force, the Democrats agreed to evacuate the area, and by the end of November it was completely in the hands of the Iranian Army. Shortly after midnight, on December 10, the Iranians attacked Democrat positions in the Qaflankuh Pass, south of Mianeh; within twenty-four hours resistance had collapsed and the Democrat leaders were in headlong flight to the Soviet Union, a year to the day after their capture of Tabriz. In his telegram of surrender to Premier Qavam, the Democrat Governor stated that the Kurd commander, Seif Qazi, had been informed of his decision and had been told that he was expected to order his forces to cease hostilities.

On December 13, Qazi Mohammed's brother, Sadr Qazi, a deputy in the Iranian Parliament who had been in Mahabad acting as go-between for his brother and the Iranians, appeared at Miandoab. There he told General Homayuni that the Kurds were ready to receive the Iranian Army peacefully. The general said he would move his forces in as soon as the Barzanis were evacuated from the Mahabad area. He sent forward an advance party of pro-government tribesmen, including some of the Dehbokri and the Mamesh and Mangur who had returned from Iraq, under the command of Lieutenant-Colonel Ghaffari. These were stopped not far from Mahabad by a representative of Qazi Mohammed who said that the agreement with General Homayuni called for occupation of the town by regular troops, not by tribesmen who might cause disorder. The tribesmen finally retired without fighting, and on December 15, 1946, after the Barzanis had withdrawn to Naqadeh, the Iranian Army entered Mahabad, thus bringing to an end the year-old Kurdish Republic.

The Iranian Army was given a great reception, and Qazi Mohammed and the army commanders exchanged visits. But on December 17 a number of Kurds were arrested, and the following day Qazi Mohammed, Seif Qazi, and many others were imprisoned. The only members of Qazi's government to remain at liberty were Hajji Baba Sheikh, immune because of his religious standing, and a handful of Kurds who had fled to Iraq or hidden in the villages. In addition to imprisonment, Kurdish leaders were further punished by having tribesmen quartered in their homes, eating at their expense — a time-honored Iranian method of imposing a fine without holding a trial. On December 30, Sadr Qazi, who had returned to Tehran, was brought from his home to Mahabad and imprisoned with his brother, although he had throughout the year left Tehran only when his services as mediator were required by the Iranian government. The army asked all persons who had grievances against the prisoners to present their evidence and after an examination by a military court condemned Qazi Mohammed, Seif Qazi, and Sadr Qazi to death. At dawn on March 31, 1947, they were hanged in the square of Mahabad.

The Iranian military government then carried out a program to eradicate all traces of Qazi Mohammed's regime. The Kurdish printing press was closed, the teaching of Kurdish prohibited, and all books in Kurdish were publicly burned. To show the tribes it meant business, the army executed eleven petty tribal chiefs of the Faizollah Begi and the Gawrik of Saqqiz.

One feature in the reconquest of Mahabad needs to be noted. Everywhere else in Azerbaijan, peasants, workers, and shopkeepers massacred the Democrats at the first indication of their collapse. This spontaneous reaction clearly indicated the hatred felt by the people for the regime. Yet in Mahabad, all passed peacefully, a circumstance especially remarkable in that elsewhere in Azerbaijan the secret police was strong and prepared for such emergencies, while Qazi Mohammed did not even have such an instrument. This fact would tend to confirm reports that Qazi Mohammed's regime was popular — at least in his own capital.

In the north, Amr Khan and the tribes under his influence took no active part in these events. The Iranian Army, evidently not wishing to incur obligations, had not informed Amr Khan of its projected move into Azerbaijan, and so by the time he had gathered his tribesmen to attack the Democrats, the war was over. Amr Khan and the other chiefs quickly sent the Iranian commander professions of loyalty. All were accepted back in the fold except Zero Beg, whose tribesmen ambushed some Iranian soldiers in Balanesh, near Rezaieh, while he was conferring there with General Homayuni. Zero consequently had to flee, accompanied by a few tribesmen and Assyrians, to Ushnuieh, where he found Mullah Mustafa and his Barzanis in a state of precarious truce with the central government. The Mullah finally refused the government's order to disarm his tribesmen or return to Iraq, and fighting broke out again. By June 1947 the Barzanis had fought their way north to Maku and seemed about to cross the border into the Soviet Union.

In Summary

This latest attempt to found a Kurdish state ended with the Iranian occupation of Mahabad. Like previous attempts it failed largely because of disunity among the Kurds themselves. One of the dilemmas of Kurdish nationalism is that while not only its leaders, but nearly all its rank and file, must come from the more enlightened townspeople, its military strength has always had to come from the tribes and their chiefs, with neither the education nor the imagination to look for anything but gain and loot in the weakening of government authority. During 1946 the Kurdish tribes, naturally opposed to government control, felt as restive under Qazi Mohammed as they had under the central government, even though he was of their own race. Because of this feeling, as well as their distrust of Qazi's Soviet connections, the tribes almost all sided with the Iranian Army.

The principal immediate reason for the collapse of the republic was the failure of Soviet support to materialize. A young and strong nationalist party which might have united a majority of educated Kurds was infiltrated by foreigners who used it for their own purposes and then let it be destroyed. The miniature state had been built under the protection of the Red Army, and continued to exist after its evacuation only because of the possibility of its return. When the Kurds no longer hoped for this, and the Iranians no longer feared it, there was no chance for Qazi Mohammed's movement to survive.

The whole episode was a serious blow to the development of Kurdish nationalism. There is now no Komala and no Democratic Party of Kurdistan, and many of the potential leaders of the Kurds are dead, in prison, or in exile. Yet this does not mean that Kurdish nationalism is finished. The Kurdish Republic found its support among those progressive elements of the population which seem bound to increase in numbers and importance, and was opposed by those elements which seem destined to disappear. It remains to be seen whether Kurdish nationalism is practical in an area where, until recently, nationalism was an unknown conception and men still give primary allegiance to their religious and tribal chiefs. The Kurds have never been combined in a stable state of their own and enjoy no ancient unifying culture. Separated from each other by mountain barriers, they have always had to look for their cultural and economic needs to the capitals of the different states in which they have lived.

If the states the Kurds inhabit allow their Kurdish populations a degree of local autonomy and give up the attempt to force an alien nationalism upon them, they may succeed in obtaining a loyalty similar to that found in Switzerland with its multi-national population. The Arab countries have made a start in this direction. A similar policy in Iran, if left free of foreign penetration, might be a cause of closer unity rather than of separatism between two of the nation's peoples.

Notes

Publisher's Note: *Archie Roosevelt, Jr., served as U.S. Assistant Military Attache in Tehran from March 1946 to February 1947. During this period he made a special study of the Kurdish situation and was one of four Americans to visit Mahabad during the brief existence of the Kurdish Republic. There is an obvious difference in tone and political orientation between this chapter and the rest of the book. It is included in this volume because of the absence of other first-hand material on the Mahabad Republic which — short-lived as it was — has constituted the only successful attempt at an independent Kurdish state in the period since the First World War. Roosevelt's account was first published in* The Middle East Journal, *Vol. 1, No. 3, July 1947.*

1. Kurdish dress consists of a tasseled turban of blue silk, embroidered vest, baggy gray pants of homespun wool, and a huge crimson cummerbund, intricately knotted in front, from which protrudes a pipe, the top of a tobacco pouch, and a long, curved dagger. The Kurds, like other Iranians forced to abandon their native dress by Reza Shah, kept their clothes hidden in their homes, a symbol of their national pride, until the Allied invasion, when they suddenly blossomed out in them. Indeed, the tribesmen, safe in their mountains, had never really abandoned them. The Kurds are incorrigible dandies and a poor man among them would rather spend his last coins on a fine sash than on a good *kebab*. Reza Shah's restrictions on their dress had served to make him and his regime all the more hated.

2. For a discussion of the Tudeh Party, see George Lenczowski, "The Communist Movement in Iran," *Middle East Journal*, I (1947), pp. 29–45.

3. Zero Beg was a bandit chief originally associated with the famous Shikak rebel chief, Simitko. Upon the latter's defeat and murder by Reza Shah, Zero Beg fled to Iraq, returning in 1941 to carve out a domain for himself in the Baranduz Valley. He was often seen with Soviet political officers and seems to have been their favored protégé. Although of little importance in his own tribe, the Herki, most of whom still followed their hereditary chiefs, these Soviet connections enabled him to play an important role in developments in Kurdistan.

4. Other officials of the new government were Hajji Baba Sheikh, local religious leader, Prime Minister; Sadiq Haideri, Minister of Works and Propaganda; Nanaf Karimi, Minister of Education; Mohammad Amin Mu'ini, Minister of Commerce; Ahmad Ilahi, Minister of the Treasury; Seyyid Mohammad Tahazadeh, Minister of Health, and Khalil Khosrovi, Minister of the Interior. Only one of these men had been among the founders of the Komala, but all belonged to the middle or upper classes — small merchants, officials, landlords.

5. The treaty was signed in Tabriz by Pishevari, Biriya, Dr. Javid, and Sadiq Padegan for the Azerbaijani Democrats, and by Qazi Mohammed, Seyyid Abdullah Gilani, Amr Khan Shikak, Zero Beg Herki, and Rashid Beg Herki for the Kurds.

6. Senandaj (Senna) was the capital of the province of Kurdistan, the former independent principality of Ardelan. It included Saqqiz and Baneh, but not Sardasht, which was administratively part of Azerbaijan. In the present article the word "Kurdistan" has been used to designate Qazi Mohammed's territory, none of which was in the province of Kurdistan.

7. The Red Army finally evacuated Iran on May 9, 1946.

8. Hama Rashid was of dubious value to the Kurds, as he was continually carrying on secret negotiations with the Iranian army for his reinstatement as Governor of Baneh, and was also suspected by both Kurds and Iranians of a mysterious connection with the British. In August, hearing that plans were being made in Mahabad to have him murdered, Hama Rashid fled back into Iraq.

9. The Kurdish liaison officer was "Colonel" Mohammad Nanavazadeh, one of the original founders of the Komala, later killed when the Iranian army plane in which he was traveling crashed near Baneh.

10. A number of other Kurdish periodicals had been published during the Komala period, such as *Kelavizh* and notably *Nishteman*, official organ of the party, which bore a picture of Saladin on the cover and circulated in Iraq as well as Iran.

11. The last of these Soviet advisers, one Asadov, is said to have been in Mahabad until the last days of the republic, when he fled to the Soviet Consulate in Tabriz.

5

Kurdistan in Iraq

Ismet Sheriff Vanly

Introduction

Ever since the end of the First World War when the great powers imposed their ill-suited solutions to the problems of the Middle East, the Kurdish people have constantly suffered from various forms of national oppression in each of the newly constituted states. In some cases this oppression was brutal, as in Kemalist Turkey; in others, it was more cunning, as in Iran. Whether the regimes in power called themselves socialist or democratic and pro-Western, the essential core of oppression has remained constant. For instance Iraq, strengthened by the March 6, 1975 Algiers Agreement — and with the active complicity of the Imperial Iranian government — launched a policy of Arabization in the 1970s involving the mass deportation of Kurds and the implantation of Arabs on their lands.

Over the years the Kurdish national movement's center of gravity has shifted regularly; flourishing first in Turkish Kurdistan from 1925 to 1938, it then moved to Iraqi Kurdistan from 1943 to 1945, then to Iranian Kurdistan during the 1946 Mahabad Democratic Republic and then back to Iraqi Kurdistan from 1961 to 1975. The revolution in Iraqi Kurdistan from September 1961 to March 1975 proved to be the longest, most sustained and most important political and military manifestation in the entire history of the Kurdish movement, the very odd manner in which it came to an end notwithstanding.

Geographic and Demographic Features

Kurdistan in Iraq is often referred to as Southern Kurdistan but in fact it occupies a more or less central position in the Kurdish territories. It is the link between what is variously known as Turkish, Northern or Western Kurdistan to the north and north-west, and so-called Eastern or Iranian

139

Kurdistan to the east and south-east, and it also borders on the mainly Kurdish areas of the Syrian Jezireh.

This part of Kurdistan is a rich country which extends over a partly wooded region of mountainous terrain curving from the River Zagros in Iranian Kurdistan to the mountains of Turkish Kurdistan. The highest peak, Hasar-Rost in the Hilgurd chain, dominates the strategic "Hamilton" route near the Iranian frontier and is 12,225 feet high. The mountains slope away to the south and west and give way to the fertile plains of Arbil, Harir, Shahrezur and Kirkuk. These plains are separated from those of Lower Mesopotamia by the low but arid Hamrin mountain chain which acts as a natural frontier between the Kurdish and Arab territories.

The climate is wet and mediterranean in the plains, cold and snowy in the mountains. Several rivers cross the area: the Tigris, the Great Zab, the Little Zab and the Diyala, which the Kurds call the Sirwan. Copses of Italian poplars dot the valleys. In the mountains, notably in Badinan south of the Turkish frontier, oak trees predominate. The country's produce is similar to that of the rest of the Kurdish territories: tobacco, cereals, wood, vines, fruit, hides, wool, mutton and goatmeat, eggs and dairy produce.

In certain areas the sub-soil is very rich, especially in iron and chrome, but it is not properly exploited. The country's great source of wealth is obviously oil, a resource from which the Kurdish people draw very little benefit.

Government estimates clearly seek to underplay the size of the Kurdish population in the area. The Baghdad government either has no statistics concerning the size of the Republic's various ethnic groups or has decided not to make them public. In a work written in 1970,[1] I tried to make some estimates of my own, based on the results of the 1957 Iraqi census. I concluded that the population of Iraqi Kurdistan, including non-Kurdish minorities, represented about 22% of the 6,538,109 inhabitants of the Republic in 1957.

Since the reorganization of certain administrative boundaries following the March 11, 1970 Agreement, the Iraqi Republic is divided into sixteen *muhafazats* (counties or provinces). Four are located entirely within Kurdistan, namely Suleimanieh, Arbil, Dehok and Kirkuk; the first three constitute the autonomous region. Dehok is in fact a truncated Badinan. Certain other provinces are partially situated in Kurdistan: for instance, Nineveh (Mosul) includes the Kurdish constituencies of Aqra, Sheikhan, Sindjar and the mainly Kurdish areas of Zammar (from Tel-Afar to Tel-Kotchek and Fish-Khapur north-west of Mosul), all of which should really be part of Badinan (Dehok); likewise the province of Diyala, with the Kurdish constituencies of Maidan, Qaratu, Khanaqin and Mandali, and the small mainly Kurdish area north-east of Badra in the Arab province of Wasit.

Given all this it is worth trying to assess the total population of Iraqi Kurdistan for 1975, the figures being based either on official Iraqi statistics or on personal estimates whenever statistics are not available, as in the Kurdish constituencies and regions falling within provinces which are only partly situated in Kurdistan.

Iraqi Kurdistan

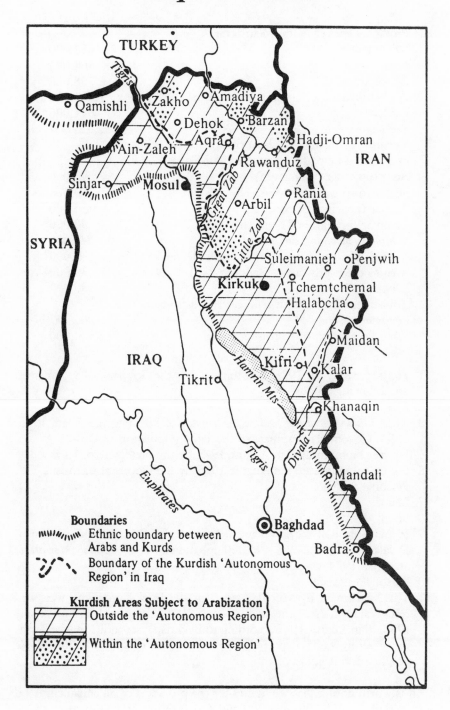

Boundaries

ᴵᴵᴵᴵᴵᴵᴵᴵᴵᴵᴵᴵ Ethnic boundary between
Arabs and Kurds

Boundary of the Kurdish 'Autonomous
Region' in Iraq

Kurdish Areas Subject to Arabization

Outside the 'Autonomous Region'

Within the 'Autonomous Region'

Estimate of Population of Kurdistan in Iraq

		Population *(May 31, 1975)*
A.	Provinces entirely within Kurdistan	
	Suleimanieh	653,000[1]
	Arbil	564,000[2]
	Dehok	168,000[3]
	Population of the "autonomous region"	1,385,000
	Kirkuk	641,000[4]
	Sub-total	*2,026,000*
B.	Kurdish (or mainly Kurdish) constituencies in provinces only partly situated in Kurdistan	
	Aqra (province of Nineveh)	90,000[5]
	Sheikhan (province of Nineveh)	50,000[6]
	Sindjar (province of Nineveh)	54,000[7]
	Zammar (province of Nineveh)	50,000[8]
	Sub-total (including Badinan)	*244,000*
	Qaratu, Maidan, Khanaqin, Mandali (Diyala)	180,000[9]
	Area to the north-east of Badra (Wasit)	50,000[10]
	Sub-total	*230,000*
C.	Adjustment for Kurdish refugees and deportees	
	Sub-total	*300,000*[11]
	Total Population of Kurdistan in Iraq	2,800,000

1. Figure for May 31, 1975 communicated by the Governor of Suleimanieh the following August.
2. Idem.
3. Cf. *Annual Abstract of Statistics*, Ministry of Planning, Baghdad, 1975, p. 34. Government estimate of the 1974 population of Dehok.
4. Figure communicated in August 1975 by the prefecture of Kirkuk.
5. Figure communicated in August 1975 by the Governor of Mosul.
6. Personal estimate.
7. Idem.
8. Idem.
9. Idem. Note that the government estimate for the 1975 population of Diyala as a whole was 496,000 inhabitants (Cf. *Annual Abstract of Statistics*, 1974, op. cit).
10. Personal estimate.
11. This adjustment is twofold: firstly, for the Iraqi Kurds who were still refugees to Iran at the end of May 1975, roughly 100,000 people (93,000 in August 1975 according to Baghdad); secondly, for the Kurds the government has deported to Arab Iraq, very roughly 200,000 people at a hazardous guess.

It is worth noting that the figures for the provinces of Suleimanieh, Arbil and Kirkuk — 653,000, 564,000 and 641,000 inhabitants respectively —

were obtained from the governors of these provinces in August 1975 during a journey made through Iraq at the invitation of the Baghdad government. They are significantly higher than the official government estimates for 1975 as laid out in the Iraqi Ministry of Planning's 1974 *Annual Abstract of Statistics* (555,000, 491,000 and 600,000 inhabitants) but are more recent and therefore more exact.

The government calculated that the overall population of Iraq grew from 8,261,000 registered in the 1965 census[2] to 11,124,000 in 1975.[3] With its population of 2,800,000, Kurdistan accounts for 26.07%, a slightly smaller proportion than the 27.2% in 1957. For the total number of Kurds living in the Republic, one must subtract from this figure of 2,800,000 the 250,000 non-Kurdish inhabitants of Kurdistan and add the 300,000 Kurds who live in the capital itself, the 50,000 Kurds who live in the city of Mosul and the approximately 100,000 Kurds living elsewhere in southern Iraq; this brings the total number of Kurds in the Republic up to 3 million for 1975, some 28% of the population as a whole.[4] This is a slightly higher percentage than the 27.5% I gave in *Le Kurdistan Irakien, Entite Nationale*. The difference is probably due to my original underestimation of the urban population in Arab Iraq and hence of the number of Kurds who live in the Iraqi towns.[5] In 1974 Baghdad had 2,800,000 inhabitants and Mosul 500,000. Changes in the deportation and Arabization measures taken by Baghdad should have no bearing on our figure of 3 million Kurds, as long as these "transfers" remain within the Iraqi boundaries.[6]

At an estimate, Iraqi Kurdistan covers about 29,000 square miles (see the table below).

Total Area of Iraqi Kurdistan (in square miles)

Provinces	Total Area*	Area within Kurdistan	Autonomous region
Suleimanieh	4,677	4,677	4,677
Arbil	5,973	5,973	5,973
Dehok	3,804	3,804	3,804
Kirkuk	7,622	7,622	
Nineveh	14,847	4,300	
Diyala	6,140	2,150	
Wasit	5,777	350	
Iraqi Kurdistan		29,000	14,454**

* *Annual Abstract of Statistics*, 1974, op. cit., p. 34.
** Area of "Autonomous Region" till November 1975.

The roughly 29,000 square miles of Iraqi Kurdistan account for 17% of the Republic's 170,994 square miles.[7] The difference between the territorial and demographic percentages accounted for by Kurdistan, 17% versus 28%, is due to the vast areas of desert in Arab Iraq, notably to the south-west of the Euphrates. The population density of Kurdistan is 101 inhabitants per square mile as compared to 57 for Arab Iraq and 65 for the Republic as a whole.

Given that the Autonomous Region is representative of the social structures of Iraqi Kurdistan as a whole, we can say that the peasantry represents
55% of the country's population. The "nomad tribes," which are still equated
with the Kurds in Western minds, do not in fact exist in Kurdistan. At most
0.5% of the population is made up of semi-nomadic elements who go up to
the mountains to graze their flocks during the spring but remain in their
villages throughout the winters.

The most important town in Iraqi Kurdistan is Kirkuk, right in the middle
of the oil fields. In 1961, before the wars in Kurdistan, the town had about
150,000 inhabitants, 60% Kurds and 40% Turkomans. In both Kirkuk and
part of the province of which it is the capital, the government systematically
set out to reduce the percentage of Kurds and to replace them with Arabs. Its
population in 1975 was probably around 250,000.

Arbil and Suleimanieh are the two largest entirely Kurdish towns in the
country and the two most important centers of its national culture.

Situated in the middle of a vast intensively cultivated agricultural region,
Suleimanieh, with its population of 160,000 in 1975,[8] is the urban center of
Southern Kurdistan. Suleimanieh is dear to all Kurds for its well laid out and
exemplarily clean streets, its climate which is brisk, even in summer, its
industrious population, its lively shops and for the young people who flock to
its university.

Arbil, the capital of the Autonomous Region, has as many inhabitants as
Suleimanieh and is just as much a major city, both in terms of culture and also
economically, thanks to its light industries and many businesses. But it is in
many ways less urban and has retained more of the old traditions.

Other important and entirely Kurdish towns in the country include Koy-
Sanjak in Arbil province, with a population of some 70,000[9] and Khanaqin,
once a famous center for artisans and trade on the old road from Baghdad to
Kermanshah and the Iranian plateau, a town whose Kurdish character is
threatened by the regime's policy of Arabization.

There are also a great many small towns, of from 10,000 to 15,000
inhabitants; Amadiya is by far the most beautiful, with its many historic
buildings and splendid setting.

Historical Background

During the First World War, Britain's Indian Army seized two *vilayets* from
the Ottomans: Basra and Baghdad, that area of Lower Mesopotamia which
the geographers of the Middle Ages knew as Arab Iraq. It was these two
vilayets that Sherif Hussein of Mecca claimed for his proposed new state[10] in
his letter to the British on October 15, 1915. On October 24, London
agreed to these demands, which were his price for raising a revolt against the
Turks.[11] The area claimed did not include Mosul.

Once the British had established their hold over the two *vilayets* of Baghdad and Basra, they explained that they "expected the Arabs to understand
that Great Britain's interests and position forced her to take certain
measures."[12] It was only after the Armistice between the Allied Powers and

the Sultan's Turkey was signed at Mudros on August 30, 1918, that the British proceeded to occupy the Ottoman *vilayet* of Mosul. Even then, they only occupied parts of it. As early as 1919 the whole Suleimanieh region slipped from their grasp when a well respected local chief, Sheikh Mahmoud Berezendji, raised troops over an area extending to Kurdistan in Iran. Later, after this movement had been defeated by the British Army, Sir Arnold Wilson, who had been the main British Political Officer in Baghdad at the time, was to write that: "the Kurds wish neither to continue under the Turkish government nor to be placed under the control of the Iraqi government." Wilson confirms that: "in Southern Kurdistan, four out of five people supported Sheikh Mahmoud's plan to set up an independent Kurdistan" and adds that "the idea of Kurdistan for the Kurds was already popular . . . nearly all the Kurds were anxious to break their ties with Turkey."[13]

But the British imperialists who were in control had already decided that, in order to appropriate the oil fields of Southern Kurdistan, they were going to ride roughshod over the Kurdish people's aspirations. They were quite determined to set up a client state which would bring together the three ancient *vilayets* of Basra, Baghdad and Mosul. The British chose to name these Arab and Kurdish territories "Iraq"[14] and selected as their "Arab King" Emir Faisal, the son of the Sherif of Mecca, whom they had exiled. In April 1919, before the Eastern Committee in London, Sir Arnold Wilson recommended to his government that it "include within Iraq all those areas of Kurdistan which at present form the *vilayet* of Mosul, as well as those of the regions to the north of this *vilayet* which are not to be included in the future Armenian state, notably the whole Great Zab basin." He also advised London not to commit itself in favor of the Kurds: "As for the question of granting the Kurds of Kurdistan some form of autonomy, it would be best to leave the matter to be settled at our own discretion and not to have it raised at the Peace Conference if at all possible."[15]

But this was not to be. In his project for a League of Nations pact, the U.S. President, Woodrow Wilson, had already prescribed that the principle of nationality be adhered to when it came to dealing with non-Turkish countries which were to be detached from the Ottoman Empire. Indeed he specifically mentioned three countries which should attain statehood under League of Nations mandate and which should not be broken up, namely (in this order) Armenia, Kurdistan and Arabia.[16]

The Kurds themselves were by no means passive. General Sherif Pasha, a high ranking Kurdish officer who had served in the Ottoman Army and been Turkey's Ambassador to Sweden, was sent to Paris to inform the Conference of his people's demands. He was in fact given some satisfaction. Section III of the Treaty of Sèvres, signed August 10, 1920 by the Allied Powers and the Constantinople government, is entitled Kurdistan. Articles 62, 63 and 64 envisaged the creation of an independent Kurdish state which would, at first, be set up under a League of Nations mandate. This state was to extend over most of the old Ottoman Kurdistan (now Turkish, Iraqi and Syrian) and its frontier with the future state of Armenia would be decided later by an international commission according to procedures laid down. Article 64 of the Treaty ended with the stipulation that: "Kurds living in that part of Kurdistan which has till now been included in the *vilayet* of Mosul should be given the option of joining this independent Kurdish state."

However, there was a contradiction between London's stated policy as set out in the Treaty of Sèvres and the policy it actually carried out in the Middle East. On August 23, 1921, following a faked referendum, Sir Percy Cox, the British High Commissioner in Baghdad, had Emir Faisal, a prince who was not even Iraqi, enthroned as King of all Iraq, including the *vilayet* of Mosul. In his official report to the Commission on League of Nations Mandated Territories, Sir Percy Cox noted that: "the Kurds feared for their interests if Baghdad should hold the reins of industry and the economy in Iraq. They assumed they would be cheated. The Suleimanieh region decided not to participate in the election of the King of Iraq. In Kirkuk the Emir's candidacy was rejected and the Kurds demanded a government of their own race . . . Suleimanieh was almost unanimous in rejecting outright any form of inclusion under Iraqi government."[17]

In 1922 in Turkey, Mustafa Kemal finally defeated the Turkish government of Constantinople which, as heir to the Ottomans, had signed the Treaty of Sèvres. Born in Erzurum province and helped to victory by the Kurdish people, the Kemalist Movement originally proclaimed its intention to create a modern Republic of Turkey in which the Kurdish and Turkish peoples would live as equals and with full "ethnic rights." Kemalism rejected the Treaty of Sèvres, which may have been a just treaty in that it guaranteed rights of independence and self-determination to the non-Turkish nationalities of the Empire but which was also grossly unfair towards Turkish Turkey, which it effectively reduced to the rank of a protectorate under joint British, French, Italian and Greek military occupation.

In the name of the fraternity between Kurds and Turks which Kemalism had adopted as one of its slogans, the Kemalists called on the British to hand back the old *vilayet* of Mosul to Turkey. In order to stave off this threat to London's plans for Iraq, the British, who had been appointed by the March 19–26, 1920 San Remo Allied Conference to exercise a League of Nations mandate over Iraq "*and* the vilayet of Mosul," joined with King Faisal's government in issuing a declaration which solemnly recognized the right of the Kurds of Iraq to form an autonomous Kurdish government within the frontiers of Iraq. This was the Anglo-Iraqi Joint Declaration which the mandatory authorities communicated to the Council of the League of Nations on December 24, 1922. Its authors hoped to obtain international confirmation of the contested *vilayet's* inclusion within the Iraqi frontiers, and thus to secure for the British the right to exploit the oil fields of Southern Kurdistan:

His Britannic Majesty's Government and the Government of Iraq recognize the right of the Kurds who live within the frontiers of Iraq to establish a Government within those frontiers. Our two Governments hope that the various Kurdish groups will reach some mutual agreement as quickly as possible as to the form they wish this Government to take and as to the boundaries within which they wish to extend its authority. These groups will send responsible delegates to negotiate their future economic and political relations with His Majesty's Government and the Iraqi Government.[18]

The December 24, 1922 Declaration gave little satisfaction to the province of Suleimanieh, which as we have seen had no desire to come under the authority of the King of Iraq and sought to pursue the struggle for a free and united Kurdistan.

As soon as the British released him from prison, Mahmoud Berezendji returned to his native Suleimanieh, again raised forces on both sides of the frontier with Iran, formed his second administration, proclaimed the establishment of a Kurdish state and, in order to stress his opposition to King Faisal, had himself declared "King of Kurdistan." This was in 1923. However, his movement eventually came round to accepting the December 1922 Declaration and recognizing that the Kurdish government should remain as an autonomous formation within the Iraqi framework.

The victory of the Kemalists forced the Allies to convene the Lausanne Conference (1922–23) so as to negotiate a new peace treaty with Turkey which was to replace the Treaty of Sèvres. Neither the Kurds nor the Armenians nor the Arabs attended this Conference. Kemalism had already accepted that the Arab countries were lost to it, but it wanted Mosul and claimed it from Britain, the mandate power. At the Conference, Ismet Inonu and Lord Curzon, as heads of the two countries' respective delegations, each claimed deep concern for the interests of the Kurds and presented this as an argument for their respective theses.

But the fate of Kurdistan was not the real bone of contention for either London or Ankara. However important or vital it might be to the Kurds, as far as these two powers were concerned, the whole affair was simply a dispute over the frontier between the Republic of Turkey and the Arab Kingdom of Iraq (represented by the British Colonial Office).

The Conference did not manage to resolve the conflict. It ended in the signature of the Treaty of Lausanne on July 24, 1923, which superseded the Treaty of Sèvres and officially established republican Turkey as a new power, in exchange for which Ankara accepted a few articles which insisted on respect for the linguistic and national rights of Turkey's non-Turkish minorities; not that these articles were ever applied of course. Article 3 note 2 of the Treaty stipulated that the Turkish-Iraqi frontier was to be fixed along "a line to be determined in conformity with the decision of the Council of the League of Nations."

From January to March 1925 an International Commission of Inquiry, sent by the Council of the League of Nations, visited the contested *vilayet* of Mosul. On July 16 the Commission presented its report in Geneva; it did not take sides but put forward various suggestions, leaving the Council to decide the issue.[19]

The report stated that the great majority of the population were Kurds and that they lived as a group apart from the Arabs. They were neither Arabs nor Turks; they spoke an Aryan language and their growing national consciousness was definitely Kurdish in orientation. The Commission's report added that, apart from a few literate Arabs in the town of Mosul, there was no sign of an Iraqi national consciousness in the *vilayet*. Relations between Arabs and Kurds "seemed shaky" to the Commission, which added that something should be done to guarantee some protection to the Assyro-Chaldeans. On the ethnic level, the Commission concluded, in one of its proffered suggestions, that:

> If one was to base oneself on ethnic arguments, one would have to conclude that the best solution would be to set up an independent Kurdist state, seeing as the Kurds account for five-eighths of the population. If such a solution was envisaged, one would be justified in augmenting this figure to include the Yezidis, who are in fact Zoroastrian Kurds, and the Turks, who would be easily assimilated into the Kurdish population. According to this estimate, Kurds would represent seven-eighths of the *vilayet's* population.

Nevertheless, in order to ensure Iraq's economic survival, the Commission finally suggested that the *vilayet* be attached to the Iraqi state, "given satisfaction of the following preconditions":

> 1) The country will remain under League of Nations mandate for a period of about 25 years.
> 2) The desire of the Kurds that the administrators, magistrates and teachers in their country be drawn from their own ranks, and adopt Kurdish as the official language in all their activities, will be taken into account.

The discussion of the report before the XXXVth session of the League of Nations Council in September 1925 in Geneva was marked by new bouts of oratorical jousting between the British and Turkish representatives. It is worth remembering that at the time the Turkish Army had just completed the bloody repression of a major Kurdish revolt led by Said of Piran whose aim had been to secure the independence of Northern Kurdistan; as for the British Army it had only recently quelled a second revolt, led by Mahmoud Berezendji, in Southern Kurdistan.

On December 16, 1925, during the XXXVIIth session, the Council of the League of Nations finally settled the conflict in favor of the British. The contested *vilayet* was attached to Iraq and the frontier between the two states was fixed. The following riders were added, however:

> 1) As the mandate power, the British Government is invited to present before the Council the administrative measures it will take to ensure that the Kurdish populations mentioned in the Commission of Inquiry's report enjoy the type of local administration recommended by the Commission in its conclusions.
> 2) The same Government is invited to present before the Council a new treaty with Iraq which will secure the extension of the mandate regime over 25 years or until Iraq is admitted to the League of Nations.

In the following year (1926) Baghdad issued the so-called Local Languages Law, which however was not enforced with any vigor. The Kurds of Iraq were allowed some Kurdish-language education, but only at the primary school level, and even this was restricted to Suleimanieh province and some districts of Arbil. Private publication of books in Kurdish was also allowed and Kurdish ministers participated in all the governments under the monarchy.

In June 1930, a new Anglo-Iraqi Treaty ended the British mandate and recognized the nominal independence of the Kingdom. The Kurds were not mentioned. The Suleimanieh region immediately rose up in protest, again under Mahmoud Berezendji, and the Barzan region followed suit in 1932 when Iraq was admitted to the League of Nations. Once again, the British Army was charged with re-establishing order in Kurdistan. The "rebels" sought to remind the League of Nations of its promises concerning an autonomous Kurdish administration,[20] but on January 28, 1932 the relevant Council committee declared that "discussion of the question of the autonomy of certain minorities in Iraq did not fall within its ambit."

On July 8, 1937, Turkey, Persia and Iraq signed the Saadabad Treaty. Article 7 of this document was aimed against "the formation and activity of associations, organizations, or armed bands seeking to overthrow established institutions," in other words it was aimed against the Kurdish movement.

In 1943, Mustafa Barzani rose up in Barzan and the revolt soon spread. The Iraqi Army was overrun and was forced to abandon vast areas of Arbil and Badinan. In 1945 Britain's RAF managed to force the Kurdish rebels to retreat into Iranian Kurdistan, where an autonomous democratic republic was set up in 1946 in Mahabad. A year later this small Kurdish republic collapsed. In June 1947, Barzani and his best troops forced their way through the lines of their numerically superior enemies, crossed the mountains of Northern Kurdistan and sought refuge in the Soviet Union. This "retreat of the Five Hundred" has passed into the annals of the Kurdish national movement. Barzani and his men were granted asylum in the Soviet Union. They were to stay there for eleven years.

The War of Liberation, 1961–1975

From 1961 to the 1970 Agreement

In the period following the Second World War, three main left-wing parties, all clandestine, can be distinguished amongst the forces opposing British influence and the Iraqi monarchy: the Iraqi Communist Party (ICP) made up of Arabs, Kurds and other minority elements; the Iraq-based Kurdish Democratic Party (KDP), composed entirely of Kurds; and the National Democratic Party led by M. Tchadertchi, which drew much support from the Arab intellectual left, mainly thanks to the personality of its president.[21]

Founded in 1946 on the same lines as the Iranian KDP, on the recommendation of Mustafa Barzani and his colleagues before their withdrawal to the Soviet Union, the Iraqi KDP was a "Marxist-Leninist inspired party," to quote its program. It recognized the existence of an oppressed and splintered Kurdish nation, and struggled for that nation's right to self-determination. But this was a distant goal. The immediate task for the Party was the democratization of Iraq, its liberation from imperialism and reaction. An autonomous Iraqi Kurdistan would emerge later, within the framework of an

Arab and Kurdish state. Apart from the issue of "Kurdish autonomy," the immediate goals of the KDP in Iraq did not differ very much from those of the Iraqi Communist Party (ICP) and the National Democratic Party (NDP). The ICP and the NDP both set out to become mass parties and succeeded in their aim. The ICP had an entirely Kurdish "Kurdistan section" and its leadership was ethnically mixed. Both parties drew their inspiration from Marxism-Leninism and the bulk of their recruits came from the same social classes. Both strove to build up their membership in Kurdistan. The ICP, with its entirely Kurdish "Kurdistan section" and its ethnically mixed leadership, easily emerged as the victor in this recruitment drive, at least till the fall of 1960.

The Iraqi Communist Party reproached the Kurdish Democratic Party for its "petty-bourgeois Kurdish nationalism," its attacks on Iraq's "Arab King," its demands concerning "Kurdish oil" and its refusal to participate in "the common struggle" of the opposition parties. The KDP, in turn, complained of the ICP's equivocal position on the national question and its refusal to admit the existence of the Kurdish nation. The situation remained unchanged till 1956, when the ICP's Second Congress passed the following important resolutions:

> Article 1: The territory inhabited by the Arab people of Iraq is an integral part of the Arab homeland. In its political unity, Iraq is an Arab state, both nationally and internationally, and is one of the main members of the family of Arab states.
> Article 2: Within its present frontiers, as established by Imperialism, Iraq includes part of Kurdistan.
> Article 3: Iraq is therefore made up of two main nations, the Arab nation and the Kurdish nation. The Kurdish people of Iraq are an integral part of the Kurdish nation, whose country, Kurdistan, is at present split up between Turkey, Iran and Iraq. The Kurdish nation has all the inherent characteristics of a nation; its people form a stable group with a common historical formation and territory, they have a common tongue and have the possibility of establishing a national economy geared towards liberation and national unity.

When Abdul Karim Qasim overthrew the monarchy and proclaimed the Republic on July 14, 1958, it was no mere coup d'etat. It was a revolution. The entire democratic opposition supported him, including the KDP. The provisional constitution he promulgated on July 27 re-established all democratic liberties and notably stipulated that:

> Iraqi society is based on complete co-operation between all its citizens, on respect for their rights and liberties. Arabs and Kurds are associates in this nation; the constitution guarantees their national rights within the Iraqi whole (Article 3).

For the first time a state which included part of Kurdistan had recognized the "national rights" of the Kurdish people in its constitution. Qasim legalized the KDP, welcomed Mustafa Barzani as a hero on his return from the USSR, and authorized the publication of 14 Kurdish journals, including *Khebat* (Struggle), the organ of the KDP, *Kurdistan*, another organ of the same party, *Jin* (Life), *Hetaw* (Sun) and *Azadi* (Liberty), the latter being the official organ of the Kurdish section of the ICP.

Unfortunately for the Arabs and the Kurds, this liberalism was short-lived. Qasim soon sought to strengthen his authority through military dictatorship. Concessions were revoked, and one by one the political parties were attacked. The ICP, which had never been legalized, was formally outlawed and was persecuted right from July 14, 1958. By 1960 it was the Kurds' turn to suffer this new repression. Gangs of feudalists were armed by the government and set against the family of the Kurdish leader in Barzan, as well as against the local branches of the KDP. Qasim had rejected Kurdish autonomy, for all that it figured in the program of his party. Ibrahim Ahmed, General Secretary of the KDP and editor of *Khebat*, was brought to trial charged with "inciting hatred between citizens" for having published a speech I delivered in Baghdad in October 1960 before the Congress of the International Union of Students.[22] Various other Party leaders were arrested or forced back underground. One by one the legal Kurdish journals were closed down. The climax came when *Thawra* (Revolution), an Arab journal edited by a close associate of Qasim, published a series of editorials calling for the outright assimilation of the Kurdish people.

Since Baghdad was no longer safe for him, General Mustafa Barzani, the President of the KDP, left the capital for Barzan, which was to be bombed on September 13, 1961. In fact all Kurdistan was subjected to a program of air bombardment initiated on September 9, 1961.

After the Second World War, with the Mahabad Republic, and now even more so with the Revolution in Iraqi Kurdistan, a democratic revolutionary phase had replaced the old traditionalist phase in the struggle of the Kurdish democratic movement.

There are several points to bear in mind when considering the 1961 Revolution.

1) It was a Kurdish movement whose national aims were actually quite moderate; it sought to secure the autonomy of Iraqi Kurdistan while remaining within the framework of the new republic.

2) Although it was a Kurdish movement, it nonetheless also remained an Iraqi one. Geographically, it concerned only Iraq; Turkish and Iranian Kurdistan were not implicated. It was also Iraqi in its goals, since its aim was to re-establish democracy in Iraq.

3) It had an "advanced social content," which was clearly in favor of the working classes of both Iraq as a whole and particularly of Kurdistan, as can be seen from the reforms proposed in the KDP's program.

4) It was a popular national movement which involved nearly all classes of Kurdish society, joined together under the political and military leadership of the KDP and its president.

5) The KDP gave the movement a solid political, military and administrative structure. The Revolution of 1961 started as a simple movement of self-defense but soon spread and organized. A Kurdish Revolutionary Army (KRA) grew out of it very quickly; numbering about 1,000 in September 1961, this force was 20,000 strong when Qasim fell from power and had reached 50,000 in 1975. The Revolution extended its control over ever larger areas. Between 1964 and 1975, 12,000–15,000 square miles of Kurdistan

were liberated and a special administration was set up. In 1964 a constitution and various laws were adopted, empowering a Revolutionary Command Council to establish an executive office, a civil administration, a judiciary, a fiscal system and an excise system. The executive office headed departments of national education, public health, justice, finance, foreign affairs, defense and national security, the latter of which incorporated an office of information known as *Parastin* in Kurdish.

General Qasim underestimated the Kurdish people's capacity to organize and resist. The war weakened him militarily and, perhaps even more so, politically. The Iraqi Communist Party, in particular, found itself in an embarrassing position. It had begun by supporting Qasim's stand against the rebellion and then gradually shifted its ground. In a long "Report of the Central Committee of the Iraqi Communist Party concerning the just solution of the Kurdish national question in Iraq," the ICP criticized Qasim "for having neglected the Kurdish question and denied the existence of Kurdistan." The Report also criticized "the Kurdish bourgeoisie which has placed its nationalist interests above common interests, thereby exposing its national cause to isolation and danger." The ICP admitted that "under existing conditions, the only valid solution is to make the Arab-Kurdish union truly democratic by setting up an autonomous government in Kurdistan which would operate within the overall unity of the Iraqi Republic."

The main beneficiary of the situation was that old enemy of both the Kurdish movement and the Communist Party, the Baath Party. On February 8, 1963, Baathist officers in the Iraqi Army eliminated Qasim and inaugurated a reign of terror: the first victims were some 7,000 communists. After a brief cease-fire with the Kurds, which lasted only as long as it took the new Baathist regime to re-arm with hastily ordered British weaponry, the government, led by two generals, President A.S. Aref and Prime Minister A.H. al-Bakr, launched a new offensive in Kurdistan on June 10, 1963. Three hundred civilians were massacred and buried in a mass grave in Suleimanieh. In Kirkuk, an Arabization program began with the expulsion of Kurds and the implantation of Arabs.

In an official communique published by Tass, the Soviet government declared that: "the USSR cannot but be interested in what is going on in Iraq today, since the Iraqi government's present policy towards the Kurds continues to undermine peace in the Middle East."[23]

Meanwhile the Iraqi Army was once again finding it impossible to crush the resistance of the Kurdish partisans, despite having been joined in Badinan by a Syrian expeditionary corps sent by the neighboring Baathist regime.

On November 18, 1963, the President of the Republic, Marshal Abdul Salam Aref, who was not actually a member of the Baath, dismissed his Baathist Prime Minister, General Ahmed Hassan al-Bakr, as well as the whole Baathist governing team. On February 10, Aref concluded a cease-fire with General Barzani. The Second Kurdistan War was over.

Barely two years later, on March 4, 1965, the war began again with a spring offensive launched by the Marshal-President. Not long afterwards, Aref died in a helicopter accident. His brother, General Abdul Rahman, succeeded him and continued the war in Kurdistan. Armed combat continued until June 15, 1966, culminating in an Iraqi debacle at the battle of Hendrin. Aref II then concluded a new cease-fire.

On July 17, 1968 the Baath took its revenge on the Aref family by staging a military putsch. The generals who led this so-called "July 17 Revolution" were presided over by General Ahmed Hassan al-Bakr, the Baathist Prime Minister dismissed in 1963; Saddam Husseiñ became the new Vice-President.

In April 1969 the new Baathist regime launched the fourth war in Kurdistan. The most bitter battles were fought in the Arbil plain. In the Kirkuk plain the Kurdish peasants were expelled from their lands or massacred.

While these struggles were taking place, General al-Bakr, anxious as ever to appear in the role of "father of the nation," made overtures to the left and sent an emissary, Aziz Sharif, to negotiate with General Barzani. These secret talks led eventually to the March 11, 1970 Agreement.

The March 11, 1970 Agreement and the "Period of Transition"

The March 11 Agreement was the direct result of the long struggle waged by the revolutionary forces of the Kurdish people. It was the outcome of laborious negotiations between the two belligerents. However, it was not presented to the Iraqi people as a joint declaration bearing two signatures but as a Revolutionary Command Council (RCC) communique concerning a change in policy by the Iraqi "regional directorate," in other words by the governing Baath Party. True, the preamble to this long communique did mention "the talks" between the RCC and the "President of the Kurdish Democratic Party, Mustafa Barzani," specifying that "the two parties have jointly agreed to the terms of the following communique and have decided to start putting it into practice."[24] However, to preserve appearances, it was left to the RCC to promulgate the 15 articles of the Agreement as such. The preamble also indicates that the seventh regional congress of the Baath Arab Socialist Party held in late 1968/early 1969 had adopted a number of new principles, in the light of which the RCC had:

— Recognized "the existence of the Kurdish nation."
— Created a university in the town of Suleimanieh, as well as a Kurdish academy of science.
— Recognized "the linguistic and cultural rights of the Kurdish nation."
— Set up a "general administrative framework" to develop Kurdish culture.
— Introduced Kurdish as the medium of instruction in "the schools, the institutes, the universities and teacher training colleges as well as in the police and military colleges."
— Authorized "Kurdish men of letters, poets and novelists to set up a union and have their works published."
— Decided to increase the number of Kurdish programs on television in Kirkuk by building a Kurdish language TV station in the town.
— Passed an edict calling for "the decentralization of local administration" and notably for the creation of a new "district" around Kirkuk.

— Decreed "a general amnesty for all civilians and soldiers who participated in violent action in the north."

Finally, we are told of the RCC's decision to work towards "a coordinated development of both Arab and Kurdish nationalism."

It was thus supposedly merely to "deepen and broaden existing measures" that the RCC and KDP adopted the 15 articles of the March 11 Agreement, the salient points of which are outlined below.

Article 1 recognizes the Kurdish language as well as Arabic as the official languages of the Region in which a majority of the population is Kurdish. Kurdish is to be "the language of schooling in these regions" and Arabic will be taught in all Kurdish schools. Correspondingly, "Kurdish will be taught as a second language in the rest of the country," namely Arab Iraq, "within the limits laid down by the law."

Article 2 stipulates that "our Kurdish brothers will participate in Government as equals, with no distinction between Kurd and non-Kurd" in any matter involving "nominations for public office, including ministerial office and military command."

Article 3 speaks of "helping the Kurdish nation make up the ground it has lost over the years in the field of education and culture" notably by implementing various concrete measures to promote teaching in Kurdish.

Article 4 envisages that "as far as possible" senior government posts such as prefects, police and security chiefs, etc., will be held by Kurds in the mainly Kurdish areas.

Article 5 is the Article in which the Iraqi government unambiguously "recognizes the Kurdish people's right to set up its own organizations for students, young people, women and teaching staffs, and that these organizations will be autonomous members of the corresponding Iraqi organizations."

Article 6 stipulates that all "employees, workers and officials, whether civil or military" having fought on the Kurdish side during the war "will be unconditionally reinstated in their jobs."

Article 7 envisages a "special commission" attached to the Ministry of Northern Affairs which will establish a plan to "promote every aspect of the Kurdish areas," notably their economic development, to compensate for the accumulated disadvantages of the area in such matters; a "special budget" will be allocated for the purpose.

Article 8 envisages "the return of Arab and Kurdish refugees to their place of origin," in other words that the Arabs implanted in Kurdistan by the government during the war would have to leave and make way for returning Kurds who had been expelled.

Article 9 deals with the extension of land reform to Kurdistan, including some redistribution of land to peasants.

Article 10 is crucial and reads as follows:

The Provisional Constitution will be amended in the following respects:
1) Two main nations, the Arab nation and the Kurdish nation, make up the Iraqi people. The Constitution recognizes the national rights of the Kurdish people and

of other minorities within the overall context of Iraqi unity.

2) The following paragraph will be added to Article 4 of the Constitution: "Kurdish and Arabic are the official languages in the Kurdish areas."

The above provisions will be inserted in the final draft of the Constitution.

Article 11 stipulates that the broadcasting station and "heavy weapons" deployed during the Kurdish revolution would be "handed back to the Government."

Article 12 lays down that "one of the Republic's Vice-Presidents will be a Kurd."

Article 13 envisages changes in the law on administrative boundaries in keeping with the spirit of the Agreement.

Article 14, which deals with Kurdish autonomy and Kurdistan's resources (notably the oil fields), stipulates that:

> Following the publication of this communique, appropriate measures will be taken, in collaboration with the relevant High Committee, to unify the mainly Kurdish districts and administrative units, as established by official statistics drawn up for the purpose.
>
> The Government will take steps to promote this administrative unity and will do what it can to ensure that the Kurdish people enjoy a growing degree of self-government, and hence internal autonomy. While the way is being paved for this administrative autonomy, the co-ordination of Kurdish national affairs will be assured by regular meetings between the High Committee and the Governors of the northern areas. Since internal autonomy will be exercised within the framework of the Iraqi Republic, the exploitation of the region's natural resources will proceed under the authority of the Republic.

Finally, Article 15 lays down that "the Kurdish people will participate in legislative authority in a measure proportionate to their number within the Iraqi population as a whole."

The signing of the March 11 Agreement was greeted by both sides as a historic event. A Kurdish delegation was officially invited to Baghdad to attend a broadcast on Iraqi television in which the President of the Republic and the RCC, General al-Bakr, declared that: "Our people, Kurds and Arabs, have regained their unity. Our fraternal relations are henceforth firmly based and will not be undermined." In an interview broadcast the same day General Barzani, who remained in Kurdistan, praised the "wisdom" of the Baathist leaders. His son Idris read out a telegram in which he assured President al-Bakr "of the support of the Kurdish people for the just struggle waged by the Arab nation against its enemies."

As evidence of goodwill, the Kurdish revolution abolished the administrative structures set up in 1964, notably its executive office and RCC, retaining only the organizational structure of the KDP, henceforth supposedly a partner of the Baath.

The Iraqi government was reshuffled to include five Kurdish Ministers, all sponsored by the KDP. Kurdish prefects and governors were appointed to administer the Kurdish districts. But the High Committee mentioned in Article 14, a bipartisan committee made up of Baath Party and KDP representatives and charged with supervising the implementation of the Agreement, soon ran into serious difficulties. Which territories should be included in this autonomous Kurdistan? What institutions and prerogatives would it be endowed with? What budgetary resources would be available to it? During the negotiations which led up to the March 11 Agreement, the two parties involved had settled two specific issues which were not mentioned in the RCC communique. The first point was that the period of transition should not extend for more than four years and that the autonomy of Kurdistan was to be proclaimed by March 11, 1974 at the latest. The second envisaged completion of a census of the population of Kirkuk by March 11, 1971, in order to determine the still undecided fate of the region. The Baath, however, constantly put off holding such a referendum, and in fact it never took place. Baghdad was all too conscious that most of the population of Kirkuk province was Kurdish.

On July 17, 1970 the Government proclaimed the new "provisional" Constitution (the fourth since 1958) but the amendment laid down in Article 10 of the Agreement was not included. The Article concerning the Kurds laid great stress on their duties but remained ambiguous as to their rights.

A major problem was the Baath's reluctance to share power. Article 15 of the Agreement envisaged the Kurdish people's "participation in legislative authority." But what legislative authority could they partake of? Ever since 1958, during the twelve years of the Republic's existence, there had been neither Parliament nor elections. One dictatorial regime had followed another, with self-appointed executives turning out "constitutions" and "laws" at will. According to the 1970 Constitution legislative authority was the prerogative of the RCC of the Baath Party.

In practice it turned out that the five Kurdish Ministers had no decision-making power at all; everything was settled in advance by the RCC. The new Minister for Northern Affairs (Baghdad's term for Kurdistan), Mohamed Abdul Rahman, a member of the KDP's Political Bureau, had to fight tooth and nail to obtain even partial implementation of Article 1 of the March 11 Agreement. In 1971 Kurdish was introduced as the language of instruction in the primary schools of certain predominantly Kurdish regions such as Kirkuk and Khanaqin, but not in the secondary schools. This concession was not extended to Dehok province not to the Kurdish districts of Nineveh (Mosul), not to mention those Kurds living in Baghdad. Furthermore, Kurdish did not become an official language, contrary to the stipulation of the article in question.

The Kurdish Democratic Party would probably have accepted all this and been content to hope that time would eventually bring change in the right direction. But it could not ignore the fact that the policy of Arabization was still in force throughout the transitional period, not only in Kirkuk but also in Khanaqin, in the Kurdish districts of Mosul (notably in Zamar, Sheikhan and Sindjar) as well as in areas of Arab Iraq settled by Kurds.

In late September 1971, there was a new development: the Iraqi government responded to Iran's occupation of a few small islands in the Persian Gulf by expelling some 50,000 "Iranian nationals," including 40,000 Kurds, mainly Faili Kurds who had been established in the capital or south of Khanaqin near the frontier for generations. They were forced to leave the country immediately, leaving all their possessions behind.

On February 9, 1973 an Iraqi army artillery unit opened fire on the village of Yostan in Sindjar. On February 26 particularly brutal house-to-house searches in the same area forced thousands of Yezidi Kurds to seek refuge in Upper Badinan, around Zakho. The exodus had begun. On March 6, Kurdish peasants from the village of Ghere in Kirkuk province were forced to cede their lands to an Arab tribe and expelled. On March 7 the same thing happened to the villagers of Qazan-Belagh, also in Kirkuk; on March 26, it was the turn of Dinatru, in the Aqra Plain. Villages in Sheikhan were next to suffer, on May 15 and 22. And on May 24, June 8 and 28, 1973, villages in the Khanaqin area were similarly struck. In February 1974 Kurdish workers and technicians employed in the Kirkuk oil industry were expelled and replaced by Arabs. Four hundred families had to leave.

Tension came to a peak following two attempts to assassinate General Barzani, both carried out by the Iraqi Security Services. Efforts were also made to split the KDP and to break its alliance with the Iraqi Communist Party.

The first attempt to assassinate the Kurdish leader took place on September 29, 1971, while he was receiving a delegation of *ulemas* (Muslim religious leaders) sent by Baghdad to his home in the Shuman Valley, near the Hamilton Road. The second occurred on July 1, 1972 and was certainly the work of Nazim Khazzar, the Chief of the Iraqi Security Services.

On November 15, 1971 General al-Bakr and the RCC invited the other political parties to form a Progressive National Front led by the Baath Party. In response, the KDP set the precondition that the future political partners in such a front would also be political equals. Free general elections, a parliamentary system and a definitive Constitution would also be necessary.[25]

In his November 15 speech, al-Bakr had proposed the setting up of a National Council, with 100 members "nominated by the RCC," some on the recommendation of the Baath's future partners.

A few days later Mustafa Barzani rejected the proposal. He reaffirmed "the immutably Kurdish character" of the Kirkuk and accused "the handful of men who govern Baghdad" of working towards the Arabization of this province. Barzani also protested against "the abuse of power" and "the tortures inflicted on Iraqi Communists." "My door is open to all who seek refuge," he added.[26]

This reference to the right of asylum in fact concerned the Communists. Since 1963, Iraqi Communist Party (ICP) leaders and many of its cadres had not only sought refuge in Kurdistan but had also been authorized by Mustafa Barzani to form some fighting units as an integral part of the KRA, the Peshmerga Army. These units, made up of both Arab and Kurdish Communists, had been more or less autonomous although under the overall authority of the Kurdish High Command. They fought alongside the regular Kurdish

Revolutionary Army (KRA) forces right up to the March 11 1970 Agreement. But when the Baath invited the ICP to join the Progressive National Front, the ICP accepted.

As a result, there were difficulties in 1972 between the KDP and the ICP. On July 17, 1973, the anniversary of the Baathist "Revolution," the Progressive National Front was formed. In its ranks, under the officially proclaimed political supremacy of the Baath, it included the "Central Committee" fraction of the ICP and one dissident representative of the KDP, Aziz Akrawi, who became a Minister of State. The ICP was also rewarded, first with one ministerial post, then with a second, neither of which carried any decision-making power. One should note that the ICP had split beforehand into two rival parties: a Moscow-aligned majority, namely the "Central Committee" tendency allied to the Baath, and a pro-Chinese tendency, the "Central Leadership" which still remained alongside the KDP.

This sudden change of tack was not due to the Kurdish leadership's links with Tehran (not that this is any reason not to be critical of KDP policy in this respect). The ICP was well aware of the existence of such links before, when its units were fighting side by side with the KDP in Kurdistan. ICP militants of both tendencies who were seriously wounded during the war were evacuated to Iran and treated in the hospitals of Tehran in the same way as their KDP comrades.

On April 9, 1972 the USSR and Iraq concluded a "friendship and cooperation treaty." In November 1973 units of the ICP Central Committee still posted in that part of Kurdistan held by the KRA, notably in the Derbandi-Khan area, took up arms against the (Kurdish) *Peshmergas* who had until then been their comrades. Naturally there are two differing accounts of what happened; the KDP explains that the blame lies with the ICP Central Committee which had been receiving Iraqi government military aid just before the "aggression," whilst the ICP claims it was "provoked and attacked."

From December 1973 to February 1974, after the KDP *Peshmerga* units had managed to expel the ICP Central Committee forces from Derbandi-Khan, sometimes even forcing them to seek refuge in Iraqi Army bases, Communist Parties throughout the world launched a vast international campaign accusing the KDP of "oppressing the Communists in Kurdistan."[27]

During the period of transition, the Baath proved to be an untrustworthy interlocutor for the Kurdish movement, whilst the ICP Central Committee was seen to submit to pressure and turn against its erstwhile ally. And sad to tell, the arms that Baghdad were receiving came from the Soviet Union. Under such conditions, when war seemed imminent, Barzani had little choice but to re-establish his links with Tehran. Was the Kurdish movement too hasty and too violent in its rejection of the offer to participate in the Progressive National Front led by the Baath? That may be. But did the Arabization program which was well under way leave it any other option?

Discrimination and Economic Exploitation in Kurdistan

Behind the Baath's progressive phraseology there lurks a policy of discrimination and economic exploitation directed against the Kurdish people.

Two KDP documents make the point and provide specific examples. The first, *On the Kurdish Question at the United Nations*, was submitted to the UN Secretary-General on June 6, 1974. The second, a little pamphlet entitled *A Paper on the Kurdish Problem in Iraq*, was presented during a UN-sponsored seminar on minority rights held in Ohrid (Yugoslavia) from June 25 to July 8, 1974.[28]

Political discrimination was reinforced by the "policy of terror" aimed at Kurdish citizens during the transition period, as is illustrated by the 35 cases of Iraqi Army attacks on the civilian population, from June 9, 1963 to May 8, 1974, mentioned in the first of these documents. For instance, on August 19, 1969 a unit of the Iraqi Army occupied the village of Dakan in the Sheikhan district some 25 miles north of Mosul; the villagers, 67 people in all, sought refuge in a cave. All the men of an age to fight had already left to join the Peshmerga; only women, children and old men remained. The soldiers gathered wood and lit a big fire at the entrance to the cave. There were no survivors. In September 1969 the village of Sorya, in the Zakho district of Badinan, was surrounded by tanks and completely flattened. The villagers, Kurdish Chaldean Christians, were all killed, no doubt to intimidate and exact revenge upon the Christians of Kurdistan who had participated in the revolution just as much as their Muslim or Yezidi compatriots.

Discrimination in education was rampant. On September 13, 1971, Arbil, the richest of the Kurdish provinces, had only 70 schoolchildren per 1,000 inhabitants, while the Arab province of Basra had 120 per 1,000. The proportion of students from Kurdistan in Iraq's various universities, including the one at Suleimanieh, was only 6.4% of the total in 1970–71 and 6.1% in 1971–72. Between March 11 and December 31, 1970, more than 110 schools — all of which were in any case teaching in Arabic — were closed in Dehok province and in the Kurdish districts of Nineveh province. Not long after Kurdish schools had been started up in Khanaqin, in 1971, the administration exercised such pressure on the parents of pupils that they intimidated them into taking 400 of their children out of Kurdish schools and putting them into Arabic-language schools. Only 3 to 4% of student grants went to Kurdish students. Kurdish students represented less than 2% of the intake at the Military Academy and Police College where Army officers and the Police Force are trained; Kurdish officers were no longer admitted to the Staff College. The same went for the Air Force Training School; not surprisingly, since Kurdish villages and towns were the Iraqi pilots' main target.

Discrimination was prevalent in the civil administration. Out of 500 high-ranking Iraqi diplomats attached to the Ministry of Foreign Affairs, including 80 ambassadors, only ten were Kurdish, one of whom held ambassadorial rank.

Discrimination was also exercised in the acquisition of Iraqi citizenship.

Thousands of Kurds whose families had been established in Iraq for generations were refused Iraqi citizenship.

Iraqi Law No. 36, promulgated in 1961 and later reinforced, states that nationals of other Arab countries who have settled in Iraq are not to be considered as "foreigners" — even Moroccans from the other side of the Arab world. Yet such privileges were not extended to Kurds from Iranian, Syrian or Turkish Kurdistan, areas lying on Iraq's very frontiers. An RCC decree issued in February 1974 debars any Iraqi student married to a foreigner from holding any job in the public sector, unless of course the spouse in question is of Arab origin; no such exception is made for spouses of Kurdish origin.

Finally, we have economic exploitation. During the four years of the transition period, the Kurdish areas received only 7 to 12% of the Iraqi development budget. Out of 150 industrial projects, only 4 were planned for Kurdistan. The steel-making projects were all to be situated in Arab Iraq, even though the iron ore deposits were all in Kurdistan. The oil refinery promised for Kirkuk in 1970 was eventually built at Hamman al-Alil in Arab Iraq, despite the 20% increase in costs involved. As for road building, it is quite clear that the Kurdish towns were being systematically disadvantaged. For instance, the planned new road between Kirkuk and Mosul bypassed Arbil. No doubt it was conceived as an avenue for Arabization, rather like the irrigation projects in Kirkuk which were geared to irrigate the plains lying to the south-east of the town where it was intended to implant Arab population as a priority.[29]

Tobacco was also a problem for the Kurdish peasantry. It is grown on a large scale in Kurdistan, particularly around Suleimanieh, and nowhere else in Iraq. The government monopoly is used to impose draconian restrictions on the Kurdish tobacco growers, in terms of both the acreage they are allowed to sow and the price they can get for their produce. The Kurds only consume about 15% of the tobacco grown in their country; most of the rest is smoked in Arab Iraq although some is profitably exported to Kuwait and Saudi Arabia by the state. Would it not be sensible to make adjustments, establish a better internal equilibrium and reduce the disastrous effects of internal colonialism? The KDP had good reasons for demanding a just solution to the tobacco problem in its 1970 program, which also called for the protection of Kurdistan's forests.

In 1964 the Iraqi government passed Law No. 80 which extended its control over those oil fields not yet being exploited by foreign companies such as Iraqi Petroleum. The Iraqi National Oil Corporation was set up the same year, but this body's scope for activity was restricted by an agreement signed with ERAP and only came into its own later, under the Baathist regime. On June 1, 1972 the Baath government issued a decree nationalizing the foreign oil companies, but still controlled only 65% of production as the companies refused to submit to the nationalization. On March 1, 1973 the companies finally accepted the Iraqi arguments. During the October 1973 Arab-Israeli war, the government nationalized those parts of the industry still held by the Gulbenkian group, Holland and the U.S., thereby achieving an 85% control of production.

The Baath ran its campaign under the slogan "Arab oil for the Arabs," with no indication that much of the oil in question was actually Kurdish. Nonetheless, the nationalizations were entirely justified, and perhaps more importantly, they were successful. But it is worth asking how much of the resulting oil revenue was provided by Kurdish oil fields and how this revenue was used. The Kurdish oil fields are at Kirkuk (the most important in Iraq), Khanaqin, and Ain-Zaleh, the last two being situated north-west of Mosul between Sindjar and the Sheikhan. They are linked to the Mediterranean by three pipelines running across Syria to the port of Banias and to Tripoli in Lebanon. Three further pipelines link the Rumaila and Zubair oil fields situated near Basra in Arab Iraq to the Persian Gulf port of al-Fao.

In 1961, the total through-put of the pipelines linking the Kurdistan oil fields to the Mediterranean reached "over 40 million tons a year"; in comparison, the through-put from the pipelines linking the oil fields of Arab Iraq to al-Fao was only about "10 million tons of crude per annum," although they had been designed "with a higher level of production in mind."[30] In other words, Kurdistan contributed 80% of Iraqi oil production for that year. Total royalties amounted to $200 million, represented 67% of state revenue and 90% of total exports (92% in 1956 and 88% in 1957). Kurdistan's oil fields, therefore, provided the Iraqi state with an annual income of $150 million, 53.6% of its total income and 72% of its total exports.

Between 1969 and 1974 increases in oil revenue nearly tripled the Iraqi national income, as can be seen from the figures presented in the "Political Report adopted by the Eighth Regional Congress of the Arab Socialist Baath-Iraq Party" in January 1974. The Report indicates that Iraqi national income more than doubled between 1972 and 1974, going from 1,218 million dinars to an (estimated) 2,550 million. This jump was of course due to the increase in oil revenue as the price of crude went up from $2.8 a barrel to $11.25 or $12 (depending on the country).[31]

Generally speaking, less than 30% of Iraqi oil revenue is allocated to the regular state budget. The Baath tells us that the remainder goes to meet the Government's public sector expenses and investment programs; what they do not say is that it also pays for armaments purchases.

With Iraq's 1975 price for crude at $11.25 a barrel, the country's oil revenue can be estimated at around 2,834 million dinars or $9,571 million. According to the *Financial Times*,[32] the Kirkuk oil fields alone accounted for 70% of Iraqi oil production, which, added to the 5% accounted for by the Ain-Zaleh and Khanaqin fields, gives us a figure of 75% for Kurdistan's contribution, a little less than in previous decades, no doubt because of expanding production from the Basra fields. By extrapolation, export of Kurdistan's oil earned the Iraqi Treasury more than $5,762 million in 1974 and $7,178 million in 1975.

Iraq's per capita and per annum GNP naturally leaped upwards following the quadrupling of the price of oil. Per capita GNP reached $970 in Iraq in 1974.[33] Development plans were put into operation, but all the benefit went to Arab Iraq. The years 1974 to 1975 brought only war and ruin to Kurdistan. There can be no doubt that the considerable increase in oil revenues, most of which were provided by Kurdish areas, was a key factor in the Iraqi government's decision to launch the fifth war in Kurdistan.

The Project for an Autonomous Kurdistan Collapses

Despite the extremely tense situation, the KDP constantly sought to reach a negotiated agreement with the Baath concerning Kurdish autonomy as projected in the March 11, 1970 Agreement. On January 17, 1974, a KDP delegation opened negotiations with the government. Major differences emerged immediately on a variety of key points including the territorial and institutional definition of the region's projected autonomy, the referendum, the future of the Arabization policy in Kirkuk, and the share of state revenue, notably oil revenue, due to autonomous Kurdistan.

Negotiations first came to a halt and were then called off by the Baath. On February 22 another KDP delegation set out for Baghdad hoping to re-open negotiations but the government refused to receive it. On March 3, the Progressive National Front announced that the government would pro-mulgate its own law on autonomy, without consulting the KDP, contrary to the stipulations of the 1970 Agreement. On March 8, 1974, in a last effort to prevent war, General Barzani's son Idris was received by Saddam Hussein in Baghdad where he proposed that the government put off unilateral promulgation of its law and extend the transitional period for a year, till March 11, 1975; even the *status quo*, however unstable, was preferable to war. On March 11, 1974, however, the Baath's RCC went ahead and issued its "law on the autonomy of Kurdistan."[34]

The following day, the Political Bureau of the KDP published a declara-tion entitled "The KDP's Case for Autonomy in Kurdistan,"[35] revealing the secrets of the negotiations, especially the positions adopted by the respective parties on the major issues of disagreement.

The most important obstacles in the negotiations concerned the territorial delimitation of the "Autonomous Region," the fate of the Kirkuk and the Arabization policy. Article 1 of the law stated:

A. The area of Kurdistan enjoys autonomy. In the present law it is referred to as "the Region."
B. The area only extends over those sectors with a majority Kurdish population. The general census will establish the area's frontiers, as laid down in the March 11 Agreement. The 1957 census figures will be used as a basis to determine the majority Kurdish regions in which the new census will be held.
C. The area forms a single administrative entity with its own civic responsibilities, existing autonomously within the framework of the legislative, political and econom-ic entity which forms the Iraqi Republic. The administrative divisions within the area will be established in keeping with the law on Governorships and within the stipulations of this present law.
D. The area is an integral part of Iraqi territory. Its people form an integral part of the Iraqi people.
E. The town of Arbil is the administrative center of the autonomous regime.
F. The autonomous regime's institutions are part of the Iraqi Republic's institu-tions.

The whole point of Article 14 of the March 11 Agreement between the KDP and the Baath was to set up a population census which would determine the territorial extent of the autonomous area. There would then be some real basis on which to fix the area's frontier. But on March 11, 1974, the Baath decided to delimit "Autonomous" Kurdistan according to figures of their own choosing. This was quite contrary to Article 3 in the secret provisions of the March 11 Agreement, which stipulated that the census was to take place by March 11, 1971 at latest. The KDP had also proposed that the census be subject to the following conditions, to ensure its validity:

a) Measures should be taken to enable all those Kurds who had been displaced or expelled since 1961 to return to their homeland and be counted amongst its inhabitants.

b) The census figures should not be framed in terms of the administrative units set up by the government following the March 11 Agreement since these units had artificially carved up the area and reduced the Kurdish territories.

c) The "changes" in the ethnic composition of the population resulting from "the racist policy of Arabization" should be annulled.

d) The KDP and the Baath should co-operate to set up a "joint administration" to govern Kirkuk and the contested regions, Nineveh and Diyala; the resulting peaceful climate would be conducive to the smooth operation of the census.

e) The conditions under which the 1957 Census was carried out should be open to examination, as should the circumstances under which people from other parts of Iraq were implanted in Kurdistan.

f) Finally, the new census should be conducted under joint KDP and government control.

The government accepted, in principle, the idea of a joint administration for Kirkuk, Khanaqin and Sindjar. But then it put off the census indefinitely and did nothing to set up the joint administration in the contested areas. In the meantime, it continued to pursue discriminatory policies "towards Kurdish and Turkoman citizens" in Kirkuk. During the January 1974 negotiations, it had clearly manifested its intentions: at most it would "cede" two of the six districts in Kirkuk province, namely Chemchemal and Kalar which lie alongside Suleimanieh province. The government evinced no willingness to change the status of the Kurdish districts in Nineveh and Diyala provinces.

The Baath thus determined the area's territorial extent quite arbitrarily; only Suleimanieh, Arbil and Dehok provinces were to be included, a total of 14,454 square miles, which was a mere half of Kurdistan in Iraq's 29,000 square miles.

During the negotiations, the KDP insisted that the "Autonomous Region" receive a share of "the general state budget and the national development plan budget" — and hence of oil revenues — proportionate to the percentage of the total Iraqi population represented by the Region's inhabitants. In this very moderate demand, the KDP even agreed that Kurdistan's share of budget revenue be calculated after deductions had been made for national defense and public sector projects of national importance.

The government made no response to these proposals and sought to retain complete control over the sums which would be allocated to the Region's budget.

Another area of disagreement was the whole issue of judicial control over administrative decisions and the constitutionality of laws. The Baath wanted to subject the validity of the autonomous authority's decisions to control by the Court of Appeal, whose president and members are all nominated by the government. The KDP proposed that this control be exercised by a special judicial body presided over by the president of the Court of Appeal but made up half of members designated by the President of Kurdistan's legislative assembly and half by the President of the Iraqi legislature.

The Baath rejected any proposition aimed at ensuring that the people of Kurdistan would be fairly represented in a genuine legislative body. The KDP held that an Iraqi National Assembly should be freely elected within six months of March 11, 1974 and that this body should then exercise full legislative power in the name of all the citizens of the Republic. This was seen as a necessary precondition to bringing the "period of transition" to an end. The government only agreed to set up an Iraqi Assembly with very limited powers which would remain subordinate to the Baath's RCC.

The government refused to allow the regional authority any rights of supervision over the police and security forces in the area. Judgements about nationalization, legal structures and the keeping of municipal records were also to be placed beyond their competence.

The regional executive was also to be denied the relevant powers concerning irrigation and industrialization projects in Kurdistan.

Out of the 80 members of the so-called "Legislative Assembly" for the Autonomous Region, 72 were actually appointed by the President of the Iraqi Republic.[36] Hashem Akrawi, a dissident KDP member who was Minister for Local Government at the time, was chosen as the President of the Executive Council. The man selected to be President of the Kurdish Legislative Assembly was Babakr Agha Peshderi, a traditional chieftain who had never played any role in the national movement. A third Kurd, Taha M. Maaruf, an independent ex-diplomat, was appointed Vice-President of the Iraqi Republic.

On October 5, 1974, this Parliament which supposedly represented the Kurdish people, held its first session in Arbil, the Region's capital. General al-Bakr, president of both the executive and legislative branches of the Iraqi government and General Secretary of the (Iraqi) regional leadership of the "leading party of the revolution," the Baath, sent Taha M. Maaruf as his representative. By then, in any case, the fifth Kurdistan war had been underway for several months. Kurdish and Iraqi forces had clashed repeatedly. During the last phase of the negotiations between the KDP and the government, the latter, having clearly decided to continue the war come what may, and whatever the attitude of its opponent, created a new Iraqi Army division (the Eighth) to be stationed in Arbil. In February 1974, General Taha al-Shakartchi, a man famous for the atrocities he committed during the 1963 campaign in Kurdistan, was appointed as commander of this division.

Then came the mass firings of Kurdish workers and technicians in the oil industry. Four hundred families were expelled. On February 8, 1974, the inhabitants of 15 Kurdish villages in the environs of the town of Kirkuk were forcibly evacuated. On February 21, the same fate befell the Kurdish inhabitants of Kifri, a Kurdish and Turkoman town in Kirkuk province. Their homes were bulldozed by the Army. *Brayeti* (Fraternity), a Kurdish daily, was closed down by the authorities and then, on February 24, the RCC's Edict No. 176 banned all political organizations not aligned with the "Progressive National Front." The main target of this decision was the KDP, but it was also aimed at the ICP (central leadership faction) and the left wing of the Iraqi Baath, which had sought refuge in Damascus.

On March 11 the government gave Mustafa Barzani 15 days to accept Decree No. 33. The ultimatum was rejected and the Kurdish radio announced that "the struggle will only cease when the national rights of the Kurdish people have been fully guaranteed." Battle proper was not engaged immediately however, as the Iraqi Army had not completed its campaign preparations. Between March 11 and 15, nearly 100,000 patriotic Kurds, mostly from the towns the Baathist Army had taken or was threatening to occupy, left their homes and jobs and went to swell the population of Free Kurdistan, which already numbered some 1.5 million people. Most of them had taken no part in the previous four wars. A strong contingent amongst the new arrivals represented the nation's intellectual and scientific elite, which put its knowledge at the disposal of the resistance forces. On March 11, five Kurdish ministers resigned from the Iraqi Cabinet and sought out the headquarters of the KDP in the Shuman Valley.[37] The fifth Kurdistan war had begun.

The Fifth Kurdistan War

Throughout the war, the regime never lost sight of its Arabization project. The outlying regions of Free Badinan, such as Sheikhan, were particularly heavily bombed. Other methods were used in Zammar, in the Kirkuk Plain and in Sindjar. Police brutality and military violence forced tens of thousands of villagers and townspeople to take to the open road. The exodus flowed mainly into Upper Badinan, near Amadiya, and into the Shuman Valley, which was soon so overpopulated that the Kurdish General Staff was forced to evacuate part of this ever-growing mass of people into Iranian territory, with the assistance of the Iranian Red Crescent — the Lion and the Sun Society. This was the beginning of the Kurdish refugee problem in Iran.

At our request a delegation from the International Federation for Human Rights visited the Shuman Valley from October 31 to November 11, 1974. The delegation, made up of a French author, Dominique Eudes, and two French lawyers, Patrick Baudoiun and Thierry Mignon, arrived via Hadji-Omran, where the Hamilton Route meets the Iranian frontier.

Their report stated that:

Signs of war are noticeable as soon as you cross the frontier. The very pass which marks the frontier is the site of a camp holding 25,000 people. Even the most elementary facilities are lacking. The people huddle here and there on either side of the road, with no shelter except their scanty baggage and a few blankets. They are lucky that they only have to face rain, cold and wind; at this time of year it could already be snowing. These unfortunate civilians, who for the most part come from the villages and towns of Badinan in the north of the country, sometimes have to wait over a month for the chance to ride in one of the seven trucks which arrive each day to take them to the Iranian Red Crescent and Lion camps in Iran. Just next to the camp a newly-dug cemetery grows larger day by day. Ten to thirty people are buried there every morning, mainly children and old people who have succumbed to malnutrition, cold and exhaustion.

The exodus was accelerated by the economic blockade Saddam Hussein imposed on Free Kurdistan. We also invited representatives from the humanitarian medical organization "Médecins sans frontières." The three French doctors, who stayed from September 13 to October 2, 1974, Jacques Beres, Bernard Kouchner and Max Recamier, traveled through the Shuman Valley and also in the south, near Dargala and Ranaga, not far from the Betwata Front. They noted that:

There are no facilities for hygiene, no permanent structures, no tents and no sanitation. Whole families wait . . . in this completely temporary setting, with only their baggage and some blankets. Where have these refugees come from? Apparently from Kalat-Diza and other southern regions, as well as from Badinan to the east, which have all been intermittently bombed. Many of the refugees are reluctant to leave Iraqi territory and have done what little they can to set up camp in villages in the valley or in market squares; some supplies are getting through to them thanks to the road but the settlements themselves are often bombed. Here and there cob houses are being built and there are attempts to set up tent villages.

Tuberculosis, typhoid, measles, meningitis, anthrax and chronic lung diseases are all prevalent and aggravated by anemia and malnutrition.

The many disease victims in the civilian population are receiving more and probably more efficient health care than the wounded, whether civilian or military; this is because there are practically no significant surgical facilities within Kurdistan. An operating theater is being built but it is ill-equipped. People with wounds requiring surgery, who have sometimes traveled twelve hours by jeep or mule to get there, often have to be taken in the only ambulance to the Piranshan and Rezaiyeh hospitals . . . Those with head, chest or stomach wounds have little chance of arriving alive.

From 145,000 in the fall of 1974, the number of Kurdish civilians seeking refuge in Iranian territory rose to between 250,000 and 300,000 before the end of the war in March 1975. Baghdad committed practically all its forces to the front: eight Army divisions (about 120,000 men) with 700–800 of the Iraqi Army's 900 tanks and some 20 battalions of mobile artillery; also the entire air force (11,000 men), equipped with several hundred planes including modern Tupolev-22 and Mig-23 bombers. One should also mention the 20,000 strong police force.

Facing this array of military might were some 50,000 *Peshmergas* and a popular militia of several thousand men whose role was not to clash with the Baghdad forces but to make life more bearable for the citizens and to watch over the territory's security. Despite the gross imbalance in military power, notably in armaments, the *Peshmerga* Army rarely had to give ground, thanks to the nature of the terrain and the level of popular support.

In August 1974, during the dry season, the Iraqi Army's armored divisions reached the foothills and began to penetrate the mountains. One brigade even managed to take Rawanduz, a town protected by the deep gorges of Spilik and Gali-Ali-Beg and surrounded by mountain peaks, including the rocky and practically unconquerable Korak. The town's Kurdish brigades replied with a similar feat of arms as soon as they could get hold of anti-tank guns and some long-range artillery. Rawanduz was taken and re-taken several times, and in the process was entirely destroyed.

Baghdad tried to cut Badinan off from the rest of Kurdistan by heading north of the Hamilton Route. The attempt did not succeed but — just in case — a parallel route was cut through the mountains, between the threatened areas and the Galala peaks. In Badinan the civilian exodus continued as the shortage of food reached alarming proportions. From the Syrian to the Iranian frontier on foot is a two-week journey; many children and old people died on the snow-covered roads.

Meanwhile the *Peshmerga* forces fought desperately but in vain to hold the enemy back from Mosul, Arbil, Khanaqin and the Kirkuk Plain.

The fifth Kurdistan war came to an end following some international horsetrading at the expense of the Kurdish people, which showed that the Kurdish High Command had made a fundamental and very serious mistake.

It was the most violent and bloody of the five wars. According to an Iraqi High Command communique, government forces lost 1,640 men, including 66 officers; 7,903 were wounded, including 88 officers.[38] As for the Kurdish casualties, they are difficult to estimate, since the civilian population was one of the main targets—not to mention the many victims of the winter exodus to Iran.

The Algiers Agreement and the Reasons for the Disaster

I cannot hide the unease and outrage I feel when I consider the circumstances which led to the Kurdish people being dragged into this war. Unease at the way it ended and at the autonomous movement's strategy and choice of external alliances; outrage at what Baghdad has been doing in Kurdistan since its victory.

From 1970 to 1975 the Iraqi Baath chose different accomplices and foreign allies to achieve its ends in the light of the changing political situation. Saddam Hussein only launched the offensive once he was assured of the co-operation of the Iraqi Communist Party Central Committee and of substantial Soviet military aid. He brought the war to a close by bringing in the Shah's Iran, Kissinger's United States and President Boumedienne of Algeria.

The first major Baathist victory in this game of diplomatic chess was the signing of the Treaty of Friendship and Co-operation between Iraq and the Soviet Union on April 9, 1972. The USSR promised Iraq weapons and experts in exchange for the use of Iraqi ports by its navy.

From Moscow's point of view, the 1972 Treaty was *not* a declaration of principle against the Kurdish movement. The Soviet leaders, who had until then shown considerable understading of the Kurdish people's struggle, believed the Treaty was justifiable not just in terms of immediate self-interest but also because of Baghdad's continuing struggle against the giant oil companies.

Furthermore, they also hoped to bring about a reconciliation between the Baath and the KDP. Moscow was not unaware of the facilities which the Shah had granted the KDP, and then withdrawn following the March 11, 1970 Agreement. The Soviets were well informed about the situation and regularly briefed by the Kurds concerning the difficulties they were having with the Baath. Apart from the usual diplomatic channels, Kurdish grievances were also expressed at the party level, notably in 1970 when the Soviet Union was celebrating Lenin's birth, then in 1971 when a KDP delegation attended a CPSU Congress, in 1972 when Kosygin visited Baghdad and finally in August the same year, this time in Moscow at the Soviet's own request.

Nevertheless, the Treaty was concluded with a partner who had already launched the peacetime deportations in Kurdistan, a policy which *Izvestia* had described as "Hitlerian" in 1963. Once the Treaty was signed, the Soviets no longer had any leverage with which to force the Baath to give up this policy, nor of course to persuade its victims to accept it. By arming the authors of this policy to the teeth and effectively granting them a "certificate of progressive good conduct" in the eyes of the world, the Soviet Union left the Kurdish movement with its back to the wall. The Kurds were thus forced to accept the Shah's offer of military aid and the concomitant unnatural alliance.

Following the signing of the Iraqi-Soviet Treaty, the Soviet leaders invited General Barzani to Moscow. Although he himself could not leave Kurdistan, he sent a KDP delegation to meet Suslov, a member of the Soviet politburo, in late August 1972, and later Ulianovsky, the man in charge of the Soviet Party's relations with popular liberation movements, in early September. The Kurdish delegation outlined its grievances and called on the Soviet Union to use its influence with the Iraqi government to persuade it to open negotiations. Suslov answered with generalities, evoking the difficulties involved in settling frontier conflicts between nationalities. In late 1972, when Ponomarev visited Baghdad, Moscow's attention was once again drawn to the Kurdish grievances, again with no effect. Meanwhile, Soviet arms had reached Iraq. It was then that Barzani accepted the alliance with the Shah.

How did it happen? We are reduced to drawing on revelations in the U.S.[39] and world press,[40] which are themselves based on the Pike Report to the U.S. House of Representatives on the clandestine activities of the CIA. Dated January 19, 1976, the Pike Report was published, and then only in an edited version,[41] on February 16, but leaks had enabled the *New York Times* to print various details before hand. The Report and the three articles mentioned above provide the basis for our estimate as to what actually took place.

Mustafa Barzani and his colleagues were thus forced to accept the Shah's offer of military aid, but by no means trusted him. Fearing that he would abandon them once the war was under way, they demanded guarantees. This

was in 1972, after the signing of the Soviet-Iraqi Treaty. When President
Nixon came to visit the Shah in Tehran on May 30, 1972, following a
summit conference with Brezhnev in Moscow, the Shah raised the problem.
He asked the U.S. president to "help him help the Kurds make life difficult
for his Iraqi neighbor and enemy."[42] According to the Pike Report: "The
Kurdish leader expressed his lack of faith in the Shah, as opposed to his
confidence in the word of the United States."[43] At first, the U.S. "had no
wish to get involved, even indirectly, in operations which might prolong the
insurrection and thereby encourage separatist aspirations, perhaps even provide the Soviet Union with an opportunity to make trouble (for our
allies)."[44] Meanwhile, at a U.S. government meeting held under conditions
of almost unprecedented secrecy, John B. Connally, ex-U.S. Secretary for the
Treasury, who had played a major role in the campaign to re-elect the
president, personally urged Nixon to accept the project.[45] The U.S. aid
program to the Kurds, "which would ultimately involve total aid of $16
million," was finally approved by the president "following a private meeting
between the Shah and Kissinger."[46] The CIA was entrusted with carrying out
the program, and the State Department was not brought in on the secret.
Barzani, too, was unaware of what was going on. As far as he was concerned,
he was dealing with the U.S. president and his secretary of state.

Of course the Shah, whose coffers were soon to overflow with dollars
thanks to the oil price increase in the fall of 1973, was hardly desperate for
the $16 million profferred by Nixon and Kissinger; nonetheless the gesture
was helpful in overcoming the old Kurdish leader's suspicions. The Pike
Report is quite explicit: "It is clear that the project was originally conceived as
a favor to our ally (the Shah) who had co-operated with the United States
secret services and felt threatened by his neighbors." The Report goes on to
say that: "The Shah's own aid could not but make ours seem insignificant by
comparison. Our contribution must thus be considered as largely symbolic.
Indeed, documents presented before the commission of inquiry indicate that
the U.S. acted only as a guarantor that the insurgents would not be abandoned by the Shah."

Nonetheless the whole operation was also American — that is to say,
Nixonian — right from the start. The Pike Report stresses that: "Neither the
foreign head of state (the Shah) nor the president and Dr. Kissinger desired
victory for our clients (the Kurds). They merely hoped to ensure that the
insurgents would be capable of sustaining a level of hostility just high enough
to sap the resources of the neighboring state." According to a CIA memorandum dated March 22, 1974 and quoted in the Pike Report, the Shah saw his
policy of "aid" to the Kurds "as a card to be played in the contest with his
neighbors." The CIA went on to say that: "We believe that the Shah would
by no means welcome the official establishment of an autonomous (Kurdish)
government. Both Iran and the U.S. hope to benefit from an unresolvable
situation in which Iraq is intrinsically weakened by the Kurds' refusal to give
up their semi-autonomy. Neither Iran nor the U.S. would like to see the
situation resolved one way or the other."[47] For Henry Kissinger, this policy
was "merely an instrument to dissuade Iraq from any international

adventurism."[48] The Pike Report authors' own judgement was that: "Our clients, who were encouraged to fight, were not told of this policy. It was a cynical enterprise, even in the context of a clandestine aid operation." Barzani was unaware of Kissinger's cynicism: apparently, he even sent presents to the good doctor when the latter got married, although this was kept secret in the U.S.[49]

Interestingly enough, the CIA memorandum outlining the U.S. and Iranian governments' position was circulated just before the arrival in Baghdad of Marshal Andrei Gretchko, the Soviet Minister of Defense. According to the *New York Times*, the Marshal brought with him a "plan for a settlement between the Iraqi client and the Kurdish rebels" which "Barzani rejected on the advice of Iran and the United States."[50]

According to the press, the aid Iran and the U.S supplied to the Kurds was "far from generous; rifles, automatic weapons, some out-of-date anti-aircraft guns and low-power artillery."[51] Nonetheless, the *Peshmergas* successfully resisted the 1974 Iraqi summer offensive. Consequently Saddam Hussein made overtures to the Shah in the hope of finishing with the whole affair by other means. This was all done very discreetly, through Egypt and Algeria whose representatives were approached on the subject during the Rabat Pan-Arab Conference in October 1974.[52]

As *L'Express* put it,

> The initiative was well timed. Kissinger was in the middle of attempting to secure a disengagement between the Israelis and Egyptians in the Sinai. These efforts were looked on with disfavor by the Syrians, who thus had to be isolated in order to prevent them from drumming up support on the basis of Arab nationalism. Kissinger and the Egyptian president, Anwar Sadat, estimated that, if they could help Iraq rid itself of the Kurdish thorn in its flesh, a grateful Baghdad would allow Egypt to pursue negotiations with Israel. An Egyptian diplomat, Ashraf Marwan, was sent to open exploratory talks in Baghdad and Tehran. Tehran declared that it was willing to abandon the Kurds in exchange for some territorial concessions in the Persian Gulf. Implicit in the deal was the idea that Baghdad would stop conducting an overtly hostile policy towards Iran and would not back Damascus's objections to the Sinai Agreement. Mohamed Yazid, Algeria's ambassador in Beirut, conveyed President Houari Boumedienne's support for the scheme to Saddam Hussein. A settlement seems imminent.[53]

The settlement was in fact concluded in Algiers during the OPEC conference on March 6, 1975. The Shah undertook to close off his frontiers with Iraqi Kurdistan, to block the mountain passes and to prevent the infiltration of "subversive elements," namely those Iraqi Kurds whom he had only recently acclaimed as heroes and whom his official press had presented as "our Kurdish brothers, those combative Aryans who are the spearhead of the Iranian nation." In exchange he obtained some significant concessions: the frontier near Abadan would henceforth run along the mid-channel line of the Shatt al-Arab, in keeping with the Ottoman-Persian protocol signed in Constantinople in 1913 which had been superseded by the 1937 British-sponsored settlement placing the Shatt in Iraqi waters. The Algiers Agreement was confirmed and fleshed out by the Iranian-Iraqi Treaty signed in

Baghdad on June 13, 1975 by the respective foreign ministers and Abdul Aziz Bouteflika, the Algerian foreign minister, who acted as a "neutral" intermediary and guarantor of the two other governments' good intentions.[54] President Boumedienne even sent a detachment of officers from the Algerian National Popular Army to help the Iranian and Iraqi forces close off the Iranian side of the Kurdish frontier.

In late February 1975, only a few days before the Algiers Agreement was signed, the leadership of the Kurdish revolution, worried by the negotiations between Tehran, Baghdad, Cairo and Algiers, sent a KDP delegation to Egypt where it was received by President Sadat. The delegation called on him to ensure that "Egypt would seek to preserve the rights of the Kurdish people" should Baghdad and Tehran reach an agreement. The Egyptian president reassured them by denying the existence of any such negotiations. They had only just returned to Kurdistan when the news of the March 6 Algiers Agreement was broadcast on the radio.[55]

The Shah welcomed the Algiers Agreement for a variety of reasons. Firstly, he did not wish to see an autonomous Kurdistan. Secondly, he sought to detach Baghdad from Moscow through a deal at the Kurds' expense. Finally, he wanted to be recognized as the "major Gulf power," even if this effectively meant simply being imperialism's regional policeman, as in Dhofar.

The Shah's aim was to conclude a deal with Saddam Hussein. The Pike Report notes: "The CIA had long-standing information indicating that our ally (the Shah) would abandon the ethnic group (the Kurds) the moment he reached an agreement with his enemy (Iraq) over their frontier dispute. A CIA memorandum dated October 17, 1972 explained that two months after proposing the project (helping the Kurds) to us, our ally had let his enemy know, apparently through the Foreign Affairs Ministry of a third country, that he would agree to a return to peaceful conditions, should his enemy publicly abrogate an old frontier treaty."

It goes without saying that the Shah's overtures to Iraq had received Kissinger's blessing, since the two were clearly agreed that the Kurds were merely a "card to be played" and a bargaining counter. But in 1972 Saddam Hussein was not yet prepared to compromise with his neighbor. Nor was he so inclined in August 1974 when Iraqi and Iranian diplomats met in Istanbul at the Shah's request. Saddam Hussein still hoped to settle the matter military and thus avoid having to make a deal, hence the Iraqi Army's general offensive in August.

An article by Mr. Gueyras in Le Monde informs us that, in order to render the Kurdish Army even more dependent on him, the Shah increased the flow of military aid, introducing "ultra-modern anti-tank missiles and Iranian 155mm artillery batteries" to the Ravanduz front and the Shuman Valley. However, he made sure that the Kurds never had more than three days' ammunition. "It is now clear that the Iranians imposed draconian controls upon the military assistance they gave the Kurdish Army, precisely so as to prevent the Peshmergas from building up armaments and ammunition depots which could have given them room for maneuver . . . According to reports from British and American journalists who were in Iraqi Kurdistan at the time of the Algiers reconciliation, the Shah enforced the clauses of the Agreement even more firmly than Baghdad had dared to hope for. In the eight hours following the embraces in Algiers, Iranian trucks began to tow 155mm cannons back towards the frontier. Since then convoys have trundled inexorably along the Hamilton Route — but this time in the opposite direction, taking back all the equipment which had been furnished to the resistance fighters: their artillery, their ammunition, their military equipment and even some of their food supplies."[56]

The Algiers Agreement embodies the "unholy alliance" policy which has been a constant theme of the main states amongst which Kurdistan has been carved up. As we have seen, the Algiers Agreement has a direct ancestor: it was called the Baghdad Pact.

In fact, Baghdad's strategic goals had not changed. The 1955 Pact with London, the 1972 Treaty with Moscow and the 1975 Agreement with Tehran were merely political ploys while the basic aim remained constant: to become ever stronger, drawing on the technology and armaments of this or that industrial power in order to smash the enemy within. The nature of the industrial power and foreign ally in question hardly came into it. Socialist or capitalist, it made no difference to Iraq.

Right at the beginning of the Kurdistan war, Saddam Hussein, in his April 8, 1974 speech celebrating the anniversary of the Baath Party's foundation, assured Turkey that it would continue to receive cheap Iraqi oil: "We consider Turkey as one of the first groups, one of the friendly nations. It is on this basis that we have supplied Turkey with oil and are prepared to give favorable consideration to any eventual Turkish requests."[57] For its part, Turkey kept its border with Iraq firmly closed throughout the war. Following the March 6, 1975 catastrophe, many Iraqi Kurds sought to flee to Turkish Kurdistan, but were all turned back.

The Algiers Agreement was greeted with amazement in Iraqi Kurdistan. Barzani was already in Tehran. When the Shah returned from Algiers, he presented the Kurdish leader with three choices: to surrender to the Iraqi forces before the end of the month when the general amnesty decreed by Baghdad would expire; to seek refuge in Iran; or to continue fighting with the frontier closed, policed by the Army and kept under Iranian-Algerian control as stipulated in the Agreement.

From Tehran, Barzani sent a coded telegram to Kurdistan, asking the KDPs Central Committee to meet and take a decision. The Committee met in Hadji-Ouiran on March 7, while its president was still in Iran. There was no unanimity, but the decision was taken to continue the war with reduced partisan forces. Meanwhile the fighting went on as fiercely as ever. The KDP leadership were really waiting for their chief to return, hoping that he would confirm their decision.

General Barzani came back to Kurdistan and, on March 11, presided over a meeting of the main political and military leaders which lasted until the following day. Having informed those present of his talks with the Shah,

Barzani congratulated the Central Committee on its "correct decision." The war continued.

However, Barzani was in fact hesitant. On March 17, through the Political Bureau of the KDP, he sent a telegram to President al-Bakr proposing renewed negotiations: to avoid further bloodshed, the Iraqi law on autonomy would not be accepted. Baghdad's answer, by telegram on March 18, was outright rejection.[58]

On the night of March 18, during a new and broader meeting of the Political Bureau and the military leaders, Mustafa Barzani informed his followers of his personal decision not to continue the struggle, but instead to retreat to Iran. If others wished to carry on with the fighting, they were free to do so. However, everybody accepted his decision and followed him into exile, including all the KDP leaders and army chiefs, even those who had argued vehemently to prolong the war.

The exodus to Iran began on March 22, starting with the civilian administration who burnt their files before leaving. The partisans destroyed their weapons and threw the heavier pieces into lakes and rivers. On March 27 Barzani, his family, the leadership of the KDP and the main army chiefs also crossed the frontier, which was, in principle, open in both directions so as to allow the Kurds "freedom of movement." For a while there was in fact considerable two-way traffic, especially amongst the civilian population. Although many civilian Kurds followed the General Staff into exile, others — refugees who had fled to Iran on previous occasions — came in the opposite direction. Despite this two-way flow, the number of Iraqi Kurdish refugees in Iran went up in a few days from about 150,000 to over 300,000, of whom 35 to 40,000 were *Peshmergas*.

As everyone was given a free choice, several thousand *Peshmergas* surrendered to the Iraqi forces rather than go into exile. A few thousand scattered through the country and went underground, so as to avoid either surrender or exile. Amongst the soldiers who opted for this solution, it is worth mentioning the *Peshmergas* under Issa Swar, the commander of a military region in Badinan. In an act of rebellion, they put their leader to death the moment he transmitted the order to retreat to Iran.

Notable amongst the KDP leaders who chose surrender to the Iraqi forces was Saleh Yussefi, the leader of the left wing within the Political Bureau who had opposed the alliance with the Shah and the U.S., albeit without success as the left had lost its majority in 1972. He now hoped to save what could be saved, but in vain.

Why did General Barzani change his position between March 11 and 18? Was it just that when he heard that the Baath had refused to re-open negotiations he could not face the prospect of a hopeless war?[59] Perhaps the U.S. disengagement also played some part in changing General Barzani's attitude. On March 10 he had sent an SOS to Kissinger, reminding him of his promises. Kissinger did not reply, which caused a certain anxiety amongst the American secret service. Not that they were concerned that their Kurdish "ally" might lose. They were simply worried that the Kurds might reveal

President Nixon's promises. On March 22, Colby, the head of the CIA in Washington, who had been informed by his men that "as yet Barzani had received no answer to his message from Secretary of State Henry Kissinger," questioned Kissinger about it, and was told that "secret service operations are not missionary work."[60]

There were other considerations which must have influenced the Kurdish High Command to opt for retreat to Iran: how were they to feed the displaced, pauperized masses piled on top of one another in the Shuman Valley and in certain areas of Badinan? How could they protect them? Finally, on the military level, how could they get hold of the ammunition and equipment necessary for a long guerrilla war against a large and modern Iraqi Army? But this way of looking at the matter ignores the fact that the Kurds helped to create their own problems. It would be irresponsible to skip over the major errors committed by the Kurdish leadership; two stand out particularly. The fundamental error in political strategy was made in 1972 before the beginning of the fifth Kurdistan war: relying on American imperialism and its main agent in the area, the Shah, to supply and finance a popular war of national liberation. The second crucial error was one of political judgement: the revolution was liquidated by its own leadership and the result was the retreat to Iran and the end of the war.

These two political errors were committed in 1972 and 1975 respectively, when international constraints were particularly pressing; in fact the Soviet-Iraqi Treaty on the one hand and the Iraqi-Iranian Treaty on the other could be said to amount to extenuating circumstances. They explain the leadership's mistakes, but cannot be taken as a justification.

Responsibility for the errors should not be laid entirely upon General Barzani and his family but on the whole leadership. Naturally this includes Mustafa Barzani, his children and his family, but it also refers to the KDP Political Bureau and the Kurdish secret services, known as *Parastin*,[61] who played an efficient and increasingly important part in the revolution following March 11, 1970. No doubt it was thanks to *Parastin* that the Political Bureau learned of the dealings between Tehran and Baghdad just before the Algiers Agreement was signed.

With his patrician background, Mustafa Barzani's role in the revolution was much more than that of a party president. He was the national hero, the supreme and unchallenged chief to whom all non-KDP elements could turn. It was he who authorized the communists to bear arms within the revolution shortly after the Baath began massacring them in 1963. This was a significant change in policy.[62] Later, in 1964, the composition of the Political Bureau was extensively modified, again on Barzani's authority, during the Party's Sixth Congress.

The principle of collective decision-making was effectively disregarded by the revolutionary leadership. Important decisions were taken by a small handful of people, and especially by Barzani himself. Nonetheless the mistake in political strategy made in 1972 must be laid at the door of the entire leadership. Certain members of the Political Bureau took the steps which eventually led to the alliance with the Shah and the U.S. In the end, the whole Bureau was let in on the secret. No one except Saleh Yassefi protested. The leadership was certainly wary of the Shah, but it had great faith in the American guarantee given by Nixon and Kissinger. This bogus guarantee was effective only for a short while, and it was not long before the Kurds were simply just another "card to be played." The situation was quite absurd: the Kurds, an oppressed people fighting a war of national liberation, were drawing support from imperialism and its agents while their oppressors enjoyed the moral and material backing of the socialist camp and the progressive forces in the world.

Did the leadership at least do everything it could to avoid the break with the Baath and the re-opening of the war? We can probably say that they did, but perhaps we do not know the whole story. The leadership rightly rejected the "autonomy" unilaterally promulgated by the Baath on March 11, 1974. But if they had not felt bolstered by the American guarantee and the Shah's promises of aid, they would surely have used a thousand little tricks to draw out the negotiations for as long as possible, building up their strength all the time.

Did the leadership do everything in its power to win the war? Unfortunately, the answer is no. There were many serious errors in this respect. A popular war against an established government is not won only on the battlefield. It must also be an economic, political, psychological and publicity offensive. It demands a rational and efficient mobilization of every energy, rigorous execution, combined with exemplary austerity. This is particularly true for the Kurdish people, whose geopolitical situation makes them especially vulnerable.

The U.S. guarantee bred a dangerous and excessive self-assurance in the movement, which did nothing to win the solidarity of the Iraqi Arab left, the friendship of the Arab world or the support of its governments. True, the Iraqi Communist Party had aligned itself with the Baath. But even the Kurdish communists fighting alongside the national movement were alienated. The *Parastin* secret services killed Fakher Mergasori,[63] a Kurdish communist accused of spying for the Baath, even though he had been the hero of Hendrin in May 1966, when he won the revolution's greatest victory. He was executed without trial, along with members of his family. No proof of his treason was ever presented before a revolutionary tribunal.

The Baath were allowed to monopolize world progressive opinion and they made good use of it both at home and abroad. No effort was made to explain the Kurdish cause in the Third World. Nothing was done to promote friendship and understanding among socialist and progressive forces in Europe: the Kurds in Europe who tried to bridge this gulf had completely inadequate means at their disposal.

Within the Kurdish camp itself, both in terms of socio-economic strategy and in terms of human relations, the excessive self-assurance of the leaders was to prove disastrous. Cockily secure in the knowledge of the U.S. guarantee, the leadership took itself for an already established state and acted accordingly. Entire mini-ministries were set up. Administrative offices multiplied to the point of bureaucratic time-wasting and conflict. The Revolutionary Army's ranks were swollen with troops, at the expense of efficiency. Communications between the front and the supply centers and hospitals were particularly badly organized.

Nor was there any thought of the economic autarchy which would have been so salutary. Nobody saw the point of carrying out the agrarian reform the Party program had promised, now that everybody was in the middle of a war. And what was the point of organizing wheat and rice production when the Shah was sending in truckloads of supplies? There was not even any move to buy up the peasants' tobacco crop when the coffers were full. No doubt this was thought unnecessary since there were plenty of American cigarettes to be had: as a result, the crop rotted in the fields and the peasants were deprived of the income they were entitled to.

Right from the start of the war, nothing was done to prevent Saddam Hussein dividing up the country into what he called two sections. On the contrary, the Kurdish leadership began by calling the local and regional cadres of the Party, the youth organizations, the student bodies and the women's groups to come to the revolution's headquarters. Next it was the technical and scientific cadres, the intellectuals and the students who were deliberately attracted to the center. Most of these cadres found themselves concentrated in the Balek area (the Shuman Valley) without work or responsibility appropriate to their aptitudes. Many were left unemployed, others swelled the ranks of the administration. The result was a clear reduction in the Party's ability to organize underground revolutionary activity in the towns under Iraqi control.

The Kurdish radio station's over-zealous denunciation of the Iraqi bombing spread panic among the population and triggered the mass exodus. Tens of thousands took to the road. The leadership tried to deal with the problem by entrusting the first 150,000 refugees, mainly drawn from the families of the *Peshmergas*, to the Iranian authorities. In so doing they unwittingly helped the Iraqi Air Force create the Kurdish refugee problem in Iran, refugees whom the Shah could later use as hostages to blackmail the Kurdish leaders. But the exodus continued and nothing was done to settle the population and get them to return to their usual tasks. In early 1975, out of a population of some 1.5 million in Free Kurdistan, one-third was made up of displaced persons. How could a war economy possibly be set up when so many peasants had abandoned their villages? How could one win the fifth war when one had failed to mobilize the Kurdish people, and when much of the human capital which could have been organized and associated with the revolutionary struggle was allowed to become a burden instead?

But there is more. Since a state had practically been established and there was no lack of money, clientelage began to emerge, and bureaucratism and elitism developed in the higher ranks of both the Army and the Party. Fortunately there were many exceptions to this rule, but little was done to prevent it and a new privileged group was allowed to install itself.

On the purely military level, despite the adoption of out-dated orthodox tactics, a huge effort was made and it is fair to say that few other oppressed peoples have fought so fiercely for their liberation. Nonetheless, the whole thing was conceived on the basis of the false assumption that foreign assistance would never be cut off. When the heavy artillery arrived, the Kurdish Army began to wage an increasingly conventional war against the Iraqi forces, a war between two states with the usual head-on confrontations and battles for position concentrated around the Shuman Valley, where the High Command, the infrastructure, most of the logistics and a growing proportion of the Kurdish population were all entrenched.

However, the increasingly sophisticated weapons supplied by the Shah enabled the *Peshmergas* to face their adversary with better equipment than before. In the end, the Kurdish forces were so anxious to retain the Shah's aid that they handed over to him many Iranian Kurdish opponents of the Imperial regime who had sought refuge amongst their compatriots in Iraq!

The final political error was the retreat to Iran. I can think of no other example of a popular war ending so lamentably following a leadership decision at a time when the people were still willing to fight and had the means to do so. This is what happens when the fundamental choices in a party's program are accepted enthusiastically by the rank and file but remain intangible because, as far as the leadership is concerned, they are merely tactical considerations of no great importance.[64]

Baghdad's Policy in Kurdistan

Roads to Servitude

From August 18 to September 6, 1975, I was the guest of the Iraqi government, which had invited me to come and inform myself directly of the situation of my Kurdish compatriots in Iraq. My delegation was to hold talks with Iraqi leaders about "how to improve the law on Kurdish autonomy," how to "extend its territorial scope," how to "heal the wounds of nearly fourteen years of fratricidal war," and how to "renew the ties of friendship and fraternity betwen Arab and Kurd." These goals had been agreed by my Iraqi interlocutors before I set out. They had also guaranteed, in the name of their government, that I would be free to move about and make contacts throughout the Republic, including Kurdistan. They even went so far as to give me *carte blanche* in my choice of companions for the journey.

Bechir Boumaza, one-time member of the Political Bureau of the FLN, several times minister in the Ben Bella and Boumedienne Cabinets, and a member of the Algerian opposition, kindly agreed to join the delegation. He hoped that his contacts in Baghdad would help to further my political negotiations with the government and thus re-establish the ties of Arab-Kurdish friendship. Jean-Claude Luthi of Geneva also agreed to come with me, in his capacity as a delegate of the International Federation of Human Rights (IFHR), with a precise mandate to investigate the human rights aspect of the problem and not to take sides in political matters. Finally, I called in Father Joseph Pari, a priest of the Chaldean Church, who was born in Suleimanieh.

After three days spent in Baghdad, where we met the two Kurdish ministers in the Iraqi Cabinet, and also the minister of justice, we left the city, early in the morning of August 21, in two cars put at our disposal by the minister of information. We were accompanied by "A" and "B," two Ministry officials who were both members of the Baath Party. Our first stop in Kurdistan was Khanaqin. From there, we went on to Darbandi-Khan, Suleimanieh, Kirkuk and Arbil, where we stopped for five days, during which time we flew by helicopter to Rawanduz, the Shuman Valley and various villages in the province. We had frequent discussions with officials charged with the administration of the "Autonomous Region." Jean-Claude Luthi returned to Baghdad and then Switzerland on August 27, when our stay in Arbil came to an end. He had decided that the preconditions for an objective human rights enquiry had not been met. On August 28, the rest of us continued our journey, first to Mosul and then Badinan, where we visited, amongst others, Aqra, Dehok, Swara-Tuka, Sheikhan, Sarsang and Amadiya. On August 30 we went back to Baghdad for five days of talks with various Baathist leaders.

On August 20, we met the minister of justice, Dr. Mundhir al-Shawi, who is, like the president and the vice-president of the Republic, an Arab from Takrit. He spoke excellent French and presented himself to us as an independent and apolitical minister, a technocrat, a jurist as it happened, and a member of the commission which had drawn up the law on Kurdish autonomy. We asked him why the government was not respecting its own law's explicit stipulation that the "Autonomous Region" be extended to include "all areas with a Kurdish majority population." "That is a political question, you should ask it of the political Ministers," he answered, and added that: "Some regions, such as Kirkuk province, are ethnically mixed, which makes it difficult to apply the law." We pointed out that the province has always had a Kurdish majority, and we asked him why, since the Kurds were a minority in Iraq, the same should not apply to the Arab minority of Kirkuk province within the framework of an autonomous Kurdistan which would include that province. Once again we were invited to refer this "political" question to a political Minister. We also asked him why, given that the Yezidis are Kurds with their own particular religion and the area they live in is ethnically homogenous, this area was not included in Autonomous Kurdistan. His answer provided us with our first surprise: "The Yezidis are Amayyad Arabs!" Perhaps we should have remembered that their territory lies close to the oil-rich Ain-Zaleh area.

On August 21, at the Government Palace in Khanaqin, our delegation was invited to an official reception organized by the town's prefect. When we sought to visit the town in order to pursue our investigations, all the officials, fifteen of them in all, wanted to go with us. Only after endless negotiations did the officials consent to let us go alone. In fact, everywhere we went we had to battle with local officials before we were allowed to exercise that freedom of movement and contact the government had promised us.

On August 26, our delegation was received by Hashim Aqrawi, president of the executive council of the "Autonomous Region." He had recently been expelled from a political group calling itself the Kurdish Democratic Party which had disassociated itself from the real KDP during the fifth Kurdistan war. This party had set up offices in Baghdad and joined the Baath's National Front. Some days previously, we had met its general secretary, Aziz Aqrawi, whom I had known well during the campaign in the sixties; when I managed to see him alone, he revealed himself as a broken man, a patriot tormented by conscience.

His ex-colleague, the president of the executive council, was very different. We asked him if he belonged to a political party and he answered that all the members of the executive council had decided to "resign" from their respective parties and that they were all "independents." It was quite obvious to us that the members of the executive council were officials, appointed by the Baath and under its orders; in no way were they representative of the political desires of the Kurdish people. When we challenged him about the deportations and the incidents at Kalor-Kharma Luja, he answered that: "Our progressive government has constitutionally and legally recognized the autonomy and national rights of the Kurdish people — that is the important thing." When we pressed him about the Yezidis and Khanaqin, he gave us the same reply. He seemed to care more for the text of the law than for the human lives involved, and clearly preferred legal fiction to the real world.

The president of the executive council was in fact nothing but a sort of "Super-Governor," and the "Autonomous Region," little more than an artificial superimposition on three governorships, all entirely subordinate to the central government.

The traditional administrators of the three provinces, for all that they came under the Iraqi minister of the interior, were, in some senses, doing fairly worthwhile work. They carried out their tasks without any political pretensions. In contrast, the "Autonomous Regime's" self-justifications were repugnant. Instead of being the democratc expression of the Kurdish people's national will, this institutionally shaky and impoverished instrument of the Baath allowed itself to be used as the alibi for a policy of Arabization in a truncated Kurdistan.

While Father Pari and the International Federation for Human Rights delegate went to visit the local church, Boumaza came with us to the souks and commercial areas. The town is Kurdish and the population speaks only Kurdish. Khanaqin and the surrounding area, which are integral parts of Iraqi Kurdistan, were nonetheless not designated part of the "Autonomous Region"; Khanaqin is, after all, situated in an oil-rich province.

In the souks, we spoke with a group of schoolchildren, who confirmed two of our suspicions. Firstly, since the collapse of the armed revolution in Kurdistan, Arabic had replaced Kurdish as the language of instruction. Also, the authorities had given the schools new names more evocative of Arab history. Secondly, more and more Kurds from Khanaqin and the surrounding area were being sent by the authorities to work in Basra and Arab Iraq. Officials, teachers, technicians and employees in the oil fields were all being replaced by Arabs.

We put the same questions to the Kurdish shopkeepers, who gave us the same answer. A hundred or so people soon gathered round us in the crowded souk. One man, an Arab schoolteacher who had been transferred to one of Khanaqin's schools some three or four months previously, came forth and spoke to us. He explained that "Barzani's treacherous clique had imposed Kurdish as the language of instruction in this town. When the clique collapsed, justice was re-established and education in Arabic restored." We pointed out that the population was Kurdish, and spoke no Arabic; that it was natural for the inhabitants to want their national language to be used in the schools. We asked the shopkeepers and passers-by if such was indeed their wish, and both they and the schoolchildren all agreed. The teacher then asserted that: "We have proof that the population wanted this change. The children's parents sent petitions calling for a return to Arabic-language schooling."

When we returned to the Palace in Khanaqin around noon, "A" came up to us and said: "Any foreign ambassador would have been expelled immediately for doing one-hundredth of what you did this morning. Our government guaranteed you freedom of movement, not the right to incite unrest amongst citizens." "This journey cannot go on like this," he added, "I will have to telephone Baghdad to ask for new instructions from the regional (Baath) leadership." We nevertheless continued our travels.

Both in Suleimanieh province and in Kirkuk, notably in the Chemchemal district some 15 miles east of Kirkuk itself, we saw several little blocks of recently built small one-story cement maisonettes. These as yet uninhabited strategic hamlets and villages were built along the more usable roads with the intention of rehousing peasants from the mountains. During a stopover at the Bayzon Straits, "A" took it upon himself to explain these developments. "Our revolutionary government has set up a Rural Resettlement Bureau to regroup the rural population and provide it with modern social, sanitary and educational services." He added that: "Our revolutionary government is anxious to give certain advantages to the Kurdish peasantry, which has suffered so much. This is why the plan is being applied in the north first, although it will eventually be extended to all Iraq."

The villages of Kurdistan have evolved out of a centuries-old equilibrium between people and nature. Each mountain village has its stream or river, its field, its orchards, its cemetery and, often enough, its oak forest. The strategic hamlets were like an oven in the summer and freezing cold in the winter. They represented an inadmissibly brutal intrusion into the life of a society whose equilibrium they would disrupt.

That same day, we visited a village called Hashimaya, in the Khanaqin area, about a quarter of an hour's drive from the town. The people there were all Kurds. In the village chief's house, we met his son, a man of about thirty, who had come from Basra to spend the end of his vacation with his parents. He explained that: "For the last five years I have worked in the Khanaqin oil industry and lived with my parents, but a few months ago the authorities decided to send me to work in the south." The figures gathered by the International Federation of Human Rights representative, Jean-Claude Luthi, bore him out; in Khanaqin alone about 5,000 Kurds had already been exiled to southern Iraq, supposedly to fill new jobs. But perhaps this is typical of how the Baath intended to "respect the Autonomous Region's moral personality."

On August 23, in Kirkuk, our delegation was invited to the offices of the province's teachers trade union. The president of the union, Akram Hardan, an Arab teacher, was accompanied by a Kurdish and a Turkoman vice-president, neither of whom said a word throughout the meeting. Hardan explained to us that, before March 11, 1970, Arabic was the only language of instruction throughout the province, but that since 1971 the Ministry had opened schools where teaching was carried out either in Kurdish or in Turkish, according to the ethnic balance and wishes of the population. We asked him why, given that most of the province's inhabitants were Kurds, with Turkomans as the next largest group, most schools were still teaching in Arabic. Hardan gave us a technical answer: there had not yet been time to complete the re-orientation which began in 1971.

We left Kirkuk on the afternoon of August 23 on the road leading northwards to Arbil. We knew that the area we were going through had been victimized and was subject to the policy of Arabization that was in force all the way to the town of Altun-Keupri on the Little Zab, which marks the border between Kirkuk province and the "Autonomous Region." Most of the villages we could see from the road appeared to be deserted. From time to time we noticed a site with trucks and bulldozers. About twenty minutes from Kirkuk, we asked the driver to bear eastwards towards a village a few hundred yards from the road. We chose it quite at random and did not even know its name. "B," the delegate from the Ministry of Information, remained silent. The cars drew up about a hundred yards from the houses, as children and a few adults rushed up to meet us. They were Kurds, speaking their national language. The adults had only a smattering of heavily accented Arabic. The children were a little more familiar with Arabic, no doubt through having learnt it as a second language at school. They were all of school age, from twelve to fourteen years old; one of them carried his schoolbooks, which were printed in Kurdish, under his arm. Did this mean that what Hardan had told us an hour before was true and that the stories about the Arabization policy were mostly exaggeration? The eldest of the children, a boy of about sixteen, claimed to have been a *Peshmerga*. We were told that the village, lying some 15 miles north of Kirkuk, was called Kalor-Khurma-Luja and that the plain we were crossing, between Kirkuk and the "Autonomous Region," was entirely Kurdish. However we still had doubts. The villagers might be frightened of telling us the truth; our two big official cars bore the insignia of the Ministry of Information. The moment we told the villagers we were an international delegation and that they had no reason to fear telling us the whole truth, the schoolchildren informed us that: "Our village has already received an official evacuation order. We are ninety families, all Kurdish, and we are to be deported to Basra. Our lands will be given to Arabs brought from the south, for whom a modern village is being built." And there was indeed a building site a few hundred yards away on the other side of the road. The children added: "Dozens of villages have already been evacuated in the Zur-Guzraw Mountains, in Ketka, Gurzay and Dibis."

As we turned back to our cars, the schoolchildren ran after us, imploring us to do something. One of them said, "We do not want to be exiled! We want to stay in our village." We glanced at "A" who looked away.

The first thing which struck us in Arbil, the capital of "autonomous" Kurdistan, was a banner stretched right across the town hall, proclaiming, first in Arabic, then in Kurdish, that "The Baath way is our way." Since there is a legal Kurdish Democratic Party in Baathist Iraq, a party which is a member of the Progressive National Front and whose general secretary, Aziz Aqrawi is a Minister of State, one wonders why the Baath should enjoy such a political monopoly in "autonomous" Kurdistan. In all the Region's larger settlements, as in other parts of Kurdistan, the Arab Baath had prosperous looking local branch offices. We often visited them during our journey, but somehow we were never led to the offices of any other party belonging to the so-called Progressive National Front. We saw no Communist Party premises either, in Kurdistan or in Arab Iraq. One well-established Baathist confided in us when we asked him about it: "The communists? We have admitted some of their better known leaders to the Front on what amounts to a purely individual basis, but we do not allow them to form cells or an organization, or to publish their views or to take any form of action. When these leaders eventually die, the Communist Party will be a thing of the past in Iraq."

On the morning of August 28, our delegation — now down to three members, Luthi having left for Baghdad the previous day — left Arbil by road and headed for Mosul. Some 15 miles from Mosul, we passed through villages which had just been renamed. Qaraqosh, for instance, was now known by the Arab name Hamdaniya.

The Governor of Mosul, Flayyih Hassan, drove us personally to the small town of Baashiqa, lying about fifteen minutes by car to the east of Mosul itself. The population in that particular area was mixed. We were led into a room in which there were about 15 people, mainly young. The governor introduced them: "These are Yezidis, Amayyad Arabs"! When we disagreed with this designation, he invited us to ask them what they thought about it. They answered as one, in Arabic: "We are Yezidis, Amayyad Arabs." We asked these young Yezidis whether they were members of the Baath, and they agreed that they were. To make the scene a little more credible, a Yezidi sheikh had also been brought along. This sheikh spoke not a word of Arabic, and knew only Kurdish. We reminded him that the Yezidis' holy book was written in Kurdish, but the saintly old man insisted, still in his national language, that he was an Arab.

Not long after, we drove on to the Aqra Plain, where an astonishing sight was awaiting us. The entire population of an agricultural area some 45 miles long and 20 miles wide, encompassing dozens and dozens of villages had been ordered by the governor to line the roadside in honor of our arrival. Tens of thousands of Kurdish peasants had been told to stand there, along the whole length of the plain; they had been waiting under the burning sun since morning. It was past eleven when we arrived and it took at least a further two hours to cross the area. The governor seemed delighted by this shocking performance. He saw nothing wrong in citizens being conscripted by the authorities in this manner. Bechir Boumaza later attempted to console us with the thought that "they do exactly the same thing in the countryside of Arab Iraq."

We were told that all the Kurds who had sought refuge in Mosul during the war had now been settled on the Aqra Plain, along with the Kurdish tribes who had fought on the government side, such as the Herki. This may be true. Some villagers did tell us they were Herkis. However, during a stopover on the plain, one villager tried to slip a folded piece of paper in my pocket: our host, the governor, noticed and, once we were back in the car, asked me to hand it to him. What the note said was this: "We are 500 Kurdish families from Sheikhan and Ain-Sifni. We fought in the revolution but in the end we accepted the government amnesty and gave ourselves up. The government confiscated our lands and sent us to *Dashte Aqra* (the Aqra Plain) where we have no means of subsistence. We are only asking for justice." The governor continued to insist we turn the note over to him. We let him glance at it, after having got him swear on his honor that he would take no measures against the plaintiff, but we kept it.

Sheikhan and Ain-Sifni are an "Arabization zone." The Kurds, at any rate the Muslims amongst them, are being expelled. Christians and Yezidis are allowed to remain only on condition that they admit "that they are Arabs." But even the inhabitants of the Aqra Plain may not be safe from Arabization. It is already bad enough that the district has been attached to Flayyih Hassan's Nineveh province, but there is probably worse to come. During our journey across the plain, the governor claimed that the population of the province was not happy with Kurdish as the language of instruction in (primary) schools. Apparently he "had received petitions demanding that education in Arabic be restored."

When we arrived in Aqra, we found a hundred people waiting for us, lined up in front of a building, carrying flags and banners. Most of them were young Kurds, who gave tongue the moment we opened the car door. They were cheering the Baath Party, both in Arabic and in Kurdish — another of those delicate attentions we had the governor to thank for.

On the morning of August 29 we left Mosul for Dehok province, in Badinan. We spent the afternoon on the immense rock of Amadiya, over-looking a beautiful valley. Without any malice aforethought, I observed that "the citadel of Amadiya was once the seat of a Kurdish principality." The Kurdish officials present, who knew the history of the town, all agreed, but "A," our guardian angel, had different views. In expressing them he managed to link the history of Amadiya with "the imperialist maneuvers against Iraq." I confess my anger got the better of me. How on earth could Kurdish medieval history be a "creation" of 20th century imperialism? Why should the Kurds of Iraq be forbidden to find out and be proud about their pre-Iraqi history. I asked "A" whether he was aware that the state of Iraq had been set up only in 1921 by the British, who had attached this part of Kurdistan to it. Did he think that the Kurds were "a people without a history"? "A" was eventually forced to concede that the Kurds did have "a history of their own." But what do the officials put down in the schoolbooks they write in Baghdad?

In Baghdad, Boumaza was with us the two times we met Tariq Aziz, the Baathist regional leader and then Minister of Information. He also attended our meetings with Naim Haddad, the Baathist Minister of Youth and General Secretary of the Progressive National Front, and with Dr. Zayd Hayder, a Syrian member of the (inter-Arab) national leadership of the Party, who directed its Bureau of Foreign Affairs. They received us very courteously. We asked them to stop the deportations and to put an end to the policy of Arabization, to allow deported Kurds to return to Kurdistan and to transfer the Arabs who had been implanted on their lands. We also asked them to extend the "Autonomous Region" to other mainly Kurdish regions and districts, even if it meant we had to accept some compromise over Kirkuk.

Tariq Aziz attempted to defend the deportations, claiming that they were entirely due to "vital necessities in the oilfields," the requirements of "frontier security" and "the demands of the internal labor market." As part of his justification of the Arabization program he told us that: "Suleimanieh is still Iraq, it is part of my homeland and, if I wanted to settle there, you could not stop me." On the subject of autonomy and the extension of the territory involved, he said: "It is the rights that have been recognized that matter; you cannot measure autonomy in square miles." Like his colleagues, Tariq Aziz also admitted that "everything was far from perfect," stressing that "improvements were always possible." We agreed to a second meeting in order to present the Party and government with our written proposals on how to remedy the situation.

Naim Haddad greeted us very affably. When we first met him, he treated us as "dear brothers" and addressed us as intimates. As for the problems, not to worry, everything would work itself out for the best eventually. "Teaching in Kurdish will be re-established" in the Khanaqin schools. Even the population transfers were "a temporary matter to which a solution can be found." He had just been to Iran to investigate the Kurdish refugee problem, and had "exceptionally good news" for us. He had managed "to convince 50,000 of them to return to the homeland within two months." It was only two months later we found out that what he was talking about was a forced repatriation.

We asked Dr. Zayd Hayder, a disciple of Michel Aflaq, whether the national leadership of the Baath recognized the Kurds as one people, and as a nation with an inalienable right to self-determination, for all that they were oppressed and torn apart from one another. We explained to him that the recognition of this principle and a just solution to the Kurdish problems in Iraq were the two preconditions to any strategic alliance between the Arab and Kurdish national liberation movements as a whole. He asked us to submit these questions in writing, since only the National Congress of the Baath was qualified to answer them. We never received a reply.

More than anybody, Tariq Aziz drew our attention to the fact that Iraq had constitutionally recognized the Kurds as one of the Republic's two nationalities, that their national rights were guaranteed by the principle of autonomy. He reminded us that: "You'll find no such rights in Iran or Turkey, even though there are many more Kurds in those countries. And the

Syrians have done no better, for all the crocodile tears they shed over our Kurds."

At this stage, it is worth noting the following points:

(a) It was indeed very important that the Iraqi Republic constitutionally recognized the rights of Kurdish nationality, and it was true that none of the neighboring states granted similar status to their Kurdish populations.

(b) It was also no minor matter that in the so-called Autonomous Region, Kurdish children could study in their mother tongue, and that there was a University in Suleimanieh which had a Kurdish section.[65]

(c) However, everything which was conceded to the Kurds of Iraq was won by force. Autonomy and national rights had been officially promised by the League of Nations as far back as 1925, by the Iraqi government and the Mandate Power in 1922, and again in 1925. But the Kurds had to fight for half a century before they gained even a few of the rights that had been originally recognized as theirs. The old Mandate Power had conceded that there should be Kurdish primary schools in Suleimanieh and Arbil.

(d) Whatever one thought of this "positive side" which the Baath leaders put so much emphasis on, it made no sense for Kurdish rights to be recognized in one half of Kurdistan and ignored in the other. Did this "autonomy" accorded to one half of the Kurdish people excuse the destruction of the other?

(e) It was also clear that the "autonomy" granted to one half of Iraqi Kurdistan was largely illusory, involving no decision-making powers or definite budget and in no way representing the will of the people.[66]

(f) Economic development was planned in terms of the enrichment of Arab Iraq, especially Baghdad, at the expense of the Kurdish people. The Darband and Dokan dams built in the Kurdish territories were mainly used to supply Baghdad with electricity. The list of achievements and projects in the "Autonomous Region" was very far from impressive: a couple of cigarette factories at Suleimanieh and Arbil, a cement factory, a carpet factory, a chicken farm and cattle ranch, a sugar refinery and a marble quarry.

By late April 1976, some 200,000 Kurds[67] had been uprooted from their lands in Kurdistan, mostly to be deported to the south, where they were scattered, in groups of three or four families, amongst the Arab villages of the Lower Euphrates, notably in Thi-Qar (the old Nasiriyya), Qadisiyya (Diwaniyya), Muthanna (the deserts near Samawa), and in the Ramadi (the Habbaniyya marshlands west of Baghdad and the surrounding steppes), as well as in Maysan Province (the old Amara, near Basra). Some, about 30 or 40,000 at a guess, were "only" moved within Kurdistan itself, resettled in Kurdish regions further east.

The 200,000 Kurds who had already been deported could be classified as follows:

(1) Those from the Kurdish or mainly Kurdish areas not included in the "Autonomous Region." The policy affected the oil-rich regions of Kirkuk, Khanaqin and Ain-Zaleh and frontier regions such as Sindjar, Arbil province, Zamma and the Qaratu-Bamo-Maidan area north of Khanaqin.

(2) The *Peshmergas* and revolutionaries who surrendered to the Iraqi forces

when the amnesty was declared but who came from areas not included in the "Autonomous Region" and which were thus subject to Arabization.

(3) Refugees from Iran, whether forcibly or willingly repatriated, whether civilian or military, who had the misfortune of coming from an area subject to Arabization.

(4) Residents within the "Autonomous Region" itself, especially in certain frontier or strategically important districts. In Badinan, the policy affected Zibar and Barzan, Atrush (north of Sheikhan), and Zakho. Thousands of Kurds were even deported from the Makhmur Plain, which lies right next to Arbil, the capital of supposedly autonomous Kurdistan. The point of all this was to evacuate the frontier regions of Iraqi Kurdistan, thereby cutting off links with Turkish and Iranian Kurdistan.

On November 18, 1975, the Baath detached Kalor and Chemchemal, the two districts it had officially recognized as Kurdish, from Kirkuk province and attached them to Suleimanieh as integral parts of the "Autonomous Region." The implication was that all the rest of Kirkuk was to be subject to Arabization. Kifri District (population 50,000), which was no less Kurdish than the other two, was attached to Diyala Province: like Khanaqin, it was to be Arabized.

What remained of the mainly Kurdish province was dismembered by official RCC decree on February 8, 1976.[68] The decree reduced the province to two of its six districts — Kirkuk itself, with its town, and Hawidja. It was given a new Arab name, Taamim, which means "nationalization." The sixth district of Old Kirkuk, Toz, with its Kurdish majority and Turkoman and Arab minorities, was attached to an entirely new province created partly out of the old province of Baghdad, notably by the inclusion of the Arab districts of Samarra, Balad and Tikrit. The new province, with Tikrit as its capital, was named Salaheddin (Saladin). Ironically, the name of this Kurdish hero of medieval Islam was used in an operation whose sole purpose was to further the crushing of the people from whom he sprang.

With the addition of Chemchemal (57,000 inhabitants and 908 square miles) and Kalar (33,000 inhabitants and 1,071 square miles), the population of the "Autonomous Region" went up from 1,385,000 to 1,475,000 on May 1, 1975. Even if one ignored the deportations, this still represented only 51% of the population of Iraqi Kurdistan and 47.6% of all Kurds living in Iraq. The Region's geographical extent also only went up from 14,454 square miles to 16,434 square miles, which represented about 57% of Iraqi Kurdistan.

The government abolished the Ministry of Northern Affairs and eliminated all reference to the history and geography of Kurdistan in schoolbooks. The Kurdish Academy, the chief agency concerned with education in Kurdish, was frozen. Teaching in Kurdish had already been abandoned in Khanaqin; then it was dropped in Kirkuk, Aqra and the rest of Badinan. Kurdish was no longer to be the second language of Iraq and the School of Kurdish Studies at Baghdad University was closed. Nor was the Kurdish section of the (Iraqi) University at Suleimanieh spared. Eighty member of its teaching staff were transferred to posts in Arab Iraq and all teaching positions were taken over by Baathist Arabs.

On the international level, despite numerous efforts, the United Nations has always refused to examine the Kurdish national question in Iraqi Kurdistan and has declared that the issue is an internal Iraqi matter. This decision did not prevent the Baghdad government from submitting an official report on "The restoration of peace and national unity following the solution of the Kurdish question in the north of the country," which was presented to the United Nations Committee for the Elimination of Racial Discrimination at Geneva on April 2, 1976. It was quite understandable that the Baathist administration in Iraq should present the Kurdish defeat in 1975 as "the solution of the question." What was puzzling was that the United Nations should have praised the Report in an official communique which states that: "Committee members unanimously agreed that the Report was satisfactory, complete and fully in accord with the stipulations of Article 9 of the Convention. They particularly praised the law on the autonomy of the Kurdish region, which, when promulgated, led to changes in the Interim Constitution and seems likely to bring about peaceful coexistence between Arabs and Kurds, the country's two main ethnic groups. The Kurds are now recognized as forming a national entity with its own political institutions and with rights equivalent to those enjoyed by the Arab majority."[69]

It really was quite intolerable that this Committee attached to the Human Rights Commission should have officially congratulated the Iraqi government for its Kurdish policy at the very moment when human rights were being trampled on in Iraq.

The Guerrilla War Resumes

Right from early May 1976 there were battles between Iraqi Army detachments and Kurdish partisans. The major confrontations took place in Badinan, notably in Amadiya, Dehok and Zakho, but there were also clashes in the mountains of Balek, in Zeyno, Ranya, Sidekan, to the north of Rawan, and Surdash, north of Suleimanieh. The Iraqi Air Force flew several missions over Badinan, particularly at Surdash in the Rawanduz area, and bombed concentrations of partisans who had gained a foothold in the mountains of Bamo-Maidan-Qaratu, between Khanaqin and Suleimanieh, an area whose population had been evacuated and deported by Baghdad.

Although the country was fully patrolled by the military, the struggle continued. In mid-June 1976, the partisans retaliated by setting fire to oil installations at Jambur and blowing up an arsenal in Kirkuk.

The partisans who took up arms in Kurdistan did so spontaneously, without consulting or co-ordinating with pre-existing political bodies. Two rival political groups aspired to the leadership of the movement, and tried to establish themselves in a *maquis* to fill the political vacuum which was created by the retreat to Iran. Both these groups called themselves Marxist-Leninist.

The first was the Patriotic Union of Kurdistan (PUK) led from Damascus by Jalal Talabani and friends. The second was a "provisional leadership" of the KDP, set up in exile by co-opted surviving members of the old leadership, some of whom had managed to leave Iran for Western Europe.

The PUK was extremely critical of all the old leadership, including General Barzani. It accused them of having conducted the revolution "by tribal methods" and of being "in cahoots with imperialism." Nor was the KDP "provisional leadership" spared; they were condemned for "having retained links with the Shah and with imperialism." The "provisional leadership" of the KDP had in fact adopted a radical program. Action might be a different matter.

The divergences, one might even say the fumblings, of the Kurdish political "class" did not prevent the partisans at home from pursuing their movement of popular resistance.[70] They persevered, and found many echoes in the Kurdish population. Eventually, in late June 1976, Saddam Hussein came to Kurdistan and published a declaration[71] in which he referred to the measures taken in Kurdistan (the transfer of populations from strategic and frontier regions) and stated that they would no longer be enforced, as the policy they were part of had achieved its goals. "Since order in the region has been re-established and the foundations of national unity secured, it has been decided that all the above-mentioned measures will no longer be applied. This is most important and will enable the inhabitants of the region to develop some confidence in their security."

The Morals of the Iraqi Baath

Five months have elapsed since the lines above were written, in late August 1976. In the meantime, on October 7, 1976, the Baghdad leadership attempted to have me assassinated in my home in Lausanne. When the government invited me to Iraq in 1975, they no doubt hoped I might be won over to their side. When this failed, they turned to crime in an effort to still one of the voices opposing them and to frighten others.

On October 2, 1976 at my home in Lausanne, I received a very surprising telephone call from Nabil al-Tikriti, Iraq's one-time Consul-General in Geneva, now promoted to ambassadorial rank as Baath adviser on foreign affairs. Claiming to be on a brief mission to the United Nations in Geneva, he suggested he would like to meet me again "on a friendly basis." Nabil al-Tikriti, like his first cousin, Vice-President Saddam Hussein, and like President al-Bakr himself, comes from the town of Tikrit. I had had occasion to speak to him just before and just after my journey to Iraq in 1975. When this mission proved a political failure, he had assured me that he "would plead our case before the government, in the hope of renewing the ties of friendship between Arabs and Kurds."

I agreed to see him and two other Iraqi "diplomats" he had told me were members of a trade delegation. The next day (October 3), at three o'clock, Nabil al-Takriti and his two companions arrived at our house. My wife and I were with two Kurdish exiles in Lausanne, Dr. Kordou Noorjan and Dr. F. Redha. I had invited them to witness what was said during the meeting.

Before leaving, Nabil al-Tikriti mentioned a present he had brought for us from Baghdad, a packet of fresh dates, which he had apparently accidentally left behind in Geneva. "I'll have them delivered," he said. "I'm taking the plane back to Baghdad tomorrow."

On October 7, one of Nabil al-Tikriti's so-called diplomats rang at my door. I invited him in and he put the packet of dates on the table in the living room, "with the compliments of Nabil al-Tikriti." I asked him if he would like coffee or an alcoholic drink. The killer, who knew the layout of my house, opted for coffee. I went to the kitchen to make some. I had just turned on the electric stove when a shot rang out. The "diplomat" had fired at point-blank range two 7.65 mm bullets which both smashed into my head, one behind the left ear, the other breaking my lower jaw. The medical report stated that the victim of this assassination attempt "escaped death only by an extraordinary fluke."

Poor People's Colonialism

Within the artificial frontiers inherited from imperialism, many Third World states practice a "poor people's colonialism." It is directed against often sizable minorities, and is both more ferocious and more harmful than the classical type. The effects of economic exploitation are aggravated by an almost total absence of local development and by a level of national oppression fueled by chauvinism and unrestrained by the democratic traditions which in the past usually limited the more extreme forms of injustice under the old colonialism. In the Middle East the Kurdish people are one of its victims.

The Kurdish movement has always proclaimed the people of Kurdistan's right to self-determination, although they have never fought for complete exercise of this right. In Iraq, the KDP hoped for a resolution of the Kurdish question which would remain within the context of the Iraqi Republic, being based on a form of internal autonomy. The Party demanded a solution on the level of provincial autonomy, and never even went as far as to propose a federalist structure.

It is high time the Kurdish question was posed as a question of national liberation, as an example of the right to self-determination. It is time to forge the political instruments necessary for such a struggle.

The Kurdish people's right to self-determination is incontestable. It includes the right to set up an independent and united Kurdistan. This right is inalienable, and no Kurdish political party, no fraction of the Kurdish people, and no one generation of Kurds can give away that right. No oppressor, no government can force the Kurdish people to renounce it. It is a right which belongs not only to the fractured Kurdish people as a whole, but also to each fraction of that whole, in each of the states of the area. Every part of Kurdistan is entitled to say whether it will continue as part of the present encompassing states[72] or whether it will split off, to live an independent life, be it as a single entity or in unison with some other fraction of the Kurdish people.

The exercise of this right by the Kurdish people does not automatically imply secession. Various solutions are possible, including national independence, binational or multinational federalism, and even internal autonomy within existing state frameworks.

But it might be stated that simple internal autonomy on the provincial level, as demanded by the KDP during the revolution, would not resolve the Kurdish national question in Iraq. It would leave the uninational structures of the Iraqi state quite unchanged, and would not provide the people of Iraqi Kurdistan with the necessary binational constitutional base. Under such conditions the Kurds would not be assured of full equality with the people of Arab Iraq, through equal participation in the making and carrying out of domestic and foreign policy. The central authorities would soon undermine this sort of provincial autonomy, which would in any case eventually be abolished or confiscated by dictatorial decree.

If the adjoining states do not wish to be dislocated by the creation of an independent Kurdistan sitting astride their frontiers, they should show that they deserve unity with the Kurdish people, rather than seeking to benefit from Kurdish misfortune or sitting unmoved on the sidelines. They could earn the trust of the Kurdish people by recognizing the latter's national identity and the rights it implies, by giving effective support to the struggle to do away with the "poor people's colonialism" their ruling classes impose on the Kurds. The Kurdish people's final choice will depend to a great extent on the attitude displayed.

The majority populations who wish to establish freely agreed unions with the Kurdish people should never forget that such unions can only be built on the basis of equality between national partners. *A fortiori*, the Kurds will retain their right to "unite amongst themselves" and to overthrow the inter-state frontiers which at present dismember their country.

Notes

1. *Le Kurdistan Irakien, Entite Nationale*, La Baconniere, (Neuchatel, 1970), p. 419.
2. The 1965 official census did not cover the Kurdish regions (14,000 square miles in extent) held at the time by the revolutionary army.
3. *Annual Abstract of Statistics, 1974*, op. cit., p. 34. Disregarding the Baathist inspired transfers of population, and basing oneself on the relative size of the country's various ethnic groups in 1961, one can estimate that, in 1975, some 8.6% of the population of Iraqi Kurdistan was non-Kurdish (250,000 out of 2,900,000). 130,000 (45% of the 8.6%) are probably Turkish-speaking Turkomans, who live mainly in the towns of Kirkuk province. There are also about 100,000 nomadic and sedentary Arabs who live close to the Arab-Kurdish demarcation line, notably in Hawidjeh, a mixed quarter in eastern Kirkuk. As for Kurdistan's Assyro-Chaldeans, who all speak Kurdish and who have participated in the country's national movement, they should be counted as Christian Kurds, just as the Chaldeans of Iraq are counted as Arabs. There are about 60,000 of them in Kurdistan — 12,000 in Arbil, the rest mainly in Badinan.
4. In 1919 the British administration in Iraq estimated the population of Basra, Baghdad and Mosul at about 2,750,000, 28.65% of which was accounted for by Mosul (788,000). This is about the same as the proportion of Kurds in Iraq, since Mosul's Arab and Turkoman populations are balanced out by the Kurds of Baghdad. Cf. Arnold Wilson, *Loyalties in Mesopotamia*, Oxford, (London, 1936), Vol. 1, p. 13.
5. Cf. *The Europa Yearbook*, (London, 1975), Vol. II, p. 714 ff.
6. The Iraqi Ministry of the Interior estimates that Kurds represent about 15% of the Iraqi population (Cf. *Iraq, A Tourist's Guide*, Tourist Office, Baghdad, 1975, p. 95). In his book, *L'Iraq d'aujourd'hui*, (Paris, 1963), p. 59, Bernard Venier suggests that the population is 70% Arab, 28% Kurdish and 2% other.

7. *Annual Abstract of Statistics, 1974*, op. cit. The figures concerning the surface area of the state and the provinces given in this recent book of Iraqi statistics are somewhat lower than those in the three volume *Larousse* (1967), which gives 173,332 square miles for Iraq and 4,700, 6,100 and 7,800 square miles for Suleimanieh, Arbil and Kirkuk respectively.
8. Figure provided in August 1975 by the Town Prefect.
9. Figure provided by the Governor of Arbil.
10. See J. Pichon, *Le Partage du Proche Orient*, (Paris, 1938), p. 77, for the full text of this letter.
11. Ibid., p. 80.
12. Ibid., p. 80ff. (Letter from London to Sherif Hussein).
13. A. Wilson, *Mesopotamia 1917–1920*, (London, 1931), pp. 103, 127, 129, 134 and 137.
14. See Lord Curzon's speech as leader of the British delegation to the Lausanne Conference, January 23, 1923, section 21.
15. A. Wilson, op. cit., p. 117.
16. Cf. H.D. Hall, *Mandates, Dependencies and Trusteeships*, (London, 1948), p. 37.
17. *Report on the Administration of Iraq, October 1920–March 1922.*
18. Cf. *League of Nations Special Report on Progress in Iraq.*
19. League of Nations, *The Council and Member States*, doc. 1925, c 400 M.147, a "Report by the commission set up by the September 30, 1924 resolution to investigate the question of the frontier between Turkey and Iraq."
20. League of Nations *Official Journal*, July 1932, pp. 1212–6.
21. See thesis by the late Jean-Pierre Viennot, *Contribution a l'etude de la sociologie et l'histoire du mouvement national kurde (1920 a nos jours)*, (Paris, 1969, unpublished) and Jean O. Pradir, *Les Kurdes, revolution silencieuse*, (Bordeaux, 1968).
22. In this speech I stressed that for all that it is in Iraq, Iraqi Kurdistan is also part of the Kurdish nation, just as Arab Iraq is part of the Arab nation; in doing so, I was criticizing Article 2 of Qasim's Constitution, which asserts that: "The Iraqi state is an integral part of the Arab nation."
23. Cf. *Le Monde*, July 14, 1963. On July 3, 1963 the government of the People's Republic of Mongolia proposed that the XVIIIth General Assembly of the UN consider the problem of the "policy of genocide implemented by the Iraqi government against the Kurdish people." On July 9 in Moscow, Andrei Gromyko, the Soviet Foreign Minister, sent notes to the ambassadors of Iraq, Turkey, Iran and Syria warning the latter three states against any pro-Iraqi military intervention in the war in Kurdistan.
24. All our information concerning this RCC communique and the text of the March 11 Agreement is drawn from the French translation issued by the Iraqi Baath, in a pamphlet entitled *La Solution du probleme Kurde en Iraq*.
25. See the "Charter of National Activities of the Progressive National Front" proposed by the RCC on November 16, 1971 in *Al-Jamahariyya*, the official mouthpiece of the Iraqi government.
26. Cf. *L'Orient — Le Jour*, the French-language Beirut daily, November 18, 1971.
27. Cf. World Conference of Communist Parties, Prague, January 1974.
28. See the excellent Minority Rights Group's Report No. 23 on *The Kurds* (London, 1975). See also *Pogrom* No. 15 (in German)(Hamburg, 1974).
29. Nothing illustrates the bad faith of the Iraqi government more clearly than the fate of the United Nations plan "for the reconstruction of northern Iraq" after the fourth war in Kurdistan. Baghdad itself had asked the specialized agencies of the UN to prepare such a plan on May 20, 1970. A UNESCO mission was sent to Iraqi Kurdistan from October 9 to 28, 1970, and submitted a two-volume report in January 1971. The commissioners observed that, in the Region's 29,000 square miles, 300 villages had been affected, 40,000 houses destroyed and more than 30,000 people rendered homeless. Furthermore, there was a marked shortage of food, especially proteins, in the ravaged areas. The development of northern Iraq, concluded the Report, would require a complete reorientation of existing economic programs. The commissioners recommended an aid scheme backed by IMF financial assistance. The Iraqi government completely ignored these proposals.
30. B. Vernier, *L'Irak d'aujourd'hui*, op. cit., pp. 387–9.
31. Cf. *Le Monde*, February 17, 1976.
32. *Financial Times*, August 20, 1974.
33. Cf. report in *Le Monde*, February 4, 1976, based on UN documents. In the same issue the *per capita* GNP is given as $1,060 for Iran, $690 for Turkey and $490 for Syria.
34. See Ministry of Information Documentary Brochure No. 33 (Baghdad, 1974).
35. Cf. "The KDP's Case for Autonomy in Kurdistan," *Kurdistan Review* No. 1, published by the KDP.
36. Cf. Pierre Rondot's article "Les Kurdes" in the 1975 supplement to the *Encyclopaedia Universalis*.
37. Including practically the entire police force of the Kurdish towns, consisting of some 5,000 men and 250 officers, 30 lecturers and professors and 600 students from Suleimanieh University, 70 doctors (there were only 6 before), 150 engineers, 4,200 school-teachers, 100 non-commissioned officers, etc.
38. Communique quoted in *Le Monde*, May 6, 1975.

39. Cf. two articles by W. Safire — "Mr. Ford's Secret Sell-Out" and "Son of Secret Sell-Out" — in the *New York Times*, February 5 and 12, 1976.
40. Cf. Emile Guikovaty, "Comment les Kurdes ont ete trahis," in *L'Express*, March 8–14, 1976.
41. Extracts from the Pike Report reproduced in *The Village Voice* (New York), February 23, 1976.
42. Cf. the first of the above-mentioned articles by W. Safire.
43. In the Pike Report, the Shah is referred to as an "Allied Head of State," Iraq as "our ally's neighbor," Mustafa Barzani as "the leader of the ethnic group."
44. Words in parentheses inserted by editor of *The Village Voice*.
45. Cf. Pike Report.
46. Ibid.
47. Memo quoted in Pike Report.
48. Pike Report.
49. Ibid.
50. Second of W. Safire's articles.
51. Guikovaty's article in *L'Express*.
52. Ibid.
53. Ibid.
54. For the complete English translation of this treaty, see *The Baghdad Observer*, June 23, 1975.
55. Algeria has been independent for many years. The Berbers of Kabylia and the Aures contributed to that victory, yet have still not been granted cultural rights. How can one ignore the existence of several million Berbers, whilst recognizing the right to self-determination of the population of ex-Spanish Sahara, numbering less than 100,000, whatever the rights of the latter?
56. "La Proie pour l'ombre," *Le Monde*, April 3, 1975.
57. Saddam Hussein, *Propos sur les problemes actuels*, published in French by *Al-Thawra*, a Baath mouthpiece, (Baghdad), p. 123.
58. For the text of the two telegrams released by Baghdad, see *Le Monde*, March 21, 1975.
59. According to sources close to the KPU (notably a KDP preparatory commission opposed to both the Barzani family and the Party's "provisional leadership"), on March 6, 1975, shortly before the retreat to Iran, the Kurdish High Command had under its control 60,000 partisans (50,000 according to my estimate), 16,000 square miles of territory (12,000 according to my estimate), at least 15 million rounds of rifle and machine gun ammunition, more than 5,000 mortar shells and bazooka rockets, as well as funds amounting to 22 million Iraqi dinars (about $70 million). Only the funds were taken along by the High Command when they went into exile.
60. Cf. Pike Report and *New York Times*, February 4, 1976.
61. "Security."
62. Either Ibrahim Ahmed or Jalal Talabani.
63. Fakher Mergasori's murder was particularly gratuitous in that it was done while he was in prison. Sources close to the KPU also claim that in 1973 the *Parastin* assassinated 12 Kurdish and Arab ex-members of the Central Committee of the Iraqi Commnunist Party. They were on their way back from a European socialist country and had decided to enter Free Kurdistan, where they expected to be welcomed, as in 1963. They were picked off by the *Parastin* at Zakho, near the Syrian frontier. The Kurdish *Parastin* were taking a leaf out of Savak's book.
64. General Barzani's responsibility for the disaster is, in one sense, less heavy than that of the "intellectuals" of the KDP Central Committee who failed to give a lead to the Party at the moment of truth. The KDP completely collapsed when disaster struck, abandoning a "decapitated" people to their fate.
65. When we visited Suleimanieh, the university was closed for holidays. A teacher told us that it comprised Faculties of Science, Agriculture, Engineering, Medicine and Literature, as well as Institutes of Administration and Economics. There were 2,900 students of whom 65% were Kurds and 35% Arabs; more than a third of the students were women. Science subjects were taught in English, Humanities in Kurdish or Arabic, according to the section concerned. Arab students studied Kurdish.
66. See Chris Kutschera's report in *Le Monde Diplomatique*, August 1977.
67. 60,000 according to Iraqi sources.
68. See English text in *The Baghdad Observer*, February 9, 1976.
69. UNO Press Communique HR/362, Geneva, April 5, 1976.
70. On June 9, 1977, a third Kurdish political group emerged, the Kurdish Democratic Union (KDU), which set itself apart from both the KPU and the KDP. The KDU called itself a socialist organization and sought to create a front which would bring together all three political forces in Kurdistan as well as "a broad Arab and Kurdish democratic front in Iraq," which would oppose "the dictatorship of the Tikrit clique" in the Iraqi Baath. On the national level, the KDU intended to work towards a "strategic alliance" between the Arab and Kurdish nations as a whole. Finally, the Union supported the idea of a "National Kurdish Conference," which would not be restricted to the Iraqi context, so that the representatives of the Kurdish nation could reach agreement as to its future. The idea was a good one and dear to the hearts of many Kurds. In the fall of 1977, the Iraqi regime decided to adopt Arabic as the language of instruction for various subjects such as

geography and history which had, until then, been taught in Kurdish in the secondary schools of the "Autonomous Region." This policy of acculturation, approved by Hashim Aqrawi, leader of the Kurdish "executive," was no doubt another example of efforts to promote the Kurdish people's "cultural fulfilment," just like the closure of the Kurdish section of Baghdad University and the Arabization of Suleimanieh University.

71. Circular published in *Irak* (Baghdad), July 5, 1976. Having announced on July 5 that the deportations would stop, Saddam Hussein proceeded to contradict himself on August 21, 1976 by officially announcing his new "cordon" policy, which consisted of evacuating the entire Kurdish population from a twelve mile deep strip along the frontiers. This confirmed the Iraqi regime's intention to continue in its attempts to eventually destroy the Republic's second main nationality.

72. In which case, they should be entitled to set up their own government on their own territory wherever they form a majority, to enjoy the fruits of their labor and the benefit of their resources, and to share in decisions as to the nature and form of their union with the neighboring majorities.

6

The Kurds in Syria

Mustafa Nazdar

A great deal of information about the Kurds of Syria and the Jezireh can be found scattered here and there in medieval Arab and Muslim writings. In contrast, the modern literature on the subject amounts to a mere handful of articles.[1]

There are no official statistics on the number of Kurds in Syria. Even if there were such figures, they would not be particularly trustworthy. One is reduced to making estimates region by region, drawing on as wide a range of sources of information as possible. On this basis, one can say that in 1976 there were something like 825,000 Kurds living in the Syrian Arab Republic, amounting to 11% of the population of 7.5 million.[2] Their regional distribution was as follows:

Kurdish Population in Syria by Region

Region	Population
Kurd-Dagh	290,000[3]
Jebel Samaan and Azaz	30,000
Ain al-Arab	60,000
Northern Jezireh	360,000
Southern Jezireh	10,000
Aleppo	10,000
Hama	5,000
Damascus	30,000
Other towns or regions	30,000
Total	*825,000*

One-third of the Kurds in the capital, Damascus, live in various parts of the town. The other two-thirds live in the Kurdish Quarter, in the foothills of Mount Qassioun.[4] Leaving aside Kurds who live in Arab towns or regions (the bottom five figures in the table above), we are left with three Kurdish or mainly Kurdish regions in the north of the country. The 740,000 Kurds who live there represent about 10% of the Republic's total population.

The Kurd-Dagh, meaning "Mountain of the Kurds," lies north-west of Aleppo, bordering on the Antioch and Alexandria Plain. With its dense, entirely Kurdish population and its 360 prosperous villages, the Kurd-Dagh is the westernmost region of Kurdistan and the only Kurdish populated mountainous area in Syria. Cereals, vines, fig trees and mulberry bushes all grow there. A little higher up, as elsewhere in Kurdistan, there are oak forests and, since the Mediterranean is not far away, olive trees. Apart from these 290,000 Kurds, there are 30,000 others who live in the nearby partially Kurdish mountain districts of Jebel Samaan and Azaz, just across the Afrin River Valley. To the north, the Kurd-Dagh gives way to the Anti-Taurus Mountains of Turkish Kurdistan.

The Ain-Arab (or Arab-Pinar) region lies to the north-east of Aleppo, just east of where the Euphrates enters Syrian territory. There are 120 villages in this entirely Kurdish area. In the Middle Ages Arab/Muslim geographers did not classify this region as part of Syria (al-Sham) at all but as the beginning of the Jezireh, the Island between the Tigris and the Euphrates. It was thus considered as part of Upper Mesopotamia. Similarly Iraq, the Arab word for Lower or Desert Mesopotamia, was used to designate an area which stopped somewhere between Baghdad and Tikrit, leaving the whole of southern Kurdistan, today's northern Iraq, as part of the *adjami* (Iranian) world.

The northern part of the Governorship or Province of Jezireh, with its 450,000 inhabitants, has the country's largest Kurdish population, numbering some 360,000.[5] This predominantly Kurdish area stretches over 175 miles along the northern section of the Iraqi frontier (Iraqi Kurdistan). The strip varies in width from 12 to 36 miles and constitutes most of the "duck's bill" formation in the north-east of the country. There are 700 villages in the area, all of them Kurdish since the Arab population is nomadic. During the Ottoman era this was the area where the nomadic Shammar, Tai and Bakkareh Arab tribes grazed their camels, alongside the Kurdish semi-nomadic Milli, Dakkori and Haverkan tribes, who would drive their sheep down from the Anti-Taurus Mountains to spend the winter there. From 1920 onwards, this part of the Jezireh was settled by the Kurdish tribes, along with mountain peasants and some town dwellers who had fled from Turkish Kurdistan after the failure of the revolt against Kemalism. They gradually became permanently settled and established a *modus vivendi* with the Arab tribes, who remained nomadic but accepted withdrawing their herds from the areas of cultivation. Thanks to the labors of the Kurdish peasantry, it was not long before small burgs and trading posts began to spring up amongst the wheatfields won from the desert. In a few decades the Syrian Jezireh had become the country's main granary.

The southern part of the Jezireh Governorship, including its chief township, Hasaka, has no more than 100,000 inhabitants, mainly nomadic Arabs. Amongst them live some 10,000 Kurds, 5 to 7,000 of whom are Yezidis settled around Lake Khatun. This small group represents the extension into Syrian territory of the Mount Sindjar zone of Yezidi population in Iraqi Kurdistan.

Are these three regions — Kurd-Dagh, Ain-Arab, and Northern Jezireh — part of Kurdistan? Do they form a Syrian Kurdistan, or are they merely regions of Syria which happen to be populated with Kurds?

Leaving aside the definitions of the medieval Muslim geographers, the areas are, in terms of the state, as much an integral part of Syria as is Damascus. But in terms of ethnography these three areas are clearly extensions of Turkish Kurdistan, the area they border on.

The Kurdish areas of the Jezireh also border on Iraqi Kurdistan. The March 9, 1921 London Agreement, between France (Syria was then under French mandate) and the Kemalist government of Turkey, did not fix the Syrian-Turkish border in strict accordance with the existing ethnic demarcation line between Arabs and Kurds. Three Kurdish enclaves were turned over to Syria, while in the north an Arab majority pocket south of Harran was left as part of Turkish Kurdistan, as was a mixed population of Kurds and Arabs to the east of Kilis. Furthermore, in 1938, Kemalist Turkey seized the Sandjak of Alexandrette, including the Plain of Antioch with its mixed Arab, Kurdish and Turkish population. It is now known as Hatay.

In Syria, the three regions in question are separated one from the other by Arab populated areas. Syrian Kurdistan has thus become a broken up territory and we would do better to talk about the *Kurdish regions in Syria*. The important thing is that 10% of Syria's population are Kurds who live in their own way in well-defined areas in the north of the country. What matters is that these people are being denied their legitimate right to have their own national and cultural identity.

The Kurds of Syria are essentially a peasant people, whose system of cultivation is intensive in the mountainous Kurd-Dagh area and extensive in the other two regions. They also own herds of sheep and goats, produce dairy products, weave Kilims and, in the Kurd-Dagh, make olive oil and charcoal which is exported to Aleppo. The town dwellers, representing barely 20% of the overall population, live mainly on petty trading and handicrafts. There are six small Kurdish towns in Syria, and the four main ones are all in the Jezireh: Qamishli (population 40,000), Amuda (15,000), Derbasiya (15,000) — all three of which are situated near the Turkish border — Derik (about 6,000) near the Iraqi border, Ain al-Arab (about 8,000) the chief township of the area of that name, and Afrin (about 20,000) the chief township of the Kurd-Dagh.

The Kurds in Medieval Syria

In his study of the *Historical Topography of Ancient and Medieval Syria*, Rene Dussaud notes that the Kurd-Dagh and the plain near Antioch had been "occupied by Kurds since Antiquity."[6] In his Ph.D. thesis, Claude Cahen, now Professor of Islamic Studies at the Sorbonne, mentions that the town of Hama was a Kurdish fiefdom held by Ali ben Wafa, known as Ali the Kurd, who died in 1114.[7] His two sons, Nasir and Kurdanshah (which means literally "King of the Kurds"), became vassals of Toghtekin, the Seljuk or Turkoman Emir of Damascus.[8] Ali the Kurd's family were masters of Rafanya, as well as of Hama and the mountainous region separating it from Tripoli and Lattaquie.[9] In his monumental work on *Nur ad-Din, a Great Muslim Prince at the Time of the Crusades*, Nikita Elisseef, Professor of Islamic Studies at the University of Lyons, describes the social structures of Syria at the time: "If we look at the population in terms of the classical social categories, we get the following pyramid. At the top, a Turkish and Kurdish military aristocracy which lived in the towns, along with civilian government representatives and tax officers. Apart from these 'foreigners,' the towns were also inhabited by a group of privileged Muslims, those who could claim descent from the Prophet."[10] Unlike the Kurds, the Turkish or Turkoman followers of Nur ad-Din Zangui (whom the Crusaders knew as Nuradin) and the Toghtekin were recent arrivals in the area. The Arabs, who formed the bulk of the population, went through a period of military decadence, and had to entrust the defense of the country against the Crusader armies to their Kurdish or Turkish Emirs.

The Krak des Chevaliers, the famous fortress taken by the Crusaders, and which still stands proudly not far from Masyaf, was built by Kurds.[11] Indeed, Claude Cahen tells us that "as a result of the frequent political unions between northern Syria and the Jezireh, Kurdish Mamelukes and Kurdish military colonies also settled there. In the eleventh Century, one of these colonies founded Hisn al-Akrad, the future Krak des Chevaliers."[12]

Before occupying Jerusalem, the Crusaders had established themselves without much difficulty along the coast, notably at Antioch and Tripoli. The Syrian Muslims were divided amongst themselves. "Bedouins, Kurds and Turkomans frequently massacred each other," and "the struggles between Shias and Sunnis continued. However, they were soon to have common enemies: the Franks from the outside and the Assassins within."[13]

The Abbasid Caliph in Baghdad exerted only moral authority. The Muslim Emirs of Mesopotamia and Iran almost came to the the rescue, but the Syrians feared that they would seize the country for themselves. In fact the Turkoman Emirs of Aleppo and Damascus did not hesitate to form an alliance with the Franks to repel any such military "assistance."

It was not until 1148 that the Muslims won their first victory over the Franks. Nur ad-Din Zangui, the Turkoman Emir of Mosul, had been entrusted with the leadership of the Jihad. As Elisseef remarks: "The young Zanguid prince had under his command a great many Kurdish Emirs as well as Turks. This mixed Turkish and Kurdish army was essentially foreign to the population of Syria."[14] The army he sent to Syria, while he himself remained in Mosul, was commanded by two Kurdish brothers, descended from the Rawand tribe. Najm ad-Din Ayyub and Sherkuh, father and uncle respectively of the great Saladin. The future hero, then a young man, was with them at the time. Sherkuh and Ayyub took Aleppo and chased Toghtekin from Damascus. Ayyub was appointed Viceroy of Syria, while Sherkuh was designated *isfah-salar*, an Iranian word meaning "Commander-in-Chief" of the Army. On Nur ad-Din's behalf, the brothers went on to occupy Egypt and do away with the rival Fatimid Caliphate. Sherkuh died in Cairo and his nephew, Saladin (Salah ad-Din), was elected *isfah-salar* by the chiefs of the Muslim army, much to the displeasure of various Turkoman Emirs close to Nur ad-Din. Saladin was then thirty-seven and was soon to set himself up as a rival to Nur ad-Din. His army was no longer "Turkish and Kurdish," it had become "Kurdish and Turkish," with a preponderance of Kurdish Emirs. He eventually returned to Syria, received the title of Sultan from the Abbassid Caliph, defeated the Franks at Hattin and in 1187 brought down the Frankish Kingdom of Jerusalem. Some time before, Saladin had seized Libya, the Sudan, the Hejaz and the Yemen. The Kurdish Emirs of Diyarbekir and Mosul gave him allegiance. In Palestine he victoriously withstood the Third Crusade, waged by Philip Augustus, King of France, Richard the Lion Heart, King of England and the troops of the German Emperor, Frederick Barbarossa. On October 4, 1189, at the battle of Acre, the Muslim army under the Kurdish Sultan had fourteen Generals, half of whom were Kurdish Emirs. Before he was killed by one of his own Mamelukes in 1249, Turanshah, the last Kurdish King of Egypt and Syria and heir to the great Saladin, managed to capture the King of France, St. Louis.

The "Legal" and "Ideological" Basis for Oppression

During the long period of Ottoman domination, relations between the Arab and Kurdish people were neighborly, in the context of the Umma or Muslim community. When the French and British troops pulled out in 1946 and the country became independent, Arab-Kurdish relations were still fairly good.[15]

However, independent Syria, governed by an Arab bourgeoisie which emerged from the latifundist-based National Front, soon adopted a pan-Arabist ideology and refused to recognize the Kurds' rights as a national minority. The very existence of the Kurds was ignored, as happened to the religious and national minorities of all the other Arab states, be it the Berbers of North Africa, the Copts of Eygpt, the Maronites of Lebanon or the Druze and Alawites of Syria. But the Kurds of Syria were not the target of direct repressive measures. From 1946 to 1962 the popular poet Geguerxwin was free to publish his *diwan* in Latin characters and in his own national language. In the Kurdish townships of Qamishli, Amuda and Afrin, state education was in Arabic only, but Kurdish schoolbooks were circulated freely.

In 1957 a group of intellectuals, workers and peasants founded the Kurdish Democratic Party in Syria, on the model of the Iraqi KDP. Its program was to obtain recognition for the Kurds as an ethnic group entitled to their own culture. It also planned to join with other political organizations in the struggle for agrarian reform and the setting up of a democratic government in Damascus. In 1959 various leaders of the Syrian KDP were arrested. This was at the time of the union with Egypt, under the aegis of Colonel Sarraj, who took his orders directly from President Nasser of the United Arab Republic.

In September 1961, Syria split from Egypt and the big latifundist bourgeoisie led by Qudsi and Azm seized power. The new government intensified the policy of national oppression directed against the Kurds, who were accused of taking an anti-Arabist stance. The Kurds were suspected of being "in league" with the Kurds of Iraq, who had just launched the September 1961 insurrection aimed at securing autonomous status within an Iraqi framework.

On August 23, 1961, the government promulgated a decree (No. 93) authorizing a special population census in Jezireh Province. It was claimed that Kurds from Turkish Kurdistan were "illegally infiltrating" the Jezireh in order to "destroy its Arab character." The census was carried out in November of that year; when its results were released, some 120,000 Jezireh Kurds were discounted as foreigners and unjustly stripped of their rights as Syrian nationals. In 1962, to combat the "Kurdish threat" and "save Arabism" in the region, the government inaugurated the so-called "Arab Cordon plan" (*Al Hizam al-arabi*), which envisaged the expulsion of the entire Kurdish population living along the border with Turkey. They were to be gradually replaced by Arabs and would be resettled, and preferably dispersed, in the south. The discovery of oil at Qaratchok, right in the middle of Kurdish Jezireh, no doubt had something to do with the government's policy.

In March 1963, Michel Aflaq's Baath Party came to power. Its socialism was soon shown to be mainly of the national variety. The Kurds' position worsened. In November 1963, in Damascus, the Baath published a *Study of the Jezireh Province in its National, Social and Political Aspects*, written by the region's Chief of Police, Mohamed Talab Hilal. The work gained him first the Governorship of Hama, then a Baathist cabinet post as Minister of Supply in Mr. Zouayyen's government, a job he retained for years in successive cabinets.

Hilal had set out to "prove scientifically," on the basis of various "anthropological" considerations, that the Kurds "do not constitute a nation."[16] His conclusion was that "the Kurdish people are a people without history or civilization or language or even definite ethnic origin of their own. Their only characteristics are those shaped by force, destructive power and violence, characteristics which are, by the way, inherent in all mountain populations." Furthermore: "The Kurds live from the civilization and history of other nations. They have taken no part in these civilizations or in the history of these nations."[17]

A zealous nationalist, Hilal proposed a twelve-point plan, which would first be put into operation against the Jezireh Kurds: (1) a *batr* or "dispossession" policy, involving the transfer and dispersion of the Kurdish people; (2) a *tajhil* or "obscurantist" policy of depriving the Kurds of any education whatsoever, even in Arabic; (3) a *tajwii* or "famine" policy, depriving those affected of any employment possibilities; (4) an "extradition" policy, which meant turning the survivors of the uprisings in northern Kurdistan over to the Turkish government; (5) "a divide and rule" policy, setting Kurd against Kurd; (6) a *hizam* or "cordon" policy similar to the one proposed in 1962; (7) an *iskan* or "colonization" policy, involving the implantation of "pure and nationalist Arabs" in the Kurdish regions so that the Kurds could be "watched until their dispersion"; (8) a military policy, based on "divisions stationed in the zone of the cordon" who would be charged with "ensuring that the dispersion of the Kurds and the settlement of Arabs would take place according to plans drawn up by the government"; (9) a "socialization" policy, under which "collective forms," *mazarii jama'iyya*, would be set up for the Arabs implanted in the regions. These new settlers would also be provided with "armament and training"; (10) a ban on "anybody ignorant of the Arabic language exercising the right to vote or to stand for office"; (11) sending the Kurdish *ulemas* to the south and "bringing in Arab *ulemas* to replace them"; (12) finally, "launching a vast anti-Kurdish campaign amongst the Arabs."

The Burden of Oppression

Many of the measures listed above were put into practice. The 120,000 Kurds classified as non-Syrian by the "census" suffered particularly heavily. Although they were treated as foreigners and suspects in their own country, they were nonetheless liable for military service and were called up to fight in the Golan Heights. However, they were deprived of any other form of legitimate status. They could not legally marry, enter a hospital or register their children for schooling.

The euphemistically renamed "Plan to establish model state farms in Jezireh Province," the so-called "Arab Cordon" plan, was not dropped in the years that followed. Under the cover of "socialism" and agrarian reform, it envisaged the expulsion of the 140,000 strong Kurdish peasantry, who would be replaced with Arabs. In 1966, there were even thoughts of applying it seriously, and perhaps extending it to the Kurd-Dagh. But those Kurdish peasants who had been ordered to leave refused to go. In 1967 the peasants in the Cordon zone were informed that their lands had been nationalized. The government even sent a few teams to build "model farms," until the war against Israel forced it momentarily to drop its plans.

Following the construction of the Tabqa Dam across the Euphrates, it was suggested that those Arab peasants whose villages had been submerged be resettled in Kurdish Jezireh. In 1975, the state built 40 "model villages" in the Cordon Zone, between Amuda in the west and Derik in the east, including in the Qamishli region. Seven thousand Arab peasant families were armed and implanted. The plan was carried out gradually, so as not to attract too much attention from the outside world. The Kurds were subjected to regular administrative harassment, police raids, firings and confiscation orders. Kurdish literary works were seized, as were records of Kurdish folk music played in public places. The little town of Derik lost its Kurdish name and was officially restyled Al-Malikiyyeh. Syrian KDP leaders were imprisoned for years, charged with "anti-Arabist actions."[18] Between 1965 and 1975, some 30,000 Jezireh Kurds were forced to leave, to find work and safety in Lebanon or in the towns of the interior. In the Kurd-Dagh, the banditry encouraged by the state forced a growing number of Kurds to leave the region and settle in Aleppo.

True, the Assembly retained a certain number of Kurdish deputies, but they could not stand as such since the official fiction decreed that all Syrian citizens are Arabs. In all the official publications of the Syrian Arab Republic, the Kurds — and every other non-Arab group — are never mentioned. Since the Republic is "Arab," the Kurds must be as well.[19]

However in 1976, President Assad officially renounced any further implementation of the plan to transfer the population, and decided "to leave things as they are." The Kurdish peasants of the Jezireh would not be harassed any more, and no further Arab villages would be built on their lands. But the villages which had already been built would stay, as would the newcomers transplanted from the Euphrates Valley. The radio began to broadcast Kurdish music and the Kurds in the country felt much safer. They wondered, however, if this was the beginning of a new policy *vis-a-vis* the Kurds of Syria or if it was just a government maneuver predicated on the rivalry between Damascus and the Iraqi Government.

Notes

1. During the twenties, Roger Lescot, the orientalist who was then serving as a French officer in Syria, produced some interesting studies including one on "Proverbes et Enigmes Kurdes" (*Revue des etudes islamiques*, Paris, 1937, Chapter IV, pp. 307–50) and his excellent *Enquete sur les Yezidis* (Beirut, 1938). Father Thomas Bois's writings contain descriptions of the cultural renaissance among the Syrian Kurds. The orientalist Pierre Rondot, also a one-time French officer in Syria, has left us a good study of "Les Tribus montagnardes de l'Asie anterieure . . ." (*Bulletin d'ethnologie orientale de l'Institut francais de Damas*, Vol. VI, 1937, pp. 1–50) which deals with the sociology of the classic Kurdish tribes, as well as an article on "Les Kurdes de Syrie" in *La France mediterranienne et africaine*, (Paris, Sirey, 1939, Vol. II, Sect. I, pp. 81–126). Other unpublished works by the same author, including his article on *Les Kurdes* (1937), can be consulted in the CHEAM Center library at the University of Paris.
2. In its *Statistical Abstract, 1975*, the Damascus government gave the population of Syria in 1975 as 7,346,104, with a projected population of 8,623,044 in 1980.
3. The figure for the Kurd-Dagh is based on the number of representatives it sends to the People's Assembly. The region sends four delegates, one for each 60,000 inhabitants, and was only narrowly refused a fifth.
4. According to *Statistical Abstract, 1975*, the city of Damascus and its suburbs had a population of 836,688 in 1970.
5. *Statistical Abstract, 1975*, gives the total population of the Governorship of Jezireh as 545,899 in 1975.
6. R. Dussaud, *Topographie historique de la Syrie antique et medievale*, Geuthner, (Paris, 1927), p. 425.
7. C. Cahen, *La Syrie du Nord . . .*, Geuthner, Institut francais de Damas, (Paris, 1940), p. 272, note 27.
8. Ibid.
9. Ibid.
10. N. Elisseef, *Nur ad-Din*, Institut francais de Damas, (Damascus, 1967), Vol. III, p. 835.
11. The Arabic word *Hisn* means "fortress," whilst *Akrad* is the plural of "Kurd." The Krak des Chevaliers is still known as the "Fortress of the Kurds" in Arabic.
12. C. Cahen, op. cit., p. 186.
13. Ibid.
14. N. Elisseef, op. cit., Vol. III, pp. 721–2.
15. V. Minorsky, *Studies in Caucasian History*, Annexe: "Notes on the Kurds under the Ayyubids," (London, 1953).
16. M. T. Hilal, "Etude sur la province de Djazira . . .," (Damascus, 1963), pp. 3–5.
17. Ibid., pp. 45–8.
18. Amongst them, Daham Miro, Kenaan Aguid, and the lawyer Nazim Mirkan. The first two were "adopted" by Amnesty International.
19. It seems clear that a country like Syria, which calls itself socialist and modern, ought to renounce oppressive policies directed against the Kurds and ought to constitutionally recognize their existence as a national group, entitled to their own language and culture, within the Syrian people.

7

The Kurds in the Soviet Union

Kendal

The frontiers of the USSR do not include any mainly Kurdish territory contiguous with Kurdistan. The 1921 treaty between the Kemalist government of Turkey and the authorities in Soviet Armenia took the ethnic composition of the areas concerned into account when it fixed the new frontiers. The "mainly Muslim" (meaning Kurdish) province of Kars was turned over to Turkey and the district of Gumru — today's Leninakan — was attached to Soviet Armenia.

Although there are no Kurdish territories in the USSR, there is a Kurdish community — or rather several compact Kurdish colonies similar to those of Turkish Anatolia — scattered throughout the Transcaucasian and Central Asian Republics, in Armenia, Azerbaijan, Georgia, Kazakhstan, Kirghiz and the Turkoman SSR.

These small scattered, disparate colonies implanted in various cultural and geographic contexts are worth considering for two main reasons. Firstly, despite their reduced numbers, the Soviet Kurds, especially those of Armenia, occupy a very important place in Kurdish cultural life and are a focus of attraction for their compatriots in Kurdistan. Secondly, it is interesting to see the metamorphoses that these fractions of the Kurdish people — once the most backward and disinherited Kurds of all — have undergone under the Soviet regime. In this study I have drawn on the documents and accounts I gathered during two visits to Kazakhstan, the Kirghiz SSR, and the Caucasus (Armenia and Georgia) as well as on the official sources available. Unfortunately I did not have the occasion to visit Azerbaijan and the Turkoman SSR, so my information concerning those areas is all second-hand.

Population

According to the 1970 General Census, there were 37,486 people in the Kurdish colony in Armenia. One-third lived in Erivan, and the rest in the twenty-two villages in the Alaguez and Talinn "Kurdish district" (*Kurdskij rajon*); there were also a few mixed villages, usually Kurdish and Azerbaijani, less often Kurdish and Armenian.

In another section the Census mentions 20,960 Kurds living in Georgia, mainly in Tbilissi, in the town's Kurdish quarter.[1] The Kurds of Georgia and Armenia are mainly Yezidis.

In Azerbaijan, things look very different. The fifty odd villages and burgs in the Kelbajar, Latchine, Koubatly, Zenguiler and Nakhtchivan districts were populated entirely by Kurds until the end of the 1930s, but they gradually became ethnically mixed. However, the official statistics concerning the number of Kurds in the territory are full of contradictions. For instance, in 1926 the Census registered 42,000 Kurds in the area, in 1959 the figure had shrunk to 303, then in 1970 it jumped to 5,488. These changes hardly fit in with what we think of as the normal growth pattern for a population! Even if one takes into account the fact that religious affinity might have led the Muslim Kurds to assimilate through marriage with their Azerbaijani co-believers, the census figures still make practically no sense.

It seems clear that, until about 1965, the authorities in the Azerbaijan Republic repeatedly expressed their Great Turk chauvinism and actively sought to assimilate the "Muslim, hence Azerbaijani" Kurdish community. In 1929 this same nationalistic zeal had led to the liquidation of the Autonomous Republic of Kurdistan set up in 1923 in Latchine, Kelbajar and Nakhtchivan, "as a beacon to the entire Kurdish people."[2] The precise consequences of this liquidation are still relatively unknown.

Given the absence of credible statistics, I can only offer an estimate for the Kurdish-speaking population of Soviet Azerbaijan. According to my Kurdish sources in the Soviet Union, the correct figure is around 150,000 to 200,000.

A similarly peculiar situation prevails in the Turkoman SSR, another Turkish and Muslim Soviet Republic. The 1926 Census mentions some 22,000 Kurds living there. Thirty years later the official estimate was 20,000.[3] In 1970, the official figure had fallen to 2,933. The Kurds had not been subjected to any deportations during this period and one can hardly be expected to believe that "voluntary assimilation and intermingling" is the sole explanation. It would therefore seem very likely that the Turkoman authorities were applying a nationalistic policy which manifested itself in two ways. Firstly, on the cultural level, assimilation was actively encouraged and there were no structures through which a Kurdish identity could express itself. Secondly, on the administrative level, Kurds were being systematically put down as Turkoman in the official registers.

My Kurdish sources estimate the population of the Kurdish-speaking colony in the Turkoman SSR at about 50,000, implanted in Achkhabad, the capital, in the townships of Baguire and Bayram Ali and in various other districts such as Ciok-Tepe, Kakhka, Kara-Kala, Tejen, etc.[4]

In Kazakhstan, the Kurds live in small communities at Tchimkent, in Jamboul and around Alma Ata. According to the 1970 Census, there were 12,313 of them, and a further 7,974 in the Kirghiz SSR, mainly in Oche. I was struck by the fact that, in the middle of the steppes, the Kurds had chosen to settle in the very occasional mountainous zones, where they could continue to graze their herds.

The table sums up what we know about the size of the Kurdish colonies in the Soviet Union.

The Kurdish Population in the USSR

Soviet Republic	Kurdish Population (1970)
Armenia	37,486
Azerbaijan	150,000*
Georgia	20,690
Kazakhstan	12,313
Kirghiz	7,974
Turkoman	50,000*
Total	278,463

*Estimate, lower limit.

Historical Outline

There are historical reasons for the wide dispersion of the Soviet Kurds. From the second half of the 18th century certain Kurdish tribes gradually extended the range of their pastoral wanderings, venturing first into the Erivan Plain, and later far beyond into Azerbaijan, all the way to Baku. During this slow expansion, Kurdish villages were set up here and there. To some extent, the Czarist authorities seem to have welcomed the Kurdish incursion, no doubt bearing in mind that the known warlike qualities of the Kurds would come in useful during any future Russian clash with the Ottoman or Persian Empire. Later, the wars between Russia and Turkey (1828–29, 1853–56, 1877–78) and the Kurdish revolts throughout the 19th century swelled the ranks of the Kurdish population with a flood of refugees seeking safety in Czarist Russia. Many Yezidis came, Kurds who had been persecuted both by the Ottoman authorities and the traditional Muslim Kurdish chieftains for having their own religion, with its many and vivid Zoroastrian elements.

The wave of immigration continued to grow in the early 20th century. Just before the outbreak of the First World War, there were 40,159 Kurds in the Governorship of Erivan alone, 68.5% of whom were nomadic, the rest being settled.[5]

Religious factors often played a part in the Kurdish immigrants' decisions to settle this or that area in the Czarist Empire. The Yezidis, who had suffered long and extensively from the repressive practices of the Muslims, including a few real pogroms, preferred to settle in Christian Armenia and Georgia, where their religious practices aroused less hostility. The Muslim Kurds, on the other hand, settled mainly in Muslim Azerbaijan or, more rarely, in Azerbaijani colonies in Armenia. Even under the Soviet regime, religious affinities and differentiations continued to play an important role in the behavior and development of the Muslim and Yezidi Kurdish communities. Despite their small numbers, the Yezidi Kurds did the most to defend their Kurdish identity, jealously guarding their national particularities and resisting any attempts to absorb them into the Georgian or Armenian whole. Assimilation had a much greater impact on the Muslim Kurds who, despite their much greater numbers, played only a very secondary role in the development of Soviet cultural life.

After 1915, the flow of Kurdish immigration diminished considerably. The vicissitudes of the First World War, the terror inspired by the nationalist Dachnak government which held power in Erivan till November 20, 1920, and the chaos of the Russian Civil War caused a panic. Both Kemalist and pro-Sultan propaganda assured the Kurds that Bolshevism meant an end to the family, to religion, to all morality. Most of the Kurds fled, till in 1922 there were only 8,650 of them left in the Governorship of Erivan.

The setting up of the Soviet regime introduced a twofold break in the life of the Caucasian Kurds. Firstly, there was the break with their previous way of life. The nomads were permanently settled and gradually transformed into agricultural wage laborers. The children began to go to school. And these somewhat heterogeneous and scattered colonies started to develop a national life of their own. Secondly, there was a complete break in the links they used to maintain with the Kurds of Kurdistan. The frontiers were now impassable, a barrier between two separate worlds which nonetheless retained a degree of fellow feeling.

As for the Kurds of Central Asia, they are all Muslim but this should not be taken to mean that they share a common origin. Those in the Turkoman SSR are descended from the Kurdish tribes which Persian sovereigns forcibly implanted in Khorassan from the 16th century onwards to guard the Empire's eastern frontiers.[6] The Kurdish colony in Afghanistan, numbering some tens of thousands, has the same origin.

The arrival of Kurds in Kazakhstan and Kirghiz is a more recent development. It was only in 1937–38 that these Caucasian Kurds were accused of having provoked frontier incidents and several thousand of them were deported to these distant Asiatic Republics.

The Economic and Social Situation

Unlike their compatriots in Kurdistan, who were very disadvantaged compared to the respective dominant nations, in the mid-1970s the Soviet Kurds were amongst the most prosperous citizens of the USSR. Hard workers on the Sovkhoz and Kolkhoz collective farms, they also had their own herds and allotments to look after. The climate was very favorable and in general they enjoyed a privileged position.

This prosperity was immediately noticeable in the quality of their dwellings, modern houses in stone or brick, usually equipped with central heating and sometimes with a telephone. In a corner of the courtyards one invariably found a *tandoor*, the traditional clay oven for bread, etc. The standard of public utilities was also very high. The villages had broad, well lit streets, linked to the urban centers by reasonable roads. In each village was an adequate supply of drinking water and electricity, a telephone service, a food store, a secondary school or technical college, access to a doctor, a dispensary, a veterinarian and an agronomist, and a cultural club which provided a public library, a projection room and, in some cases, sports facilities.

The Kurdish town dwellers in the USSR were not subject to any form of discrimination. Their economic and social position was in no way inferior to that of their colleagues. Even in a Republic as evolved as Armenia, the relative proportion of Kurdish intellectuals was as high as the proportion of intellectuals in the Armenian population. They occupied very responsible posts, both in the Party and in the administration. In Armenia, where the Kurdish community represented barely 1% of the population, a Kurd sat on the Central Committee of the Armenian Communist Party. There were Kurdish Deputies in the Supreme Soviet and in the Soviet of Nationalities. These Kurds were Vice-Ministers (Transport, Rural Economy, and Justice).[7]

The situation was broadly similar in the other Republics. Despite their small numbers, Kurds reached the highest positions. For example, in Kazakhstan, the Minister of Irrigation was a Kurd. There were several Kurds teaching at Kazakh Universities.

Cultural Life

On the cultural level, the various Kurdish colonies, separated from one another by considerable distances and inserted into such different contexts, have undergone different evolutions, although they do have a few things in common.

One of these is that illiteracy was eliminated in the 1930s. Just after 1917, less than 1% of Kurds were literate. Considerable effort was put into providing education for all children of school age and into teaching illiterate adults to read and write. At first, teachers and tutors were given an intensive six months training course. Later, as more competent cadres were formed, compulsory schooling for four years was introduced. This was later extended to seven years, then to ten years.

The "battle for learning" was at its most intense from 1930 to 1937. This spread and democratization of education and access to culture are indubitably amongst the Soviet regime's most remarkable achievements.

However, it was not carried out everywhere by the same means. In Armenia, Georgia and to some extent in Azerbaijan, Kurds were taught to read and write in Kurdish. A Kurdish alphabet, developed in 1921 on the basis of Armenian characters, was used in Georgia and in Armenia's ten or so Kurdish schools until 1929, when Latin characters were adopted as more appropriate to the Kurdish language.[8]

In 1931 the Armenian SSR boasted 27 Kurdish schools, and a Kurdish teacher training college — the Transcaucasian Pedagogic Technicum — opened its gates in Erivan. Under the guidance of Academician Orbeli, a worker's college near the Leningrad Institute of Oriental Studies began to train Kurds in Kurdish studies for the first time. The students went on to promote their national culture.[9]

During the 1930s nearly all subjects were taught in Kurdish in the Kurdish schools. Most of the 30 or so Kurdish language books published every year in Armenia were textbooks, of physics, arithmetic, geography, agronomy, natural history and animal husbandry. But there were also some translated novels and poems from the Russian or the Armenian, brief biographies of Marx, Engels and Lenin, a few political pamphlets, copies of the Communist Manifesto and an Armenian-Kurdish dictionary. The first literary work by a Soviet Kurd, Ereb Semo's autobiographical *Sivane Kurd* (The Kurdish Shepherd), appeared as late as 1935, and was followed in 1936 by *Folklora Kurmanca*, an important collection of popular stories, legends and songs.

In Azerbaijan, however, during the (theoretical?) existence of the Autonomous Republic of Kurdistan (1923–29), not a single book was published in Kurdish and no Kurdish schools were set up. The main literacy program were based on Azerbaijani, and only very secondarily on Kurdish. The first Kurdish book published in Baku, in 1930, was an ABC. Each year thereafter one or two manuals in Kurdish were published, until 1937 when, exceptionally, twelve books came out.

In the Turkoman Republic, the sizable Kurdish colony was provided with only a half dozen mediocre volumes from 1933 to 1935. The literacy campaign was based on the official language of the Republic, in this case Turkoman, as it was in Azerbaijan. It is worth noting that after 1938 no Kurdish book appeared either in Azerbaijan or in the Turkoman SSR, and there have been no Kurdish schools in either territory.

In Armenia, which became the center of cultural life for the Soviet Kurds, no books were published in Kurdish from 1937 to 1946. Obviously the "nationalities policy" was suspended during this period, but the particular needs of wartime do not entirely explain the turnabout in Soviet policy. Once the Second World War was over the cultural production of the non-Russian nationalities fell to a very low level compared to what had been happening before 1938. The Kurds, for instance, only managed to publish two or three books a year, all dealing with language, literature or folklore. The Cyrillic alphabet was adopted "so as not to disorient Kurdish children who will also need to learn Georgian or Armenian characters, according to where they live." Similarly, "to ensure greater mobility for Kurdish children," only Kurdish language and literature were taught in Kurdish in the Kurdish schools; the other subjects were taught in Russian, Armenian or Georgian.

Later, when Khrushchev came to power, the "nationalities policy" was revamped so as to "repair the errors and injustices committed under Stalin." In 1957 twelve books in Kurdish were published, including a 30,000 word Russian-Kurdish dictionary compiled by I.0. Farizov; this was in notable contrast to the previous year, 1956, when a grammar book was the only new title produced.

All in all, from 1921 to 1960, 238 works, with a combined print-run of

370,000, were published in Kurdish in the Soviet Republics.[11] This may not be much in itself but it is still something when one bears in mind the Soviet Kurds' starting point and especially when one considers that in half a century the millions of Kurds in Turkey were only allowed to publish about a dozen titles.

In 1976, the Kurds of Armenia and Georgia, and to some extent those of Kazakhstan and the Kirghiz SSR, enjoyed cultural rights. Kurdish language and literature were taught in Kurdish in the Kurdish village schools. In the mixed villages, the parents of any children in a class with more than five Kurdish pupils could demand that their children be taught their national language and literature. All the schoolbooks were produced by the Armenian publishing houses, which also published the work of poets and writers affiliated to the Kurdish sections of the Armenian or Georgian Writers Unions. Poetry played a particularly important part in these publications, but they also included many plays, novels, essays and collections of folklore.

The four page Kurdish newspaper, *Riya Teze* (New Path), a mouthpiece of the Armenian Communist Party, came out in Erivan every two weeks after March 1930. Printed in Cyrillic from 1946 onwards, its circulation rose from the original 600 to 5,000 in 1976.[12] And from 1956 onwards Radio Erivan broadcast excellent daily Kurdish programs which attracted a very wide audience throughout Kurdistan as a whole and served to hold the Soviet Kurdish community together. In 1976 the programs ran for about 90 minutes every day.

But the cultural facilities provided for the Soviet Kurds were not everything. At the Moscow, Leningrad and Erivan Institutes of Oriental Studies, and to a lesser extent at Baku, Tbilissi and Tashkent, students of Kurdish history, language and classical literature were producing some remarkably interesting work. Many of these students were, of course, themselves Kurds and the armed struggle of the Kurds in Iraq did a great deal to stimulate research into the subject. There were more than 100 Kurdish postgraduates contributing to this new scholarly endeavour by the mid-1970s.

After 60 years of separation, one may wonder what the Soviet Kurds still had in common with their compatriots in Kurdistan, apart from the language. It is certainly true that over the years a distinct national community emerged, with its own traditions and ways of thinking. The community even had its own heroes, the most illustrious of whom was Ferik Polatbekov, the son of a Kurdish chieftain deported to Siberia. This young revolutionary poet, who became the main leader of the Red Army in Siberia and was finally killed by the Whites, remained totally unknown in Kurdistan.[13] The same applies to a number of Kurdish writers and poets who achieved fame in the Soviet Union.

Nonetheless, an unshakable and ancient cultural heritage continued to act as a powerful bond between this community and its country of origin. The children and grandchildren of "immigrant" or "exiled" Kurds knew the names of their ancestral villages and grazing grounds by heart. They still remembered to what tribe they belonged. Some Soviet Kurds painstakingly preserved customs and dress typical of the nomadic Kurds at the turn of the century, along with various archaisms which had actually disappeared in Kurdistan itself. Their justification was that, if they allowed their customs to fall into disuse, they would find themselves on the road to assimilation.

Although the Soviet Kurds were grateful and loyal to the regime, they continued to keep an eye on what happened in "their Kurdistan" and to entertain the hope that one day they would return to their homeland, to contribute to its development. The Kurdish national movement in Iraq gave new life to these hopes. The Soviet Kurds listened attentively to "The Voice of Free Kurdistan," broadcast by the Kurdish maquisards. They also kept up contacts with Kurdish students from Iraq and Syria, who came to attend Soviet universities. In fact, I found them remarkably well informed about what was going on in the various parts of Kurdistan.

From Georgia to the Kirghiz SSR which borders on China, I saw portraits of Barzani in many Kurdish homes, including those of senior Communist Party officials. "We know that Barzani is no revolutionary, that he is in fact more of a conservative," one communist told me, "but for us he is a symbol, a symbol of our Kurdishness. When people come in, they can see that we are Kurds. During your stay, you must have been told that, when the Kurdish uprising collapsed in Iraq, everybody in our community went into mourning."

In conclusion, it is fair to say that the Soviet Kurds, the descendants of the most persecuted groups in the old Kurdish society, had become the most prosperous and well educated section of the Kurdish people. Economic and cultural development resulted in no Russification or loss of identity whatsoever. However, it was only in Armenia and Georgia that this identity could truly express itself. The status of the Kurds of the Soviet Union would be greatly improved if the Soviet authorities had taken steps to ensure that the Kurds of Azerbaijan and the Turkoman SSR enjoyed the same rights as their compatriots in Armenia and Georgia. Given the numbers involved, it would have been even better to regroup the scattered Kurdish colonies in a single region, a territory of their own if not an autonomous republic.

Notes

1. My Kurdish interlocutors estimated that in 1975 there were 48,000 Kurds in Armenia and 35,000 in Georgia. They explained that the gap between the official figures and the reality was due to the fact that many Yezidi Kurds put themselves down as Yezidis rather than Kurds and that certain Muslim Kurds who live in mainly Azerbaijani villages are registered as Azerbaijanis.
2. A. Bukchpan, *Azerbaidjanskije Kurdy (The Azerbaijani Kurds)*, (Baku, 1932), p. 8.
3. T.K. Bakaev, *Govor Kurdov Turkmenii (The Speech of the Kurds in the Turkoman S.S.R.)*, (Moscow, 1962), p. 3.
4. Ibid., p. 6.
5. K.M. Tchatoev, *Kurdy Sovetskoj Armenii (The Kurds of Soviet Armenia)*, (Erivan, 1965), p. 22.
6. Notably Shah Ismail (1502–24), Shah Abbas (1587–1629) and Nadir Shah (1736–47). Shah Abbas I alone had over 15,000 Kurds deported to Khorassan. (Cf. Bakaev, op. cit., p. 3.)
7. Mahmoudov, former shepherd and Vice-Minister of Transport, was also the author of an important work in Armenian on the history of the Kurds and Kurdistan, and was a member of the Kurdish section of the Armenian Writers Union. Samande Siabend was born the son of a porter and became a Hero of the Soviet Union for his valor in the defense of Moscow and at the Battle of Minsk. He was also a writer in Kurdish and a member of the Kurdish Fine Arts Committee.
8. *Bibliografia Ktebed Kurdieye Sovetiye (Bibliography of Soviet Kurdish books) 1921–60*, (Erivan, 1961), p. 10. (In Kurdish and Russian)
9. Ibid.

10. For further details see *Bibliographia* . . ., op. cit.
11. Ibid., p. 15.
12. K.M. Tchatoev, op. cit., p. 143.
13. Amongst the many works on the life of this famous revolutionary, the two most recent are *Salnikov, Fedor Lytkin (Ferik Polatbekov)* (Moscow 1976) and an important work in Kurdish by Cindi, *Hewari*, (Erivan, 1967).

8

Iranian Kurds under Ayatollah Khomeini

Gerard Chaliand

After the fall of the Shah on February 10–11, 1979, Iranian Kurds faced an entirely new situation. The Kurdish community participated most actively in the demonstrations which brought the Pahlavi regime to its knees, especially in Sanandaj, Kermanshah and Mahabad. These demonstrations were not led by the Shi'ite clergy (the Kurds are Sunnis), but by the KDPI (the Kurdish Democratic Party of Iran), a movement headed by one of the authors of this book, A.R. Ghassemlou. The KDPI's program was based on the autonomy of Iranian Kurdistan within the framework of a democratic, hopefully secular and federal Iran.

The political vacuum created by the overthrow of the monarchy was quickly exploited by the Kurds. Revolutionary councils were elected to manage local affairs, armed popular militias were set up and equipped from captured arsenals. Cultural life flourished; Kurdish language publications, which had been banned for three decades, began to appear.

On March 3, after 32 years underground, the KDPI, assembled at Mahabad, proclaimed its own legalization and sought to get the new Iranian authorities to recognize the *de facto* autonomy which had been established in Kurdistan. A few weeks later, the Turkoman and Arab communities followed suit and also demanded autonomy.

Iran, which was known as Persia until 1934, is a multinational empire dominated by the Persians, who represented only about 40% of the population. Out of an overall population of about 36 million, there are roughly 13 million Turkish-speaking Azerbaijanis, 6 million Kurds, 2 million Arabs and a certain number of Baluchis and Turkomen. The Pahlavi dynasty, which only goes back to 1926 when a career officer, Reza Khan, the deposed Shah's father, was crowned, adopted a policy of systematic centralization, involving forcible settlement of nomads and tight control over the national minorities.

On March 28, 1979, a Kurdish delegation went to Qom to present the Kurds' demands to Ayatollah Khomeini, who answered that the demand for

autonomy was unacceptable. The following month there were clashes between the *Pasdars* (Revolutionary Guards) and the Kurdish militia in a small
town called Naghadeh. Further incidents occurred throughout the summer.
Meanwhile, the KDPI organized itself and co-ordinated popular activity. For
the first time the Kurds had a modern leadership. The referendum on the
Islamic Republic was massively boycotted in Kurdistan; 85 to 90% of voters
abstained. While negotiations with the government dragged on, the KDPI
called for a "Congress of Oppressed Peoples in Iran," to be held on August
25 and to which Turkoman, Arab, Baluchi and Azerbaijani delegates were
invited. But on August 17 the Ayatollah took the minorities unawares by
ordering the army to launch an offensive against the towns of Iranian
Kurdistan. After a brief resistance, notably in Mahabad, the Kurdish towns
were taken. By September 5 they were all under army control. The *Pasdars*
then carried out a violent repression, especially in Saqez and Qarngh. But the
Kurdish forces were able to pull back into the mountains, having suffered
only very minor losses, and the Iranian Army, having no taste for the pursuit,
contented itself with occupying the main urban areas and communication
centers.

In fact, the army was itself divided and insecure following the fall of the
Shah and the events leading to the rise of the Ayatollah. The different services
— land, air and sea — had their own divergences and in each branch there
were both supporters and opponents of Khomeini, especially the latter. By
late November, the Kurdish forces were able to take advantage of the enemy's
paralysis and reoccupied all the towns in Kurdistan.

Ayatollah Khomeini's regime, based on Shi'ite fundamentalism, was essentially ambiguous. On the one hand, he called himself primarily a Muslim,
committed to the universal community; on the other, his regime was mainly
Persian and imperial in its implicit orientation. Until mid-December the
government was still refusing to recognize the principle of autonomy demanded by the minorities.

In mid-December, the Tehran government, well aware of existing tensions
and of the widespread reservations concerning the projected Constitution
inspired by the Ayatollah, published its own 14 Point Program granting
limited autonomy to the national minorities. This was clearly a victory —
albeit perhaps only a provisional one — for both the Kurds and all the other
minorities — the Turkomen, Arabs and Baluchis — who manifested their
aspiration for autonomy during 1979. The Azerbaijani attitude, however,
was far less clear-cut, although some autonomist tendencies did emerge
during November and December 1979.

The 14 Point Program, which was more akin in scope to a measure of
administrative decentralization than to any real autonomy project, could at
least serve as a starting point. The cultural rights of the minorities were
unambiguously recognized, although the Program did not contain a conception of autonomy which might eventually give rise to a federal state. Furthermore, the project did not deal with the question of the extent of the
territories occupied by the minorities, and thus did not specify precisely who
would enjoy autonomy. In the case of the Kurds, for example, the KDPI

demanded that four administratively distinct provinces be brought together within the framework of autonomy, namely Kurdistan, the Kurdish districts of Western Azerbaijan, of Kermanshah and of Ilam. The government rejected this proposal and apparently intended to divide even the existing province of Kurdistan into two separate administrative units, one centered on Mahabad and the other on Sanandaj.

Quite conceivably, this idea might have been a tactical concession unwillingly granted by the government and doomed to be eaten away at until it became unacceptable to the minorities, and especially to the Kurds. The KDPI had in effect created a state within a state, a situation which no government could endorse enthusiastically. In the long term, an eventual trial of strength seemed inevitable.

The Shah's regime collapsed for a wide range of reasons, most notably because very unbalanced economic growth from 1975 to 1978 greatly intensified existing distortions between the various social categories.

In the light of the new level of financial liquidity resulting from oil revenue in 1974, Iran's Fifth Economic Plan was revised; the expected annual growth rate was raised from 11.4% to 25.9%. The Shah was promising nothing less than the achievement, in a dozen or so years, of the "Great Civilization" which would make Iran the world's fifth industrial and military power. But the decision to opt for ultra-accelerated growth was disastrous. The Shah had overestimated Iran's financial resources and the country's technical and cultural capacity for absorbing the surplus. Right from 1975, the initial boom was dragged down by 35% inflation. The 40% increase in imports created bottlenecks at every level of the infrastructure, beginning with the ports. Despite the presence of tens of thousands of American technicians, the shortage of skilled staff grew acute. Excessive centralization accentuated all the imbalances. Military expenditure became exorbitant. The price of building land in the large cities increased tenfold in three years. The crisis struck particularly hard in the countryside and greatly augmented the rural exodus, although the standard of living of the urban masses was also declining appreciably. The impact of rampaging modernization destabilized society and marginalized the disinherited masses. Along with the identity problems that this sort of savage modernization cannot help but create, these were the main causes of the Iranian Revolution. Religion, serving both as an ideology of resistance and as a sign of identity, mobilized the disinherited masses who rejected a process from which they were excluded.

But the support given to the Ayatollah by the urban masses should not blind one to the existence either of the peasantry or of a powerful and numerous middle class. The economic situation went from bad to worse; in 1980 about 20% of the active population was unemployed.

Iran was regionally isolated. The mainly Sunni, mainly conservative Arab states in the area were all hostile, as was emphatically demonstrated when Iraq's invasion of Iran in September 1980 began the eight-year Iran-Iraq war. Beset by major economic and military problems, the Iranian regime under Khomeini was certainly not going to grant its national minorities autonomy. Once again the Kurdish movement was crushed.

9

The Two Gulf Wars: The Kurds on the World Stage, 1979–1992

*Kamran Karadaghi**

As on many previous occasions, the Kurds had an appropriate popular expression for what happened in Iraqi Kurdistan as a result of the agreement between Iraq and Iran on March 6, 1975. Faced with the almost immediate collapse of the Kurdish military movement once the deal had been made, the weary murmur of *Ash batal!* (The mill has stopped), was on every lip.

"The mill has stopped!" In the past, each group of Kurdish villages had one mill to process its wheat. At times, exhaustion so overtook the miller that he would simply stop and go out to shout *Ash batal!* — to the disappointment of the no less tired, newly arrived villagers, who had covered long distances only to hear the shout.

The response of the armed Kurdish movement (numbering around a hundred thousand fighters) to the Iran-Iraq agreement was without precedent in the history of the Kurdish struggle. It dissolved itself, within a period of two weeks, by a decision from its own command, taken against the backdrop of a combined Iraqi-Iranian threat to destroy it if it refused.

The psychological blow to the fighters and civilians in the liberated areas of Kurdistan was indescribable, as it was for the tens of thousands of their families who had taken refuge in Iran.

By the beginning of April, more or less all of the fighters and civilians who had joined or supported the armed uprising in March 1974 had left Iraqi Kurdistan. The vast majority soon took advantage of the general amnesty declared by the ruling Revolutionary Command Council. (The amnesty excluded four people — the movement's legendary leader Mustafa Barzani, his two sons Idris and Massoud, and their uncle Sheik Mohammed Khaled.) Everyone else returned home, resigned to their fate under the mercy of the Iraqi authorities.

* Kamran Karadaghi is a senior political correspondent at *al-Hayat* Arabic daily in London.

To Barzani himself, there was an added humiliation. The late shah of Iran, his erstwhile ally, refused to meet him on his return from Algiers, although the Kurdish leader had been waiting for him in Tehran since March 7. The meeting was not held until March 11, and it is quite possible that the shah chose that date deliberately. It was on that day, five years earlier, that Barzani had signed the fateful March Agreement with Saddam Hussein, ignoring the shah's strong pressure not to do so.

The agreement gave the Kurds autonomy, recognizing also their cultural identity and establishing a Kurdish university in Suleimanieh, and including teaching the Kurdish language as a subject in all academic institutions throughout Iraq. But in the following four years the government gradually scaled down its commitments. The Autonomous Region Law, when it was eventually published in March 1974, subjected all decisions by the Autonomous Legislative Council to Baghdad's approval, and demanded the Kurds recognize the leading role of the Baath Party.

Barzani was later to remark that, during that meeting, there was something new in the shah's demeanor. Alongside the usual imperial *hauteur*, there was a barely disguised satisfaction at the humiliation of the Kurdish leader.

On March 13, Barzani returned to Hajj Omran, his headquarters in Iraqi Kurdistan. I was among a group of Kurdish intellectuals he invited to meet him on that same day.

His speech, recounting his long and truly heroic history of struggle, had an unmistakable note of farewell. He called on those present not to give in to despair, reminding them that he started his armed campaign against Baghdad with a band of no more than seven fighters. He said he would never stop serving the Kurdish cause, but added that he was now an old man, both tired and ill.

This was indeed the end for the legendary leader, who was soon to die of cancer. In March 1976 he left Iran, where he had lived since the collapse of the Kurdish movement, to seek treatment in the United States. He died in a hospital there in 1979.

The Kurdish defeat was so complete this time that even the most optimistic did not expect the movement to regain its strength before many years had passed. Among the Kurdish intellectuals and activists who returned to Iraq, there appeared views, nourished by despair, on the futility of armed struggle. It was thought that there was no alternative but to accept the status quo, to attempt coexistence, somehow, with the central authority in Baghdad. The regime, they argued, had demonstrated its unbreakable will to gain mastery over everyone and everything. The Iraqi agreement with the shah, brokered by Algeria, in which Baghdad yielded on all points in the historic dispute between the two countries, including control of Shatt al-Arab and several strategic border areas, in return for his abandoning the Kurds, proved there was no price the Iraqi regime would not pay to achieve total domination.

The defeat of the Iraqi Kurds in 1975 led to wide debate among their intellectuals over the direction the movement should take. There were calls for a unified movement for "Greater Kurdistan," in which there would be no deals between Iraq's Kurds and those neighboring states which oppress their own Kurds. Another proposal was to link the Kurdish movement firmly to the Iraqi context, throwing in its lot with the Baathists' opponents.

Some even argued that it would have been better for the Kurdish leadership to have avoided armed conflict and accepted the conditions demanded by the Baathists in March 1974 for the implementation of the Autonomy Agreement of 1970. Foremost among these was the demand to recognize the Baath Party as sole leader of the whole of the Iraqi people, with sole right to organize within the armed forces and the security and intelligence structures.

There was also of course the disagreement on the demarcation of the Autonomous Region. The Kurds demanded that it must include all of the areas traditionally known as Kurdish; in other words, what were formerly known as the northern *liwas*, with Kirkuk among them. This was utterly rejected by Baghdad.

But all notions of coexistence very quickly lost credence, thanks mainly to the activities of the authorities themselves. The Baathists saw the collapse of the insurrection as the signal to proceed to the "final solution" of the Kurdish problem. The wave of terror unleashed soon after exceeded the Kurds' worst fears. (Much worse was to come later, and the events of the seventies pale before the atrocities of the eighties.)

Waiting only a few weeks, until most Kurds had returned to their homes, the government started a wave of expulsions from Kurdistan to the southern and mid-Euphrates areas of Iraq. Estimates of the numbers involved ranged between 120,000 and 300,000. They were kept there for around a year, before the government allowed them to go back home. During their period of exile, the government supported them financially as well as with provisions. Large amounts of money were promised to encourage intermarriage with the local Arab population. The aim was to make the Kurds permanent residents there and to absorb them into Arab society.

By now, the area officially known as the Autonomous Region had been mapped out; from it the Iraqi authority excluded Kirkuk and some hundreds of villages along the borders with Iran, Turkey and Syria.

The border area, a strip hundreds of miles long and between five and fifteen miles deep, contained within it more than 1,500 villages. All of these were destroyed and more than 750,000 of the inhabitants deported to hastily erected new villages. At the same time, Arab tribes were brought in and settled in Kurdish areas, especially in Kirkuk, where deportations were not confined to the Kurds but affected the Turkomans also, dozens of whose villages around Kirkuk were destroyed.

The pretext was "strategic security," and the Baathists had used it before, during their brief period in power between February and November 1963. At that time a limited expulsion operation was launched in the Kirkuk area, involving 21 villages, from which around 1,500 peasant families were deported. "Strategic" for the Baathists involved not only borders but the oil-producing areas.

The expulsions, the building of new villages, and the compensations to expellees, cost the government hundreds of millions of Iraqi dinars after 1975. The real cost, including the destruction of the economic structure of these agricultural areas, ran into billions. Money was certainly spent in Kurdistan at that time, but its purpose was not redevelopment so much as to change its demographic balance through piecemeal Arabization. It was thought that this would eventually lead to the Arabization of the Kurds themselves.

"The final solution" to the Kurdish problem, within the framework of "strategic security," envisaged the removal of the "Kurdish threat" to Iraq's future by denying it strategic depth: destroying its base in the countryside as well as preventing access to fellow Kurds in Turkey, Iran and Syria. It reflected the central authority's mistrust of the Kurds; the assumption was that they would always be Iraq's potential enemies. This explains why the Kurds are always accused of being "instruments" in the hand of foreign powers, ever ready to be used against the interests of Iraq and the Arab nations as a whole.

All this, together with the continuing persecution of Kurdish militants, especially students and teachers, with imprisonment, torture and executions, explains why resistance and the armed struggle soon resumed, although, to begin with, only on a very limited scale. In fact, Kurdish parties and movements began to reorganize only a few months after the disaster of March 1975, and the new wave of armed action began as early as June of that year, undertaken by small groups infiltrating from Iran and Syria.

Iran, ostensibly starting to normalize relations with Iraq, together with Syria and even Turkey at times, appeared to look away while those incursions took place. Iraq's neighbors, it seemed, were worried by the increasing power of the regime. In any case, Iran and Syria always chose to maintain relations, in one form or another, with Iraqi opposition forces. The Kurdish Democratic Party (KDP) at the time had stronger relations with Iran, while the Patriotic Union of Kurdistan (PUK) was in the stage of establishing links with Syria. At the same time, Iraqi Kurds maintained clandestine contact with the illegal Kurdish organizations in Iran and Turkey, to obtain their help in establishing bases for military and political action against the Iraqi regime.

This was also the time when internal resistance began, first as clandestine work in towns, later developing into a movement to join the *Peshmerga* in the mountains. The decisive development here came in the middle of 1976, when three distinguished political-military leaders, appointed to administrative posts in southern Iraq after their return in 1975, defected back to the mountains with between 200 to 300 fighters.

One of these was Omar Mustapha, a PUK founder member who later became a member of its Politburo and died in Irbil, during the PUK conference in April 1992. The second was Ali Askari, a top *Peshmerga* commander who had supported Jalal Talabani in the split he led against Barzani in 1966. Askari was, together with Omar Mustapha and Mamend Rasoul, founder of the Social Democratic Movement, one of the two major organizations later comprising the Patriotic Union of Kurdistan (PUK). Third was Khaled Saeed, also a noted military leader and a founder of the

Social Democratic Movement. Saeed, Askari and a large number of their followers were killed in a single incident in 1978, ironically not by the Iraqi army, but by fellow Kurds, in the power struggle raging at the time between the KDP and PUK.

Foundation of Parties

The political void left by the collapse of the Kurdish armed struggle, and the illness and later death of its undisputed leader Mustafa Barzani, led to violent struggles among the parties, movements and leading personalities in Kurdistan. There appeared within the KDP itself tendencies hostile to the leadership of Barzani and his family. The Kurdish Democratic Party was the acknowledged leader of the Kurdish movement for the period between the signing of the Autonomy Agreement in March 1970 and the collapse of March 1975. The struggle within the party after that led to the formation of the Provisional Command, headed by Sami Abdul Rahman who became the KDP's secretary general, with the leadership including both Idris and Massoud Barzani. This power structure continued until 1979 when the party held its ninth general conference, which ended with Abdul Rahman splitting to form the Kurdistan People's Democratic Party. For the KDP itself, Massoud was elected leader, while Idris remained Politburo member, although he was regarded the party's strong man, until his death in 1987.

Early in 1976, Dr. Mahmoud Othman formed an organization under the name of KDP-Preparatory Committee. A member of the KDP's Politburo during Mustafa Barzani's time, he was also his main foreign relations advisor. He had visited the U.S. with Idris Barzani in 1973, to form the first American link through the CIA. Othman moved to Syria soon after forming his new organization, where he was joined by others, among them Qader Jabbari and Shams al Din Mufti. He continued to lead the group until 1979, when, together with Mamend Rasoul and other members of a dissident wing of the Kurdish Social Democratic Movement, one of the major groupings within the PUK, he established the Kurdistan Socialist Party, one of the eight members of the present Kurdistan Front.

The oldest party in Iraq is the Communist Party (founded in 1934) and its Kurdistan branch has been active within the Kurdish movement since the sixties. But in 1974 it was part of the Patriotic and National Forces Front formed and led by the Baath Party, and its armed formations, accordingly, fought against the Kurdish uprising of that year. The communists maintained support for the government until 1978, when the Baathists launched a campaign of terror against them, in yet another attempt to liquidate the party. The final break between the two sides came in 1979, and the communists resumed their activities within the Kurdish armed struggle.

The period immediately following the defeat of 1975 was marked by a proliferation of leftist ideas, especially of Marxist and Maoist orientation. A number of smaller leftist parties and organizations were formed at the time, including the Kurdistan Workers Party, founded by Ibrahim Khalil. The KWP's ideas proved particularly attractive to young people, large numbers of whom joined the party. It conducted effective clandestine operations in the towns and cities of Kurdistan, and the security forces waged relentless war against the party. One of its leaders, Shehab Nuri, was arrested and executed in 1976, and its founder Ibrahim Khalil himself was soon captured by the government. He broke down under interrogation and revealed details of the party's organization, enabling the government to smash it.

The most complicated and difficult birth was that of the Patriotic Union of Kurdistan (PUK). At the time of the collapse, Jalal Talabani was Barzani's personal representative in Syria. The two had been back together since the 1970 Agreement with Baghdad, when Talabani returned for a time to Barzani's headquarters in Hajj Omran. The Kurdish chief had decided to forgive his "son," as he always called Talabani, after the latter had split from him in 1966, forming an "alternative" Kurdistan Democratic Party and fighting alongside the government against Barzani. The struggle leading to the split started in 1964, and it was caused by accusations of authoritarianism and tribalism against Barzani. After a short stay in Hajj Omran, Talabani left again, staying for a while in Beirut where he established relations with a number of Palestinian organizations, settling at last in Damascus as Barzani's representative.

Immediately in the aftermath of the collapse of 1975, attempts began to unite two Kurdish groupings, the Kurdistan Workers League and the Social Democratic Movement, in moves which were to result in the emergence of the Patriotic Union of Kurdistan. Talabani was, along with Nusherwan Mustapha (in 1992 a member of the PUK leadership), Shehab Nuri and Shaswar Jalal (later to die in battle), a founder member of the Workers League. Among the leaders of the Social Democratic Movement were Ali Askari, Khaled Saeed, Omar Mustapha and Mamend Rasoul. Talabani was seen as the man most fit to lead the emerging Union, and he resigned his position in the Workers League to ensure his impartiality. After his election, his charisma attracted a large number of activists from outside the two organizations. These were at first known as "the general tendency." Before long, however, they solidified into the third organization within the PUK, itself regarded as a new departure in the course of the Kurdish movement.

Kurdish observers have said that the experiment was perhaps modeled on the Palestine Liberation Organization; it was during that period that the PLO had emerged as a formidable political and fighting force in the Middle East. Talabani had developed particularly close relations with a number of Palestinian leaders, among them George Habash of the Popular Front for the Liberation of Palestine and Naif Hawatmeh of the Democratic Front. He worked for a while in *Al Hadaf*, organ of the Popular Front. At the same time, a number of young Kurdish leftists joined the military wings of the two Palestinian organizations. Among their motives was securing a source for arms, as well as contact with the Syrians. One disadvantage here was that tensions between the Syrians and Palestinians tended to reflect adversely on the relations between the former and the Iraqi Kurds.

The period between 1975 and 1976 was that of the establishing or reestablishing of all Kurdish parties, movements and organizations. All sides agree that the new phase of armed struggle started toward the end of this period, and that the earliest operations were launched simultaneously by the two major groupings, the KDP and PUK. The conditions were of extreme harshness and danger. Small bands had to infiltrate into Iraqi Kurdistan from Syria and Iran, often forced to enter hostile Turkish territory. Yet for all its limitations, the armed movement played a vital part in raising the morale of the population, in the face of continuing terror, expulsion and forced Arabization.

It has to be noted here that, from the beginning of the Kurdish armed movement in 1961, no real distinction can be made between the political and military aspects of the various organizations. In fact, it is no exaggeration to say that, with the exception of the KDP which was founded in 1945 in circumstances far removed from the post-1958 revolution in Iraq, all Kurdish movements were born on the battlefield.

The situation was made worse by fighting among the parties, after the loss of Barzani, the movement's historic leader. The limited fighting against the government was paralleled by internal fighting among the Kurds.

This situation remained until the start of the Iran–Iraq war in 1978, which ushered in a new phase for the Kurdish movement in Iraq, in which external factors regained greater importance. Although the armed struggle posed no real threat to the Baghdad regime, two attempts at negotiation were made in 1978 and 1979, the first with the KDP-Preparatory Committee and the second with the PUK. Both attempts failed, as Baghdad insisted on nothing less than total surrender from all Kurdish sides, although the Kurds wanted no more than the ending of mass expulsions, Arabization and arbitrary arrests, in addition to demands well within the government's own Autonomy Law.

The Iran–Iraq War

The start of the Iran–Iraq war afforded the Kurdish armed struggle the opportunity to expand greatly, as Baghdad had to withdraw a large proportion of its forces to support its central and southern fronts.

In addition to the hundreds of *Peshmerga* veterans who remained with their leaders outside Iraq after the defeat of 1975, returning soon after to take up the fight against Baghdad, there were thousands who flocked to the mountains from the "new villages" established by the government for those expelled from their land. The Kurdish population always hated those villages, considering them no more than concentration camps.

But tensions within the movement were such that, between 1979 and 1980, Kurdistan was divided into two areas. One part, Badinan, roughly the northern and western parts of Iraqi Kurdistan, was controlled by the KDP; the other, Sooran, the south and east, by the PUK. Each guarded its territory jealously, and armed confrontations occurred whenever a band from one side tried to trespass, even if the purpose was to attack the Iraqis. At the heart of the tension was the power struggle between the two main groupings to fill the political vacuum and take over the leadership of the movement as a whole.

The scale of the confrontations was at first limited, if only because of the limited military capacity of the combatants. But as the Iran–Iraq war continued, these capacities grew, and the Kurdish parties were soon raising veritable armies of *Peshmerga*. The fighting among them intensified, to the alarm of the leaderships on both sides.

At this time, in the early eighties, an agreement was made between the KDP, the Iraqi Communist Party, the Kurdish Socialist Party and a number of other Iraqi parties, to form the National Democratic Front. More importantly, in the summer of 1982, the KDP and PUK held a meeting in the Pisht Ashan valley near Hajj Omran, on the slopes of Mount Kandil which straddles the Iraqi–Iranian border. The PUK was represented by Fraidoun Abdul Qader, while Mulla Mohammed Lajani represented the KDP. They signed an agreement in which all claims to area control were nullified and Kurdistan declared open to all fighting groups, no matter from what party. The two sides, however, stopped well short of forming a joint military command.

In addition, Syria and Libya mediated wider efforts to bring Iraqi opposition groupings closer. On February 6, 1983, nineteen Iraqi parties and movements signed a declaration in Tripoli, pledging "irrevocable moves toward unity within a wide patriotic front," to be announced "within a month." The aim was the destruction of the Baathist regime, replacing it with "a democratic, popular, unity-seeking government." The declaration included a clause on the necessity of "giving Iraqi Kurdistan real autonomy, with the rights of Turkomans and other minorities guaranteed." The signatories also called for "an immediate ban on all propaganda campaigns, differences and clashes" among the parties.

The meeting was convened under the chairmanship of Major Abdul Salam Jalloud, Libya's second in command, and attended by Mohammed Haidar, member of the Pan-Arab Command of the Syrian Baath Party, together with several Palestinian leaders. The 19 Iraqi groupings taking part included the KDP and PUK, the Iraqi Communist Party, the Kurdistan Popular Democratic Party and the Democratic Patriotic Turkoman Organization. But the solemnity of the occasion and the pledges notwithstanding, the settlement did not last long, and public mutual recrimination resumed within a few weeks.

The source of dissension among the opposition was (and remains) its ideological, religious and national diversity. The opposition fell into four major blocks: Islamic Shi'ite, Kurdish, Arab nationalist (pro-Syrian Baathists, Nasserists and others) and the communists. These last were the only ones who recognized the national rights of the Kurds, including the right to self-rule.

In Kurdistan itself, the parties started to mobilize. The situation came to a head in the spring of 1983 with an attack by the National Democratic Front of Iraq (mainly the KDP, the Communist Party, the Kurdish Socialist Party and the Kurdistan Socialist Party) on the PUK positions in the Balisan area in the Irbil governorate. The PUK retaliated with an attack on Communist and KDP positions in Pisht Ashan and Karnakao, as well as Kurdish and Kurdistan Socialist positions in Ashkolka. Terrible damage was inflicted on the

Communists, with about a hundred combatants killed, a number of leading cadres captured, many offices totally destroyed and their broadcasting station silenced.

ICP politburo member Karim Ahmed was immediately dispatched to meet with PUK leader Talabani. The latter had an abiding affection for the veteran communist, who had been his teacher in Kwaisanjak in the early fifties. The two issued a joint declaration on May 5 addressed to "all combatants on both sides," in which they ordered "resolutely and most urgently immediate cessation of hostilities," and deplored "the unnatural situation which has developed between them." They called for the resumption of moves toward "uniting their efforts . . . against the dictatorship and for the creation of a democratic, patriotic coalition regime capable of realizing true national independence for Iraq and real autonomy for Kurdistan." The real outcome of the events, however, was the liquidation of all Front presence within the PUK areas, while the propaganda war between the two sides continued to escalate throughout 1983 and 1984, with mutual accusations of treachery and subservience to the Baathists or foreign powers.

Despite the internecine fighting, the KDP and PUK *Peshmerga* were increasing their pressure on the Iraqi forces. Their military capacity grew to the extent that parts of the areas in which they operated really became "liberated zones." At times, small contingents could even undertake hit and run operations in the towns. The authorities often had to withdraw forces from the fronts with Iran to confront the growing menace of the Kurdish fighters.

In the period between 1983 and 1984, Kurdistan witnessed the growth to remarkable dimensions of a phenomenon which has long accompanied the Kurdish struggle with the central authority in Iraq: that of government mercenaries among the Kurds. The recruitment of mercenaries (called *fursan* or knights by the government and *jash* or donkeys by the Kurds) expanded greatly in that time because of the pressure of the war with Iran. In return for weapons, money and privileges, Kurdish tribesmen played a part in containing the onslaught of the *Peshmergas*.

The efforts to destroy Kurdistan's rural economy and social life through expulsions and the destruction of villages reached new levels. Those parts which were not the object of direct attack were denied all social, health and education services, to force the inhabitants to leave for the towns and cities. A dramatic example was the announcement in 1985 of the closure of 748 primary schools in the Irbil, Suleimanieh and Dhouk countryside, denying education to some 15,000 children. The pretext was that the schools were within "sensitive security areas," in which the education authorities could not be expected to function. The villagers asked for the children to be registered in schools in nearby towns and villages, outside the designated areas. The request was refused.

In 1983 something occurred which signaled the new dimension of horrors to come. Around eight thousand members of the Barzani tribe, boys and men between the ages of 12 and 80, were rounded up and taken to an unknown destination. The Barzanis were living in the Qash Taba government-built compound, about six miles to the south of Irbil. A unit from the Republican Guard surrounded the compound one night and completed the round-up of the males by early morning. The fate of the detainees remained unknown, and there was no satisfactory answer from the government when the question was raised by the Kurdish side in the post-Gulf War negotiations. The conviction grew among the Kurds that the captured Barzani men had been exterminated.

The Road to the Kurdish Front

Early in 1984, Iran's military pressure on Iraq forced the regime to offer negotiations to the PUK, which had by then become a formidable fighting force. The talks went on for almost a year, but ended in complete failure. Paradoxically, the event triggered the start of a long and complicated dialogue among the Kurds themselves, culminating in the formation, in 1987, of the Kurdistan Front.

The background to the contacts between Talabani and Baghdad was the former's friendship with Abdul Rahman Ghassemlou, leader of the Kurdish Democratic Party in the Iranian part of Kurdistan, and one of the contributors to this volume. Ghassemlou was an ally of Iraq in the struggle against Tehran, and brokered the initial meetings between Talabani's side and the Iraqi Baathists in 1984. In 1989 Talabani was to return the questionable favor, with a disastrous result. The meetings he brokered between Ghassemlou and the Iranian side were held in Vienna, and Ghassemlou was assassinated there, allegedly at the hands of Iranian agents. Thus it appeared that both Baghdad and Tehran used the relations between the two Kurdish leaders to their advantage.

The start of the negotiations between Talabani and Baghdad marked an escalation in the propaganda war among the two main Kurdish sides, the PUK and the Patriotic Democratic Front (the KDP, Communists and Socialists). Two weeks after the talks began, PUK leader Talabani returned to his headquarters in Kurdistan, to hold a series of meetings in order to explain and defend his position. In a meeting with a number of Kurdish intellectuals, the question was raised as to whether overall reconciliation, if that was the aim, should not start nearer home, among the two major Kurdish factions, before involving the Iraqi regime.

This, in fact, marked the start of the intra-Kurdish dialogue, in which the Communist Party played a particularly positive role. Publicly, the Front kept up its propaganda campaign against the PUK, calling for an end to the negotiations with Baghdad, while privately the two sides kept on talking.

At the same time, Talabani established secret contacts with Ali Akbar Hashemi Rafsanjani, then speaker of the Iranian parliament (and later to be president of Iran). He explained to the Iranian leader that the PUK had been forced to negotiate, that it would really prefer a settlement to the Kurdish problem in the absence of the Baathist regime, but that the movement did not have sufficient means to oust it.

Talabani thus found himself negotiating simultaneously on three fronts:

with Baghdad, with the other Kurds, and with Tehran. The failure, in the end, of the negotiations with Baghdad gave impetus to the dialogue with the other two, to the point when, in 1986, a delegation representing the KDP, the Communists and the Kurdistan Socialist Party, arrived at the PUK headquarters in Yakhsamar in the Suleimanieh governorate, for a meeting which ended with a statement calling for unity against the rulers of Baghdad.

As for the negotiations with Tehran, an early result was the daring operation in October 1986, when PUK fighters bombarded the Kirkuk oil installations with artillery supplied by Iran. More far reaching was the change in Iran's attitude once the PUK terminated contacts with Baghdad. After years of diligent work to keep the Kurds apart, Iran became an enthusiastic supporter of their unity. A possible motive was that Tehran felt the military balance shifting against it by then, and hoped that a united Kurdish front would lead Baghdad to withdraw more troops from the central and southern fronts to meet the pressure in the north. To that end, Iran allowed the Kurds greater freedom of movement across its borders with Iraq, as well as the right to establish military bases near the borders.

Iranian–Kurdish relations reached their highest point when, in 1987, Rafsanjani invited Jalal Talabani and Idris Barzani for a meeting in Tehran, where he told them that Kurdish unity would mean even more help from Iran. Idris Barzani died a short while after the meeting. This was a bitter blow to his brother Massoud, but it left him undisputed master of the Kurdistan Democratic Party.

On May 7, 1987, the formation of the Kurdistan Front was officially declared, with the aim, as the announcement had it, "of augmenting our struggle and escalating the resistance in Iraqi Kurdistan to the war of genocide waged by the Iraqi regime on the Kurdish inhabitants." A joint command was to oversee all military and political activities. The Front demanded the recognition of Kurdish national rights within Iraq.

Six parties signed the document: the KDP, the PUK, the Kurdistan Socialist Party, the Kurdistan People's Democratic Party, the Kurdish Socialist Party and the Iraqi Communist Party. Two groupings joined later, the Kurdistan Toilers' Party and the Assyrian Association.

Chemical Weapons and "Anfal"

In the closing stages of the war with Iran, Iraq established such a clear military predominance that it felt able to increase its deployment in the north and escalate the fighting against the Kurds. Beginning in the spring of 1987, it increasingly resorted to indiscriminate use of chemical weapons, hitting rebel positions as well as civilians in towns and villages. Kurdish documents and sources agree that the army first used chemical weapons in mid-April 1987. But there are reports that the first case goes back to the summer of the previous year, when an artillery-fired chemical bomb exploded harmlessly near the village of Yakaskhamar in the Irbil governorate.

In any case, there is agreement that the first organized chemical attack took place on April 15, 1987, when, in one day, war planes used what the Kurds described as a "hitherto unknown type of bomb" on Hiladeen, Pirgalo, Seerwan, Awazik, Noljika, Chinara, Kanito, Lutar, Sidar, Awjah, Jalawa, Saraghalo and Awazeh, all towns and villages in the Suleimanieh governorate. By the end of the month, at least thirty towns and villages, in addition to numerous *Peshmerga* positions, had been subjected to similar treatment. From the middle of that year, chemical weapons were in daily use.

In the first phase, up to the start of the infamous *Anfal* operations in February of the following year, mustard gas was the type most commonly used. With the beginning of *Anfal*, between February and October 1988, nerve gas was added. *Anfal* is an Arabic word meaning "spoils of battle." It is the name also of a chapter in the Quran on the rules of war and rights of conquest. For the Baathists, however, it was the code name for an operation for the pitiless devastation of the Kurds. The operation was carried out in four phases. The first was from February 1988 to March of the same year; the second from April to May; the third from May through August, when the fourth was unleashed, ending in September. The operation took the form of mass, indiscriminate air raids, followed by ground assaults in which towns and villages as well as agricultural areas were destroyed.

Early on in the operation, on March 16, 1988, Halabja took its place in the tragic history of the Kurds, when a chemical attack on the town of that name from the air left five thousand of its civilian inhabitants dead. The last *Anfal* phase took the horror to even greater dimensions, where it undeniably reached the level of genocide. The operation targeted the Badinan areas near Turkey, where thousands of civilians were killed and tens of thousands made refugees. Thousands of others were captured, many of whom died in mass executions, torture, and harsh conditions in prisons and concentration camps. Some sixty thousand managed to escape to Turkey, where around half of them remained in 1992.

It has to be mentioned that Tehran and Baghdad exchanged accusations over the responsibility for Halabja. The former said that the operation was Iraq's punishment for the town after an uprising there in support of an Iranian advance toward it. Baghdad said that it was attacked by Iran in support of that same advance. American intelligence claimed that both sides had used gas against it. One thing, however, is certain. Halabja was subjected to devastating chemical attacks, and the victims were all Kurds.

The Kurdish leadership could do nothing in the face of the onslaught, except issue calls almost daily, to the UN, international public opinion and world powers. To the increasing despair of the Kurds, the world hardly troubled to notice, let alone condemn, Baghdad's crimes. There were honorable exceptions, mainly a number of human rights groups and journalists friendly to the Kurdish cause, who tried to alert the world to the tragedy. But the international and regional powers had something else in mind, which was how best to take advantage of the new situation, in which it appeared that Saddam Hussein was emerging as the area's new strong man.

The situation in Kurdistan was such that no resistance, armed or unarmed, could be maintained. By the end of 1988 the Kurdish leadership, together with the *Peshmerga* survivors, had to withdraw across the borders to Iran and Syria. The regime could thus go on quietly with its "strategic security" plans for the border areas.

Exile

The early days of exile for the Kurdistan Front and the leadership of all the parties were a time of bitter reflection. In a history full of tragedy, the experience of 1987–1988 was by far the most tragic. Mustafa Barzani had always taught that, ultimately, the mountains were the Kurds' only friend. Now they learned that the mountains could no longer protect them; that nothing availed against chemical warfare. History had showed them that it indeed repeats itself, in a series of deepening catastrophes. What happened to the Kurdish movement in the fall of 1988 was, in a way, an exact repetition of the situation in the spring of 1975. At both times the fate of the Kurds was sealed as a direct result of an agreement between Iraq and Iran.

But we have also to consider that the Barzani leadership believed American promises of support against Baghdad. This was an important factor in its decision to reject the conditions Baghdad laid down for the implementation of the Autonomy agreement, leading to the outbreak of hostilities in March 1975. Kurdish leaders who at the time were working closely with Barzani still say that privately the Americans even promised support for the Kurds for a federal solution to their longstanding dispute with Baghdad. These hopes collapsed when it became clear finally that the real aim of U.S. policy, as drawn by then Secretary of State Henry Kissinger, was to use the Kurds as a means to pressure the Iraqi regime towards meeting Iran's demands and drawing it away from the Soviet Union. The Kurds remember with bitterness Kissinger's reported answer to Barzani, who had reminded him of former promises, that, as far as Washington was concerned, the whole affair amounted to "no more than a covert operation."

There is a kind of bitter comfort in explaining everything by the fact that "the Kurds have no friends," but, at the same time, the Kurdish leadership cannot be fully exonerated from its share in the tragedy. It is certainly true that lack of regional and international support drove the Kurds to their fate. But it is also true their leadership, in both cases, failed to understand how the situation was developing, and so committed fundamental mistakes. The Mustafa Barzani leadership knew, prior to the spring of 1975, that Iraq and Iran were moving towards an agreement, and had indeed discussed the possibility more than once. But, through political narrowness, it failed to see the full implications, refusing to believe that Iran would go so far as to cut all aid to the movement and threaten to destroy it if did not surrender to Baghdad.

Essentially the same mistake was made in 1988, where the leadership discounted totally any possibility of an end to the Iraq–Iran war before the destruction of the Baghdad regime. This, after all, was the substance of a solemn oath taken by Iran's leader Ayatollah Khomeini. But the late Ayatollah soon faced the choice of either accepting the ceasefire or risking the destruction of the Islamic Republic, and as he put it at the time, had to "drink the cup of poison" and order a halt to the war with Saddam Hussein.

There are signs that the Kurdish leadership learned from the two experiences. This was reflected in the cautious position taken in the period between the start of the second Gulf War and the popular explosions in the south and north of Iraq, which were bloodily suppressed by the end of March 1991. Some of the most important leaders made it clear they were not prepared to fight and sacrifice the Kurdish people for the interests of others. Even more strikingly, Dr. Mahmoud Othman who was the Front's chief spokesman, demanded putting Kurdish interests first, even talking to Saddam Hussein if he proved really ready to concede their demands. Although the *Peshmerga* were deployed on Iran's and Syria's borders from the start of the Gulf crisis, many of the leaders were reluctant to go into action once the disturbances leading to the uprisings in the north and south had started.

The Kurdish leadership's exile lasted just over two years. But, unlike the similar situation in 1975, the Front did not disintegrate. Massoud Barzani himself had described the 1988 disaster as "unprecedented," and it is true that its scale was such that it dwarfed any possible disagreement or ambitious rivalry among the leaders. Everyone realized that there was no other way but to remain united; that any falling out would be fatal to all parties. The Front concentrated on wide campaigns in the West to explain the Kurdish issue and expose the Iraqi regime's crimes.

On the political level, there were calls for more unity among the parties and movements of the Front. In a newspaper interview, Barzani said that all had agreed on a single overall political command, an executive committee to control day to day affairs, a unified information center, a newspaper and offices abroad. In fact only the first objective was achieved. The political leadership, in which all sides are represented, has obtained effective control of much of Iraqi Kurdistan. Its decisions are reached through consensus, each party having ultimately the right of veto. Although no party has yet exercised that right, it is seen as a possible source of future difficulties, whenever the Front is called on to make fundamental decisions. This is one of the reasons why the Front decided to speed up elections for "liberated" Kurdistan, i.e. those parts of it not under the control of the Baghdad regime.

With all this, the Front's political and military effectiveness remained limited. Although isolated raids were made from across the border, there was no concerted military action. Politically, the Front still suffered almost total regional and international isolation, the only exception being Syria, which continued to play host to the Iraqi opposition generally. On his visit to London in March 1992, Massoud Barzani contrasted the full media attention and official welcome he enjoyed, including meetings with Prime Minister John Major and leader of the opposition Neil Kinnock, with his previous visit in 1989, when he was met by a junior official in the Foreign Office, on the condition that the meeting take place in a restaurant.

In contrast to this international isolation, the cohesiveness provided by the Front enabled the Kurds to extend their relations to the other sides in the Iraqi opposition. This largely fell into four major groupings: the Islamic block (The Higher Council for Islamic Revolution, *Al Da'wa* Party, the Organization of Islamic Action and others), the Democrats (the Communist Party and a number of other left-wing organizations), the Nationalists (pan-Arab socialists, Syria-orientated Baathists and others) and of course the Kurdistan Front. Relations among the sides remained fluid, in part because of their deep ideological and political differences, but also because of the enormous influence on them wielded by Syria, Iran and Libya. The quest for unity among the Iraqi opposition forces remained unfulfilled, despite repeated attempts during the eighties.

One of the last of such attempts before the second Gulf War was sponsored by Syria in 1989, with Barzani and Talabani representing the Kurds. After three months of talks, the attempt failed, with the Islamic side delivering the death blow in a last minute change of mind. For the Kurds, the problem had always been the refusal of the Islamic and pan-Arab factions to support their central demand for autonomy, or the right to self-determination as they sometimes put it. In addition, the Islamic side had never been able to give unambiguous support for a democratic system as the only viable solution for Iraq. In fact, Iran's coldness toward the Iraqi opposition had reached such a stage that by the end of 1989 and in the context of renewed talks between the Iraqi opposition and Damascus, it asked all sides of the opposition, including the Islamists, to leave for Damascus.

The Kurdistan Front prepared for what it thought would be a long winter indeed, with no real hope of a sufficient weakening of the Iraqi regime to allow the Front to return and reorganize itself in Kurdistan. For its part, the regime felt strong enough in 1989 and 1990 to send emissaries to all opposition leaders, including the Kurds, to return to the "patriotic fold." The condition for this, however, was the same: recognition of the absolute dominance of the Baath Party. Most active of Baghdad's emissaries was Mukarram Talabani, an ex-Communist Kurd who had served as minister, who had managed to retain the respect of the opposition, especially the Kurds. Prominent Kurdish and Communist leaders were not unreceptive, declaring a willingness to withdraw their call for the destruction of the regime in return for talks to find a basis for agreement. Saddam Hussein, however, was unbending. First there had to be public recantations, then an unconditional return to Baghdad, where the Baath Party would look into their demands.

The Second Gulf War

It is impossible to tell how this stalemate might have ended. The Gulf crisis which began in August 1990 with the Iraqi invasion of Kuwait changed the picture irrevocably, for Iraq as well as for the Middle East as a whole. Regional and international capitals soon rediscovered the existence of the Iraqi opposition, especially the Kurdish side within it. There were speedy joint moves by the Saudis, Iranians and Syrians, in support of efforts to unite the opposition, which had meanwhile returned to its call for the removal of the Baathist regime.

In the autumn of 1990 the Kurdistan Front remobilized along the borders, and secret contacts were made with the leaders of the Kurdish tribes still loyal to Baghdad. These had at their disposal thousands of armed followers — the formerly despised *jash* who were soon to play a major part in the uprising against the regime, thereby losing their old nickname and gaining the more dignified one of "armed revolutionaries." It appeared that their leaders knew that the Baathist regime was entering a major crisis, and decided accordingly that it was wise to negotiate with the Front. They asked the Front to declare a general amnesty for all those who had fought alongside government forces. The Front agreed to the request and the amnesty was soon proclaimed.

Contacts among the various elements of the Iraqi opposition intensified in the weeks leading up to the war. A coordination committee was formed, with Syrian, Saudi and Iranian backing. The committee had six members, two Kurdish representatives, two from the Islamic side, and one each for the pan-Arabists and democrats. Several opposition leaders visited the Saudi capital Riyadh, among them the Kurds Jalal Talabani and Sami Abdul Rahman. The contacts led to the publication of a statement on January 27, 1990 in Beirut signed by more than 20 parties and movements, as a result of a meeting held in Damascus. The opposition condemned the invasion of Kuwait and promised to struggle to destroy the Baathist regime and secure "Kurdish rights."

The efforts toward unity were complicated by the continuing rivalry among the regional sponsors, especially between Syria and Iran. Also, at this time, London became active in this context, amid reports that Washington had decided to leave the matter to its British ally. Damascus exercised tremendous pressure to ensure that the Iraqi opposition hold its first conference under its protection in Beirut. This duly took place on March 11.

Toward the end of January 1991, the Kurdistan Front opened clandestine contact with Turkey. This was the first of its kind since the start of the Iraqi Kurdish movement. The talks were overseen on the Turkish side by President Turgot Ozal himself, and on the Kurdish side by Barzani and Talabani. Barzani kept in touch with developments from his headquarters on the Iranian side of the border with Iraq, while continuing to supervise the *Peshmerga* preparations to enter Iraq. Talabani traveled to Europe and the United States to talk to officials there, before going to Damascus early in March to meet President Hafez Assad. On March 9 he left for Ankara for secret talks with Turkish officials. Also taking part was Muhsin Deza'i, Barzani's personal representative. After two days both left overland to Damascus, on their way to Beirut to attend the opposition conference.

The conference opened on March 11, a day late to allow Talabani to join. By then the uprisings in the south and north of Iraq had begun. In a short time, the *Peshmerga* secured control over three quarters of the Kurdish areas, including cities and towns like Suleimanieh, Irbil, Dhouk and Kirkuk. Toward the end of March Talabani crossed the Syrian border into Iraq. Kurdistan's Spring, however, lasted only a few weeks as Baghdad's forces, having subdued the south, moved north to settle accounts with the Kurds.

230 A People Without a Country

The attack on Kirkuk started on March 29, and within a few days the uprising collapsed, with around two million Kurds making for the mountains, from there to cross into Turkey and Iran. The public dimension of the impending human tragedy was such that President Bush agreed to designate safe areas for the refugees. That human concern had two days earlier made the Kurdish leadership accept Baghdad's offer of negotiations, and a team was dispatched there under Talabani.

Like so many times in the past, however, these negotiations broke down without a workable agreement between the two sides. The collapse of the uprising in the north and the failed negotiations with Baghdad marked the start of a new, and perhaps most crucial chapter in the history of the Kurdish movement, one which is still being written.

None of the parties on its own could have survived the defeat of the uprising. Without the political and administrative cohesion provided by the Front, the Kurds would not have been able to run the vast areas under their control after the uprising was crushed, involving three major provincial capitals and some three million people. International protection was of course the reason why the Iraqi regime could not go back into these areas, but it was the Front, the symbol now of Kurdish unity, which prevented total social and economic disintegration.*

---

* Information in this article is based on first hand experience, interviews with Kurdish officials and documents from parties and movements in the Kurdistan Front.

10

Operation Provide Comfort:
False Promises to the Kurds

*Bill Frelick**

The U.S.-led response to Iraq's invasion of Kuwait has had many immediate repercussions on the international humanitarian network set up at the dawn of an earlier "new order" — the close of World War II. It also has more than a few similarities with the protection scheme set up then to assist and protect refugees and displaced persons, and similarly reflects the values and concerns of its time.

While both the post-World War II and Persian Gulf War interventions succeeded in responding to the immediate needs of an abused population high in the consciousness of the Western public, both also failed to recognize equally endangered but less visible or strategically useful populations. They failed to establish a more equitable and far-reaching system for responding to humanitarian needs based not on the popularity of the oppressed group or its usefulness in promoting particular ideological or geopolitical ends, but rather on its vulnerability and need for protection.

The international regime established for refugees has been created and maintained less for their protection than to preserve the prerogatives of powerful states. Many heralded the U.S. aid to Iraqi Kurds at the end of the 1991 Gulf War as a precedent for future interventions in defense of human rights and humanitarian assistance. In retrospect, the U.S. move appears as yet another exercise designed to enhance the prerogatives of state power by a stronger against a weaker state.

* Bill Frelick, a senior policy analyst with the U.S. Committee for Refugees, visited Kurdish refugee camps in Iran in April 1991. This article appeared in the May/June 1992 issue of *Middle East Report* and is based on a longer paper presented at the Middle East Studies Association conference in November 1991.

Eurocentric World Order

The 1951 Convention Relating to the Status of Refugees was drafted when Europe was attempting to cope with millions of people displaced by World War II and facing the prospect of coping with millions more fleeing a Soviet-dominated Eastern Europe. The Convention explicitly limited its legal force to refugees affected by events occurring prior to 1951 in Europe — excluding the rest of the world's refugees from the protection mandate. Although the geographic and temporal limits were subsequently dropped in the 1967 Protocol, the implicit Western and Eurocentric state bias remained untouched.

The definition of "refugee" incorporated in the Convention and Protocol was limited to persons fearing a narrow spectrum of human rights violations based on "race, religion, nationality, membership of a particular social group, or political opinion." Determination of refugee status — whether a person's fear of persecution was indeed based on one of these five criteria, and whether it was genuine — was left exclusively to states. The notion of a well-founded fear of persecution based on deprivation of civil and political rights accorded easily with the Western view of Soviet-style repression of dissidents and minorities, accommodating the legitimate need of those people while at the same time scoring Cold War points by encouraging disaffected elements within the East bloc to "vote with their feet." The five enumerated grounds of the Convention and Protocol encompass many serious human rights violations, and the term "persecution" appropriately invokes the torture, arbitrary arrest, and the like that have befallen untold numbers of people in the second half of this century. What it excludes, however, remains a source of concern, as does the prerogative of interpretation and implementation left to the states.

The universality of the international human rights regime is based on two Covenants. The first, the International Covenant on Civil and Political Rights, addresses rights protected by the Refugee Convention of 1951. The second, the International Covenant on Economic, Social, and Cultural Rights, addresses additional fundamental rights such as the right to food and shelter (Article 11), and the more elusive right of self-determination (Article 1). These do not fit the prototype of the Refugee Convention, despite the obvious relevance of such rights to many forced migrations during the past 40 years.

The incompleteness of the Convention mandate has been acutely felt in the Third World. In Africa and Latin America, it has been superceded by a more inclusive definition that more closely comports with the reality of forced migration in those parts of the world. Both the Organization of African Unity's (OAU) Convention Regarding the Specific Aspects of Refugee Problems in Africa and the Cartagena Declaration of the Organization of American States (OAS) extend protection to persons compelled to flee their country due to foreign aggression (OAU and OAS), occupation (OAU), foreign domination (OAU), internal conflicts (OAS), massive violations of human rights (OAS), and other circumstances that have seriously disturbed public order (OAU and OAS). Within Africa and Latin America, the UN High Commissioner for Refugees (UNHCR) acts in accord with these regional instruments and extends protection to refugees of war and civil strife.

Double Standards

The development of different legal standards for refugees in the industrialized West and the Third World is most acutely apparent when Third World refugees seek asylum in the West. In most Western states, the Refugee Convention definition has been adopted in national legal codes. The narrow "persecution" standard of the Convention is insufficient ground for granting asylum when the asylum applicant's life or freedom is endangered by one of the broader causes of flight recognized by the OAU or OAS.

The problem is not only definitional. The heart of the matter is state power to grant or to deny asylum. In drafting the 1951 refugee Convention, Western governments rejected a right to asylum.[1] They were unwilling to make legally binding a right they had all recognized in principle in Article 14(1) of the *non binding* Universal Declaration of Human Rights: "everyone has the right to seek *and to enjoy* in other countries asylum from persecution." This was no mere oversight. A UN conference, convened in 1977 with the idea of correcting the problem by drafting an internationally binding convention on the right to asylum, was an abject failure.[2]

The OAU Convention speaks specifically about the obligation of states to endeavor to "receive refugees and to secure the settlement of those refugees." Western states have assumed no such obligation. Their only obligation under the terms of the Refugee Convention and Protocol is not to "expel or return (*refouler*) a refugee . . . to the frontiers of territories where his life or freedom would be threatened on account of his race, religion, nationality, membership of a particular social group, or political opinion." This principle of *nonrefoulement* is interpreted by states, principally the U.S., to mean that an obligation of nonreturn only exists if the person is already in the country of refuge. By this restrictive interpretation, the obligation does not hold for persons interdicted on the high seas, such as Haitian boat people, nor to people turned away at the border they are seeking to cross, such as Iraqi Kurds on the Turkish border.[3]

The refugee crisis that arose on the heels of the Gulf War owes much of its tragic character to the failure of the 40-year-old Refugee Convention to address the right of asylum or to curb state power from manipulating the refugee definition to suit other-than-humanitarian ends.

The cause of the sudden flight of approximately 1.5 million Iraqi refugees in March and April 1991 can be traced to a combination of factors, including the Iraqi regime's history of aggression, brutal repression of minority groups and political dissenters, and disregard for human life. Under the U.S.-led Operation Provide Comfort, a protective shield was supposedly erected for a repressed and endangered minority in flight. In fact, true safety in the form of asylum was denied. The assistance that did arrive was as much to shore up

U.S. alliances with friendly governments as to assist the refugees.

The *principle* of a right to seek and enjoy asylum from persecution is recognized universally by the community of nations through the Universal Declaration of Human Rights. Turkey, a key U.S. ally, has remained among the most recalcitrant European states regarding the applicability of the Refugee Convention and Protocol. While most other European states have dropped the Convention's European-specific limitations, Turkey (along with Yugoslavia and Hungary) has steadfastly limited its definition of refugees to persons fleeing Europe. Turkey, for instance, has neither recognized nor protected the vast majority of the hundreds of thousands of Iranians who have fled to Turkey in the past decade.

Refugees from Iraq are likewise barred from consideration as refugees, and a Turkish refugee policy that excludes Kurds accords with Turkey's repression of its own Kurdish minority. Tens of thousands of Iraqi Kurds fled the Iraqi army in 1988 — this offensive included the poison gas attack on the Kurdish town of Halabja — but Turkey has refused to characterize refugees as "refugees" or the places where they have been held — often behind barbed wire and armed guards — as "camps." "We are not calling these groups refugees — yet," said Hayri Kozakcioglu, a regional governor, to the *Christian Science Monitor* in September 1988.

> The reason is just because the word "refugee" has very different legal meanings and understandings throughout the world. These groups haven't yet expressed their wishes about staying here. We understand they may go back to Iraq. So we call them "Iraqis who are staying here awhile." And we are not calling [the places where they stay] "camps." We are calling them "temporary residence places."[4]

If official circumlocutions seem bizarre, conditions in the three camps holding the Kurdish refugees still in Turkey from 1988 were appalling. For the three years prior to the Gulf War, the camps were surrounded by barbed wire and troops. International visitors were denied access, and movement in and out of the camps was strictly limited. Children were denied educational opportunities, and employment was either barred altogether or severely restricted. Residents of all three camps say that hundreds fell ill from alleged food poisonings in 1989 and 1990.

The smallest camp, Mus, was operated like a prison, according to observers. Residents were allowed out only for a couple of hours per day, and residence structures were reported to be unsafe and overcrowded. The larger camp at Diyarbekir was overcrowded, with intermittent electricity and unclean water. At the Kiziltope camp at Mardin, residents were forced to remain in tents from the time of their arrival. Kurds claimed that children died from exposure, malnutrition and disease. In the summer, the dilapidated tents absorbed terrific heat and sanitation broke down. In 1990, international donors pledged $14 million to relocate these refugees into permanent shelters in Yozgat province, in central Anatolia, but the Turkish government canceled these plans without explanation.

There have been persistent reports since 1988 of Turkish authorities returning Kurdish refugees to Iraq against their will. Coercion has reportedly been more intense during times when Baghdad announced amnesties. Allegations against the Turkish government include delays and reductions in rations, veiled threats, beatings and stepped up "security" measures.

No New Day

Ankara decided not to repeat what they saw as their mistake in 1988, when, in the Turkish view, they received plenty of Western criticism for their treatment of the Kurdish refugees but very little support either in the form of offers to resettle them or to provide adequate financial support for them in Turkey. It came as no surprise, therefore, that when a mass exodus of Iraqi Kurds arrived on Turkey's borders at the end of March 1991, they were left to fend for themselves, clinging to the sides of mountains.

A picture of misery and death briefly riveted the Western public's attention. The response to that outpouring of concern was neither the use of moral suasion nor the more taxing pressures governments such as the U.S. were in a position to exert to get Turkey to open its border and provide refuge. Turkey, the good ally, was essentially let off the hook with the creation of a "safe haven zone" inside Iraq. As so often happened before, the needs of refugees were a considerably lower priority than the need to cement political alliances.[5]

Creating a safe haven inside Iraq was a convenient "single-edged sword" for the U.S. — blunt on the Turkish side to protect its ally from any encroachment, yet razor sharp on the Iraqi side. The U.S., joined by Britain and France, justified the creation of a safe haven zone in northern Iraq by citing UN Resolution 688, adopted by the Security Council on April 5, 1991. The resolution is important both for what it says and for what it does not say. It frames its condemnation of Saddam Hussein's repression not in terms of the human rights violations committed against Iraqi citizens inside Iraq, but rather in terms of the "massive flow of refugees toward and across international frontiers" caused by the repression. The concern is not primarily about Baghdad's threat to the Kurds of Iraq, but rather the fear of the Kurds themselves — that their flight to other countries will "threaten international peace and security in the region."

Resolution 688, therefore, should hardly be read as ushering in a new day for human rights, sheltering citizens from government abuse committed under the umbrella of state sovereignty. The resolution pointedly reaffirms the "sovereignty, territorial integrity and political independence of Iraq and all the States in the area."

Resolution 688 did insist that Iraq "allow immediate access by international humanitarian organizations to all those in need of assistance in all parts of Iraq." This was a genuine advance, in that it expressed a consensus that international humanitarian organizations should be allowed free access to assist within Iraq. In compliance with the resolution, Iraq concluded a Memorandum of Understanding with the UN Secretary General's Executive Delegate, Prince Sadruddin Aga Khan, on April 18, 1991, that allowed the UN to provide humanitarian assistance whenever it believed necessary.[6]

But this was not enough to satisfy the Western powers. Nowhere in 688 was the U.S. Army defined as an international humanitarian organization. Straining their interpretation of Resolution 688, Britain, France and the U.S. created an occupied military zone in the name of international stability with the intent to destabilize the government of Iraq. This may have been a legitimate political goal, but it misrepresented the intervention under an essentially humanitarian facade.

Disparate Treatment

The self-serving character of the U.S.-led intervention is apparent from the grossly disproportionate U.S. response to the needs of Kurds in northern Iraq compared to the many more Kurds who fled at the same time to Iran. Total funds allocated and designated for Iran by mid-May 1991 was about half of that allocated for Turkey, although there were an estimated 1.3 million Kurdish refugees in Iran, about triple the estimated 330,000 in Turkey. Iran received $128.9 million in international assistance compared to $248 million spent on the Turkish/Iraqi border.[7] For every dollar spent for an Iraqi refugee in Iran, $7.60 was spent on an Iraqi refugee on the Turkish border. The U.S. contribution was even more heavily weighted in favor of Turkey. Of the $207.6 million spent by the U.S. government between the time the Iraqi refugee crisis erupted and mid-May, only 10% at most went to assist refugees in Iran.

It did not matter that the person was a refugee in need of assistance, or that the person was a Kurd, or a victim of Saddam Hussein's wrath. What mattered was the direction of flight — toward U.S. friend or foe. In effect, the Kurdish refugees in Iran were punished for the poor relation between Tehran and the West.

In August 1991, a year after the Iraqi invasion of Kuwait — the attack on national sovereignty that precipitated an unprecedented international military response — Turkey mounted a military incursion across its border with Iraq. Ankara claimed that it was attacking guerrillas of the Kurdish Workers Party (PKK) who had fled into northeastern Iraq. Turkey announced at the end of the first week of August — shortly after the allied withdrawal from the security zone — that its F-4 and F-104 fighters had conducted a total of 92 air raids and that 2,000 Turkish commandos, supported by helicopter gun ships, had crossed into Iraq. According to UN officials, the attacks targetted two Iraqi Kurdish villages, killing 20 civilians and wounding 15 but inflicting no known PKK casualties.[8]

The Turks announced at the time their intent to create a three-mile buffer zone along the Iraqi side of the border between the two states.[9] Although Ankara did not pursue this, the Turkish air force continued to violate Iraqi territory. On October 11, they bombed five Kurdish villages in northern Iraq that had been within the allied security zone, including Begova, which was being assisted by the International Rescue Committee, a U.S. voluntary agency. Kurdish sources reported that three Iraqi Kurds died and 11 others — including civilians — were wounded.[10] The U.S., Britain and France made no effort to protect the Kurds from Turkish bombs and bullets. In late March 1992 there were further Turkish air raids across the border.

Far from being a breakthrough for human rights and humanitarian assistance to displaced persons, the allied intervention on behalf of the Kurds of Iraq instead affirmed the power politics and hypocrisy that have long characterized the actions of states with respect to refugees and other powerless victims of official terror.

Iraq's egregious aggression and human rights violations created an opportunity for improving refugee policy, but this opportunity has been squandered. In the meantime, we must deal with the crises engendered by the actions of states, including the U.S., that compromise the rights of refugees, most especially the right to asylum and against forced return to conditions of political violence and persecution. Denial of asylum is a human rights violation. The U.S. supported Turkey's violation of the Kurds' right to asylum. Just to make it absolutely clear that there is no "new order," the U.S. adopted the same approach with the interdiction and forced return of boat refugees to Haiti. Who is left to intervene?

Notes

1. G. Goodwin-Gill, *The Refugee in International Law*, p. 74.
2. *Ibid.*, p. 111.
3. Kay Hailbronner articulates this view: "Codified refugee law is plainly inapplicable to persons fleeing from generalized violence in their home countries. A customary norm of *nonrefoulement* for humanitarian refugees, however merited on humanitarian grounds, is not now supported by the requirements of broad and consistent state practice and opinion juris . . . Despite the efforts of some observers, international law should not be viewed as demanding an obligation of states to adhere to *nonrefoulement* or provide temporary refuge for all humanitarian refugees." See *"Nonrefoulement* and 'Humanitarian' Refugees: Customary International Law or Wishful Legal Thinking?"* in D. Martin, ed., *The New Asylum Seekers: Refugee Law in the 1980s* (Kluwer Academic Publishers, 1988), p. 144.
4. September 20, 1988.
5. "If the refugees had been permitted to cross the border — even by half a mile — to enter more hospitable Turkish valleys and facilities, some of the tragic loss of life could have been minimized during those desperate early days in April." "Aftermath of War: The Persian Gulf Refugee Crisis," *Staff Report*, Subcommittee on Immigration and Refugee Affairs, US Senate Committee on the Judiciary, 102nd Congress, First Session, May 20, 1991, pp. 36–7.
6. See James Fine, "The Iraq Sanctions Catastrophe," and Attalah Kuttab, "Dilemmas of Relief Work in Iraq," in *Middle East Report* No. 174 (Jan–Feb 1992).
7. The UN Disaster Relief Operation (UNDRO) situation report, May 17, 1991. The $248 million figure for the money spent in Turkey combines the UNDRO accounting of $57 million with the $140.1 million in US Department of Defense contributions and $31.6 million in Food for Peace assistance, both of which were distributed as part of Operation Provide Comfort.
8. *Washington Post (WP)*, October 12, 1991.
9. *WP*, August 8, 1991, A27.
10. *WP*, October 12, 1991.

11

Turkey's Kurds After the Gulf War:
A Report from the Southeast

*Aliza Marcus**

The Cihan Hotel in Sirnak rarely had any running water in 1992, like most businesses and homes in that city in southeast Turkey. The few kebab shops along the main road kept tanks filled with water so their customers could wash off the dust before eating, but the Cihan's guests had to make do with a splash of lemony cologne kept on a shelf in the main room.

There was no real point in the Cihan Hotel arranging for a water tank because guests, mainly truck drivers picking up coal from the nearby mines, were used to the hard life of the impoverished southeast. And it was no wonder the manager didn't prepare his six dank rooms for a tourist onslaught: The last time anyone could remember seeing a tourist was in 1989, when a lost German motorcyclist suddenly appeared, much to the bemusement of the locals. Despite breathtaking views of the surrounding mountains, and the cool, clean air of the summer, few foreigners dared enter this region.

The battle between Turkish troops and Kurdish guerrillas seeking self-determination turned much of the southeast into a war zone. In 1992 the PKK, the Kurdish initials of the Workers' Party of Kurdistan, had 5,000 to 10,000 guerrillas fighting the Turkish army there. Hundreds if not thousands more were training in bases located in northern Iraq and the Syrian-controlled Bekaa Valley. Despite the estimated 120,000 Turkish troops stationed in southeast Turkey, backed up by tanks, helicopters and a 30,000-strong government-financed Kurdish militia, Ankara was unable to end guerrilla attacks, which began sporadically in 1984 and by 1992 occurred almost daily. About 4,400 people — civilians, guerrillas and soldiers — had died in the fighting.

* Aliza Marcus is a journalist, and a frequent contributor to the *Christian Science Monitor*. She lived in Turkey from 1988 to 1990.

"For 150 years the Kurdish movement was a fire, sometimes stronger, sometimes weaker, but it was never put out completely," said Faysal Yilmaz (who asked that his real name not be used), a prominent and wealthy Kurdish human rights lawyer in Sirnak. The town is in the center of the Botan province, as the Kurds call it, and like many of the surrounding villages, the 29,000 people of Sirnak supported the guerrillas. "This fire is always in the people," added Yilmaz, who said ten of his relatives had joined the guerrillas.[1]

Since the founding of the Turkish Republic in 1923, successive governments have tried, with occasional respite, to eradicate manifestations of Kurdish nationalism and identity. Use of the Kurdish language, especially written Kurdish, was at times unofficially and sometimes officially banned. Whole villages were uprooted and people relocated, history was rewritten to treat Kurds as "mountain Turks," people who forgot their Turkishness while living in inaccessible and remote mountain villages. While the degree of repression always fluctuated, the overriding policy was one of forced assimilation. But Turkey's approach, "which has relied on ignorance and avoidance," could not make the problem go away, according to Ismail Besiksi, a Turkish sociologist who spent over 10 years in prison for his attempts to explore and chronicle Kurdish life in his country.[2]

In the aftermath of the 1991 Gulf War, the government took steps to appease the Kurds and to liberalize laws aimed at dissent (laws which were harshly employed against ethnic Turks as well as Kurds, especially in the repressive years following the 1980 military coup). In April 1991, the National Assembly abolished penal code articles which prohibited communist, religious, and separatist activities. Thousands of prisoners were released and a 1983 law forbidding the use of the Kurdish language was repealed.

The repeal of the 1983 law was met with derision by Kurds. "It was a trick of the government, an attempt to stop the Kurdish movement," insisted a member of the pro-Kurdish People's Labor Party (HEP), who pointed out that Kurds had continued to speak their language, despite government harassment. "The people want their freedom, they are dying . . . and they are not dying for the right to speak Kurdish, they are dying for independence, for freedom . . . The Kurdish problem is a human rights problem."

For most Kurds, the government's liberalization efforts did not begin to redress their grievances. (Other changes included Ankara's new willingness to tolerate pro-Kurdish publications, greater mention of the Kurdish conflict and even a private Kurdish Institute — opened by Ismail Besiksi in Istanbul in 1992.) They complained of continued and widespread human rights abuses, and many demanded a referendum on the future of the southeast, home to about half the country's 10 to 12 million Kurds and an area that has been governed by emergency rule since 1987. The Turkish military was largely responsible for the human rights violations in the region, and Kurdish activists pointed out that even were the government inclined to change the situation, it wouldn't be easy. In southeastern Turkey, the military was barely under civilian control. Furthermore, the government in Ankara had always had a strained relationship with the army, which saw itself as the guarantor of the Turkish nation, and had staged three coups to prove it.

In effect, parliament assured the military of a continuing free hand when it passed the "Anti-Terror Law," which took effect on April 12, 1992. For all intents and purposes, this reinstated the repealed ban against separatist propaganda. One article in the law forbade "written and oral propaganda . . . aiming at damaging the indivisible unity of the State of the Turkish Republic." Its vague wording, coupled with the law's ambigious definition of terrorism, invited easy abuse of human rights by security officers.[3]

This law was used by the police and military to confiscate pro-Kurdish newspapers, ban books about Kurds and arrest proponents of Kurdish rights. A lawyer who defended someone charged under it could in turn be prosecuted. Likewise, the law could be applied against vocal human rights workers and, of course, anyone suspected of aiding the guerrillas.[4]

The new Turkish government that was elected in October 1991 (headed by Suleyman Demirel, leader of the conservative True Path Party) promised to promote human rights, but violence by security forces against residents in the southeast continued. In increasing numbers, local human rights monitors were harassed and detained, torture of political detainees remained endemic, journalists working in the southeast were threatened and some were mysteriously murdered.[5] Kurds who refused to join the government-backed militia were victimized by security forces; whole villages were forcibly evacuated either because residents would not take up arms against the PKK or because guerrillas were thought to be nearby. Or, merely because the army told residents to move.[6] Security forces opened fire on non-violent demonstrations, and during the Newroz, or Kurdish New Year celebrations in 1992, over 70 people died when troops shot demonstrators lining the streets in various towns in the southeast.[7]

The southeast was also struck by a series of mysterious killings; over 60 outspoken Kurdish activists were assassinated between early 1991 and mid-1992, many last seen in the company of men claiming to be police. Dozens of others received death threats. Turkish authorities strongly denied charges of complicity. Local Kurdish residents blamed shadowy "counterguerrillas," who they contended were supported by the government's security forces, tacitly if not directly.[8]

The ongoing violence only strengthened Kurdish support for the guerrillas. Hatip Dicle, former chairman of the Turkish Human Rights Association's office in Diyarbekir, the largest city in the southeast, easily recited a litany of abuses, including the 1991 bombing of the association's office. "The government is losing authority in this region and they are trying to solve the problem with violence." Dicle, who was elected to parliament in the 1991 national elections added, "But they never can solve it with violence. The government must open peaceful and democratic channels . . . If it really wants to solve this problem . . . it must negotiate with the PKK. The PKK is the organization which is struggling for the Kurds."

One reason why the PKK commanded such widespread support was that it had established an active network of organizations that went beyond its battles with Turkish security forces. From its allied organizations in Europe (especially in Germany, home to hundreds of thousands of Kurds) the PKK published magazines and printed books, organized women and youth groups and generally worked to develop and reinforce Kurdish identity. In Turkey, a number of illicit groups, particularly aimed at teenagers, operated out of high schools and tea houses.

The PKK also worked through its support base in the southeast, the untold number of sympathizers who staffed Turkish government offices, political parties, legal aid societies and private businesses. When the group needed to inform people to stay inside one night because of a planned attack on a nearby army base, for example, word traveled fast, residents said.

The PKK also sought to influence Turkish politics, mainly by promoting certain Kurdish candidates for local and national offices. The PKK gave at least tacit support to some of the Kurdish candidates who ran in the 1991 national elections, while guerrilla sources said the group also offered to help defray campaign expenses for some people who wanted to run but could not afford it.

By mid-1992, the PKK exerted some control over parts of the southeast. At night, guerrillas would set up roadblocks, killing the few soldiers and village guards who still dared travel after dark and confiscating Turkish identity cards from Kurds, handing out PKK-issued replacements. Foreigners were advised to obtain special travel visas from PKK-support organizations in Europe before entering the area.[9]

Development of the PKK[10]

The PKK was founded in 1978 by Abdullah Ocalan, a Kurdish university student in Ankara. In 1984, it staged its first attack, and Turkey's Kurds initially responded hesitantly. For many of them, the pronounced Marxist-Leninist rhetoric of the PKK was anathema to their Muslim way of life. Furthermore, the group's widely applied policy of attacking "collaborators" with Turkey was often indiscriminate, and uninvolved women and children were also killed. Many Kurds were angered by this bloodshed.

Local residents, especially those in mountain villages, quickly found themselves caught between the guerrillas and the army. The PKK's army, officially called the People's Liberation Army of Kurdistan (ARGK), was initially not very discriminating; schools and health clinics — some of which the army had occasionally used to store weapons or quarter troops — were burned; relatives of members of the government's Kurdish militia were killed; and there were reports that teenaged boys were being forcibly conscripted.[11] The PKK's activities were funded through a tax on Kurds, and political refugees and other Kurds living in Europe are said to have been major financial supporters. The group always remained fairly independent. The bulk of its "foreign aid" came from Syria, which allowed the PKK to set up bases in the Syrian-controlled Bekaa Valley.[12]

Slowly, the PKK changed its methods. After a few years of fighting, the group realized that some of its actions were alienating Kurds. It also had achieved dominance over the handful of other groups that had sought to gain followers. Around 1990, the PKK announced it would try to avoid killing civilians. In 1991 it instituted a year-long amnesty for the government's Kurdish militia members, giving them a chance to quit without facing retribution. Stories of boys being kidnapped had long since died. The number of young men and women who wanted to join had grown so large there was no longer enough room to train them, PKK sources in the region explained during 1991. These moves, coupled with the group's increasingly successful assaults against Turkish security forces, attracted more adherents.

With the majority of Turkish leftists and intellectuals slow to address the Kurdish problem, many Kurds saw the PKK as the only force interested in their plight, and certainly the only group exacting retribution for human rights abuses. "We are all guerrillas, the only difference is some of us are in the mountains and some of us are here," insisted a 31-year-old Kurdish truck driver. He said that in 1990 he was tortured and spent a month in jail for having a Kurdish music casette. It was not an unusual story.

"In a way, the government made the PKK as strong as it is today," said a 24-year-old man from a village near Sirnak, a university graduate now working as an organizer for the PKK. "The security forces think it's a solution that if they kill they will scare the people, but they don't understand that when they kill they make more enemies."

After 1990, the PKK, while still Marxist-Leninist, toned down its rhetoric, acknowledging a place for Islam. National rights, rather than economic questions were emphasized. At the same time, the original demand for total independence was modified. In 1992 Ocalan was quoted as calling for a federal solution, with Kurds granted self-rule over the southeast, which would remain part of Turkey.

"The PKK is not inevitably insisting on organized violence," Ocalan told a leftist Turkish magazine in March 1992, in an interview clearly aimed at Turkish readers.[13] The Kurdish problem, he said, must be resolved through "dialogue with legitimate and official organizations which represent our people. Let the bloodletting be stopped . . ." He indicated that he would accept a ceasefire, assuming the security force violence against Kurds ceased and the government opened talks with Kurdish leaders.

He was not alone in this demand. In the 1991 national elections, 22 Kurdish parliamentarians who were members of the pro-Kurdish People's Labor Party (HEP) were elected on the left-of-center Social Democratic People's Party ticket (SHP). Some of them argued that Turkey had to open talks with the PKK and allow a referendum on what sort of links Kurds wanted with Turkey. Ankara was clearly not interested. Ever since a deputy spoke in Kurdish during the swearing-in ceremony — one of the few times Kurdish had ever been used in the Turkish parliament — there had been various calls to strip the parliamentarians of their immunity and charge them with "sedition" for statements calling for recognition of Kurdish rights.[14]

"Our goal is not to divide Turkey, but to share it," continued Ocalan, in that interview, one of his most wide-ranging on the future of the Kurdish southeast. "I don't see it as either reasonable or necessary that [a Kurdish region should] be detached from the country as if cut by a knife. But the Kurds will determine their own fate."

While a later interview in the PKK's European-based magazine indicated that Ocalan had not given up his desire for a Kurdish independent state, his comments aimed at a Turkish audience showed a certain flexibility, at least in the short-run.[15] If nothing else, Ocalan's willingness to discuss solutions short of independence was a sign of increased political maturity.

The Gulf War and After

The Gulf War and the subsequent safe haven for Iraqi Kurds created by the U.S.-led allied forces after the failed uprising in northern Iraq had little direct impact on Turkish Kurds, although it did aid the PKK's armed struggle. The PKK successfully took advantage of the power vacuum in northern Iraq to move more training bases into the region. The group was also quick to buy up military hardware abandoned by the Iraqi army and to avail itself of the more loosely patrolled border.[16]

The Kurds in Turkey were certainly heartened by the nominal autonomy established in northern Iraq and the international attention focused on Iraqi Kurds. The two groups had always had economic and familial ties, and Turkish Kurds had generally sought to aid the various groups of Iraqi Kurdish refugees that streamed across the border at different times. Still, the Gulf War did not change the reality (PKK rhetoric about greater Kurdistan aside) that the Turkish and Iraqi Kurds were fighting separate battles despite various agreements at times between their leaders.

If anything, relations after the Gulf War were strained by attempts by Jalal Talabani and Massoud Barzani, the two main Iraqi Kurdish leaders, to gain favor with the Turkish government despite its oppression of its Kurdish population. Both leaders sought to distance themselves from the PKK, even though Turkish bombing of supposed PKK camps in northern Iraq had killed Iraqi Kurdish civilians. While there were some claims by both Iraqi and Turkish Kurds that this reflected "realpolitik" rather than true sentiment, the aftermath of the Gulf War might have revealed real differences.

The situation certainly made it easier for Turkey to continue its heavy-handed approach toward its Kurds. The lack of clear control over the Iraqi-Turkish border enabled the Turkish army to stage frequent cross-border raids. The allied military protection afforded the Iraqi Kurds against Iraqi President Saddam Hussein meant little for the Turkish Kurds, who remained at the mercy of the Turkish security forces.

At the same time, Talabani and Barzani's stated support for Turkey did not quell Turkey's wariness of Iraqi Kurdish autonomy, despite their repeated promises to honor Turkey's territorial integrity. The Turkish government continued to believe that autonomy in northern Iraq could only strengthen Turkish Kurds' calls for self-determination, a point not without merit. Turkey did not support the May 1992 Kurdish elections in northern Iraq and it made its displeasure clear. A few days before the elections Turkish military planes embarked on a cross-border bombing raid in which they hit a local

Barzani campaign office. The Turkish government also issued a statement saying the elections could lead to a power vacuum and more violence in northern Iraq.[17]

Arguably, the Gulf War's main effect on Turkish Kurds was economic, weakening a region already near collapse from decades of government neglect and years of battle. The southeast had always suffered from a lack of private investment and a scarcity of government-financed factories, partly because of the lack of infrastructure and security fears.[18]

Nevertheless, for decades the Kurds were able to maintain themselves — albeit it at a relatively low standard of living — by relying on agriculture, sheep and cows, a few privately-owned coal mines, a brisk smuggling trade across the borders with Iran and Iraq, and, in towns along the Iraqi border, a bustling service industry for the thousands of truckers crossing between Turkey and Iraq daily. In the late 1980s, the military started closing coal mines for weeks on end (charging the workers with supporting the PKK), fields were placed off-limits, and nomadic families prohibited from traveling to their mountain pastures and seasonal camping areas.[19]

When Turkey complied with the economic embargo against Iraq after Baghdad invaded Kuwait in August 1990, the truckers abandoned their brightly-painted cabs on the roadsides and smuggling became very dangerous. Soon, many of the Kurdish cafes, cheap hotels and repair shops shut down, while shelves in local shops, once stocked with Iraqi tea, cigarettes and toiletries, lay empty. The only real source of income became itinerant work in western Turkey. Kurds complained, however, that they were discriminated against and harassed there when they revealed their southeastern origins.

Investment — which Kurds say never got much beyond military barracks and prisons — was further limited by the guerrilla war. Part of the problem with developing the southeast was the region's lack of roads: the few that traversed the area were often of extremely poor quality, making it difficult to transport goods. But roads, which could also carry troops, were targeted by the PKK: At least one major road-building project in the southeast came under attack by guerrillas, sending a strong signal to those who might attempt projects without the PKK's approval.[20]

Guerrilla attacks on teachers in the southeast also made it impossible for hundreds of schools to open. The PKK at times targeted teachers, condemning them as purveyors of Turkish culture and its repression of the Kurds and alleging that many were spies for the army. Turkish teachers, as a result, became increasingly unwilling to work in the region, correctly believing the military could no longer guarantee their safety. Whether or not Turkish teachers ever spied for the army, the result was that schools were shut, children were not learning Turkish and many students who hoped to pass the university entrance exams or work outside the region found their chances diminished without proper schooling.

Despite the acute teacher shortage, local residents said Kurdish teachers willing to work there could not always get the necessary Turkish authorization. In any case, the educational level of schools in the southeast was very low, books were few and students mostly poor. And, of course, Kurdish school children had to deny their national identity.[21]

Despite these pressures, the PKK maintained an extremely high level of support among most Kurds in the southeast, and it was clear there would be no ceasefire until Ankara at least made a good faith effort to end human rights abuses and open discussion on Kurdish political rights. In the meantime, relations between Kurds and Turks worsened. Funeral ceremonies for soldiers killed by guerrillas began to turn into anti-Kurdish rallies, ultra-nationalist groups demanded an end to virtually any recognition of Kurdish identity, and rumors of civil war were rife.[22]

Prime Minister Suleyman Demirel, who said he recognized the "Kurdish reality," promised economic development programs for the southeast, and it seemed by 1992 that he might be ready for some compromises and concessions. But the main impediment to change remained the military. Demirel, a former six-time prime minister twice deposed by the armed forces (in 1971 and in 1980), was unlikely to risk being deposed a third time by opening talks with the PKK. Meanwhile, General Dogan Gures, chief of the general staff, repeatedly vowed to crush the guerrillas. Besides military incursions into northern Iraq, the Turkish airforce bombed at least one mountanous area inside Turkey. The bloodshed following the 1992 Newroz New Year demonstrations underscored the military's position on how to address Kurdish demands for recognition.

The situation had reached an impasse. Kurds called for international pressure, and they managed to get some attention from European organizations and governments. But, ironically, the Gulf War could have minimized the importance of the Turkish Kurds to the U.S.-led allied forces. The United States, always a strong backer of Turkey, was basically unreceptive to the Turkish Kurds' pleadings, despite the sudden outpouring of support for the Iraqi Kurds. European leaders, desperate to ensure Turkish support for a continuing allied presence on Turkish soil to protect Iraqi Kurds in the safe haven, were quick to label Turkish Kurds "terrorists," a situation termed by some the "Good Kurd/Bad Kurd" syndrome.[23] Likewise, the United States and European powers were interested in using Turkey as a stabilizing force against Iranian influence in the new, mainly Muslim Central Asian nations. It was clearly not politic to point out that the Turkish security forces were committing massive abuses against Kurds in the southeast. Nor was it diplomatic to raise the logical question of why some Kurds should have freedom while others could not.

"Happy is He Who Calls Himself A Turk," read the sign hanging over the main street of Sirnak, one of the many oft-quoted phrases of Kemal Ataturk, the leader of the Turkish independence war and the first head of the republic. A few blocks away, Ayse Yilmaz, the 35-year-old wife of human rights lawyer Faysal Yilmaz, told a story about life as a Kurd in Turkey: "One time when my seven-year-old son was studying in primary school in Izmir [a city in western Turkey], he was being taught to write 'I am a Turk.' He wrote instead, 'I am a Kurd. I am smart. I never lie.' The teacher called me in and said I was brainwashing my child and warned if this happened again, she would call the police.

"I told my boy not to write these things, and he said, 'Why are you lying? Aren't we Kurds, aren't we from Kurdistan?' I was ashamed, but I said if he didn't follow this, his father could be taken away and tortured.

"We live under the same flag [as the Turks] but we are not the same nation. Our people are not struggling for their comfort, we are struggling for our future and our children's future."

Notes

1. Interview in Sirnak, October 1991. Unless otherwise noted, everyone quoted was interviewed during an October 1991 two-week trip through the southeast.
2. Interview, October 1991. Besikci was in an Ankara prison at the time, awaiting trial on charges of "separatist propaganda" under the Anti-Terror Law for his book *State Terror In the Middle East*. The interview was conducted via his lawyer Husnu Ondul. For a good English-language explanation of Besikci's history and works, see *Kurdish Times*, Vol. I, No. 2 Fall, 1986.
3. The Anti-Terror Law has been criticized by a number of groups, including the Human Rights Foundation of Turkey, Helsinki Watch and the Lawyers Committee for Human Rights (May 1992 draft report "Critique: Review of the State Department's country report on human rights practices for 1991").
   The law defines terrorism as "any kind of action conducted by one or several persons belonging to an organization with the aim of changing the characteristics of the Republic as specified in the Constitution, its political, legal, social, secular and economic system."
   Because of its vague wording, "anyone advocating non-violent economic or social change can be charged with and prosecuted for engaging in terrorism." (Lawyers Committee draft report, p. 5). Even the U.S. State Department, never very critical of Turkey, said the ambigious definition of terrorism in the law "could invite abuses of power by security authorities" ("Country Reports on Human Rights Practices for 1991," February 1992).
4. For specific examples of the law's application see information collected by the Human Rights Foundation in Turkey and the U.S.-based Committee to Protect Journalists' 1991 worldwide survey on press freedom. Analysis of the law's application based on, among other things, discussions with Lois Whitman at Helsinki Watch.
5. Interviews in the southeast, October 1991; "Urgent Action" mailings from Amnesty International; Helsinki Watch reports on human rights abuses in Turkey; Alan Cowell, *The New York Times*, "Turkey's Efforts To Quell Rebel Kurds Raises Alarm in Ankara and Europe," March 27, 1992, p. 10. During Kurdish New Year demonstrations in March 1992, a Turkish photographer in Cizre was shot by someone in a police tank as he ran to his hotel carrying a white flag, according to the Turkish Human Rights Foundation.
6. Aliza Marcus, *The Christian Science Monitor*, "Turkey Struggles With Kurdish Uprising," August 30, 1990, p. 10–11; Helsinki Watch, "Destroying Ethnic Identity," September 1990, pp. 19–26.
7. See Amnesty International Urgent Action Appeal March 27, 1992; Human Rights Foundation of Turkey, daily fax, March 26, 1992, stated: "The observations . . . [indicate] the events were caused by security forces' intention to disperse unarmed demonstrators." The report specifically referred to events in Cizre, where many of the deaths occured.
8. Interview with relatives of Vedat Aydin, a Kurdish member of the People's Labor Party, murdered July 1991 after being taken from his apartment by two men claiming to be police officers; interviews with Kurdish human rights lawyers October 1991; Cowell, *New York Times*.
9. Aliza Marcus, *The Christian Science Monitor*, "Kurds Separatists Grip Southeastern Turkey," October 24, 1991, p. 5.
10. Description of the PKK and how it has evolved is based on my trips to the region starting in 1989, extensive interviews with PKK sources and local Kurdish residents, and talks with Aram Nigogosian, a graduate student at the University of Pennsylvania, who is writing his dissertation on the Kurdish movement in Turkey.
11. Based on numerous trips to the region and interviews with PKK sources and local residents. Claims of kidnapping are hard to verify because families often told authorities their sons had been kidnapped by the PKK as a means to avoid punishment for being seen as guerrilla sympathizers.
12. Toward the end of April 1992 the PKK started to move some bases out of the Bekaa, following strong demands by Turkish officials that Syria close the camps.
13. *2000'e dogru*, March 15, 1992. Translation provided by Aram Nigogosian.

14. By the end of May 1992, eighteen of the deputies had resigned from the SHP to protest abuses against the Kurds. The deputies originally ran on the SHP ticket because their party, HEP, was banned from the elections on a technicality.
15. Serxwebun, April 1992; translation provided by Aram Nigogosian.
16. Based on interviews in the region, visits by local journalists to PKK bases in northern Iraq, and Turkish news reports.
17. Kurt Schork, Reuters, "Turkey bombs Iraqi Kurds as election approaches," May 14, 1992.
18. Almost the only large-scale government investment had been in the Southeastern Anatolia Project, which will irrigate swathes of land in the region and provide Turkey with additional power sources. This project, however, will not be fully completed for at least another decade, and its benefit for the Kurds is as yet unknown.
19. Interviews in the southeast, 1989, 1990, 1991.
20. Around October 1992, trucks and a generator for a road works project were bombed, slowing down work. A private company — probably under government contract — had been trying to put down asphalt on part of a road between Pervari and Siirt. Workers told me the guerrillas said they were afraid the new road would make it easier for the military to move troops around. In an example of how the PKK operates, the guerrillas told the workers to stay inside their trailer while the trucks and other items were being firebombed. When asked whether the guerrillas tried to propagandize the workers, one man said, "No, it isn't necessary."
21. "Every single student learns about the history of Turkey, about Turkish nationalism, and they fill your heads with these lies," Ahmet Ikinci, a 29-year-old road surveyor who grow up in Diyarbakir, told me in October 1991. "Then you come to a certain age and you realize you are from a different nation with a different history and so you try to examine your history. And then you no longer trust Turkey and you feel alienated. Maybe we struggled together," added Ikinci, referring to Kurdish support for Turks during Turkey's war of independence, "but they won and we lost."
22. Telephone interviews, 1992; Turkish press reports.
23. John Gittings, Guardian (London), "Good Kurds and Bad Kurds in the New Geopolitical Conjunction," April 25–26, 1992.

Chronology

7th Century: First record of Kurdish writing: a short text, in verse, evoking the sufferings of the people during the Arab invasion. Mazdeist temples of fire were destroyed and the devotees of Ahura Mazda persecuted for professing a religion which the Kurds had adhered to since the time of the Medes.

7th–9th Centuries: Having converted to Islam, the Kurds made an original and important contribution to Muslim civilization, notably in the military and artistic fields. A Kurdish musician from Mosul, Ibrahim Mawsili (743–806) introduced music, an art which had until then been forbidden by Islam, to the court of Harun al-Rashid: he also founded the first Muslim Conservatory. His son, Ishaq, developed and codified his work and one of their disciples, another Kurd called Ziriyab, went to the Court of Cordoba to set up his own school and spread his master's teaching in Spain and the Maghreb.

10th–12th Centuries: Emergence of independent Kurdish principalities: to the north, the Chaddadides (951–1174), with their capital at Ganja; to the south, the Hassanwaihides (959–1015); and to the west, the Merwanides (990–1096), with their capital at Diyarbekir.

1169–1250: The Kurdish Ayyubid dynasty, with Saladin as its most illustrious representative, reigns over the whole Muslim Middle East.

14th–15th Centuries: Reconstitution of the Kurdish principalities following the tidal wave of the Mongol invasion. Kurdish cultural life flourishes in the courts of Bitlis, Hakkari and Bohtan.

1514: The Kurdish princes form an alliance against Shiite Persia with the Ottoman Sultan Selim the Cruel. The Shah's army is defeated by the Turkish and Kurdish forces at Tchaldyran, north of Kurdistan. The Sultan promises to recognize the "Kurdish states" and not to interfere in their internal affairs.

1596: Cheref Khan, Prince of Bitlis, completes his *Cheref-Nameh* (Days of the Kurdish Nation), the first book on Kurdish history as a whole.

1695: Ehmede Khani (born 1651), poet, philosopher and linguist, publishes his masterpiece *Mem-o-Zin*, a saga of the Kurdish people calling for the creation of a united national state of Kurdistan.

19th Century: The Sublime Porte begins to interfere in Kurdish affairs. Feeling their prerogatives threatened, the Kurdish feudalists rise up against the Ottomans in a series of disconnected revolts led in 1806 by Abdurrahman, Pasha of Suleymanieh, in 1818 by the Bilbas, in 1832 by Mir Mohammed of Rawanduz, in 1843–46 by Bedir Khan Bey, in 1853–55 by Yezdan Sher and in 1880 by Sheikh Obeidullah of Nehri. Apart from a few provinces annexed by Persia, all the Kurdish territories fell under Ottoman domination.

1898: The first Kurdish journal, *Kurdistan*, appears and begins to propagate the idea of Kurdish national liberation.

1908: The Young Turk Revolution. A Constitution promulgating full equality between all the Empire's nationalities is proclaimed in Constantinople. But right from 1909 the Young Turks begin to apply repressive policies against non-Turkish people — the Albanians, Armenians, Kurds, etc. Kurdish organizations and publications are outlawed.

October 30, 1918: The Mudros Amnesty. Having sided with Germany during the First World War, the Ottoman Empire capitulates to the Allies.

April 19–26, 1920: The San Remo Conference. The various agreements concerning the carve-up of the Middle East concluded by the Allied Powers during the War are tabled once again, in the light of the new balance of power. Britain is given a mandate over Arab Iraq and the Turkish Vilayet of Mosul, "ceded" by France in exchange for Cilicia. There is talk of creating separate Armenian and Kurdish states on the territories which had originally been allocated to Russia.

1919–1920: The first Kurdish revolt against the British occupation of southern Kurdistan breaks out. The movement, led by Sheikh Mahmoud, aims to create a "free and united Kurdistan."

August 10, 1920: The Treaty of Sevres, concluded by the Allied Powers with the Sublime Porte, confirms the carve-up as defined at San Remo. Section III (Articles 62–64) envisages the creation of a Kurdish state on Kurdish territory.

October 20, 1921: The French and Turks sign the Ankara Agreement. France takes the Kurdish provinces of Jezireh and Kurd-Dagh which are annexed under the Syrian mandate.

August 23, 1921: Sir Percy Cox, British High Commissioner in Mesopotamia, presents the throne of Iraq to Emir Feisal, son of the Sherif of Mecca, whom the French had just expelled from Syria. The Kurds of Mosul boycott the plebiscite organized to "elect" Feisal.

1923: Sheikh Mahmoud leads a second revolt, proclaims himself "King of Kurdistan" and establishes contact with Simko, the leader since 1920 of a Kurdish revolt against Persian domination. The movement was repressed by the British Army and the Sheikh was exiled to India.

June 24, 1923: The Allied Powers and the Kemalist Ankara government sign the Treaty of Lausanne, which supersedes the Treaty of Sevres and sets the seal on the annexation of most of Kurdistan by the new Turkish state.

March 3, 1924: A Turkish decree bans all Kurdish schools, organizations and publications, along with the religious fraternities and *medressehs*. The first Turkish Assembly, which included 72 representatives of Kurdistan, is dissolved.

February–April 1925: Sheikh Said leads a revolt in Turkish Kurdistan.

December 16, 1925: The Council of the League of Nations accepts the British claim to annex southern Kurdistan (Mosul) under the Iraqi mandate.

August 1927: *Hoyboun* (Independence), the Kurdish National League, is founded to bring together all Kurdish political parties and organizations set up following World War I.

1928: The entire civil and military administration of Kurdistan in Turkey is entrusted to the "Inspector-General of the East," the Turkish High Commissioner for Kurdistan. Revolts erupt throughout the Kurdish provinces.

1930: *Hoyboun* organizes a vast insurrection in the Mount Ararat region. Turkey and Iran form a pact to repress the movement (January 1932).

June 1930: Simko, leader of the Kurdish revolt against the central authorities of Iran since 1920, is assassinated during talks with representatives of Tehran.

Autumn 1931: A new revolt breaks out in Iranian Kurdistan under Jafar Sultan.

1931: Having returned from India, Sheikh Mahmoud raises another revolt in Iraqi Kurdistan. He is eventually captured by the British and placed under house arrest in Baghdad. Immediately afterwards, the Iraqi Kurds rise up again, this time under the leadership of Sheikh Ahmed Barzani, Mustafa Barzani's brother. The British RAF is sent in to attack the Kurdish villages.

May 1932: Ankara promulgates a law for the deportation and dispersion of the Kurds. Hundreds of thousands are deported to Central and Western Anatolia.

1933: The Kurds rise up in Iraq, led by the Barzanis.

1936–1938: Armed resistance by the Kurds of Dersim (Kurdistan in Turkey).

1943–1945: Kurdish revolts in Iraq, under the leadership of Mustafa Barzani, who is eventually forced to retreat to Iranian Kurdistan.

August 1945: The Iranian Kurdish Democratic Party (KDP) is founded. Sometime later, a similar organization is set up by the Kurds of Iraq.

January 13, 1946: The first Kurdish Republic is proclaimed at Mahabad, under the presidency of Qazi Mohammed. It was destroyed in the spring of 1947. Barzani, at the head of the Kurdish forces, managed to open up a passage for himself and a few hundred followers across the Turkish-Iranian frontiers and into the USSR.

August 1953: A coup organized by the CIA brings the Shah of Iran back to power.

1956: Under the aegis of Britain and the United States, Turkey, Iran and Iraq sign the Baghdad Pact. One of the clauses envisages co-ordinated repression of any revolts in the territory of any one of the states involved. This was soon put into effect; the rebellious Kurds of Juanroj (Iranian Kurdistan) were put down by a combined Iraqi-Iranian force.

July 14, 1958: A military coup led by General Qasim overthrows the Iraqi monarchy. A Republic based on "the free association of Arabs and Kurds" is proclaimed in Baghdad. Iraq denounces the Baghdad Pact (later replaced by CENTO). Barzani returns from exile in the Soviet Union.

January 9, 1960: The Iraqi KDP is legalized.

May 27, 1960: A military coup overthrows the Menderes government in Turkey. The military convoke a Constituent Assembly which elaborates a new, more liberal Turkish Constitution.

Spring 1961: Kurdish newspapers and publications in Iraq are accused of "separatism" and are gradually closed down.

September 11, 1961: Beginning of a Kurdish armed insurrection in Iraq which eventually became a popular movement of national liberation.

February 8, 1963: Baathist coup in Baghdad. A provisional ceasefire is called along the front in Kurdistan. Several thousand communists are killed or imprisoned. Those who escape take refuge in the Kurdish maquis.

June 1963: The Iraqi Army launches a new offensive against the Kurdish maquisards. From Syria, where the Baath Party has seized power in March 1963, airforce and army units come to fight against the Kurds.

June 18, 1963: The USSR officially declares its support for the Kurdish movement.

July 9, 1963: Mr. Gromyko, the Soviet Minister for Foreign Affairs, sends a note to the ambassadors of Iraq, Iran, Turkey and Syria warning their governments not to launch a joint military intervention in Iraqi Kurdistan. Turkey and Iran give up Operation Tiger, the planned link-up with the Iraqi and Syrian troops engaged in Kurdistan.

November 18, 1963: In Baghdad, Colonel Aref replaces the Baathists and has himself promoted to Marshal.

February 10, 1964: Marshal Aref recognizes Kurdish national rights and a ceasefire is called. The political opportunities provided by the agreement provoke splits in the Kurdish leadership. The KDP Political Bureau, led by Ibrahim Ahmed and Jalal Talabani, declares its opposition to General Barzani, the movement's leader. The dispute soon degenerates into armed conflict. The Political Bureau group first seeks refuge in Iran, then returns to Baghdad and gives its support to the regime. Crisis and confusion spreads throughout the Iraqi Kurdish movement.

March 1965: Military operations begin again in Iraq, and continue till the second ceasefire in June 1966.

Autumn 1965: Foreign visitors are for the first time allowed into Turkish Kurdistan, which had been classified as "a military zone forbidden to foreigners" since 1925. There are mass demonstrations against unemployment, poverty and ethnic discrimination.

1967–1968: Peasants wage guerrilla war in Iranian Kurdistan.

July 1968: Following two successive coups (July 19 and 30) the Baath regains power in Baghdad. General Al-Bakr, Prime Minister in the 1963 Baathist government, is proclaimed President of the Republic. The war against the Kurdish partisans is relaunched in April 1969.

March 11, 1970: The Kurds and the Iraqis sign an Agreement on "the Autonomy of Kurdistan," which is supposed to be implemented within four years.

March 12, 1970: Military coup in Turkey. The Army appoints a "strong government." Left-wing parties and organizations are outlawed. Several thousand Kurdish "separatists" are arrested and brought before special military tribunals. A parliamentary regime is finally re-established in October 1973.

1970–1974: "Neither war nor peace" in Kurdistan. The Iraqi government sponsors a variety of attempted assassinations aimed against the Kurdish leaders. The Baghdad authorities' continuing policy of Arabizing Kurdish provinces, and their total disregard for their previous commitments lead to a rapid deterioration of relations with the Kurdish movement.

Spring 1972: Alliances are switched. In an effort to isolate the Kurdish movement both at home and abroad, the Iraqi government signs a friendship and co-operation treaty with the USSR, erstwhile ally of the Kurds. Discreetly encouraged by the U.S., Iran decides to back the Kurds.

March 1974: Baghdad publishes its "Law on Kurdish Autonomy," which is a very definite step backwards from the 1970 Agreement and which the Kurdish leadership rejects. From April onwards, the war starts up again on an unprecedented scale.

March 5, 1975: The Algiers Agreement between the Shah of Iran and Iraqi Vice-Premier Saddam Hussein. Iran decides to cut off logistical support to the Iraqi Kurds.

Late March 1975: The Kurdish leadership gives up the struggle and flees to Iran. Kurdish resistance collapses.

June 1976: A new phase of guerrilla operations is launched in Iraqi Kurdistan.

1977–1978: In Iraqi Kurdistan, several hundred villages along the frontiers with Turkey, Iran and Syria are systematically destroyed or depopulated. The Iraqi Army shoots on sight at anybody wandering into this eight to twelve mile-deep no man's land, whose population has been herded into "strategic hamlets." Baghdad also intensifies its Arabization and other repressive policies in the Kurdish provinces.

August 1978: Increasingly angry popular demonstrations against the monarchy spread throughout Iranian Kurdistan. In Kermanshah and Sanandaj the Army opens fire on the crowds, killing dozens of people.

February 10–11, 1979: After a year of struggles, demonstrations and marches, the monarchy is overthrown in Iran. In Kurdistan, Kurdish partisans seize the barracks and police stations, and set up a *de facto* autonomous administration. In both towns and countryside the population elects revolutionary councils to manage local affairs.

March 2, 1979: Barzani dies in the U.S.

March 3, 1979: In Mahabad, after 33 years underground, the Kurdish Democratic Party of Iran announces its own legalization to a crowd of 200,000 people gathered in the very square where the leaders of the first independent Kurdish republic had been hanged in March 1947.

March 18–19, 1979: In Sanandaj, the main center in Iranian Kurdistan, there are violent clashes between Kurdish *Peshmergas* and militiamen and soldiers supporting Ayatollah Khomeini. A special envoy, Ayatollah Taleghani, concludes a ceasefire agreement with representatives of the Kurdish national movement on March 22, and promises publicly that the new regime will grant autonomous status to Iran's "ethnic minorities." On March 23 a KDPI delegation meets with Khomeini to outline the Kurdish demands.

March 30–31, 1979: The Kurdish provinces overwhelmingly boycott the referendum on the Islamic Republic.

April 20–22, 1979: Very violent incidents at Naghadeh are followed by a whole series of clashes which culminate in August with the Iranian Army's general offensive against the Kurdish autonomous forces.

April 26, 1979: In Turkey the Ecevit Cabinet extends the state of siege, affecting 13 provinces, which had been decreed following massacres at Kahramarmaras provoked by extreme right militias. Six further provinces are put under martial law. Fifteen of the 19 provinces concerned are in Turkish Kurdistan. All progressive publications and organizations are outlawed.

August 17, 1979: In a virulently aggressive speech, Khomeini declares war on the Kurds. On September 5, following a huge offensive backed by tanks, helicopters and bombers the Iranian Army reoccupies the main towns of Kurdistan. Within a few days, Khalkhali's Islamic tribunals sentence nearly 200 people to death. The *Pasdars* (Revolutionary Guards) are let loose on the civilian population.

September 20, 1979: Saddam Hussein's army invades Iran. Gulf War continues to July 1988.

September–October 1979: Guerrilla operations are carried out throughout Iranian Kurdistan.

October 27, 1979: Khomeini appoints a delegation of four Ministers to negotiate a settlement in Kurdistan. On November 3 the Kurdish leaders proclaim a ceasefire for the duration of the talks. The *Peshmergas* regain control of the Kurdish cities.

December 2–3, 1979: The referendum on the Islamic Constitution is boycotted by nearly the entire Kurdish population. Most of the other non-Persian nationalities follow suit. In Iran as a whole, the rate of abstention is over 50%.

Summer 1982: KDP and PUK meet on Iranian-Iraqi border and agree to end each group's control of specific parts of Kurdistan.

1983–84: Repression in Iraq escalates, aimed at destroying Kurdistan's economic and social life.

Early 1984: Negotiations between Talabani and Iraqi government begin; inter-Kurdish dialogue starts.

April 15, 1987: Kurdistan Front declared.

May 7, 1987: First confirmed use of chemical weapons against Kurds by Iraqi regime.

March 16, 1988: Five thousand Kurds die of poison gas at Halabja.

End of 1988: Kurdish leadership and *Peshmerga* survivors go into exile in Iran and Syria.

1989: Kurdistan Front launches diplomatic campaign in the West to gain support for Kurdish rights.

1989–90: Saddam Hussein sends emissaries to negotiate the Iraqi Kurds' return. Negotiations bog down over Saddam Hussein's demand for public recantations and support for the Baath Party.

August 2, 1990: Saddam Hussein invades Kuwait.

January 1991: Kurdistan Front opens clandestine contact with Turkey.

March 1991: Uprising in south and north of Iraq. *Peshmerga* in control of three quarters of Iraqi Kurdistan.

March 11, 1991: Iraqi opposition conference held in Beirut.

March–April 1991: Uprising collapses. Two million Kurds flee to mountains. U.S. establishes Operation Provide Comfort.

April 5, 1991: UN Security Council passes Resolution 688, condemning Iraq's human rights violations.

April 18, 1991: Iraq signs Memorandum of Understanding with UN Secretary-General's representative.

April 1991: Turkey frees thousands of Kurdish prisoners and repeals law forbidding use of Kurdish language.

August 1991: Turkey launches military attack on PKK positions inside Iraq.

October 1991: New Turkish government elected, headed by Suleyman Demirel of conservative True Path Party. Twenty-two Kurdish deputies elected.

October 11, 1991: Turkey bombs five Kurdish villages in northern Iraq inside allied security zone. U.S. does not respond.

February 1992: Seventy Kurds killed by Turkish forces during Newroz, or Kurdish new year celebrations.

April 12, 1992: Turkey passes "Anti-Terrorism Law," forbidding separatist propaganda.

May 1992: Kurdish elections held throughout Iraqi Kurdistan.

Bibliography

This bibliography does not set out to be exhaustive. I have only mentioned works and a few articles which I thought important. The *ISK Bibliography* listed in Section V indicates a wide range of other titles.

I. History, Sociology and Politics

Afra, Hassan, *The Kurds*, Oxford University Press (London, 1966).

Barth, Frederik, *Principles of Social Organization in Southern Kurdistan* (Oslo, 1953).

Bayazidi, Mela Mahmoud, *Nravy i Obytchai Kurdov*, (a study of Kurdish customs and ways during the 19th Century), critical Kurdish-Russian bilingual edition, USSR Academy of Science (Moscow, 1962).

Bedir Khan, Emir Soureya Ali and H. Gibbons, *The Case of Kurdistan against Turkey* (Philadelphia, 1928).

Besickci, Ismail, *Dogu Anaddu'nun Duzeni*, (a study of the social and economic structures of Kurdistan in Turkey), E. Yayinlari (Istanbul, 1969), (in Turkish).

Besickci, Ismail, *Gocebe Alikan Asireti* (a sociological study of the Alikan Kurdish nomadic tribe), Sevinc Matbaasi (Ankara 1969), (in Turkish).

Blav, Joyce, *Le Probleme Kurde, essai sociologique et historique*, Centre pour l'etude des problemes du monde musulman contemporain (Brussels, 1963).

Bois, Pere Thomas, *Connaissance des Kurdes*, Khayats (Beirut, 1965).

Bozarslan, Mehmet Emin, *Dogunun Sorunlari (Problems of the East)*, (an analytical study of the key socio-economic characteristics of Kurdistan in Turkey), Is Matbaasi (Ankara, 1966), (in Turkish).

Braidwood, R.J., *Prehistoric Investigations in Iraqi Kurdistan* (Chicago, 1960).

Bukchpan, A., *Azerbaijanskie Kurdy (The Kurds of Azerbaijan)*, (Baku, 1932).

Chaliand, Gerard, *La Question Kurde*, Maspero (Paris, 1961).

Cheref Khan, Prince of Bitlis, *Cheref-Nameh (Archives of the Kurdish Nation)*, (in Persian), 1596. The basic work on the history of the post-Islamic Kurdish states and principalities.

Cherif Pasha, General, *Memorandum sur les revendications du peuple kurde*, presented at the Paris Peace Conference (Paris, 1919).

Dersimi, Dr. Nuri, *Kurdistan Torhinde Dersim (Dersim in the History of Kurdistan)*, (Aleppo, 1952), (in Turkish).

Eagleton, William Jr., *The Kurdish Republic of 1946*, Oxford University Press, 1963, (available in Arabic and Turkish editions; Istanbul, 1976). The only full-length work dealing with the ephemeral Kurdish Republic of Mahabad in Iranian Kurdistan.

Edmonds, C.J., *Kurds, Turks and Arabs*, Oxford University Press, 1957.

Ghassemlou, Abdul Rahman, *Kurdistan and the Kurds*, Publishing House of the Czechoslovak Academy of Sciences (Prague, 1965); also published by Collets Holdings Ltd. (London, 1965). Slovak and Arabic translations available.

Gokalp, Ziya, *Kurt Asiretleri Uzerine Sosyolojik Tetkikler (Sociological Studies of Kurdish Tribes)*, Komal Yayinlari (Istanbul, 1975), (in Turkish). An interesting study of certain aspects of Kurdish society at the beginning of the 20th century, written by an author who later became the main ideologue of Turkish nationalism.

Hansen, Henry H., *The Kurdish Woman's Life* (Copenhagen, 1961). A unique monograph.

Ibn-ul Ezraq, *Merwani Kurtleri Tariki (A History of the Merwanid Kurds)*, Komal Yayinlari (Istanbul, 1975). The first and most complete study of the Merwanid Kurdish state during the 10th and 11th centuries. Written by a 13th century Kurdish historian and savant, it also contains a wide range of essential information as to contemporary events in other parts of the region.

Kenane, Derek, *The Kurds and Kurdistan*, Oxford University Press, 1964.

Minorsky, Vladimir, "Kurds," "Kurdish language" and other articles in *Encyclopedie de l'Islam*.

Mr. Minorsky is the first scholar to have investigated the Kurdish peoples' ethnic origins. His work is of a high scientific standard and consequently quite demanding.

Nikitine, Basile, one-time Russian Consul in Persia, *Les Kurdes, etude sociologique et historique*, Imprimerie Nationale, Libraire C. Klincksieck (Paris, 1956).

Rambout, Lucien (alias Pere T. Bois), *Les Kurdes et le droit*, Editions du Cerf (Paris, 1947). Contains much useful and precise information about Kurdistan between the wars.

Roosevelt, Archie Jr., "The Kurdish Republic of Mahabad," *The Middle East Journal* (Washington, July 1947). Eye-witness account of events at Mahabad. (Reproduced in this volume).

Safrastian, Arshak, *Kurds and Kurdistan*, Harvil Press (London, 1948).

Spencer, William, *The Mosul Question in International Relations*, thesis, American University (Washington, 1965).

Waheed, Sheikh A., *The Kurds and their Country: History of the Kurdish People from the Earliest Times to the Present*, University Book Agency (Lahore, 1955).

Zeki, Mohammed Emire, *A Summary of the History of Kurdistan and the Kurds from Earliest Times to the Present Day*, (in Kurdish), Dar-al-Salam (Baghdad, 1931). Arabic edition annotated by Ali Ewni, *Tarikh al-Kurd wa Kurdistan*, Al Saadeh, Cairo.

Zeki, M.E., *A History of the Kurdish States and Principalities during the Muslim Era*, (in Kurdish), (Baghdad, 1937); published in Arabic by Ali Ewni, *Tarikh ad-duval vat-imarat al Kurdiyeh fi ahde-e-islami*, Al Saadeh, Cairo. Both are fascinating works of information by this eminent Kurdish historian.

II. Works on the Kurdish Movement in Iraq (1961–75)

Adamson, David G., *The Kurdish War*, Allen and Unwin (London, 1964).

Haraldson, Erlender, *Land im Aufstand Kurdistan*, Matori-Verlag (Hamburg, 1966).

Mauries, Rene, *Le Kurdistan ou la Mort*, Robert Laffont (Paris, 1967); also "J'ai lu" edition, 1970.

Pradier, Jean Otton, *Les Kurdes, revolution silencieuse*, Ducros (Bordeaux, 1968).

Schmidt, Dana Adams, *Journey Among Brave Men*, Little and Brown (Boston, 1964).

Vanly, Ismet Cherif, *Le Kurdistan Irakien, entite nationale*, (a very well documented work of reference on the 1961 revolution), La Baconniere (Neuchatel, 1970).

Viennot, Jean Pierre, *Contribution a l'etude du mouvement national kurde*, thesis presented at the Sorbonne, 1961. 2 vols. roneo. A study which contains a great deal of precise and important information, much of it culled at first hand and all carefully verified. The author's analyses of various aspects of the Kurdish national movement in Iraq up to 1969 are often very pertinent.

III. Literature, Folklore and Religion

A. Literature and Folklore:

Bedir Khan, Emir K.A. and Paul-Marguerite, Lucie, *Proverbes Kurdes*, (preceded by an essay on Kurdish poetry), Berger Levraut (Paris, 1936).

Bloch, J., *La Nuit kurde*, (a novel now in its 2nd edition), Gallimard (Paris, 1925); also Bibliotheque Francaise (Paris, 1946).

Bois, Pere Thomas, "L'ame des Kurdes a la lumiere de leur folklore," from *Cahiers de l'Est*, Nos. 5 and 6, (Beirut, 1946).

Brunel, Andre, *Gulusar, contes et legendes du Kurdistan*, Sfelt (Paris, 1946).

Chaliand, Gerard, *Poesie populaire des Turcs et des Kurdes*, Maspero "Voix" (Paris, 1961).

Hartmann, M., *Der Kurdische Diwan des Scheich Ahmad von Cezireh*, (Melaye Ciziri), (Berlin, 1904). First edition of classic works by the famous 14th century Kurdish poet.

Khani, Ehmede, *Mem-o-Zin*, (patriotic epic set in verse during the 17th Century), (Moscow, 1962). Kurdish text in Arabic characters. Russian translation with notes by N.R. Rudenko. Kurdish-Turkish bilingual edition (Istanbul, 1967).

Lescot, Roger, *Textes Kurdes* Part I: *Contes, proverbes et enigmes*, Librairie Orientale P. Geothnier (Paris, 1940); Part II: *Meme Alan* (Kurdish national epic), (Beirut, 1942). A critical Kurdish-French bilingual edition of outstanding quality.

Prym, E., and Socin, Albert, *Kurdische Sammlungen* (St. Petersburg, 1887–1890), 4 vols.

Sedjadi, Alaeddine, *Mejuwe edebe kurdi (A History of Kurdish Literature)*, (Baghdad, 1952), (in Kurdish).

Wikander, Stig, *Recueil de textes kourmandjii*, Uppsala University Institute of Sanskrit, 1959. Bilingual French-Kurdish edition.

Yachar, Kemal. *Memed, My Hawk*, Harvill Press (London, 1957).

Yachar, K., *The Wind from the Plains*, Collins and Harvill Press (London, 1963).

Yachar, K., *Memed le Mince II*, Gallimard (Paris, 1976).

Zaza, Dr. Noureddine, *Contes et poemes kurdes* (Lausanne, 1975).

There is an abundant literature written in Kurdish but it did not seem appropriate to go into great details here, in a book aimed at a public unlikely to know the language.

B. Religion

Furlani, G. *The Religion of the Yezidis: Religious Texts of the Yezidis*, translated from Italian with additional notes, an appendix and an index by Jamsedjii (Bombay, 1940).

Isya, Joseph, *Devil Worship: the Sacred Books and Traditions of the Yezidis*, Badger (Boston, 1919).

Lescot, Roger, *Enquete sur les Yezidis de Syrie et du Djebel-Sindjar* (Beirut, 1938), (Memoires de l'Institut francais de Damas, V).

Nur, Ali Shah Elahi, *L'Esoterisme kurde*, translated, introduced and annotated by Dr. M. Mokri, Albin Michel (Paris, 1966).

IV. Accounts by Western Travelers and Observers

Balsan, F., *Les Surprises du Kurdistan*, 2nd edition, (Paris, 1945).

Binder, H., *Au Kurdistan, en Mesopotamie et en Perse*, Quantin (Paris, 1887).

Bishop, I.L., *Journeys in Persia and Kurdistan*, Vols. 1–11, J. Murray (London, 1891).

Cholet, Comte de, *Armenie, Kurdistan, Mesopotamie*, Plon, Nourit et Cie (Paris, 1892).

Douglas, William O., *Strange Lands and Friendly People*, Harper (New York, 1951).

Fraser, James B., *Travels in Kurdistan and Mesopotamia with Manners of the Kurdish and Arab Tribes* (London, 1840), 2 vols.

Hamilton, A.M., *Road through Kurdistan*, Faber (London, 1937).

Hay, W.R., *Two Years in Kurdistan: Experiences of a Political Officer, 1918–1920*, Sidgwick and Jackson (London, 1921).

Kinneir, John MacDonald, *Journey through Asia Minor, Armenia and Koordistan in the Years 1813 and 1814* (London, 1818).

Maunsell, F.R., *Reconnaissance in Mesopotamia, Kurdistan, North-West Persia and Luristan*, Sinsla (India, 1899–1900), 2 vols.

Rich, Claude James, *Narrative of a Residence in Kurdistan and on the Sites of Ancient Nineveh* (London, 1836–1837), 2 vols.

Soane, Ely B., *To Mesopotamia and Kurdistan in Disguise* (London, 1912).

V. Bibliography

I.S.K.'s Kurdish Bibliography No. 1, edited by Silvio Van Rooy and Kees Tamboer, International Society Kurdistan, (Amsterdam, 1968), 2 vols. The 9,350 titles, drawn from over 40 different languages, are classified alphabetically by author. Original script and transcription in Latin characters, with English translation, of all titles from languages unfamiliar to Western Europe.

Index

257